RESISTING REBELLION

RESISTING REBELLION

THE HISTORY AND POLITICS OF COUNTERINSURGENCY

Anthony James Joes

THE UNIVERSITY PRESS OF KENTUCKY

Publication of this volume was made possible in part
by a grant from the National Endowment for the Humanities.

The University Press of Kentucky
Scholarly publisher for the Commonwealth,
serving Bellarmine University, Berea College, Centre College of Kentucky,
Eastern Kentucky University, The Filson Historical Society, Georgetown
College, Kentucky Historical Society, Kentucky State University,
Morehead State University, Murray State University, Northern Kentucky
University, Transylvania University, University of Kentucky, University of
Louisville, and Western Kentucky University.

Editorial and Sales Offices: The University Press of Kentucky
663 South Limestone Street, Lexington, Kentucky 40508-4008
www.kentuckypress.com

08 07 06 05 04   5   4   3   2   1

Library of Congress Cataloging-in-Publication Data

Joes, Anthony James.
  Resisting rebellion : the history and politics of counterinsurgency /
Anthony James Joes.
      p. cm.
  Includes bibliographical references and index.
  ISBN 0-8131-2339-9 (hardcover : alk. paper)
  1. Counterinsurgency—History. 2. Counterinsurgency—Political aspects.
I. Title.
  U241.J62 2004
  355.02'18—dc22   2004010630

This book is printed on acid-free recycled paper meeting the requirements of the
American National Standard for Permanence in Paper for Printed Library Materials.

Manufactured in the United States of America.

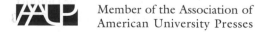

Member of the Association of
American University Presses

To my former students at the U.S. Army War College

CONTENTS

GUERRILLA INSURGENCY
AS A POLITICAL PROBLEM

THE POWER OF GUERRILLA INSURGENCY

Insurgency, an attempt to overthrow or oppose a state or regime by force of arms, very often takes the form of guerrilla war. That happens because guerrilla war is the weapon of the weak. It is waged by those whose inferiority in numbers, equipment, and financial resources makes it impossible to meet their opponents in open, conventional battle. Guerrillas therefore seek to wage a protracted conflict, winning small victories over government forces by attaining numerical superiority at critical points through speed and deception. The ambush and attacks on the enemy's lines of supply have always and everywhere been favorite guerrilla tactics.[1]

Over a century ago, an astute observer wrote that "guerrilla warfare is what regular armies always have most to dread, and when this is directed by a leader with a genius for war, an effective [counterinsurgency] campaign becomes well-nigh impossible."[2]

In witness to this dramatic statement stand the Vietnam conflict that destroyed two U.S. administrations and the war in Afghanistan that helped unravel the USSR. Those guerrilla insurgencies were waged by poor countries, but "iron weighs at least as much as gold in the scales of military strength."[3] Guerrillas mauled the Americans and the Soviets because those countries' militaries were deficient in proper doctrine and prepared troops and were slow to adapt to unforeseen difficulties. Certainly, both cases illustrate that guerrilla insurgency is not simply a scaled-down version of conventional war. Hence those who undertake counterinsurgency by treating it as such are committing an error with possibly grievous consequences.

But however dramatic, the Vietnamese and Afghan conflicts are only the most recent cases where great powers have encountered calamity at the hands of guerrillas. Everybody once knew that the American War of Independence came to an end because General Cornwallis surrendered his trapped army at Yorktown. Fewer have been aware that Cornwallis was in Yorktown in the first place because his army had been badly cut up by guerrilla forces in the Carolinas.[4]

Additional examples of the power of guerrilla insurgency abound. In Spain, the all-powerful armies of Napoleon were frustrated and bloodied by guerrillas, a spectacle that encouraged renewed European resistance to the Corsican conqueror. Indeed, the French lost more soldiers in Spain than in Russia.[5] Later, the renewal of guerrilla insurgency in western France almost certainly cost Napoleon victory at Waterloo.[6]

In South Africa, Britain eventually crushed the Boer guerrillas under weight of numbers, but the unexpectedly protracted and difficult conflict was a painful embarrassment for the British government and earned it much domestic and international opprobrium.

In Cuba, Spanish failure to suppress guerrillas provided the occasion for the blowing up of the *Maine*.

In China, Imperial Japanese forces were ultimately unable to cope effectively with widespread guerrilla resistance.

French embroilment with guerrilla war in Indochina and then Algeria resulted in a virtual army coup d'état and the collapse of the Fourth Republic.

Protracted guerrilla war in her African colonies was the principal factor bringing revolution to Portugal in 1974.[7]

Just a few years after the fall of Saigon, the North Vietnamese Army, exulting in the (partly correct) conviction that it had defeated both the French and the Americans, found itself enmeshed in a long and frustrating struggle against Cambodian guerrillas.

In Chechnya, the armed forces of post-Soviet Russia proclaimed "final" victory many times over the guerrillas. In that little region (smaller than New Jersey), with a population of less than half a million, the Russians had eighty thousand armed troops as late as 2003.[8]

Clearly, then, with regard to the question of becoming involved in combat against guerrillas, "let no state believe that it can always follow a safe policy; rather let it think that all policies are doubtful."[9]

THE SCOPE OF INSURGENCY

Many Americans who came to maturity in the Cold War era tend to identify guerrilla war with Communist subversion. But guerrilla war has not been exclusively nor even mainly Communist. Throughout history, royalist, conservative, nationalist, and/or religious movements have engaged in guerrilla insurgency. Its venerable record includes the brilliant exploits of Judas Maccabeus against the Syrians in the decade after 170 B.C. In the same period, the Romans had to confront "the peculiarly wearing and expensive character of guerrilla tactics, at which the Spaniards were so adept."[10] In fact, these Spanish tactics were remarkably similar to those used in the same country two thousand years later against Napoleon. As the nineteenth century was turning into the twentieth, guerrilla war flared simultaneously in the Boer Republics, Cuba, and the Philippines, long before the world had heard of Lenin, much less Mao, Castro, or Ho Chi Minh.

Consider the following scenario: A superpower, bearer of a universalistic ideology, invades an underdeveloped country right across its border. The superpower, having grossly underestimated the difficulty of subduing this neighbor, commits forces inadequate to the task. To a lack of numbers the invaders add atrocious conduct, including widespread rape, sacrilege, looting, and casual murder. This behavior provokes a fierce popular resistance, its morale sustained by religious fervor and outside support. This protracted and bitter conflict has very damaging effects on the superpower, and contributes to its eventual collapse.

Is this a serviceable summary of the Soviet invasion of Afghanistan? Yes, it is. But exactly the same words would describe the Napoleonic invasion of Spain in 1808, out of which conflict comes our word *guerrilla,* meaning "little war"—a misnomer if there ever was one. Spain was Napoleon's Afghanistan.

Even during the Cold War, conflicts ostensibly about Communism exhibited deep ethno-religious roots, as in Malaya, Vietnam, Tibet, Angola, Peru, and Afghanistan. The United States itself lent assistance to insurgencies in Tibet, Angola, Afghanistan, and Nicaragua. Indeed some notable guerrilla chieftains have been Americans, including Francis Marion, Thomas Sumter, John Mosby, and, in a different category altogether, William Clarke Quantrill.

ROOTS OF THE PROBLEM

The power of nationalism (and xenophobia) to generate armed conflict, including guerrilla insurgency, is well known. The most famous of these insurgencies have arisen against foreign occupation or foreign-imposed regimes. They include the Americans in the Carolinas during the War of Independence, the Spanish against Napoleon, the Boers against the British Empire, the Chinese against the Japanese, the Tibetans against the Chinese, both the Viet Minh and the Algerian Muslims against the French, the Cambodians against the Vietnamese, the Afghans against the Soviets, and the Chechens against the Russians. It is of more than passing interest that no Communist party ever came to power on its own except through identification with a nationalist struggle.[11]

Ordinarily, therefore, guerrilla insurgency has its best chance against an occupying foreign power and its local allies. But many notable eruptions have occurred against indigenous regimes; these conflicts include the Vendée, the Philippines, postwar Greece, contemporary Colombia, the Cuba of Batista, and the Nicaragua of the Somozas. The distinguished political analyst Lucian Pye wrote: "The possibility of an insurrectionary movement arising and then employing organized violence depends upon the existence of sharp divisions within the society created by regional, ethnic, linguistic, class, religious or other communal differences that may provide the necessary social and geographic basis for supporting the movement; and a central authority that is unable to maintain uniform and consistent administrative controls over the entire country."[12] While Pye's statement clearly needs fine-tuning, his wish to call attention to domestic causes of insurgency is valid and useful. In addition, therefore, to those famous insurgencies arising out of foreign occupation or intervention, other insurgency-generating circumstances also need analysis. These include defeat in war, religious rebellion, resistance to a murderous regime, a tradition of civil conflict, the desire of would-be or former elites to gain power, and the closing off of any peaceful avenue to change through rigged or cancelled elections. One or another of these causes is often dominant, but it almost always receives reinforcement from additional ones. In the case of both the Vendée (1790s) and Mexico (1920s), for example, the combination of religious persecution and rigged elections produced major explosions of guerrilla insurgency.

THE PERSISTENCE OF THE PHENOMENON

Since guerrilla insurgency transcends Communism, it is no surprise that the end of the Cold War has not meant the end of guerrilla conflict; far from it. "It is abundantly clear today that the collapse of ideology with the end of superpower rivalry has not served to dampen Third World conflicts."[13] As the twentieth century was turning into the twenty-first, Communist wars of national liberation were gone, supposedly for good, but guerrilla wars flared from Colombia to Algeria, from Nepal to Turkey, from Sri Lanka and Mindanao and Chechnya to Sudan and Kashmir and Kosovo. Endless guerrilla clashes in Kashmir have brought Pakistan and India to the brink of war more than once, and now both states possess nuclear weapons.

Many so-called states cannot maintain even a semblance of order outside the capital city, sometimes hardly even there, and the list of such failed or failing states grows longer.[14] The Balkan turmoils that so disturbed the twentieth century will not quickly fade in the twenty first. Many ethnic groups—Basques, Chechens, Kashmiris, Kurds, Moros, Uighers, and others—continue to demand, and fight for, a national state of their own. Other groups, including some unheard of at this time (because nationality arises first of all in the human mind), will do the same. Conflicts with religious causes or rationalizations, especially Islamic, will continue to spread. Wars to control drugs or diamonds will not disappear. Some of these ethnic, religious, and re-source struggles will trigger U.N. "peacemaking operations" that will look very much like traditional counterinsurgency.[15] It might be rash to predict where the next Sri Lanka or Chechnya or Kosovo or Somalia or Colombia will appear, but it would be even more rash to predict that it will appear *nowhere*.

THE NEGLECT OF THE SUBJECT

In spite of all this, crucial segments of U.S. society pay little attention to the accumulated store of experience regarding how, and how not, to fight guerrillas—that is, how to conduct counterinsurgency. The academic community generally ignores warfare. Although things have improved somewhat since he made it, there is still much truth in Bertrand Russell's observation that it has "been customary to accept economic power without analysis, and this had led, in modern times, to an undue emphasis upon economics, as opposed to war and propaganda, in the causal interpretation of history."[16]

The academy is not alone in this neglect. "Most [governments that have faced insurgency] have been quick to put their experiences out of mind, and thus they have failed to acknowledge and codify their accu-mulative understanding of how to cope with insurrections. In any case, each outbreak of insurgency seems *to call for relearning old lessons, for memories on this subject seem always to be peculiarly short.*"[17] Certainly, before and during the Vietnam wars the U.S. governing classes forgot or ignored many valuable lessons acquired from experience in the Philippines of the early 1900s or Central America of the 1920s (nor did they bother to study the perplexities of the French in Indochina). Today, those who seek to shape U.S. opinion display little clear understanding of *what* happened in Vietnam, not to speak of *why* it happened.

But a third element of American society that has ignored the counterinsurgent experience (their own and others') is the U.S. military. This has been in part an understandable, if regrettable, consequence of the events in and after Vietnam. It is also a product of American strategic culture in which "two dominant characteristics stand out: the preference for massing a vast array of men and machines and the predilection for direct and violent assault."[18] In other words, "the exercise of maximum violence for swift results has been the American way."[19] (One might add, like the Romans.) Successful counterinsurgency, however, requires almost the diametrically opposite approach: patience, circumspection, and the strict limitation of violence. Those historians who write about war focus on great battles, not guerrilla campaigns. Even so, while there are famous guerrilla leaders, from the Swamp Fox to Lawrence of Arabia to Ahmed Shah Massoud, there are no famous commanders of counterinsurgency—although there should be. All these factors contribute to the situation in which "our military is determined to be unprepared for missions it does not want, as if the lack of preparedness might prevent our going."[20] But this shall change.

AN APPROACH TO THE ANALYSIS OF COUNTERINSURGENCY

This book is concerned with answering a number of questions. Why do guerrilla insurgencies arise? Against whom are they directed? Who participates in these insurgencies? Who leads them? Are there differences in motivation and expectation between insurgent leaders and followers? Who will oppose the insurgents? What is the counterinsurgency record of the U.S.? How does that record compare to those of the British, the French, the Soviets/Russians, and others? Have any countries been successful in one counterinsurgency and frustrated in another, and if so, why? Are there replicable and nontrivial aspects common to successful or unsuccessful insurgencies and counterinsurgencies?

The search for answers to these questions will range across five continents, and from eighteenth-century Vendée to twenty-first-century Chechnya. The emphasis is on "lessons learned"; the assumption is that no insurgency is so distant from us in time or space or culture that it cannot cast some light of wisdom upon the path ahead.

This approach to the dual subject of insurgency/counterinsurgency is comparative and developmental, based on interpretation and synthesis of the extant literature, including primary sources, as well as discussions with individuals who had or have a personal involvement with the subject. Since very few, if any, internal conflicts—including guerrilla insurgency—occur in a global vacuum, the international and geographical contexts of the struggles herein considered receive much attention.

Analysis will usually be from the perspective of the counterinsurgents. This is certainly not because of any generalized lack of sympathy with insurgents per se (as the reader will soon discern). The U.S. has assisted guerrillas in most areas of the globe and will do so in the future. Indeed, Americans have sometimes *been* the guerrillas. Rather, the emphasis on counterinsurgency arises from two other reasons. First, guerrilla strategy and tactics, having been long and well studied, at least by some, are better understood than those of counterinsurgency. Second, there can be no doubt that in the twenty-first century, U.S. military personnel will find themselves cast, perhaps not infrequently, in the role of counterinsurgents. The concern here with identifying valid counterinsurgency methods therefore reflects a concern to save American lives, as well as lives of the civilian populations among whom such methods will unfold.

The central concept of this study is that guerrilla insurgency is quintessentially a *political* phenomenon, and that therefore any effective response to it must be primarily political as well. Many years ago a distinguished student of internal conflict articulated a view whose wisdom continues to impress: "Despite the many recent attempts to psychologize the study of revolution by introducing ideas of anxiety, alienation, rising expectations, and the like, and to sociologize it by employing notions of disequilibrium, role conflict, structural strain, and so on, the factors which hold up under close scrutiny are, on the whole, political ones. *The structure of power, alternative conceptions of justice, the organization of coercion, the conduct of war, the formation of coalitions, the legitimacy of the state—these traditional concerns of political thought provide the main guides to the explanation of revolution.*"[21]

Substituting "insurgency" for "revolution" neatly captures the general orientation of the present volume.

If insurgency and counterinsurgency are fundamentally political, what is the essential aim of any intelligent counterinsurgency policy? That essential aim is *peace*, here defined as "a pattern of stability acceptable to those with the capacity to disturb it by violence."[22]

Military victory is sometimes illusory and often ephemeral, and hence cannot in itself produce or guarantee lasting peace. Certainly, an insurgency is not suppressed just because the insurgents cannot be seen. Clausewitz taught that "war is the continuation of policy by other means," that "war is only a branch of political activity," and that "no other possibility exists, then, than to subordinate the military point of view to the political."[23]

Concurrence with this essential concept—the primacy of the political in war—by distinguished practitioners and/or students of war and counterinsurgency across time and culture is abundant. The following statements are only a sampling. Sun Tzu: "To win one hundred victories in one hundred battles is not the acme of skill. To subdue the enemy without fighting is the acme of skill."[24] Julius Caesar: "Victory through policy is as much a mark of the good general as victory by the sword."[25] C.E. Callwell: "Expeditions to put down revolt are not put in motion merely to bring about a temporary cessation of hostilities. Their purpose is to ensure a lasting peace. Therefore . . . the overawing and not the exasperation of the enemy is the end to keep in view."[26] J.F.C. Fuller: "A military victory is not in itself equivalent to success in war."[27] General Sir Gerald Templer: "The shooting side of the business is only 25% of the trouble and the other 75% lies in getting the people of this country behind us."[28] Michael Howard: "[A] war, fought for whatever reason, that does not aim at a solution which takes into account the fears, the interests, and not least the honour of the defeated peoples is unlikely to decide anything for very long."[29] Gene Hanrahan: "Of first importance [is] the recognition that guerrilla warfare is politico-military in nature and hence must necessarily be countered by a combination of political as well as military means."[30] Charles Freeman: "A peace based on the humiliation of the vanquished contains the germs of renewed warfare."[31] Basil Liddell Hart: "The object in war is to attain a better peace—even if only from your own point of view. Hence it is essential to conduct war with constant regard to the peace you desire. This is the truth underlying Clausewitz's definition of war as a 'continuation of policy by other means'—the prolongation of that policy through the war into the subsequent peace must always be borne in mind. If you concentrate exclusively on victory with no thought for the aftereffect . . . it is almost certain that the peace will be a bad one, containing the germs of another war."[32] In brief, "Gaining military victory is not itself equivalent to gaining the object of the war."[33]

To summarize: lasting peace—that is, lasting victory—comes through *conciliation*. This is achieved first by military actions involving minimum violence through an emphasis on conservative but effective tactics, and, second, by a political program focused on splitting the revolutionary elite from their followers: that is, attending to legitimate popular grievances, and offering the possibility of reintegration into society and a peaceful method for the adjustment of disputes. In a word, counterinsurgent victory derives from justice supported by military power, justice defined in terms of the particular society in question, justice that is seen to be done. The principal models for this kind of counterinsurgent approach are the U.S. in the Philippines (1899–1902) and the British in Malaya (1946–1954). It is notable that even in the latter case, where the counterinsurgents had the advantages of overwhelming numbers and favorable geography, the British administration thought it worthwhile to wield (with great effect) a sophisticated political strategy against the guerrillas. The point is certainly not that these counterinsurgencies were immaculate, unblemished by any errors or excesses or stupidities. Rather, they are relevant because they resulted not only in the complete defeat of the insurgents but also in reconciliation between the counterinsurgent power and the large majority of the civil population.

CHAPTER 1

GUERRILLA STRATEGY AND TACTICS

This chapter reviews the fundamental strategic and tactical aspects of successful guerrilla insurgency. Extreme asymmetries in physical power characterize most contests between insurgents and almost any state. Therefore a victory of guerrilla insurgents indicates either that they have employed excellent strategy and/or tactics, or that the regime has displayed unusual incompetence—or both.

GUERRILLA STRATEGY

Guerrilla warfare is not a phenomenon peculiar to a particular ideology, century, or culture. It is, rather, a method employed by those seeking to force a militarily superior opponent to accept their political objectives. In the ideal, guerrillas are those who fight against ostensibly more powerful forces by unexpected attacks against vulnerable targets, and who are sustained by popular support, high morale, good intelligence, secure bases, and foreign assistance.

One of the most notable aspects of guerrilla warfare is the lack of symmetry regarding the military power of the two sides, with the regime always having the advantage at the beginning. But another, and profound, asymmetry affects the strategic tasks of the antagonists. The regime (of whatever nature) usually believes it must destroy the insurgents, or at least reduce them to unimportance. In contrast, the insurgents need merely to survive, at least for the intermediate term. Guerrilla war is a kind of attrition against the regime. For guerrillas, exhausting or outlasting the enemy will produce victory. "Tactics favor the regular army while strategy favors the enemy [guerrillas]."[1] Thus, the "basic winning formula for an insurgency is as follows: if an insurgent movement can, at a cost which is indefinitely acceptable, impose costs on a government which are not indefinitely acceptable, then, while losing every battle, it is winning the war."[2] The longer the guerrilla insurgency lasts, the worse it is for the regime.[3] This is an inestimable advantage to the guerrillas, because they have the power to protract the conflict. They do this by avoiding contact with their enemies while and where the latter are strong or alert, and then carrying out spectacular operations against attention-getting targets.[4] From Vietnam to Somalia, the American public has shown particular vulnerability to such dramatic actions.

Guerrillas tend to do best when they operate in a symbiotic relationship with elements of a friendly regular army.[5] This scenario most commonly arises when guerrillas are supporting the government of their own country against a foreign invasion or occupation. Guerrilla victories can be ephemeral unless assisted or consolidated by allied regular forces. But more immediately, the presence of regular troops hostile to the counterinsurgent forces will usually prevent the latter from dividing into small units, for fear of meeting equal or larger units of hostile regular troops; they therefore will be able neither to pursue guerrilla bands nor to occupy important points nor to control the population. At the same time, well-led guerrillas will distract or exhaust enemy troops, making them unavailable to concentrate against the regular forces that the guerrillas are supporting. This pattern was clearly visible in South Carolina during the American War of Independence, in Napoleonic Spain, and in Vietnam.[6]

Thus guerrillas contribute to overall victory both by inflicting losses on the enemy and by drawing elements of his forces away from the main battlefields. If a guerrilla movement is not supporting and supported by regular forces, then it must inflict more damage on the enemy (and for a longer time) than the enemy inflicts on it—or lose. Nevertheless, in some instances guerrillas have in fact succeeded without the help of regular forces. Perhaps the most notable examples are the Cuban Fidelistas and the Afghan Mujahideen, both cases that will be considered later in this work.

A student of guerrilla insurgency once wrote that the Vietnamese Communist strategy for making war "is a strategy for which there is no known proven counterstrategy."[7] That statement needs considerable refining. Hanoi got its way in the end, at enormous cost, but the vaunted guerrilla strategy called People's War was defeated. The famous 1968 Tet Offensive "was the end of People's War, and essentially of any strategy built on guerrilla warfare and a politically inspired insurgency."[8] U.S. firepower had reduced the Viet Cong to secondary importance.

That is why the fall of Saigon in 1975 required one of the largest conventional military operations since the end of World War II.

GUERRILLA TACTICS

Mao Tse-tung wrote that the strategy of the guerrillas is to pit one man against ten, but the tactics are to pit ten men against one. He meant that strategically—in terms of the conflict viewed as a whole—guerrillas are by definition the inferior force. But tactically—in terms of particular combats—guerrillas must strive to be the superior force *at the point of contact* with the enemy.[9] The constant guerrilla aim will therefore be to concentrate strength against weakness by carrying out surprise attacks.[10] Surprise is a true force multiplier, compensating for inferiority of numbers. It is the primary and decisive weapon of successful guerrillas. And not only of guerrillas; surprise has been the "master-key of all the great captains of history."[11]

Effective guerrillas attack the enemy's flanks and rear. They interrupt his lines of communication by ambushing convoys; mining or damaging roads; blowing up railroad tracks, trains, and bridges; and isolating small enemy military units. They strike at night, or in the rain, or when the enemy troops are eating or have just finished a march.[12] The favorite tactical operation of guerrillas is the ambush; guerrillas will often attack a particular place in order to lure a relief force into an ambush.[13] All these activities create casualties and anxieties among the enemy, undermining morale. To destroy, or even to attack, one government outpost is to make all such places feel vulnerable. This is not a new phenomenon. During the Gallic wars, Caesar observed: "If I wanted the business finished off and the criminals [Gallic rebels] rooted out and killed, I had to divide my troops into a number of small detachments and send them out in different directions. If I wanted to follow the established practice of the Roman army and keep the companies in regular formation, then the terrain itself acted as a protection for the enemy, who were, as individuals, quite bold enough to lay an ambush and surround any of our men who strayed from the main body of our army."[14]

The great Boer guerrilla chief Jacobus De La Rey "masked his essentially offensive plan in continual retreats until at last his unwary enemy was lulled into a false sense of security and would think he was no longer worth much care or watchfulness; and then he would pull his forces together at a suitable opportunity and like a tiger make a terrific spring at his enemy."[15] De La Rey thus anticipated Mao's tactic of "luring the enemy in deep."

Surprise attack requires mobility, that is, quickly bringing sufficient numbers of guerrillas together and dispersing as soon as the attack is over.[16] Surprise also requires intelligence, that is, knowing how many of the enemy are in a particular place, with what weapons and what morale. Without mobility and intelligence, surprise attack—and guerrilla warfare—will be nearly impossible. Guerrillas are mobile by definition: they lack the heavy weapons and equipment that slow the movement of conventional forces. (The revealing Roman word for the equipment and baggage that a conventional army must transport is *impedimenta*.) As for reliable and timely intelligence, the most important source will be the civilian population. Mao said that the guerrillas must move among the people as fish move in the water. This statement has several meanings: a vital one is that to get good intelligence it is essential to establish and maintain rapport with the local population. An excellent method for establishing good relations with the civilians is for guerrilla units to operate in their native districts. During the Greek civil war, Communist-led guerrillas systematically violated this principle of good relations with the civilian population, to their eventual serious cost.

Guerrillas can also gather valuable intelligence, and create dissension among the foe at the same time, by sending selected members of their group to join the army, the police, the civil administration, the press, pro-regime political parties, labor unions, and so on. By such methods guerrillas and their sympathizers thoroughly penetrated the army and government of both South Vietnam and Soviet Afghanistan.[17]

Properly led guerrillas will also treat their prisoners well. Mao Tsetung taught that "the most effective method of propaganda directed at the enemy forces is to release captured soldiers and give the wounded medical treatment."[18] Such a policy will not only produce excellent intelligence but will also undermine the willingness of the enemy to fight to the death. Castro's guerrillas released large numbers of captured Batista soldiers outright, an "expression of utter contempt for their fighting potential."[19]

TO WAGE GUERRILLA WAR

Clearly, to be effective—indeed to survive—guerrillas must rely on surprise, which in turn derives from mobility and intelligence. But they also need good morale, a well-organized infrastructure, effective leadership, assistance from outside the country, and, ideally, a secure base inside it. Under these conditions, a guerrilla insurgency can flourish indefinitely.

Morale

Filled with danger and deprivation, the life of the guerrilla is rarely romantic and never comfortable. Maintaining morale is essential if guerrillas are to sustain their commitment to the conflict. High morale comes primarily and abundantly from two principal sources: first, the belief that one's cause is just,[20] and second, the feeling of invincibility generated by consistently winning small engagements.[21] The justice of the guerrillas' cause will be particularly apparent to them, and others, if their opponents are foreign and/or brutal. Under these circumstances, guerrillas will usually find it easy to obtain good intelligence from the civilian population. Religious faith has also sustained guerrilla insurgencies fighting against enormous odds, as in Napoleonic Spain and Soviet Afghanistan.

The certainty that the guerrilla will receive medical assistance if wounded will also be a major factor in maintaining morale. So will the practice of hostage-taking, to ensure that captured guerrillas will not be executed out of hand.[22]

Infrastructure

A well-organized guerrilla movement will have an infrastructure, often quite elaborate, that consists of persons who do not normally bear arms but render vital assistance to the guerrillas. Living ostensibly peaceful lives in civilian society, members of the infrastructure furnish the fighting guerrillas with intelligence, supplies, and recruits. Such infrastructures can continue to function even in areas under hostile military occupation. Their contribution to the guerrilla movement is always important and often indispensable. For example, analysts have noted that "it was the VC [infrastructure], not the guerrillas or local forces, which was the foundation of the insurgency [in South Vietnam]."[23]

Leadership

Talented guerrilla leaders repeatedly arise from the most unexpected places, recalling to us the lines of Thomas Gray:

Some village Hampden that with dauntless breast
The little tyrant of his fields withstood,
Some mute inglorious Milton here may rest,
Some Cromwell guiltless of his country's blood.[24]

Guerrilla annals are full of examples of this phenomenon. Consider Francisco Espoz y Mina. To all the world he would have seemed merely a semiliterate Basque bumpkin. Yet "underneath the simple and rustic peasant there lay dormant a complex and powerful individual."[25] In the days of the Napoleonic occupation of Spain, he emerged as "the greatest guerrilla warrior of them all."[26] Indeed, "his services were invaluable during [Wellington's] campaign in Portugal, since he was wearing out a French force fives times his own strength in fruitless marches, under winter rains, and over roads that had become all but impassable."[27] During the winter of 1811–1812, he actually led incursions into French territory. Eventually the king of Spain made him a field marshal. Espoz y Mina was unusual in his time because he discouraged camp followers, and most especially because he left the war no richer than when he took it up.

Frail and sickly as a youth, John Mosby was a young attorney, a reader of Plutarch and Byron,[28] when he became a leader of a Confederate guerrilla unit. As such "his exploits are not surpassed in daring and enterprise by those of *petite guerre* in any age."[29] Confederate Secretary of War Seddon endorsed a paper by Mosby with these words: "A characteristic report from Col. Mosby, who has become so familiar with brave deeds as to consider them too tedious to treat unless when necessary to reflect glory on his gallant comrades."[30] Mosby summed up his ideas of irregular warfare thus: "We had to make up by celerity for lack of numbers,"[31] and, "If you are going to fight, then be the attacker."[32]

Jan Christian Smuts, educated at Christ College, Cambridge, began what was to prove a long and brilliant career as an international statesman when he was appointed—at the age of twenty-eight—state's attorney for the Transvaal Republic. From this unlikely apprenticeship he emerged as one of the great guerrilla chiefs in the Boer war. Smuts's mounted guerrillas penetrated so far south into Cape Colony that they could see the night lights of Port Elizabeth on the Indian Ocean. They captured several British posts in the western area of Cape Colony and managed to maintain themselves right up until the peace negotiations.[33] The number of active guerrillas in Cape Colony never exceeded three thousand at any one time, against forty-five thousand British troops there, and more than one thousand miles separated Smuts's guerrillas in the Cape region from Boer forces in the northern Transvaal.[34]

Or consider the shy young Englishman, an Oxford student of archaeology, whose unsuspected powers won for him—in his twenties—the chieftainship of ten thousand Arab horsemen and world celebrity as "Lawrence of Arabia."

What are the qualities that make a great leader of guerrillas? An answer lies in the example of Francis Marion, the guerrilla chieftain known to history as the "Swamp Fox." General Nathanael Greene, perhaps the finest strategist of the Continental Army during the American War of Independence, wrote that Marion excelled "in all the qualities which form the consummate partisan—vigilance, promptitude, activity, energy, dauntless courage and unshaken self-control."[35] Marion was "sparing of words, abstemious in his habits, a strict disciplinarian, ever vigilant and active, fertile in stratagems and expedients that justified his nickname of Swamp Fox, quick in conception and equally swift in execution, unrelenting in the pursuit of his purposes, yet void of ruthlessness or cruelty to his victims."[36]

And, writes Marion's biographer, "Since his men had no tents, he also slept in the open."[37] This is indeed a cardinal point: the great leader leads by the force of his example. Accordingly, it is not enough for the leader to *be* brave, austere, and self-sacrificing. These qualities need to be *seen* by his followers. Long ago, Sun Tzu wrote that "the [great] commander must be first in the toils and fatigues of the soldiers. In the heat of summer he does not spread his parasol nor in the cold of winter don thick clothing. In dangerous places he must dismount and walk. He waits until the army's wells have been dug and only then drinks; until the soldiers' food is cooked before he eats; until the defenses have been completed, to shelter himself."[38]

Help from Outside

Because the true long-range aim of the guerrilla movement is to be able to meet the enemy army on its own terms—that is, to become itself a conventional military force[39]—a guerrilla insurgency will need assistance from outside the country. More immediately, because guerrillas cannot typically obtain, or produce on their own, weapons of sufficient quality and quantity, outside help will usually become essential at some point. Such assistance was of tremendous value to the Spanish guerrillas against Napoleon and to the Afghan Mujahideen against the Soviets. During World War II, outside forces indirectly but effectively opened the road to power for Mao Tse-tung: first, the Japanese badly mauled the forces of his enemy Chiang Kai-shek, and then the U.S. defeated the Japanese. The Japanese occupation of French Vietnam, and later the help of Chinese advisers and artillery, were of inestimable value to the forces of Ho Chi Minh. A noteworthy and very ominous variation on outside aid is the situation of the Revolutionary Armed Forces of Colombia (FARC) guerrillas, who have in some years obtained an annual income of close to $1 billion, mainly from narcotics and kidnapping. Thus, in lurid contrast to the usual situation, "the Colombian guerrilla war is a rich war."[40]

The Question of Base Areas

The term "secure base" normally refers to an area within the boundaries of a state into which the counterinsurgent forces of that state either cannot reach effectively or will not attempt, for whatever reason, to occupy. A secure base is invaluable to the guerrillas. Within it they can stockpile armaments, food, and medicine; care for the sick and wounded; and indoctrinate recruits and train them in tactics so as to minimize accidents in guerrilla operations.

Many guerrilla movements, including those of the Swamp Fox, Mao, and Castro, have sought to set up a secure base for themselves. In the best circumstances, such a base would exist in an area far from the developed sections of the country, close to an international border, rough in terrain, and primitive in transportation.[41] Establishing the base in a province with a history of rebellion facilitates the recruitment of local people into the guerrilla organization and the building of good relations with the civilian population. Another highly desirable aspect of the selected area is location in a lightly administered part of the country, such as highland Peru, northeastern Thailand, or southeastern Colombia. The absence or intermittent presence of state, army, and civil organizations makes the planting and growth of a guerrilla movement easier, and leaves civilians with little or no protection against threats or acts by the guerrillas. Indeed, very often what guerrillas call "liberated" areas are in fact areas that have been abandoned by the government. For example, in Peru, "by the end of the 1980s, it was difficult to determine how much of Sendero's expansion was due to effective guerrilla strategy and how much to the breakdown of governance."[42]

An especially notable instance of the influence of topography on guerrilla warfare is found in the Tibetan resistance to Chinese Communist invasion in the 1950s. The air of Tibet was too thin for the Chinese troops, who became exhausted after short marches. In addition, Tibet did not produce enough food to feed massive armies, nor did the Chinese troops like the Tibetan barley-and-dried-meat diet. Hence food had to be trucked in to Lhasa across Sinkiang, a sixteen-day trip; eventually, feeding one Chinese soldier in Tibet cost the Communist regime as much as feeding fifty in Beijing.

Clearly, a secure base can be of inestimable value to guerrillas. Still, a cardinal rule for guerrillas—perhaps the most important—is: *Never attempt to hold onto a particular piece of territory in the face of determined enemy attack.* For guerrillas, survival is the supreme consideration. Retreat before the enemy involves no disgrace; indeed, it is the highest wisdom. Guerrillas therefore must always be prepared to abandon any position, including their base. Fighting to hold a piece of territory is to give up guerrilla tactics and face the conventional enemy force on its own terms, a move that would place the very survival of the insurgency at risk.[43] Furthermore, deciding not to defend their base is one instance among many in which the guerrillas can turn their weaknesses into advantages. The guerrillas' lack of equipment and numbers allows them to move quickly and relatively quietly, while the regular troops' baggage (*impedimenta* again!) slows their progress, makes certain routes impassable, and provides plenty of warning of their approach.

During the long Chinese civil war Mao Tse-tung derived immeasurable benefits from his guerrilla base areas. Mao was able to possess such havens because of China's vast spaces, the utter inadequacy of the country's transportation network, and the limited numbers and technology of the invading Japanese. Afterward, Mao believed that it was not possible to wage effective guerrilla war in a small country.[44] Perhaps he was on the whole correct; but notable guerrilla struggles have occurred in Chechnya (with an area of 6,000 square miles), on Cyprus (3,473 square miles), and in Northern Ireland (5,459 square miles). For comparison, Connecticut is 5,009 square miles.

In any event, today, even in large countries, governments' modern, long-range aircraft, guided missiles, satellite communications, and similar weaponry may have put an end to the possibility of truly safe and extensive guerrilla bases such as Mao's forces enjoyed.[45] As a substitute for a secure indigenous base, guerrillas may find a foreign sanctuary—territory across the border where, for one reason or another, they can be relatively safe.[46] The Afghan Mujahideen possessed an invaluable sanctuary in Pakistan, as the Viet Cong did in North Vietnam, Laos, and Cambodia. The Spanish guerrillas of Napoleon's day had all the waters surrounding Spain as a sort of sanctuary, for on those seas sailed the British navy and the guns and gold it brought to the insurgents. Neither the Vendeans, nor the Boers, nor the Huks possessed secure bases or foreign sanctuaries; tellingly, all of them met an unfavorable end.

Nevertheless, possessing a foreign sanctuary can sometimes turn out to be a grave source of weakness. For years the Communist-led guerrillas in the Greek civil war enjoyed unparalleled access to foreign sanctuaries across Greece's northern frontiers. Unfortunately for them, their sanctuaries were in the territory of countries many Greeks had long considered as hostile. More destructively, the possession of sanctuaries and outside sources of supply encouraged the guerrillas to discount the importance of popular support inside Greece itself, so that they felt free to express their profound, even murderous, contempt for the Greek peasantry among whom they operated.[47]

GUERRILLAS AND TERRORISM

The essence of guerrilla warfare is to carry out swift, successful attacks on isolated posts, small units, and supply lines of the enemy. Terrorism, here understood to be the deliberate targeting of civilians for death or injury, has nothing to do with guerrilla warfare per se; nevertheless, guerrilla movements have often resorted to it. In the post-1898 Philippines, guerrillas turned to terrorism against the civilian population when it became clear that they were losing the conflict. This policy was effective at first, but soon enough turned many Filipinos to cooperation with U.S. forces.[48] During the Greek civil war and the Malayan Emergency, insurgents directed terror at the population as an integral part of their strategy; by far the majority of people killed in Malaya by guerrillas were Chinese civilians. In Algeria, "urban terrorism was a much more important factor than in most popular rebellions."[49] French Army efforts to deal with this terrorism eventually led to the mutiny of 1958 and the collapse of the Fourth Republic.[50] In El Salvador, the leftist Farabundo Marti National Liberation Front (FMLN) turned increasingly to operations and tactics to inflict pain and death on innocent civilians (e.g., planting mines near populated areas, bombing cafés), a course that eventually generated a major public split within the insurgent ranks. In Colombia during the 1980s, FARC kidnappings and murders produced the counter-phenomenon that came to be known as the self-defense groups ("paramilitaries").[51] Many contend that these groups were an unavoidable consequence of the failure of the Colombian state to mobilize civilians into legally sanctioned self-defense forces.[52] In any event, these self-defense paramilitaries were both controversial and effective.[53]

But the premier examples of deliberate terrorism by a guerrilla force remain the Viet Minh and their successors, the Viet Cong. From the beginning of the Vietnam wars, the insurgents used violence against civilians as one of their cardinal methods. "The elimination of their opponents was one of the most common means the Communists used to establish Viet Minh control over the entire nationalist movement."[54] By 1965 the Communists had assassinated literally thousands of local officials and schoolteachers.[55] This reliance on terrorism was the most notable Vietnamese Communist innovation to (or deviation from) the Maoist model of insurgency. (Another important Vietnamese addition was reliance on manipulation of opinion in democratic societies—first France, then the U.S.)[56]

Open Viet Cong terrorism, including the shelling of crowded market places, increased in the 1970s, partly because they had a firm base area in North Vietnam and Laos, and partly because they had little hope of winning over substantial new numbers of the peasantry by that point.

All but one of the instances of deliberate terrorism cited here were employed by insurgencies that were losing, or that eventually lost. This suggests that not only is terrorism not intrinsic to properly waged guerrilla war, but that it is indeed *antithetical* to it (especially if one believes Mao's adage about fish in the water). Nevertheless, those who plan and wage counterinsurgency need to be aware that their very successes may unleash an ugly terrorist campaign by the remnants of the defeated insurgents.

"URBAN GUERRILLAS"

Certain groups, usually very difficult to distinguish from mere terrorists, have called themselves "urban guerrillas." A notable example would be the Uruguayan "Tupamaros" of the early 1960s. However sensational the violence they may perpetrate, guerrilla operations in cities defy the clear teachings of Clausewitz and Mao, and they have been victorious nowhere. Insurgents attempting to operate permanently in confined urban areas expose themselves to classic sweep and encirclement actions.[57] The tragic uprising of Polish Home Army units in Warsaw in 1944 is not a true instance of urban guerrilla war, but was instead a clash—forced upon the Home Army—of two wildly asymmetrical military formations within a metropolitan setting.[58] The insurgent forces in Grozny in the 1990s, employing artillery and even aircraft in a determined effort to hold onto key locations in that city, were not engaging in guerrilla tactics as that term is used in the literature.[59]

GETTING THE PARADIGM WRONG

The victories of Mao Tse-tung and Fidel Castro spawned many would-be imitators, especially in the 1970s. All of them failed. The failures of these imitators stemmed in large part from their misunderstanding of the paradigm they thought they were copying.[60] The mythology of the Maoist revolution is examined in chapter 14. Here it may be opportune to take a brief look at the true nature of Fidel Castro's successful revolt against the regime of Fulgencio Batista. Despite the romantic myths and clouds of propaganda surrounding that event, the simple truth is that the increasingly repressive and corrupt Batista regime had alienated key strata of Cuban society, including the Church and the business elites, and earned the open distaste of the Eisenhower administration. Identified with no particular class, group, or region, by 1956 the regime was isolated. Leading a band of a few hundred guerrillas in the mountains, Castro promised free elections and a return to the constitution of 1940—definitely not the Leninist dictatorship and explosive confrontation with the U.S. that he eventually imposed. The high command of the Batista Army consisted of "corrupt, cruel and lazy officers without combat experience."[61] During its two-year conflict with the guerrillas, many units of this fifteen-thousand-man force never fired a shot; it suffered a total of three hundred fatalities—an average of three per week. Toward the end of the conflict, the Eisenhower administration imposed an arms embargo on the Cuban regime. In actuality, therefore, the Castro revolution was a Batista collapse. Inexplicably overlooking these facts and acting on a totally illusory version of the Castro revolt, Ernesto Guevara quite predictably met his premature death in the mountains of Bolivia.[62]

An arresting contrast to the isolated, personalistic Batista dictatorship existed in El Salvador. There, the solidarity of the upper and upper-middle classes with the army produced "the strongest anti-communist sentiment in Latin America."[63] Against this steely phalanx, which was both receiving aid from the U.S. and clearly implementing some democratic reforms, the openly authoritarian and pro-Castro FMLN guerrilla movement, relying increasingly on forced recruitment and terrorism, hurled itself in vain for a decade, and then disappeared.[64]

"Russia's Vietnam"

Another notable example of the dangers of getting the paradigm wrong arises from the Soviet war in Afghanistan. Many have referred to that conflict as "Russia's Vietnam." Clearly, any two guerrilla conflicts will display certain similarities, especially if they involve superpowers failing to achieve their principal objectives. Yet the differences between the Soviet experience in Afghanistan and the American experience in Vietnam are patent and profound.

In the first place, at their numerical peak, Soviet forces committed to Afghanistan were less than one-fifth of the U.S. forces in South Vietnam in 1968. Five times more Soviet citizens died in road accidents during any single year of the 1980s than in the entire Afghan conflict.[65] Second, the geographical circumstances of the two conflicts differed dramatically: Afghanistan was right across the Soviet border, whereas Washington was closer to the South Pole than to South Vietnam. Thus, Afghanistan was not Russia's Vietnam but rather Russia's Mexico; Soviet withdrawal from Afghanistan was the equivalent of a U.S. withdrawal from Chihuahua. Third, indigenous support for a noncommunist South Vietnam was incomparably greater than indigenous support for a Soviet-dominated Afghanistan; hence the conquest of South Vietnam required a full-scale invasion by the North Vietnamese Army, the largest military operation East Asia had witnessed since the Chinese intervention in Korea a quarter of a century before. Fourth, however impressive their bravery and resolution, in terms of training and equipment the Afghan Mujahideen were simply not in the same class as the North Vietnamese Army and many of the main force Viet Cong units the Americans had to face. Fifth, Hanoi was incomparably more successful at manipulating perception and opinion in Washington (and elsewhere) than the Mujahideen ever were in Moscow. And last (at least in this account), the Soviet occupation of Afghanistan contributed indirectly but effectively to the dissolution of the Soviet empire; however painful the American experience in Vietnam, its effects were ephemeral in comparison.[66]

But perhaps some sort of award for the most grandiose failure to understand a guerrilla paradigm should go to those Americans who in the 1980s displayed bumper stickers demanding "No Vietnams in Central America."

CHAPTER 2

SOME WELLSPRINGS OF INSURGENCY

Many factors have produced insurgencies, almost as many as the ways in which rulers can commit folly or self-seeking men disguise their aims. While insurgencies always have multiple causes, in almost every instance one factor predominates, by providing either the provocation, the justification, and/or the opportunity for an outbreak. The present chapter examines five elements that have played such a role in insurgency: rigged or suppressed elections, a tradition of internal conflict, the aspirations of former or marginal or would-be elites, defeat in war, and a response from those targeted for genocide. (Religiously motivated insurgencies will be considered in separate chapters.)

RIGGED ELECTIONS: CLOSING THE PEACEFUL ROAD TO CHANGE

Popular elections have achieved a quasi-universal status as the symbol of legitimate authority, or at least as the road to peaceful change.[1] "Perhaps the most important and obvious, but also the most neglected fact, about great revolutions is that they do not occur in democratic political systems."[2] Che Guevara insightfully observed that it is not possible to make a successful insurgency against a government that is democratic, or that pretends to be so.[3]

On the other hand, for at least the past two hundred years the absence, or especially the shutting down, of a peaceful means of redressing grievances has clearly contributed to the outbreak and continuation of insurgency. This section examines five cases of the connections between denied or rigged elections and the development of insurgency: France in the 1790s, Mexico in the 1920s, the Philippines in the 1950s, El Salvador in the 1970s, and Kashmir in the 1990s.

France

The French revolutionary regime would eventually wage war not only against the whole of Europe, but against its own citizens as well, devastating and depopulating entire regions of France. Such conduct was possible because the revolutionary government had come to power through elections that were totally unrepresentative of popular desires. The French elections of August–September 1792 installed a new parliament, the so-called National Convention, a body that would proclaim the end of the monarchy; execute King Louis and his wife, Marie Antoinette; carry the country into war against Britain, Spain, and Austria; impose the draft; confiscate the equivalent of hundreds of billions of dollars in private property; shut all the churches in Paris and elsewhere; initiate the Terror; publicly guillotine thousands of citizens (most of them persons of quite humble condition); and wage genocidal war against French men and women in the Vendée and other provinces. Yet in those 1792 elections, less than one eligible voter in five participated, from an already narrowly restricted pool of electors. Most of those who did vote were compelled to do so orally and in the presence of government authorities.[4] Thus the revolutionary regime, enforcing an unprecedentedly radical program while restricting the electorate to its own narrow base of supporters and beneficiaries, found itself confronted by widespread and serious insurgencies.[5]

Mexico

The revolutionary regime that ruled Mexico after 1915 "had come to power through military force. It maintained itself by authoritarian means, without free elections. The new constitution had been imposed by a small minority of revolutionaries and had never been submitted to a vote for popular approval or rejection."[6] The subsequent electoral record speaks for itself. In the presidential election of 1920, the candidate of the revolutionary oligarchy, General Obregón, allegedly received 1.1 million votes, and all other candidates together less than 50,000; in some states the vote for Obregón was actually declared to be unanimous.[7] In 1924, government candidate Plutarco Calles was credited with 1,340,000 votes; all his opponents, 250,000.[8] In 1929, the official results gave Ortiz Rubio, the government candidate, 1,949,000 votes, while the distinguished educator José Vasconcelos allegedly received but 111,000. In 1934 the government candidate Lázaro Cárdenas supposedly obtained 2,225,000 votes; the official count for all his opponents, including the famous General Antonio

Villareal, was 41,000. Furthermore, shortly before the election of 1928 officially won by Obregón (who was soon thereafter killed), the government arrested both of the leading opposition candidates, Generals Arnulfo Gomez and Francisco Serrano, and executed them.[9]

Aside from their antireligious posture, the only shred of ideological cohesion among the revolutionary general-politicians was the sacred slogan of "No Reelection" of presidents, the cry of Francisco Madero and his followers in 1910. But these men rewrote their own constitution in 1926, to permit former president Obregón to take a second term. Not only was "No Reelection" cast aside, but the presidential term was extended to six years.[10] Twenty-three members of the Federal House of Deputies who dared to criticize these changes were stripped of office.[11] President Calles (1924–1928) treated public criticism of any constitutional provisions or laws as sedition. The regime was able to impose these measures because in addition to controlling the army and the labor unions, it counted the ballots and accumulated great wealth from recurrent civil wars, the looting of the Church, and the emoluments of office.

The regime's combination of religious persecution, prodigious stealing, and electoral fraud predictably produced violent reactions. The largest of these was a rising of Catholic peasants called the "Cristeros" (a name given to them in derision by the regime and then adopted by the insurgents). The rebellion flamed from 1926 into 1929. The insurgents enjoyed at certain periods quite widespread popular support, especially in western Mexico, and they inflicted some notable reverses on regime troops. Nevertheless, the Cristeros suffered defeat for several reasons. First, the U.S. supported the regime in Mexico City and prevented vital arms purchases by the insurgents. Second, rich Catholics on both sides of the border remained aloof from the predominantly peasant movement. Third, many Mexican bishops, eschewing violence or actually welcoming the prospect of martyrdom, refused to endorse the rising. Fourth, Pope Pius XI pressured those elements of the Mexican Church hierarchy who were favorable to the Cristeros to accept his view that peace must be made at almost any price.[12]

The Philippines

After the Japanese invasion of the Philippines, one of the main resistance groups formed there became known as the Huks (short for Hukbalahap, the Tagalog acronym for "People's Army against Japan"). This organization fell increasingly under the influence of Communist elements. Less than a year after the surrender of Japan, the U.S. recognized the independence of the Philippine Republic (July 4, 1946). The Huks soon took up arms against this government.

The insurgency derived support from many sources. Its stronghold was in the central region of Luzon, an island about the size of Kentucky, which had a long history of agrarian rebellion. Dislocation following the expulsion of the Japanese was compounded by widespread corruption in the administration of Manuel Roxas, first president of the independent Philippines. Roxas had served in the pro-Japanese puppet regime, and had been saved from postwar prosecution only by the intervention of General Douglas MacArthur.[13] As the Huk rebellion spread, mistreatment of the peasantry by the military increased.

Vice President Elpidio Quirino succeeded to the Philippine presidency after Roxas's death in 1948. Corruption in the Quirino government was so blatant that the Huks supported his reelection in 1949, hoping to benefit from growing disillusionment among the population. Quirino did not ultimately need their help, however: electoral dishonesty was so egregious that the "dirty election of 1949" played directly into the Huks' hands. The only path to change appeared to be that of the insurgency.

Alarmed by Huk progress, Quirino appointed Ramón Magsaysay as secretary of defense. Magsaysay immediately set to work improving both the military's counterinsurgency tactics and their treatment of the civilian population. Above all, Magsaysay used the army to ensure the cleanliness of the 1951 congressional elections. Indeed, the opposition party won every senate seat at stake that year. Magsaysay had restored the efficacy of the ballot box, and thus "to all intents and purposes the 1951 elections sounded the death knell of the Hukbalahap movement."[14] Two years later Magsaysay defeated President Quirino in a landslide.[15] The collapse of the Huk movement followed inevitably, symbolized by the surrender in May 1954 of Luis Taruc, principal military leader of the insurgency.[16]

Kashmir

Kashmir has long been a deeply troubled region, whose conflict has its most visible roots in the partition of British India into a Hindu-dominated India and a Muslim-dominated Pakistan in 1947. At the time, the so-called princely (semi-independent) states were free to choose which of the two successor countries they would join. Everyone expected that the maharaja of Kashmir, a Hindu ruling over a largely Muslim population, would join Pakistan. But he decided otherwise, and Kashmir thus became the only non-Hindu princely state to adhere to India. No election or referendum was held to ratify this decision. Warfare between India and Pakistan, as well as within Kashmir, directly followed. Kashmir had an area of eighty-six thousand square miles, the size of Romania or Utah. Following a U.N. cease-fire in 1949, fifty-four thousand square miles of Kashmir (equal to Bangladesh or Wisconsin), with a population of 7.5 million, remained under Indian occupation; the rest was occupied by Pakistan. After the partition, Prime Minister Nehru "connived at regimentation, repression, rigged elections, corruption and nepotism in Kashmir in the name of national interest."[17]

Outside observers have maintained that the latest eruption of insurgency in Kashmir is primarily the result of India's rigging of the 1987 state elections and the imposition of a puppet regime through fraud and intimidation.[18] "The conduct and outcome of this election closed the last possible venue for the expression of legitimate dissent in Kashmir."[19] "The same boys who joined the insurgents in 1989 had been poll watchers during the 1987 elections—and then found the elections to be rigged."[20] Estimates of those killed in the fighting in Kashmir between 1990 and 2000 reach sixty thousand—more than U.S. fatalities in the entire Vietnam conflict.[21]

El Salvador

El Salvador was for generations a commodity-export economy, with grave maldistribution of land and wealth and a dreary history of oligarchical control and military dictatorship.[22] The country has the highest population density in Latin America, and the living conditions of El Salvador's lowest strata had been for decades the worst of any Latin American country except perhaps Haiti. Certainly no other Central American society had a greater potential for class conflict.

Massive government fraud against reformist candidates in the presidential elections of 1972 and 1977 effectively closed off the electoral road to change.[23] Meanwhile, the curious and combustible mixture of Marxism and Christianity called "Liberation Theology" had been finding an attentive audience among some of the clergy and other middle-class elements. In December 1979, several Salvadoran revolutionary groups gathered in Castro's Havana to organize the Farabundo Marti National Liberation Front (FMLN). (The name derived from a Salvadoran Communist contemporary of the 1930s Nicaraguan guerrilla chieftain Augusto Sandino, who himself had never been a Communist.)

In 1980, President Carter committed the U.S. to preventing an FMLN victory. His successor, President Reagan, granted increased military aid to El Salvador, which greatly improved the army's counterinsurgency effectiveness. At the same time, appreciating the importance of restoring an honest ballot to the strife-torn country, President Reagan sent Vice President George Bush to San Salvador in December 1983 to warn the Salvadoran military not to interfere with the approaching elections. A month later appeared the famous Kissinger Commission Report, which insisted that further U.S. military aid should "be made contingent upon demonstrated progress toward free elections" and other political reforms.[24] Accordingly, in 1984, José Napoleon Duarte, mayor of San Salvador, graduate of Notre Dame, and critic of the Salvadoran establishment, was elected president, the first time in the country's history that an opposition candidate had been victorious.[25] In the 1989 elections Alfredo Cristiani, a Georgetown graduate, defeated the candidate of Duarte's party and was inaugurated; this was El Salvador's first-ever transfer of power from an elected civilian president to the elected civilian leader of the opposition.[26]

The restoration of honest national elections, a centerpiece of U.S. policy during the Salvadoran insurgency, contributed to the negotiated ending of the conflict in 1992.

Summary

The record strongly suggests that denying or corrupting free elections has served to provoke armed resistance to a regime; at the very least such practices have provided a justification for such resistance. In contrast, observers have often noted that the "ballot box is the coffin of insurgency," a dictum that receives ample support from the Philippines to El Salvador.[27] Greece, Venezuela, and Colombia, among other countries, succeeded in maintaining the practice of free elections even while facing serious challenges from insurgencies—challenges that were eventually defeated.

A TRADITION OF INTERNAL CONFLICT

Many societies have experienced an insurgency that flared brightly for a period and then became extinguished, often permanently. Some others, however, seem to possess a proclivity for protracted internal conflict that continues from one generation to another and for which no realistic set of solutions or palliatives is readily available. Long internal conflict of this type has plagued Northern Ireland, Yugoslavia and its successors, Angola, Sudan, Mozambique, Algeria, and some other countries. Few if any societies, however, have exhibited the tragic syndrome of chronic internecine destructiveness as severely as Colombia.

Colombia and Its Violence

Colombia is a land of superlatives: it is at least the fourth most populous Spanish-speaking country in the world, the country with the longest record of civilian rule in South America, and the third-largest annual recipient of U.S. military aid.[28] Colombia also has the unfortunate distinction of being the locus of the longest-lasting guerrilla insurgency in the twentieth century, a conflict that has generated the world's fourth-largest internal refugee problem.[29] Although help for the guerrillas once came, at least indirectly, from the USSR and Cuba, the warfare in Colombia is not caused by outsiders. On the contrary, it is rooted in the country's history and culture, a culture of violence that solidified itself during the nineteenth century, at the latest. Yet neither class nor ethnic nor ideological divisions satisfactorily accounts for these conflicts.[30] The period 1863–1880 is known in Colombia as the "Epoch of Civil Wars." From 1899 to 1903 the War of a Thousand Days killed 130,000 people out of a total population of a few million. The Colombian army has always been too small to maintain order, and beginning in the late 1940s, the country entered into a decade of slaughter, called simply *la violencia*.[31] Estimates of the number of Colombians who perished in *la violencia* run to 200,000, out of a 1952 population of 12 million.[32] (Violence on a proportional scale in the present-day U.S. would produce 8,000 killings per week.) Moreover, *la violencia* was notable not only for the scale of killing but for the truly horrific brutality inflicted upon many of the victims, especially women. Today the homicide rate in the city of Medellín is twice that of Detroit; the Colombian national homicide rate is fourteen times that of the United States. At least ten Colombians die in political violence per day.[33] Convictions, even indictments, for these crimes are uncommon; impunity is the rule. Colombia has become a self-perpetuating "war system."[34]

It is sometimes said that an insurgency cannot end until the social conditions that caused it also end. This is misleading on several levels. First, insurgencies in Central America ended in the 1980s and 1990s without fundamental changes in social conditions. Second, the principal insurgent force in Colombia, the FARC (Revolutionary Armed Forces of Colombia), at one time the military arm of the Colombian Communist Party, was never an authentic social movement, and has little popular support.[35]

But if the FARC guerrillas lack popular support, how can they survive? The answer lies in the last and most devastating of Colombia's superlatives: it is the greatest drug producer in the Western Hemisphere. Colombia today supplies 80 percent of the world's cocaine. Perhaps as much as 90 percent of the cocaine coming into the U.S., and 75 percent of the heroin seized on the east coast of the U.S., is Colombian.[36] The drug trade annually generates $900 million for the FARC and smaller insurgent groups, mainly from "taxes" on coca. FARC also gets about $250 million annually from kidnapping and extortion.[37] Another guerrilla group, the ELN, extorts money from oil companies. Between 1985 and 2000, the ELN bombed Colombia's main oil pipelines seven hundred times, inflicting untold damage on the ecology. In short, Colombian guerrilla groups have adopted many of the key methods of organized crime; thus, unlike almost all other guerrillas in world history, the Colombian guerrillas are rich.

With 439,000 square miles, Colombia is equal in size to France, Germany, and Italy combined, or to Arizona, Colorado, New Mexico, and Utah combined. Historically the control of the central government over this sprawling area extended not very far beyond the major cities. Several ranges of the great Andes Mountain chain traverse the country. Extensive eastern regions have never been integrated into national life.[38] Large strata of the rural population have traditionally had no positive contacts with the national government. Poor communications in many areas of the country have been an advantage to the guerrillas. From the early days of the republic until today, internal violence and state weakness have fed on one another. Organized violence becomes an expected, predictable, and hence normal, element of daily life.

Worse, in the mid-1990s the administration of President Andrés Pastrana "demilitarized" (i.e., abandoned) a 16,000-square-mile region in eastern Colombia (called the *despeje*), thus handing the FARC control of an area the size of Switzerland, bigger than Massachusetts, Connecticut, and Rhode Island combined. The ELN also received an area of its own, larger than Long Island. In effect, the Colombian government provided the insurgents with a secure base area, that prize of prizes for guerrillas. (Then-president Fujimori of neighboring Peru publicly criticized President Pastrana for these surrenders.) Predictably, handing these extensive zones over to the insurgents did not promote peace; to the contrary, the rebels used these areas to train fighters, stockpile supplies, and prepare attacks. The Colombian government finally rescinded this misguided *despeje* policy in January 2002.

Despite (or rather because of) President Pastrana's granting them a safe base, it has become clear that FARC will not seriously negotiate until the national army develops the capacity to defeat it. In August 2003, estimates of FARC strength hovered around 15,000 first-line fighters. The ELN guerrillas had perhaps another 5,000. The Colombian army numbered approximately 146,000 soldiers, considerably less than one-half of one percent of the population, backed up by 120,000 national police.[39] During the 1990s the Colombian army suffered several humiliating defeats at the hands of the FARC, which was able to deploy fighting units as large as 700 men. Clearly, the national army needs significant enlargement and improvement, advances that will almost certainly not occur until all Colombian social classes accept the need to make real sacrifices in order to establish government control of their country.[40] (Army casualties have been overwhelmingly from the lower classes, while high school graduates receive exemption from serving in combat units.)

A complicating factor is the rise of self-defense groups (often referred to as the AUC—"Autodefensas Unidas de Colombia"), misleadingly labeled "paramilitaries" by the U.S. media. Attempting to fill a role that the national army and police were not satisfying, many of these groups arose spontaneously to protect villages from FARC kidnappings and depredations.[41] The self-defense groups have proven to be the most aggressive and successful anti-FARC organizations in the country. The exact nature of the relationship between the army and the AUC—beyond the obvious fact that they have a common enemy—is hotly disputed.

Colombia's fighting and its refugees have been spilling over into Panama (with its canal), Venezuela (with its petroleum), and Brazil (with its extensive borders as the fifth-largest country on the planet).[42] Meanwhile, the distribution of Colombian cocaine increasingly involves European organized crime. Thus Colombia's long-standing violence is today not only disintegrating that country itself, but it also has regional, hemispheric, and even global implications and effects.[43] And a permanent end to this strife is not on the horizon.

THE DESIRE OF ASPIRANT ELITES TO GAIN POWER

Certainly, one can offer numerous instances in which the policies of an indigenous regime or a foreign occupation predictably provoked armed resistance, and several are discussed in this volume. But popular exasperation with government oppression does not exhaust the etiology of insurgency, as distinguished students of the phenomenon labored to illustrate during the Cold War. "Put crudely, we tend to work on the assumption that there is no such thing as bad peoples, only bad governments; and the very occurrence of revolutionary violence establishes a prima facie judgment in our minds in favor of the rebels and against the authorities."[44] This belief that internal conflicts "erupt spontaneously out of conditions grown socially and economically intolerable—and can only erupt out of such conditions—is a very important propaganda weapon in the hands of sympathizers with revolutionary warfare."[45]

As the Cold War evolved, analysts of rebellion challenged the view that guerrilla insurgency is primarily and invariably a mass uprising against gross exploitation. "Guerrilla movements are not best understood as the response of oppressed peoples to government repression. . . . Rather they better fit Theda Skocpol's concept of 'marginal political elites,' heretofore excluded from full power, who turn to revolutionary organizations. Their revolts . . . are an attempt to secure that power through the unorthodox means of a military alliance with the peasantry."[46] Especially but not exclusively in Latin America, revolutionary leadership prominently displayed this elitist character. Accordingly, "few scholars would now dispute the fact that Latin American modern guerrilla movements have been led to a large extent by middle class, university-educated young men."[47]

Supporting evidence for this view is not hard to find. Fidel Castro, the son of a landowner, studied law at Havana University. Ernesto Guevara, who wished to be a sort of latter-day Lawrence of Arabia, graduated from medical school in Argentina. Abimael Guzman, founder of Peru's Sendero Luminoso, was a philosophy instructor at a provincial university. Other examples abound.[48] An even more telling instance of the elitist nature of Latin American revolutionary/leftist movements was provided by the resounding defeat suffered by the Sandinista regime in the 1990 Nicaraguan elections, which took place under ideal conditions for the regime: control of the army, the police, the media, and the labor unions. After their defeat, the Sandinistas spent their

brief remaining time in power distributing state property among themselves in the form of large landholdings. The Sandinistas' subsequent
efforts to return to office met with even more decisive rebuffs by the
electorate.[49]

Latin American revolutionary movements have not been the only
ones dominated by members or near-members of the domestic elite.
In the Philippines, Emilio Aguinaldo's best chance to defeat the U.S.
occupation after 1898 was to play the card of class war, promising to
distribute the property of the rich to the impoverished peasantry if it
would follow him. But he chose to lose the conflict rather than take
such a fateful step against his own class. Fifty years later prominent
Philippine guerrilla leaders continued to come largely from the country's
elite classes: Luis Taruc, the principal figure of the Huk rebellion, had
been a medical student and a successful candidate to the Philippine
Congress; Vicente Lava, head of the Philippine Communist Party, held
a Ph.D. from Columbia University and was a professor of chemistry at
the University of the Philippines.

While further elaboration of the elitist nature of revolutionary leadership will follow, it may be necessary here to emphasize that elites or
would-be elites who organize revolutionary and insurgent movements
are not necessarily engaging in conscious deception. On the contrary,
Pareto was assuredly correct when he observed that "many of the
counterelite [revolutionary leadership] believe that they are pursuing,
not a personal advantage for themselves and their class, but an advantage for the masses, and that they are simply struggling for what they
call justice, liberty, humanity."[50] (Traditionally, revolutionary elites
sought to enlist oppressed or disrespected elements in the country. But
in recent times—actually for some considerable period—a new constituency is available to support elite-driven violence: what Ralph Peters has called the "new warrior class.")[51]

Neither does elite leadership in itself mean that such movements
are without significant popular support. Rather, it means that the support of a majority of the population, or even a large minority, is not
necessary to explain even a successful armed insurgency. The power of
well-organized minorities under determined leaders, especially in times
of political upheaval, has long impressed students of revolutionary conflict.[52] The definitive example of the power of a self-selected and highly
restricted group of insurgent leaders, of course, is the French Revolution, especially (but not only) in its most radical phases. "Participation
in the revolutionary movement involved only a narrow militant minor-

ity. *The violence it engendered was related to this fact.* The partial failure of the revolution stems from the fact that it was a popular movement only to a very limited degree. On the contrary, it increasingly incurred the hatred of the masses."[53]

Similarly, Lenin's Bolsheviks received only 25 percent of the vote in the elections for a Russian Constituent Assembly in 1917. But their discipline and ruthlessness empowered them to disperse that representative assembly and then to lash the peoples of the Russian empire through experiences from which they have not recovered to this day.[54]

Reflecting on the upheavals of the twentieth century, Hannah Arendt concluded that armed uprisings organized by small bands of professional revolutionaries have been the predominant revolutionary motif of this century.[55] An arresting example of both the elitist-minority nature of a famous revolutionary movement, as well as the ability of such a movement to obscure that nature, is provided by the Vietnamese Communists.

The Vietnamese Revolution

Perhaps the key mistake of French colonial policy in Vietnam was to allow thousands of Vietnamese to obtain a European-style education and then deny them the positions, salaries, and status in government service and private enterprise for which their educations had prepared them.[56] In the mid-1920s, 5,000 British civil servants governed 325 million Indians, but somehow it required the same number of Frenchmen to govern only 30 million Vietnamese.[57] By the mid-1930s, French civil servants in Vietnam were three times as numerous as their British equivalents in India.[58] As late as the 1950s Hanoi actually had French traffic policemen.[59] All the top positions, and many middle-ranking ones, in both government and business were closed to the Vietnamese. Any Vietnamese fortunate enough to get a job in those spheres usually received from one-fifth to one-half the salary paid to a Frenchman in the same position.[60] Contrast the situation in the Philippines: the Americans established an elected legislature there in 1907; before World War II almost all the government services in the islands, including police, health, and education, were run and staffed by Filipinos.[61] It is no mystery why "for most of those [Vietnamese] who became revolutionaries, it was clear that their own opportunities for advancement were inseparably bound up with eliminating French rule in Viet Nam."[62]

Thus we see a familiar picture in Vietnam: elements of a social elite organizing a revolutionary movement in order to come into power.

The revolutionary icon Ho Chi Minh attended a select prep school in Hué (and then was rejected for government employment). Pham Van Dong, the future premier of North Vietnam, was the son of an Annamese mandarin. Vo Nguyen Giap, who organized the Viet Minh army and defeated the French at Dien Bien Phu, had graduated from the University of Hanoi and taught history in a private school. Bui Tin, who led the final North Vietnamese assault on the Presidential Palace in Saigon in 1975, was the great-grandson of a provincial governor and cabinet minister. Bui Tin's father, who employed a chauffeur and several house servants and possessed a degree in French literature, had also been a provincial governor and cabinet minister.[63] The Japanese invasion of Vietnam in 1940 destroyed French control and prestige and opened the way to power for this privileged but frustrated Vietnamese elite.

The Revolutionary Minority

Soon after the partition of Vietnam in 1954, the Communists began organizing the insurgency against South Vietnam. The reason why that insurgency failed—and why, even after the withdrawal of American forces, it took a massive, conventional invasion by the entire North Vietnamese Army to subdue the South—is that the Communist organization in the South, the so-called Viet Cong, was not representative of the majority of the South Vietnamese population.

The Viet Cong were a minority in South Vietnam primarily because their predecessors, the Viet Minh, who had defeated the French and their indigenous allies, had also been a minority there. This apparent paradox grows out of the political history of Vietnam, a history of division, not unity, between the North, dominated by the Red River Delta, and the South, comprising mainly the Mekong Delta. Vietnam stretches a thousand miles from north to south, equal to the distance from Rome to Copenhagen. For centuries rival kingdoms contended in Vietnam, the boundary between them usually coinciding roughly with the 1954 line of partition. Thus, history and geography explain the marked differences in accent and psychology between northerners and southerners, much commented upon by Vietnamese themselves up to the present day.[64]

Colonial experience reinforced this regional diversity. French political and economic interests were much more firmly planted in Cochin China (Saigon and the Mekong Delta) than in other parts of Vietnam. During their occupation, the Japanese had treated Cochin China as a region distinct from the rest of the country. At the same time, the Viet Minh guerrillas sought refuge near or across the Chinese border, thus necessarily establishing their base in northern Tonkin, eight hundred miles away from Saigon. After the Japanese surrender, troops of Chiang Kai-shek occupied the northern Vietnamese provinces, while British forces entered the southern ones. The returning French reestablished their control first in the Saigon area.

Another major difference between the two regions was religion. The popular Western image of Vietnam as an overwhelmingly Buddhist society is quite mistaken. The Catholic minority, 10 percent of the total population, made up fully 50 percent in some provinces; great numbers of Catholic Vietnamese moved from North to South after the partition of 1954, becoming a bulwark against the Viet Cong. Additionally, the southern provinces were the stronghold of powerful indigenous religious sects, the Hoa Hao and the Cao Dai. At the end of the Viet Minh war in 1954, the latter group mustered from 15,000 to 20,000 armed men and controlled extensive areas north and west of Saigon. In 1947, Communists assassinated the leader of the Hoa Hao religion. At the same time, while the Vietnamese Communist Party claimed 180,000 members, only 23,000 of them lived in heavily populated Cochin China.[65]

Neither was the Viet Cong insurgency able to develop much support in the cities. An assertively pro-Viet Cong source estimates that in Saigon, a city of 2.5 million people, Communist activists in 1974 numbered perhaps 500.[66] Even in their stronghold of the countryside, the Viet Cong's strength diminished over time due to their tremendous casualties, losses they tried to replace through coercion. The Saigon government's sweeping land reform in the early 1970s also dimmed the luster of Communist revolution. By the middle 1970s outside observers estimated Viet Cong support at less than a third of the South Vietnamese population.[67] On the other hand, many groups—Northern refugees, Catholics, members of the Cao Dai and Hoa Hao sects, ARVN (South Vietnamese regular army) officers and their extended families, militia members, the urban middle classes, racial minorities—were irreconcilably opposed to a Northern takeover. The ARVN and the territorial (militia) forces numbered over a million men. Assuming that each member of these forces had four close civilian relatives (a very conservative estimate for a peasant society), soldiers, militia, and their families alone comprised almost a third of the population of South Vietnam. The self-defense forces (PSDF), composed of persons too young or too old for the army or militia, counted an additional half-million members. ARVN has been much criticized for its desertion rates (which had nothing at all to do with political loyalties); but casualty rates in the territorial forces were higher than in ARVN, while desertion rates were lower. Notably, defection to the enemy (as distinguished from desertion) was extremely rare in ARVN—but not among the Viet Cong.[68] Most important of all, ARVN stood up to the supreme challenges of the 1968 and 1972 Offensives. Indeed one expert observer stated that ARVN could stand comparison to the Israeli army.[69]

In 1975, North Vietnamese premier Pham Van Dong estimated that between 50 percent and 70 percent of the Southern population would need to be reeducated about the benefits of "reunification."[70] And after the fall of Saigon, over 1.5 million persons, out of a population of roughly 17 million, fled South Vietnam. (This is the equivalent of 24 million Americans fleeing the U.S., which would be the most enormous refugee mass in Western history.) It is not unreasonable to assume that more would have fled if leaving Vietnam had been easier, or if they could have been sure they had someplace to go.

Nevertheless, by promising to redistribute wealth and especially status in the countryside, the Viet Cong were able to mobilize considerable strength, especially before 1968. "To young men and women from the countryside, the [Viet Cong] offered the idealistic vision of a unified socialist Viet Nam. It also recruited and promoted on the basis of merit and offered to the ambitious an opportunity to help govern the new Viet Nam."[71] The Viet Cong showed to rural youth a vision of a Vietnam from which the French and the landlords were gone, a Vietnam which they themselves would rule. In return for this promise of social advancement, the party "asked absolute political dedication, obedience, and a willingness to face the very real prospect of death."[72] By joining the Viet Cong, an individual broke his ties with family and village, becoming totally committed to the revolution.[73] Thus, whether or not the party had the support of the majority of the peasants made little real difference. "It is very possible that [observers] were right when they claimed that most peasants did not care who ruled in Saigon and just wanted to be left alone. The Party had what it needed, the support of the most politically aware and most determined segment of the peasantry."[74] After 1968 at the latest, the Viet Cong almost certainly would have lost an internationally supervised election in South Vietnam. But insurgencies are not elections.

A notable, if unsurprising, similarity exists between young recruits to the Viet Cong in the 1950s and those elements of Peruvian Indian youth in the 1980s who viewed membership in Sendero Luminoso as an avenue to social advancement. "By joining Abimael Guzman's movement, young people became better than whites; they went instantly from the bottom to the top of the social pyramid. For brown-skinned women this meant achieving a double equality—to whites and to men."[75]

Summary

In times of social malaise or political upheaval, the power of organized minorities to impose their will can affect the course of national and even global events. During the twentieth century, the leadership of many insurgent movements, from Latin America to Southeast Asia, was comprised quite disproportionately of young men and women from ruling, displaced, or aspiring elite groups. Revolutionary leaders from these relatively privileged social strata were able to attract recruits from elements of the depressed or marginalized classes with promises of future social advancement and political preferment.

The elite or quasi-elite leadership of revolutionary movements reminds us of Aristotle's observation that "men do not become tyrants in order that they will not have to suffer from the cold."[76] Or, in George Orwell's words: "One does not establish the dictatorship in order to safeguard the revolution; one makes the revolution in order to establish the dictatorship."[77]

DEFEAT IN WAR

Any search for understanding of insurgency requires an examination of the armed forces that an insurgent movement will challenge.

Some insurgencies have confronted regimes whose militaries were corrupt, badly trained, and/or apathetic. A classic example is the collapse of the Batista regime in Cuba. But more often, revolutionary guerrilla warfare has arisen in circumstances in which involvement in a conventional conflict had seriously weakened or even obliterated the regime's military defenses.

Lenin wrote, "The fundamental law of revolution, which has been confirmed by all revolutions and especially by all three Russian revolutions in the twentieth century, is as follows: for a revolution to take place it is not enough for the exploited and oppressed masses to realize the impossibility of living in the old way, and demand changes; for a revolution to take place it is essential that the exploiters should not be able to live and rule in the old way. It is only when the lower classes do not want to live in the old way and the upper classes cannot carry on in the old way that the revolution can triumph. This truth can be expressed in other words: *revolution is impossible without a nation-wide crisis* affecting both the exploited and the exploiters."[78]

This "nation-wide crisis" is, at bottom, the regime's loss of its military defenses. Again Lenin: "No revolution of the masses can triumph without the help of a portion of the armed forces that sustained the old regime."[79] The profoundly anti-Leninist scholar Hannah Arendt agrees: "Generally speaking, we may say that no revolution is even possible where the authority of the body politic is truly intact, and this means, under modern conditions, where the armed forces can be trusted to obey the civil authorities."[80] Whatever the precise accuracy of these pronouncements, students of political upheaval would hardly deny that "the part played by the army is decisive in any revolution."[81] Perhaps the Russian Revolution of October 1917 most persuasively demonstrates the effect of the collapse of a government's military power: "the ultimate complete loss by [Kerensky's] Provisional Government of control over its armed forces predetermined and made possible the scope and success of the social upheaval throughout the country."[82]

Disaster in war therefore has served as a crucible of internal upheaval. The crumbling or cracking of the regime's armed forces does not in itself produce insurgency, but it provides its opponents with the opportunity for a successful armed strike, and may also suggest to those not previously hostile to the regime that immediate, fundamental change in the leadership of the state is required. A generation ago an acute observer wrote that "existing theories [of revolution] focus primarily or exclusively upon *intra*-national conflicts and processes of modernization [but] modern social revolutions have happened only in countries situated in disadvantaged positions within international arenas,"[83] that is to say, countries whose military power has been broken by foreign adversaries. From France in 1789 to Russia in 1917 and China in 1945, repeated military failures, even catastrophic defeats, have destroyed ruling regimes' reputations for wisdom or even competence, and deprived them of the physical means to stave off attack by internal enemies.[84]

Most particularly, disaster in war was the fundamental circumstance leading to the rise of Communist regimes, from Russia to Vietnam. "The political function of Communism is not to overthrow authority, but to fill the vacuum of authority."[85] That was why "all Marxist revolutions, from that of Lenin to those of Mao and Ho Chi Minh, and from the First World War to after the Second, were produced in backward countries and under the impact of war. This *is* their logic, and not an accident at all."[86]

The German occupation of Greece and Yugoslavia early in World War II made possible the Communist-led insurgencies in those countries. Similarly, the severe mauling that the Imperial Japanese Army inflicted year after year on the Chinese forces of Chiang Kai-shek prepared the path to power for Mao Tse-tung after the end of World War II. "Communism in China has very little meaning apart from the trials China experienced during the war of resistance [to the Japanese]."[87]

In the same period, the prestige of the European colonial establishments in British Malaya, Dutch Indonesia, and French Vietnam suffered ultimately fatal blows from the rapid and apparently effortless advances of the victorious Japanese. Thus, before the war the French had been able to maintain order in Vietnam with a few thousand troops; after the war, many scores of thousands would prove insufficient. Between the surrender of the Japanese and the reappearance of the French, the Communist-dominated Viet Minh guerrillas marched unopposed into Hanoi. And in the Philippines, the severe dislocations produced by the Japanese occupation opened the road to the Huk rebellion.

If all this is true, or mainly true, then it strongly suggests that successful guerrilla insurgency is unlikely in a country whose army is intact and loyal. There is evidence to support this thesis: Despite all their confusion, corruption, or incompetence, the regimes of El Salvador, Colombia, the Philippines, and Peru have successfully resisted quite serious insurgencies in large part because their respective armies remained solidly opposed to the insurgents and therefore generally willing to submit to government direction.[88]

The Case of Malaya[89]

In Malaya, as in many other societies, the upheavals wrought by World War II provided the circumstances for guerrilla insurgency. Japanese operations began in northern Malaya on December 8, 1941. On December 24 they took the capital, Kuala Lumpur. And on February 15, 1942, sixty-two thousand British and Imperial troops surrendered Singapore to a considerably smaller number of Japanese, "the worst disaster and largest capitulation in British history."[90]

The British collapse at the hands of the Japanese stripped them of the aura of invincibility that had been the main source of their power. "[Singapore's] easy capture . . . was shattering to British, and European, prestige in Asia."[91] The disaster also exposed many serious flaws in the British administration of those colonies.[92] Moreover, the Allied victory in 1945 did little to restore British prestige in the eyes of the Malayans: While the peoples of Malaya had seen the Japanese defeat the British, they did not see the British defeat the Japanese, because Japan surrendered before the arrival of British forces in the peninsula. As the Japanese were advancing down the Malay peninsula in early 1942, the British trained a guerrilla force eventually called the Malayan People's Anti-Japanese Army (MPAJA), and released numbers of Communists from prison to participate in that force. At the end of the war, the crucial weeks between the Japanese capitulation and the reestablishment of British power provided the Communist-led guerrillas of the MPAJA precious time to solidify their organization. Moreover, the behavior of newly-arrived British troops often resembled that of an army occupying a conquered territory: soldiers were frequently billeted in civilian homes, some of the troops committed rape, and others either ignored or participated in petty corruption. None of this strengthened British authority.

The ethnic policies of the Japanese occupation—which favored the Malays and persecuted the Chinese—also complicated the British restoration. Elements of the ethnic Malay population had viewed the invading Japanese with equanimity, seeing them as useful allies in holding down the Chinese population.[93]

After the war the returning British had little money with which to restore an economy damaged by war and Japanese neglect, and few personnel familiar with the languages and customs of the various ethnic groups in Malaya. The administration favored British businesses over Chinese, and during the early days of the insurgency protected British plantations but not Chinese. The Chinese community wanted prosecution of those who had collaborated with the Japanese, but the returning British were reluctant to antagonize the Malay majority. Between the Japanese surrender and the British reoccupation many racial scores were settled, while bandits took hostages, especially Chinese, for ransom. Maintenance of an impartial reign of law and order had been a chief justification for British colonialism, and the widespread disorder was upsetting to many and undermined British authority probably as much as the 1942 defeat.[94] A key reason for the disorder was the devastating impact of the Japanese occupation on the police forces; the Japanese had used Malay police brutality to control the Chinese community, and low pay encouraged corruption.

By war's end the Communist-led MPAJA had little competition within the Chinese community. The only news the Chinese in Malaya received during the war was through Japanese propaganda or the MPAJA. The Chinese were inclined to believe the latter source; indeed, many of them believed that the MPAJA had won the war. The Japanese occupation had broken up many traditional social groupings, and the returning British had very few Chinese speakers or contacts in the Chinese community through whom grievances could be expressed. Chinese schools in Malaya, moreover, had for years been inculcating nationalist and anti-British attitudes. Once a Chinese joined the MPAJA guerrillas, the whole family felt obliged to protect him/her. During the insurgency, Communist guerrillas killed more Chinese than any other ethnic group, but on the whole the British authorities nonetheless tended to be suspicious of all Chinese. On the other hand, those very factors that made the MPAJA powerful among the Chinese community tended to hurt it among Malays and Indians, who comprised a majority of the total population. Meanwhile, British postwar plans for a Malayan constitution offended the Malays because the proposals seemed too friendly to Chinese interests and too limiting of the powers of the Sultans in the various Malay states. In the face of criticism, the British backtracked on their original proposals, thereby alienating the Chinese but not recapturing the trust of the previously offended Malays. In the midst of these conflicting pressures unleashed by defeat and occupation, the long Malayan guerrilla insurgency arose and developed.

Summary

After 1945, Communist or nationalist insurgencies flared across Southeast Asia, in the Philippines, Malaya, Indonesia, and Vietnam. It is not easy to imagine how these insurgencies would have been possible had there been no Japanese invasion, which swept aside the forces of the colonial or tutelary power in each case and thus stripped away the ruling authorities' aura of competence and permanence. To an equal degree, the Yugoslav and Greek insurgent movements received their opportunity from the German occupation of their countries. And it is hardly an accident that the insurgency in French Algeria broke out a few months after the fall of Dien Bien Phu.

INSURGENCY AS A RESPONSE TO GENOCIDE

It would clearly be an error to assume that all insurgencies are a reaction to oppressive practices by those in power. As has been noted, most insurgencies can be usefully understood as having multiple interconnected causes. But in some instances the approach taken by those in power toward the general population is so thoroughly hostile, so systematically destructive, that it is tantamount to genocide, and consequently provokes armed rebellion.

The Chechen conflict of recent years and the Polish uprising against Nazi occupation are two examples of insurgency as a response to a genocidal regime.[95]

The Chechen Wars

Not long after their withdrawal from Afghanistan, the Soviets found themselves facing another insurgency, this time within their own borders, in Chechnya. With an area of about six thousand square miles, Chechnya is smaller than El Salvador or New Jersey; the population in 1992 was about one million. Conquering the region that included Chechnya took the Russians most of the first half of the nineteenth century, and czarist aggression and repression were the principal instruments in forming Chechen national and religious self-identification. The Chechens' experiences of the past two hundred years "made them in fact one of the great martial peoples of modern history."[96] During and after World War II, the Stalinists deported Chechens and other groups from their traditional homelands, because they had been occupied by the German army. Six hundred thousand Chechens were packed into overcrowded railroad cars without heat or sanitation, transported thousands of miles, and often simply dumped into desolate areas devoid of shelter or food. Perhaps one-third of the deportees perished.[97] "The memory of the deportation became the central defining event in modern Chechen history."[98] After the war, scores of thousands of surviving Chechens made their way back to their homeland. By the end of the 1980s the area suffered from widespread unemployment, nearly the lowest medical and educational levels in the USSR, and very high mortality rates from infectious diseases and parasites. In light of Chechen experience with the Russians and Soviets—conquest, massacres, confiscations, collectivization, purges, deportations—it should have surprised no one when during the breakup of the USSR they sought to reclaim their independence, which they declared officially in November 1991. Thus began a cruel war that raged into the next century and exposed Russian military weakness even more glaringly that had the war in Afghanistan in the previous decade.[99]

The Polish Home Army Against the Nazis[100]

Soviet brutality in Afghanistan and Chechnya, however appalling, is overshadowed, sadly, by the enormities that the Nazis perpetrated in Poland after 1939. Out of the hell the Nazis created in that land arose one of the most desperate and tragic insurgencies of the blood-soaked twentieth century.

"The conditions of German occupation were worse for the Poles than for any other nation except the Jews."[101] Poland lost six million inhabitants in the war, 22 percent of her total population—the largest loss of any country in Europe. Many young Polish children were kidnapped, to be raised as Germans. Aiming to exterminate the intelligentsia, the Nazis systematically murdered teachers, professors, priests, physicians, and journalists. Poland was the only occupied country in which the Germans imposed the death penalty on anyone helping Jews.[102] The German occupation was so harsh that no Polish Quisling ever appeared. At the same time, in their half of Poland, the Soviets deported around one and a half million Poles, many of whom died in labor camps in Siberia and inner Asia.

The unprecedented enormities of the Nazi occupation help explain why Poles who were able to escape abroad pursued the fight against Nazism with unparalleled ferocity. In the Royal Air Force (RAF), Polish fighter squadrons accounted for 15 percent of German aircraft destroyed during the Battle of Britain. Polish ground units fought in Libya, Normandy, Belgium, and Italy; by 1944 there were two hundred thousand Polish fighting men under British command.[103]

The Home Army—Organized underground resistance in Poland began in September 1939 when, in the face of the Nazi invasion, the commander of the troops defending Warsaw authorized creation of a secret military organization, which eventually became known as the Home Army (Armja Krajowa), designated AK in the following discussion. By July 1944 the AK had 380,000 "sworn members";[104] 8,000 women belonged to the Warsaw AK.[105] The AK's principal aims were to support Poland's allies by gathering intelligence and distracting German units, and to prepare for a general uprising when the hour of Poland's deliverance approached.[106]

The Polish intelligence services had already helped to change the course of history by their role in breaking the vaunted German "Enigma" code before the outbreak of World War II.[107] The AK also made vital contributions to Allied intelligence during the war. It had warned of Hitler's approaching invasion of the USSR. It also discovered the secret activities at Peenemunde, enabling the RAF to attack the factories there in August 1943, thus setting back the German V1 rocket program by several months.[108] Polish postal workers randomly opened and photographed letters from German soldiers in Poland to their homes in Germany, a priceless source of information concerning military morale and order of battle. The AK also sheltered escaped Allied prisoners of war and carried out a vast program of sabotage, which included damaging or destroying literally thousands of locomotives and military vehicles and blowing up thirty-eight railroad bridges. All these activities slowed down delivery of Polish quotas of food and material to Germany and were worth several divisions to the Allied cause.[109]

The AK also executed officials who exceeded the usual Nazi standard of savagery, as well as Polish traitors and spies. In most of these cases, a secret panel of three professional jurists would hear an indictment. The panel could then render one of three verdicts: guilty, not guilty, or case postponed because of the nature of the evidence (the last being in fact the most common verdict). A local resistance commander could order an execution without a trial in an emergency (for example, if a spy or traitor was about to betray someone to the Gestapo). Predictably, many Polish jurists were very reluctant to serve on these panels because of the impossibility, under the Nazi occupation, of having the accused person appear in his own defense. The AK set up the panel system in order to provide some legal sanction for its use of reprisals as a means of imposing some restraint on the Nazis. No one was permitted to participate in more than three executions, in order to avoid developing a corps of professional assassins.[110]

Perhaps the most famous AK reprisal against the Nazis involved General Franz Kutschera, who had inaugurated random street executions in Warsaw. After warning Kutschera twice that if he continued such practices he would be killed, the AK executed him on February 1, 1944, in downtown Warsaw. His successor evidently took this lesson to heart because the Germans ceased to perform public executions in the capital.[111]

The AK also published its own newspaper, which it mailed regularly to the Gestapo. It detailed which execution and act of sabotage had been committed in retaliation for which German atrocity. General Komorowski (hereinafter referred to by his nom de guerre, Bor), eventual commander of the AK in Warsaw, believed that many Gestapo agents began to be more hesitant to commit criminal acts, at least openly, for fear of AK reprisal.

As the war ground on, and German troops began retreating slowly westward, the AK started preparations to liberate Warsaw before the Russians arrived. The AK had many good reasons to fear the advancing Soviets. Substantial AK units in eastern Poland had been taken prisoner by Russian troops. In the city of Wilno on July 17, 1944, AK commanders and staff were arrested by Soviet commanders, who had invited the Poles to a conference.[112] Similarly, in Lwow on July 31, 1944, the Soviet High Command called for a meeting with the AK leadership; the NKVD (Stalin's secret police) then seized the Polish soldiers, along with civilian representatives of the Polish government-in-exile in London.[113]

The Death Struggle—At the time of the uprising, August 1, 1944, Warsaw was fifty-four square miles in area with between one and one and a half million inhabitants. No European capital suffered so much destruction as Warsaw, mainly as a result of the 1944 rising. At the time, the Warsaw AK had around twenty-five thousand members, of whom only one in ten had a gun.[114] Before the rising the AK had actually managed to purchase some firearms from the Germans themselves.[115] At the outbreak of fighting about fifteen thousand German and other Axis troops were in the city; that number would soon be increased. Heinrich Himmler gave orders that everyone in Warsaw should be killed, including women and children. The Luftwaffe bombed Warsaw for the first time since 1939. Massive air attacks and artillery fire destroyed the Old Town section, the site of many medieval structures and the easternmost outpost of baroque architecture in Europe. The Germans dropped more bombs and shells on the Old Town than on any other single place in World War II. The AK in that sector suffered from 50 percent to 80 percent casualties. Fifteen hundred Old Town defenders escaped via the sewers, which the AK had been using for communications. Eventually discovering this fact, the Germans attacked the sewers with hand grenades and poisonous gas and engaged in ferocious hand-to-hand fighting in conditions of unimaginable filth.

To reinforce the German army garrison during the uprising, SS troops were brought into the city. They committed every kind of sub-human atrocity. AK members treated captured soldiers of the regular German army as prisoners of war, but they killed on the spot any captured SS men.[116]

On October 2 the Germans agreed to treat surrendering Warsaw AK members as prisoners of war under the Geneva Convention. Seeing no hope of outside help reaching Warsaw, General Bor, commander of the AK in the city, gave himself up on October 5.

Why Did the AK Rise?—The source of the AK's rising is a very complicated question. One who was not there cannot hope to understand fully the pressures felt by those in charge of the AK, men who had been living for years in a psychotic, satanic Nazi world. But motivations for the AK rising certainly included the following: First, by 1944 the AK had an "overwhelming impatience to fight."[117] Second, AK Warsaw commander Bor believed that if a rising did not take place before the end of summer 1944, the Germans would have time to send ample reinforcements into the city.[118] Third, the Germans were announcing plans to take one hundred thousand young persons out of Warsaw to dig fortifications, and the AK would thereby lose many of its members. Fourth, the AK leadership wished to prevent the destruction of Warsaw's population and structures when a general German retreat should become necessary. Fifth, Soviet armies were advancing rapidly across White Russia, and would soon roll across Poland's borders; the Poles believed they had to do something to avoid being portrayed as German collaborators by the Soviets.

The AK suffered twenty-two thousand casualties. Perhaps a quarter of a million civilians perished in the city. The German commander in Warsaw, General Bach-Zalewski, claimed twenty thousand German casualties, while Bor said ten thousand Germans were killed, nine thousand wounded, and seven thousand missing.[119] The Germans also lost 270 tanks, highly vulnerable in narrow streets to young men and women with homemade gasoline bombs ("Molotov cocktails"). Fifteen thousand AK, including two thousand women, marched out of Warsaw as German prisoners.

During the nine weeks of the rising, while the Nazis bombed and burned and killed, the Soviet armies halted their advance within binocular range of Warsaw. Stalin repeatedly rebuffed pleas from his Western allies to relieve the dying city. He even refused to allow Allied pilots who had dropped supplies into Warsaw to land within Russian lines. Because of the excessive rate of loss caused by this refusal, British flights to Warsaw from bases in Italy were soon halted. "The Soviets' conduct during the Rising should be branded as the greatest crime of that war, a worse crime even than Katyn,[120] for two hundred thousand men, women and children paid for it with their lives."[121] As the Hitlerite occupation of Poland was replaced by the Stalinist occupation, the Soviets imprisoned all the AK leaders they could locate. Many were never seen again.

The Polish Home Army believed that Poland would be enslaved forever if Warsaw did not free itself from the Nazis. After six indescribably horrible years, the Nazis were gone. Then the Russians and their native stooges subjected what was left of the country to a regime both tyrannical and incompetent for the next forty-four years. Truly, Poland's geography was her destiny, and her tragedy.

CHAPTER 3

RELIGION AND INSURGENCY IN THE EIGHTEENTH AND NINETEENTH CENTURIES

While it would be difficult to identify a guerrilla insurgency driven exclusively by religious issues, it is undeniable that a number of insurgencies have had their primary genesis in a reaction to perceived outrages against religious institutions and sentiments.

For countless millions of human beings, especially those in rural communities, religion is intimately connected to their self-definition and to their perceived well-being both in this world and in the next. Consequently, an insurgency in defense of religion will be resolute and protracted, and may have the most serious consequences for the regime that provokes it. In our own time, religious insurgency is widely and understandably associated with Islam, the result of conflicts in Afghanistan, Chechnya, Kashmir, Kosovo, Mindanao, Palestine, Sinkiang, and elsewhere. But five of the six insurgencies analyzed in this chapter and the following one were non-Islamic: in France, Spain, Mexico, Tibet, and Sudan. Three of these insurgencies arose against a domestic regime (in the Vendée, Mexico, and Sudan), and three against a foreign occupation (in Spain, Tibet, and Afghanistan). The present chapter shows as well the undeveloped and self-destructive counterinsurgency methods of the armies of Revolutionary and Napoleonic France, at home and abroad.

THE VENDÉE

As the Revolutionary regime in Paris entered its most radical phase in the early 1790s, insurgencies broke out in several areas of France. The most famous of these, in the province of La Vendée, became "the symbol of the counterrevolution."[1] There and in other areas[2] rural folk rose up, driven to desperation by a full-scale assault on their way of life, especially on their religious practices. The enormities committed by the Revolutionary regime against its own civilians, enormities perhaps assumed to be exclusive to the twentieth century, make these Vendean events all too familiar to present-day observers.

In many areas of rural France, the social life of the people revolved around the parish church.[3] The "country curates [parish priests] of the Estates General [were] the most authentic representatives of the majority of Frenchmen. They were certainly much closer to the People so freely apostrophized by the Third Estate than the lawyers, functionaries and professional men who made up that body."[4]

The Revolution suppressed religious orders and confiscated Church lands, most of which went to rich bourgeoisie. But the Revolution's main blow to the Church was the cluster of decrees known as the Civil Constitution of the Clergy of July 1790. This document provided that "the laws of the state are absolutely binding upon the clergy, even when they are opposed to the discipline or dogma of Catholicism." That is, "the state was master even in the religious sphere; it was the source of all law, authority and truth."[5] In March 1791 Pope Pius VI condemned the Civil Constitution of the Clergy.[6] Indeed, "no pope could for a moment have considered accepting it. Although there was the usual diplomatic delay, the break between the pope and the revolutionary government was inevitable, and with it *a powerful and conservative group of Catholics was forced irreconcilably into opposition.*"[7]

"The Turning Point"

The regime demanded that every bishop and priest not merely conform to the Civil Constitution but swear a public oath of allegiance to it. "If there was a point at which the Revolution 'went wrong,' it was when the Constituent Assembly imposed the oath to the Civil Constitution of the clergy, November 27, 1790. This marked the end of national unity and the beginning of civil war. *For the first time popular forces were made available to the opponents of the Revolution.*"[8] Here "was the fatal moment in the history of the Revolution,"[9] because "it brought wide popular support to its adversaries."[10] It was "certainly the Constituent Assembly's most serious mistake."[11] All but seven bishops (out of 160) and about half of the parish priests became "nonjurors," refusing the oath.

The Legislative Assembly, successor to the Constituent Assembly, imprisoned or exiled recalcitrant priests.[12] Women on their way to religious services were beaten on the streets "before the eyes of the jeering

National Guards."[13] Nonjuring priests risked harsh penalties for ministering secretly to their flocks.[14] In June 1792 local authorities began the illegal deportation of all clergy who refused the oath.[15] On March 3, 1793, (just before the first major rising), nearly all the churches in the Vendée were declared closed.[16] Soldiers carried off the bells and sacramental vessels. The regime struck Sunday from the calendar and forbade the erection of crosses on graves. It thus provided "the sine qua non of any peasant rebellion: an overwhelming conviction that the government, its officials, and friends were manifestly unjust."[17]

The Insurgency

"In the Vendée it was the republican assault on religion that turned the peasants into potential insurgents."[18] But what turned potential insurgents into actual ones was the Revolution's declaration in March 1793 that it would draft three hundred thousand peasants into the army while public officials (the republican bourgeoisie) granted themselves an exemption from this very draft.[19] These bourgeois officials were "the same people who had ejected non-juring priests in 1791; the same people who had bought up the best Church lands when they had come on the market; townsmen who had done consistently well out of the Revolution at the expense, so it seemed, of surrounding peasant communities and the Church upon which loyalties had focused."[20]

The Vendean peasantry rose up against the draft from reluctance to be sent far away from their home districts.[21] Coming on top of the assault on their priests, the peasants-only draft was "the spark in the building stuffed with combustibles."[22] And so, in the spring of 1793, extensive areas of western France erupted in revolt.

Having turned all Europe against itself,[23] the Paris regime now faced rebellion at home. It might have chosen to remove or mitigate some of the main causes of this discontent. Instead, it chose to suppress and eventually obliterate the Vendée, one of the most prosperous regions in the country, full of grain and beef and sturdy houses, supporting a population of eight hundred thousand in an area half the size of Connecticut.

"A Movement Purely Democratic"

The conflict was to a large degree a battle of town versus village.[24] Regime militia units, composed largely of republican refugees from inflamed areas of the Vendée, predictably were bent on revenge against the country people.[25] These bourgeois had always looked upon the peasants "not as potential partners to be won over but as potential enemies to be controlled."[26]

The Vendean rebellion was spontaneous and local, "a movement purely democratic in its origin."[27] The insurgents elected their own local commanders. Although at its core a religious revolt,[28] the longer the rebellion went on, and the more violent the republican response to it, the more certain that hostility toward the republican authorities would turn into support for monarchical restoration. The Vendeans first took the name of "The Catholic Army"; the phrase "and Royal" came later.[29] "Everything in this army was religion."[30] The Vendeans fought for local goals, above all the reopening of their parish churches with their former priests. This localism was to prove their main weakness.

The republicans now encountered an ideological fervor equal to their own.[31] "The insurrection was the first instance of that modern type of war in which both sides stress the ideological involvement of their troops and use tactics that attempt to exploit the enthusiasm, the sense of conviction, and the physical and moral initiative of the individual fighter."[32] Here the Vendeans had an advantage: "A patriot gained so little by dying for the republic, whilst a Vendean braved death for his God and his King."[33] Religious exaltation gave the peasants courage and a cause; it did not give them a strategic vision.

Most Vendeans were armed with farm tools. They obtained some real weapons from the republican troops, through combat or purchase, or from their own forges.[34] They received no arms from abroad.[35] The British government, facing worldwide demands on its slender military resources, believed it could not afford to waste any assistance to what appeared to be a series of peasant riots. But in March 1793, a Vendean force of ten thousand took the sizable town of Cholet; other towns fell to them the same month without a fight.

The Regime Responds

At war with England, Austria, Spain, and Prussia, the Revolutionary regime did not at first appreciate the magnitude of the revolt. When appeals by republican officials in the region could no longer be ignored, the government dispatched inadequate numbers of ill-trained troops. As late as the end of July only 80,000 republican troops had reached the area.[36] This was a major error, because it gave the Vendeans time to organize. Between 60,000 and 120,000 persons, including thousands of women, eventually took part in the rising.[37] Sometimes the Vendeans would assemble a force of 100,000 at a time.[38] The insurgency owed its early successes in part to the inadequate quality of the republican forces in the affected areas.[39] Also inadequate were the army's tactics. A further handicap of the regime's troops was their open contempt for the peasantry among whom they were operating. And political interference from Paris played its predictable role: to ensure the fidelity of republican officers fighting in the Vendée, the National Convention sent civil commissioners to oversee military operations, and imprisoned some of its best officers because they had previously held commissions in the royal army.

In contrast the Vendeans combined the skill of the American Indian, the fury of the Scots Highlander, and the zeal of the Cromwellian Ironside.[40] They fired at their antagonists from behind trees, thickets, and houses. When they suffered defeat or encountered danger at a certain place, they vanished into the countryside. These peasant guerrillas, who carried at most a gun and some ammunition, could move much more quickly than the pursuing republican troops heavily burdened with weapons and ammunition.[41] Rebel mobility, especially among the followers of Charette,[42] constantly amazed their foes. A republican general wrote: "Invincible attachment to their party, unlimited confidence in their chiefs, such fidelity to their promises that it could take the place of discipline, indomitable courage, strong enough to meet the test of all sorts of dangers, fatigues and privations; that is what makes the Vendeans fearsome enemies."[43]

In April 1793, an invading force of twenty thousand republican troops encountered thirty thousand insurgents. Operating on interior lines and unburdened by a heavy logistical "tail," the Vendeans maneuvered and struck quickly. By the end of the month the invaders had endured a severe mauling. By late May, the insurgents were organizing a government and issuing their own currency, bearing the face of the boy King Louis XVII (who would die in a republican prison). That same month the Paris regime informed the Vendean rebels that they were being misled by priests who had sold themselves for English gold. Such propaganda was ineffective.[44]

Victory of the Regime

But the Vendean forces had their serious shortcomings, principally indiscipline. Many simply left their units and went home whenever it seemed appropriate, to see to their families and farms.[45] This was especially likely to occur immediately after they had won a victory, at the very point they should have been pursuing the beaten foe. Thus, the insurgent forces were not an army but a sort of home guard: the Vendean "fought for his church and his village."[46] Local people joined together quickly from their farms and jobs to defend the local territory. This defense of hearth and Church constituted the real source of Vendean strength and fierceness. But it meant as well that it was next to impossible for Vendean commanders to make long-range plans or mount long-term operations. Unable to launch a strategic counterattack, they could not win, but only await defeat.

All this explains why, although the Vendeans captured a considerable armament, they neither entered neighboring provinces, nor consolidated their home base for a war of attrition.[47] They established no strict authority, trained no full-time formations, and made no sustained attempt to burst through the ring of steel that their enemies were slowly constructing around them.[48] "The peasants hastened forth when the 'Blues' [regime troops] were reported, but after a victory they returned to their homes. It was this fact that saved the republic."[49]

On June 9, 1793, an insurgent force of forty thousand attacked Saumur. They captured the town along with eleven thousand prisoners and sixty cannon. The fall of Saumur interrupted traffic between Tours and Nantes and left the latter quite isolated. The Vendeans now had a truly golden opportunity. Years later Napoleon said that after the capture of Saumur, with most of the republican forces engaged on the eastern frontier, the Vendeans could have reached Paris and "the white flag [of the Catholic and Royal Army] would have flown over the towers of Notre Dame before it was possible for the armies on the Rhine to come to the aid of the government."[50] After Saumur, writes Paret, "nothing could have halted the triumphant progress of the [Vendean] forces."[51] Marching straight to Paris is what the Vendeans would have done, if they had had an educated military leader. But they did not. Very few officers from the regular army joined the Vendean cause.[52] Most of the Vendean chiefs were brave and clever, but their lack of a professional military background proved decisive. They allowed their personal rivalries to impede coordination. Most of all, they lacked strategic vision: nothing demonstrates this more clearly than their decision to turn back to their own country, wasting time and lives on a fruitless siege of Nantes, rather than pressing on toward Paris after their victory at Saumur. This fateful error may well have saved the Revolution. The Vendeans gave up their attack on Nantes on June 29, 1793, in part because of the death of a widely esteemed leader but more so because it was simply beyond their ability to capture defended walled cities.[53]

Then, on October 17, the Vendeans suffered a demoralizing defeat at Cholet. This was "a true turning point in the war."[54] Repulsed before the walls of Nantes, beaten at Cholet, and faced with an increasing inundation of destructive enemies, sixty-five thousand Vendeans, including women and children and old men, fled across the Loire heading in a generally northern direction. Eventually their leaders decided to get to a seaport, where perhaps they might receive succor from England. Indeed they almost certainly could have captured Cherbourg, but this fact was unknown to them. Instead they besieged Granville, once again failing to take a fortified city.

Thus the Vendeans, with no real organization or effective leaders, with no clear idea of where to go next, wasted precious weeks wandering aimlessly and without order.[55] Yet on November 21–22, 1793, in one of the largest encounters of the entire uprising, approximately twenty thousand Vendeans repelled an equal number of regime troops near Dol.[56] But this victory was illusory; the tide had turned against the Vendeans, numerically and psychologically. On December 12, a republican army caught them in the open near Le Mans. What resulted was not a battle but a massacre, after which many prisoners were killed. General Westermann boasted that "women, priests, monks, children, all have been put to death. I have spared nobody."[57] A week and a half later, on December 23, 1793, General Kleber caught the few thousand Vendean survivors at Savenay, some miles from Nantes; another slaughter took place. This was the end of the Catholic and Royal Army.[58] "On that day," wrote Adolphe Thiers, "the column was utterly destroyed and the war of La Vendée was truly brought to a close."[59]

Genocide

Far from bringing the war to a close, the massacre at Savenay brought instead the "most abominable" period of the Vendean struggle.[60] The radicalization of the regime had "ushered in a new era of warfare."[61] The hallmark of this new era was to be "the first ideological genocide" in human history.[62] This genocidal campaign commenced *after* the armed rebels had been slaughtered and scattered at Savenay.[63]

In January 1794 more regime units invaded the Vendée. Among them were the so-called infernal columns. Their orders were that "Villages, farms, woods, heath, brush and in general all things that can be burned are to be delivered to the flames."[64] As one republican official stated, "the death of a man is quickly forgotten, but the memory of a house set afire remains with people for years."[65] The infernal columns began their work immediately after Savenay.[66] Perhaps one million cattle were also slaughtered or burned by the regime forces.[67]

But these "infernal columns" were more than incendiaries and animal-killers. They also indiscriminately killed civilians.[68] The Convention had decreed the death penalty for all rebels—meaning anybody of either sex who bore arms, or wore the white cockade, or spoke against the draft.[69] The Convention also ordained (contrary to its own statutes) that all captured Vendeans could be executed without trial. Thousands died in this manner.[70] The Vendée became "a revolutionary police state,"[71] and the Convention adopted a true "policy of extermination."[72] On October 1, 1793, it addressed the Army of the West: "Soldiers of liberty! The brigands of the Vendée must be exterminated."[73] On February 11, 1794, the Committee of Public Safety commanded: "Totally crush this horrible Vendée."[74]

"Conciliation was never seriously considered by the government."[75] After defeating and destroying the Vendean army at Savenay, General Kleber was transferred because he advocated a policy of moderation.[76] During early 1794 the Republic promised pardon to all rebels who would surrender. Thousands of Vendeans took advantage of this amnesty, only to be seized and executed. Not only legitimate prisoners but even mere suspects were shot out of hand.[77] During the first months of 1794 republican troops received orders to kill anybody, including women, whom they found in areas recently cleared by patrols.[78] Distinctions between combatants and noncombatants were erased. Old men, women, and children were forced to dig mass pits, then were shot beside them. Many were simply buried alive in the "unconscionable slaughters of the winter of the Year II."[79]

The savageries against women in the Vendée were perhaps the most revealing feature of the entire holocaust.[80] Women in particular had opposed the regime's attack on their customs and beliefs.[81] Now they would pay the price for daring to attract such attention to themselves.[82] Soldiers would gather great masses of women and rape them. Then they would kill them, along with their children, hacking them with sabres to conserve ammunition.[83] One republican officer wrote to his sister that he had seen soldiers rape women by the roadside and then shoot them or stab them to death.[84] Others wrote of the bodies of young girls, naked, their hands tied behind their backs, hanging from the branches of trees.[85]

Putting all humanitarian considerations aside for the moment (if possible), it is clear that allowing an army to sink to such acts is not good military practice. All this burning and raping and killing undermined the discipline and morale of the republican troops. French forces participating in the Vendean slaughter had the worst record for indiscipline of all the Revolutionary armies.[86] Another negative consequence was that these enormities inflamed and prolonged the fighting. The sheer terror of 1794, which offered the inhabitants no chance of survival, sent many of them back into the ranks of the formerly beaten rebels. So out of control had many regime units become that they ravaged not only the rebellious districts but also those in the hands of the loyalists.[87] Indeed, regime troops often executed local republicans along with everybody else.[88] One Revolutionary officer wrote: "The death of a patriot [republican] is a small thing when the public security is at stake."[89]

Les Noyades

Priests, usually the older ones who could not or would not escape, were loaded onto boats, which were then taken out to the middle of the Loire and sunk in the dark of night.[90] Later, all suspicious persons, including women and children, were thus executed, in the full light of day.[91] In this "generalized and daily terror" campaign,[92] plans were adopted for poisoning wells and spreading infection,[93] and for the use of poison gas against both prisoners and entire districts.[94]

At the end of 1794, one general reported: "This rich country, which supplied grain to several departments and meat to Paris and horses for the army, is now only a pile of ruins."[95] Another wrote to the Committee of Public Safety: "There is no longer a Vendée; it is dead under our sabre, along with its women and children . . . following the orders which you have given me, I have crushed the children under horses' hooves, massacred the women. . . ."[96]

It must be noted that the Vendeans, too, committed war crimes. They were often infuriated to discover that their prisoners were soldiers whom they had captured before and had released on the solemn promise to fight against the Vendeans no more. Upon capturing them a subsequent time, they executed them. Generally, however, the Vendeans treated prisoners, of which they had tens of thousands, as well as they could, and this was widely known.[97]

But rebel wrongdoing is quite beside the point: it is inadmissible to equate rebel and governmental acts of criminality in order to excuse or lessen the guilt of the latter. The Paris regime was responsible for law and order and justice. Thus its acts—systematic trampling even on its own laws, butchering and drowning its own unarmed citizens—were far worse than the lapses of the rebels. The rebels carried out their atrocities in hot blood, while the executions and burnings and drownings of the Republic were "administrative," that is, planned policy, as in the Nazi death camps.[98] "There was something horribly new and unimaginable in the prospect of a government systematically executing its opponents [its own citizens] by the carload for months on end, and . . . this occurred in what had passed for the most civilized country in Europe."[99]

But how could all this have happened? Where were Liberty, Equality, and Fraternity?

A Republican Dictatorship

In the 1790s it was not at all difficult or expensive for politicians to produce a mob in Paris, shouting revolutionary slogans and ready for sanguinary deeds. But Paris was not France. Outside of the large cities where it drew its mass support, the Revolution, especially in its Robespierrean phase, was decidedly a minority movement, with relatively little strength in most rural areas.[100] Voting was by spoken word, in public, and exercised by less than half of the quite restricted pool of eligibles.[101]

Nevertheless, the radical minority was able to maintain its grip on power because of its superior organization, because its many opponents did not coordinate their rebellions against Paris, but most of all, because of its alliance with the army. Many army officers benefited directly and dramatically from the changes the Revolution had imposed. France was in effect a military dictatorship long before Napoleon.

The events in the Vendée therefore confront us with "a central truth of the French revolution: its dependence on organized killings to accomplish political ends. [Its] power to command allegiance depended, from the very beginning, on the spectacle of death."[102] Most of the people executed by the Revolution were simple peasants and the urban poor, obscure, helpless, and forgotten.[103]

Almost every section of the country witnessed mass executions of civilians, sometimes by cannon fire. Resistance to the Revolution was "endemic throughout the south."[104] By 1795, "an enormous proportion of the population in the south and west supported movements which demanded nothing less than a return to the Old Regime."[105] In brief, "the insurrection which broke out on March 10, 1793, in [the Vendée and adjacent areas] was only the supreme manifestation, the most formidable episode, of the opposition and discontent which were seething among the mass of the populace throughout the whole of France."[106]

A Kind of Peace

Robespierre's fall from power in July 1794 signaled the end of the official Reign of Terror. The new leaders began slowly to take steps to dampen the rebellion in the West, removing local authorities whom they considered to be too provocative, and releasing thousands of peasants held on mere suspicion. In December 1794 they also proclaimed a new amnesty—which this time seemed to have been fairly well observed—to all who would lay down their arms.[107]

Paris also revised its military approach to the Vendée. In August 1794 General Louis-Lazare Hoche, twenty-six years old, son of a groom in the royal stables, received command of the Army of Cherbourg and other forces. Hoche and his masters in Paris agreed that they must settle affairs in the Vendée first.[108] Hoche's pacification plan included preventing foreign assistance from reaching the rebels, cutting communications between the Vendée and Brittany, and covering the Vendée itself with constant patrols.[109]

Hoche built numerous strongpoints all around the northern and eastern boundaries of the Vendée. Heavy patrols constantly moved back and forth between these posts, so that no large groups of guerrillas could pass near them. To the west of this line he deployed powerful mobile columns, attempting thereby to force the rebel units either to disperse or to come up against the line of strongpoints and their patrols.[110] He chose a certain area demarcated by strongpoints and then inundated that area with troops, thus forcing any rebels in that sector to move westward, ever closer to the imprisoning sea. Hoche gradually pushed his line of fortified posts deeper and deeper into the Vendée, continuously reducing the territory in which the rebels could roam. He was thus developing a variant of the clear-and-hold strategy that would become famous later in Malaya and Algeria. By making his columns support one another he deprived the rebels of the advantages of their mobility and knowledge of the territory. Confronted by overwhelming numbers of effectively deployed troops, hemmed into a small and constantly diminishing area with no place to hide or run, the Vendean rebels were doomed.

At the same time Hoche proceeded systematically to disarm the entire Vendean population. Officers would estimate the male population of a given parish, and set a quota of one musket for every four males. Then they would seize hostages and cattle, to be held until the requisite number of muskets had been handed in.[111]

In addition to these military measures, Hoche emphasized the importance of political considerations in ending the Vendean insurgency. As early as October 1793, before he arrived to command in the West, he had written that "the enemy was not the Vendée . . . the only enemy was England."[112] This interesting view would have very important consequences. "Let us never forget that politics must play a great role in this war. Let us in turn use humaneness, virtue, probity, force, cunning, and always that dignity proper to republicans."[113] That is, military operations must be supplemented by political concessions. In the last months of 1795 Hoche devoted much effort to improving relations with the local clergy. "The Vendeans have but one real sentiment, that is, attachment to their priests. These latter want nothing but protection and tranquility. Let us ensure both to them, let us add some benefits, and the affections of the country will be restored to us."[114] On the other hand, Hoche recognized that "if religious toleration is not allowed, there will be no peace in this part of France."[115]

What a lot of blood had to be spilled in order for somebody in authority to arrive at this simple idea.

In pursuit of his elementary but powerful concepts, Hoche (who himself had once been thrown into prison by the Terror) would extend tolerance to the nonjuring priests, treat the civil population leniently, and punish pillaging soldiers severely. (Despite Hoche's orders and fierce threats, many of his troops continued to kill, steal, and rape.)[116] This policy of political conciliation made Hoche many enemies among the local republicans, but his political friends were able to sustain him.[117]

In February 1795, Hoche arranged a peace between the Convention and the insurgent leader François Charette at Nantes. The treaty promised the Vendeans freedom of religion, exemption from the draft, the return of confiscated property, and indemnity for victims of the worst outrages.[118] Most of the fighting in the Vendée then came to a close.

Hoche's campaign succeeded primarily because he had sufficient troops to carry out his policy of gradual occupation of every square mile of Vendean territory. But peace was also attained because the surviving inhabitants of the countryside were physically and morally exhausted, and because the regime was finally willing to compromise with the religious sentiments of the people.[119]

The Aftermath

The conflict, and the manner in which it was waged, was quite unnecessary: Hoche showed this by conceding the Vendeans' main demands. Yet the suppression of the Vendée resulted in "the total economic devastation of the region."[120] Over ten thousand houses had been burned down and four-fifths of the male population killed or chased out. The war reduced the permanent population of the Vendée by one-third.[121] "Historians agree that this insanity cost the lives of one hundred and fifty thousand victims."[122] More French died in the Vendée than in Napoleon's Russian campaign.[123] Indeed, in relation to the total population of the time, the number of Frenchmen, soldiers and civilians, killed as a result of the Revolution—before the Napoleonic wars began—represents a greater loss than France suffered during all of World War I.[124] (The equivalent figure in the United States in the year 2000 would be twenty times the total American military losses in World War II.)[125] And within the lifetime of some of those who had been at Waterloo, the victorious armies of Prussia would parade down the Champs Élysées.

The French army learned little from the Vendean experience. It would behave the same way in Spain. Command of French artillery in the Vendée had been offered to the young Bonaparte. His refusal was good for his historical reputation, but he missed the chance to learn some lessons about guerrilla warfare that might have influenced his policy in Spain, and thus have changed the destiny of France.[126]

Reflection

The Vendean insurgents had important sources of strength. They drew inspiration from both religious fervor and a deep sense of injustice. The regime's brutal methods further alienated the population.[127] But they carried serious burdens as well. They lacked proper terrain for guerrilla war, the support of regular military units,[128] and most of all, help from outside. However brave and exasperated, the plain people of the Vendée possessed neither strategic vision nor political coherence.

Nevertheless, in the end, the Vendée had its revenge. When Bonaparte, heir and embodiment of the Revolution, escaped his Elban exile, the Vendeans (and many others) rose up once more. The thirty thousand troops Napoleon sent to suppress the Vendean rebellion might have made all the difference between victory and defeat at Waterloo, where on the climactic day Bonaparte commanded but seventy-two thousand soldiers.[129]

SPAIN

In October 1805, Nelson's victory over the combined French and Spanish fleets at Trafalgar sank Napoleon's plans for an invasion of England.[130] Consequently, Napoleon instead decided to bring the British to their knees with a Europe-wide economic blockade. As part of this grand enterprise, in May 1808 Napoleon invaded Spain; forcing its king to abdicate, he put his brother Joseph on the throne. Possession of Spain would shut out English goods, and also (presumably) bring Napoleon control of Spain's vast overseas empire and respectable fleet. Thus Trafalgar was one of the most important battles in world history. In its absence, it is hard to see how there would have been an occupation of Spain, a Peninsular War, a Duke of Wellington—or a Waterloo.

In 1808 France was a country of thirty million people, with the most puissant armies in Europe. Spain counted only eleven million, and had long ceased to be a power of the first rank. These undeniable facts, plus years of battlefield success, allowed Napoleon to underestimate most gravely the difficulty of the Spanish undertaking,[131] a fateful error similar to the one he had already committed in Haiti[132] and would commit in Russia.

From the start, things in Spain went badly. In July 1808, at Bailén, a French army of twenty thousand capitulated to the army of the Spanish national resistance government centered in Cádiz. This French force had been considerably harried by guerrillas, partly because it had earlier plundered the Cathedral of Córdoba. Two weeks after Bailén, the future Duke of Wellington landed in Portugal with a small professional British army and took command of all Portuguese forces. Throughout the war, the Royal Navy carried supplies to the Anglo-Portuguese forces, protected the flow of assistance to the Cádiz government from Latin America, and carried weapons to the ever more numerous Spanish guerrillas, who were rendering vital assistance to Wellington.[133] In the early days, the French concentrated on defeating the regular forces of the Cádiz government, thus giving the guerrillas the chance to organize themselves. As a consequence, the French could devote full attention neither to Wellington's British and Portuguese regulars nor to the Spanish guerrillas.[134]

In these circumstances, the best strategy for the French would have been to win over key strata of the Spanish population, or at least reduce the number of their enemies. Actually, notable elements of the Spanish elite and middle class were not unhappy to see a Napoleonic regime in Madrid. These "Afrancesados" hoped that French control would help to modernize a Spain that had descended to the status of a second-class power, at best. To them, the French seemed invincible; and besides, King Joseph Bonaparte was relatively enlightened and obviously well-meaning. Beyond these elite groups, the French might have tried to attract those elements of the popular classes who had reason to be dissatisfied with the status quo, and they would have been many.

But the French did not pursue a policy of attraction. On the contrary, their behavior in Spain was egregious. The depredations and atrocities of the Napoleonic troops made ready recruits for the Cádiz forces and most of all for the guerrillas—a story to be repeated again and again in the annals of insurgency.

Everywhere the French raped women of all conditions, including minors, nuns, and expectant mothers.[135] They pillaged and burned whole cities. They made little effort to distinguish the peaceful from the resistant. Most disastrously for themselves, they looted and gutted cathedrals and churches, murdered priests, and committed public sacrilege of the grossest sort. When Saragossa fell after a heroic resistance, the French made a point of desecrating the city's churches. Spain had sixty thousand parish priests and many thousands more in religious orders. "It was they, in close touch with the people . . . who instilled the spirit of revolt."[136] Under the leadership of their priests, great numbers of humble folk, who might otherwise have remained passive, took up arms against the French, in a popular resistance movement that took on the aspects of a holy war.[137]

Thus, "the war in Spain [became] the most cruel, the most pitiless, the most desperate of all wars."[138] Guerrillas frequently mutilated their French prisoners; once they actually boiled a general in a cauldron. Imperial soldiers who found themselves cut off or surrounded often committed suicide rather than fall into guerrilla hands.[139] The Spanish insurgency was thus a grisly harbinger of modern wars of national liberation.

Defeat of the French

The guerrillas concentrated on disrupting Imperial supplies and communications. Spain is the size of Austria, Belgium, Germany, and the Netherlands combined, or of Japan, Taiwan, and South Korea combined. The distance from Paris to Cádiz is greater than that from Chicago to Austin. Indeed Paris is closer to Warsaw than to Cádiz. Numerous mountain chains and rivers cross the country from east to west—major obstacles to any invading force. And the Napoleonic armies of course had no aircraft, no telephones, not even a telegraph. Hence messengers with the most urgent dispatches would take two weeks to travel from Paris to Madrid, if they arrived at all, across a barren landscape with a hostile population and ubiquitous guerrillas. Sometimes a French commander in one region of Spain would have no idea, literally for weeks, of what was going on in other areas of the peninsula. (Even before the guerrilla insurgency had really gotten started, none of the pleas for help from the commander of the ill-fated army at Bailén had reached Madrid.)

When campaigning in Belgium and Italy and the Rhineland, the victorious French had "lived off the land" (a euphemism for looting the civilian population). Hence their system of logistics was woefully underdeveloped. "Alternating between total privation on the one hand and feasting and drunkenness on the other, [the French soldier] was condemned to a life of disease. No one cared about his health. The medical service continued to be utterly neglected. . . . Napoleon's military strategy was predicated on the existence of fertile and populous lands. . . . When he invaded North Germany, Poland, Spain and Russia, geographical conditions made his system unworkable and the army was imperiled."[140] Soon enough, French forces in Spain went unpaid and unfed. Cavalry horses died by the hundreds from overwork and malnutrition.[141]

It was of course "the power of rapid movement that was the true strength of the guerrillas."[142] Eventually even columns of two thousand soldiers were not safe from severe guerrilla mauling.[143] The day came when the French controlled "only the ground upon which the soles of their shoes rested."[144] The French learned little from this hellish experience, and thus plodded on to another disaster in Russia.

From the beginning of the occupation, the French and Imperial forces had only a very marginal technological superiority over the guerrillas. French advantages lay in their superior tactics and numbers, and these proved to be waning assets. Guerrilla tactics notably improved during the course of the conflict (all guerrillas have a self-activating, Darwinian merit system: incompetently-led guerrillas soon die). Besides, Napoleon opposed static defense; hence the French relied very heavily upon sweep maneuvers. Of course these usually failed, and the guerrillas quickly returned to the swept areas.

As for the French numerical advantage, it soon showed itself to be a fatal illusion. To fight Wellington, the guerrillas, and the forces of the Cádiz government successfully, the French would have needed 825,000 troops. Such a figure would have been impossible to reach, even if all Napoleonic forces in Europe, including Polish and Italian allies, could by some miracle (or insanity) have been concentrated in Spain. And of course the Russian adventure soon drew away thousands of soldiers.

The quarter-million Imperial troops south of the Pyrenees were quite inadequate for controlling the guerrillas, containing Wellington, and conquering Cádiz, but they were more than adequate to account for Napoleonic defeats elsewhere in Europe. "The trained cavalry still locked up in Spain might well have turned the scale in the campaign of Germany [in 1813]."[145]

Napoleon's invasion of Spain thus opened up the continent to the British army, helped to train the future Duke of Wellington, sacrificed tens of thousands of Imperial troops badly needed elsewhere—more French soldiers perished in Spain than in Russia[146]—and, above all, destroyed the potent myth of French invincibility: Spanish resistance to Napoleon soon rekindled Europe's determination to rid itself of the Corsican conqueror, with disastrous results for Napoleon.

There can be little doubt that "the decision to seize Iberia was probably the most disastrous blunder of Napoleon's career."[147] At any rate, on Saint Helena Napoleon declared: "That miserable Spanish affair is what killed me."

CHAPTER 4

RELIGION AND INSURGENCY IN THE TWENTIETH CENTURY

The twentieth century witnessed religious insurgencies as violent as those of the preceding century, and in the case of Afghanistan, as consequential internationally as the anti-Napoleonic revolt in Spain.

AFGHANISTAN

For generations, Afghanistan ranked as one of the most remote and obscure places on earth. Yet the religiously inspired uprising that swept across that country beginning in 1979 is probably the best-known guerrilla insurgency of the last quarter of the twentieth century. Because several chapters of this book discuss key aspects of that conflict, only the outlines of the religious basis of the war are presented here.

The Communist Party of Afghanistan, the PDPA, came into existence in 1965. It always remained an exiguous minority, beset by bloody factional divisions. In 1978, after a coup and assassinations, the minuscule and inexperienced PDPA unexpectedly found itself in power, and it began imposing Leninist reforms. The urban membership and Soviet orientation of the PDPA had incubated a fierce hatred both of Islam and of the peasantry. The PDPA regime launched an all-out assault on the customs of the population, aiming in effect for a latter-day, full-scale Central Asian Stalinism. Forcible and arbitrary land reform offended Muslim concepts of legality.[1] As part of the PDPA literacy campaign, women were dragged from their homes to listen to antireligious lectures. The regime admitted to killing without trial 12,000 political prisoners and religious teachers in its first two years of power; the actual number was probably much larger. The regime appeared as "repulsively anti-Islamic."[2] Such egregious behavior, in a country with perhaps 320,000 mullahs, naturally called forth a widespread popular rebellion, in fact "the largest single national rising in the twentieth century."[3]

In March 1979, anti-regime riots rocked the streets of Herat. The PDPA reprisals, including aerial bombings, killed between three thousand and five thousand inhabitants of that city. Revolt swept over the country, and soon most provinces were in the hands of the insurgents. To prevent the fall of the PDPA regime, the Soviet army invaded in December 1979. The entrance of Soviet troops enflamed rather than quenched the rebellion. In the eyes of most of the Mujahideen guerrillas, the conflict became a defense of religion against foreign atheists. To the Kremlin's incredulous dismay, the resistance stalemated the Soviet forces, the first clear reversal of the "historical inevitability of Marxism-Leninism" since the 1920 war with Poland. The invincible Red Army, conquerors of Berlin, held at bay by semiliterate warriors of God, Leninism tamed by Islam—what a spectacle. Faced with this burgeoning disaster, Mikhail Gorbachev and others initiated a major reexamination of the entire Soviet national defense doctrine, a move that resulted in the Soviet withdrawal from Afghanistan, and eventually from Central Europe. Trotsky supposedly said in 1919 that "the road to Paris and London lies through the towns of Afghanistan, the Punjab and Bengal."[4] As in so many things, Trotsky was wrong about this—dead wrong, so to speak. But in a devastating way, Trotsky's aphorism about the relationship between revolution in Europe and Asia turned out to be correct. The cries of battle in the Afghan mountains found their echo in the shouts of freedom on the Berlin Wall.[5]

And even with all this, the world had not heard the last of Afghanistan.

The religiously generated insurgencies considered below are not nearly so well known as the Afghan case, even though they all produced major conflict in their respective countries, and one of them—the Sudanese—still continues after more than forty years.

MEXICO

The Cristero rebellion—"the last insurrection of the masses" in Mexico[6]—was one of the largest insurgencies in the Western Hemisphere. Yet few Americans have ever heard of it. As the foremost student of that conflict observed, "history has failed the Cristeros."[7]

The Cristero movement, called by Mexicans *La Cristiada*, fought against religious persecution by the regime in Mexico City. Although Mexico has an overwhelmingly Catholic population, the Church there suffered considerable tribulation for more than a century. After independence from Spain, "the definition of the proper role of the Church became the critical issue; the history of Mexico from 1821 to 1872 could be written in terms of the search for that definition."[8] Power in Mexico has often been in the hands of men implacably hostile to religion, a condition facilitated by the political ineptitude of many Mexican Church leaders. The civil war called the War of the Reform was "essentially a religious conflict."[9] Benito Juárez and his followers seized the Church's property and persecuted both clergy and laymen. Confiscations of Church lands led to great profits for speculators but little benefit for peasants.

In reaction to Juárez, many Church leaders joined with the Conservative Party in supporting the reign of the French-imposed Emperor Maximilian of Habsburg. The withdrawal of French backing for Maximilian and the return to power of Juárez exposed the Church to new attacks.[10] After the fall of the dictator-president Díaz in 1911,[11] prominent Catholic leaders supported the regime of General Victoriano Huerta. The price for this miscalculation was physical outrages against clergy and property, including open murder. (The Huerta regime would almost certainly have survived and established a semblance of order in Mexico, thus saving hundreds of thousands of lives, except for the opposition of President Woodrow Wilson.)[12]

The State

The post-Huerta regime "had come to power through military force. It maintained itself by authoritarian means, without free elections. The constitution had been imposed by a small minority of revolutionaries and had never been submitted to a vote for popular approval or rejection."[13] The regime desired not the separation of Church and state but rather the control of the Church by the state. Elections became fraudulent to the point of tragicomedy. The semi-sacred battle cry of the Madero revolution of 1910—"No reelection!"—was crudely cast aside by President Obregón.[14] Members of the Mexican Congress who dared to object to this power grab were expelled.[15]

General Venustiano Carranza, "Mexico's last [L]iberal,"[16] organized the convention that produced the constitution of 1917. Only his followers were allowed to vote for or be elected to this convention.[17] The new constitution was far more hostile to the Church than the Juárez constitution of 1857. "Indeed, if [the 1917 constitution had been] strictly executed, the very existence of the Church would have been threatened."[18] "From the standpoint of religious freedom, most of the restrictions bordered on the ridiculous,"[19] and "no religious body anywhere in the world could have accommodated itself to them."[20] Article 130 declared that clerics who were arrested for violating antireligious decrees could not have a trial by jury, thus acknowledging the wide unpopularity of these measures.[21] No referendum or freely elected assembly ever ratified the 1917 constitution.

Carranza's successor was General Álvaro Obregón. He and his henchman Plutarco Calles had fought against and eventually killed the populist leaders Francisco Villa and Emiliano Zapata, saving the Carranza regime. But when Carranza sought to extend his presidential term, Obregón and Calles, hungry to take office themselves, revolted, and Carranza was murdered.

At the end of his term in 1924, Obregón imposed his minister of the interior, the arch-anticatholic Plutarco Calles, as the next president of Mexico. In his earlier life Calles had been fired as a schoolteacher in Hermosillo and later suffered dismissal as treasurer of a municipality in Sonora because of shortfalls in funds with which he had been entrusted. He gathered more experience as a bartender and hotel manager. As governor of Sonora (Obregón's bailiwick) under Carranza, Calles expelled all priests from that state.

Most of the revolutionary leaders who had opposed both Díaz and Huerta were of northern origin.[22] They were men of means who had been deprived of what they saw as their share of the political spoils. Many led or joined the revolution for personal or political gain: revolution was the only way to make room at the top or the middle for new men. During the succession of civil wars that wracked Mexico after 1910, officers quickly improved their rank by switching again and again from one side to another. As the years of fighting went on, the leaders of the different revolutionary currents enriched themselves. "Palatial homes, fine estates, prosperous ranches, flourishing businesses—these were the fruits of revolution."[23] More importantly, the revolutionary men of the North "were the enemies of the Indian, of the peasant, of the priest of that Old Mexico which they never understood because they never belonged to it." They "hated the Old Mexico and despised its traditions, looking down on both its customs and its faith."[24] Their soldiers sacked cities, raped women, looted churches, burned libraries, massacred peasants, broke strikes, shot priests (including foreign nationals), and extorted money from everyone.[25]

Mexico on the Eve

In the 1920s, the great majority of devout Catholics were either peasants or upper- and upper-middle-class women. Mexican women did not have the vote, and peasants, mostly Indian, did not normally challenge governmental authority, that is, the army and police. (Thus the 1926 Cristero rising would be a big surprise to leaders of both Church and state.) There was a severe shortage of clergy, especially in the rural areas. Many of the Mexican bishops were men of learning and probity. But they, like the city priests, the canon lawyers, and Catholic intellectual and political lay leaders in Mexico City (not to speak of Vatican City) lived in a world so completely removed from that of the devout peasants who would make up the rank and file of the Cristero rebellion that they might have come from a different century or even a different planet.[26] (The peasant army of Emiliano Zapata, perhaps the most authentically popular movement of the entire revolutionary period, never attacked the Church per se.)[27]

Under Calles, clashes between government forces and Catholic citizens became more violent. In July 1925 police and troops fired on worshippers in and around churches in the city of Guadalajara, inflicting perhaps six hundred casualties.[28] Police in other cities often fired into crowds of women inside or in front of churches, causing many deaths.[29] Regime goons assaulted members of Catholic labor unions.

In February 1926, Archbishop Mora y del Rio was arrested for critical remarks regarding the constitution in a newspaper interview. President Calles used this incident to launch a determined assault against the Church.[30] Neither Carranza nor Obregón had enforced the antireligious clauses of the 1917 constitution with any vigor. But in June 1926 Calles, employing "utterly ruthless and vindictive methods,"[31] decreed the activation of the antireligious articles in the constitution (though his manner of handing down decrees often violated that very constitution). The regime confiscated what Church property had not already been nationalized. Eager for the "progressive de-Christianization" of Mexico,[32] the regime expelled all foreign-born priests. It closed down all schools, asylums, and orphanages where religious instruction had been given (this in a society with distressingly large numbers of illiterates).[33] It prohibited all religious education, even in private schools. No private school could display a religious picture, and no teacher in such a school was permitted even to mention a religious subject.[34] In the states of Michoacan, Hidalgo, and elsewhere, teachers swore this oath: "I declare that I am an atheist, an irreconcilable enemy of the Catholic, Apostolic and Roman religion, that I will endeavor to destroy it. . . ."[35]

Any cleric who criticized the regime or the authorities could be jailed for five years.[36] In many areas of the country religious practices were illegal even in private homes, into which police or troops could enter at will to look for evidence or make arrests (or steal). The governor of Campeche limited the number of priests in the entire state to five. Calles began expelling foreign-born nuns, most of them teachers or nurses. In January 1927, with the departure of four hundred foreign-born priests, there were but thirty-six hundred priests left in all of Mexico.[37] No one was permitted to remain or become a member of a monastic order. Deprived of priests from abroad, forbidden to open seminaries to train new ones, the Mexican Church was on the road to physical disappearance. Clearly, "the enemies of Catholicism were legislating it out of existence in Mexico."[38] (In practice, though, some priests were trained in secret, and others educated in seminaries in Texas.)

In protest, the Mexican bishops took an unprecedented and perilous step: they declared a nationwide cessation of all religious services to begin August 1, 1926. The coming suppression of these services made them all the more desirable and well attended. In July, huge crowds seeking baptisms and/or marriages overwhelmed the churches, especially in the great cities.

The Cristeros

In August 1926, fighting between armed Catholics and regime troops broke out in various places. The rising was most massive in the state of Jalisco.[39] With 8 percent of the country's population and 20 percent of its priests, Jalisco was the most populous and most Catholic of all the states, and the rebellion lasted longest there. The rising also found significant support in the states of Colima, Guanajuato, Guerrero, Michoacan, Puebla, Querétero, Vera Cruz, and Zacatecas. But the Cristeros were weak in Chihuahua and other states along the U.S. border. This was a grave circumstance, because of the insurgents' need for munitions from the United States.[40]

Most of the rebels used as a battle cry "Viva Cristo Rey!" (Long Live Christ the King!). From this phrase the regime contemptuously pinned the name Cristeros on them, a name they adopted with panache. Their name also reflected a great truth about their movement. Traditional Mexican uprisings took the name of a famous leader—

Juáristas, Maderistas, Carrancistas, Zapatistas. But the Cristeros had no such leader; their movement was spontaneous, local, and regional, without national organization. Even so, during 1927 most Cristero units accepted the name of The Army of National Liberation. "The Cristeros were free men who were unmoved by considerations of pay, advancement or punishment."[41] Their goal was not to overthrow the regime but to win recognition of basic religious rights.[42] "That was why the peasants took up arms—because the Revolution was trying to take their priest away from them."[43] As one student of the rebellion in the Los Altos region of Jalisco concluded: "It was a people's war in the truest sense."[44]

Estimates of the number of Cristero fighters vary widely, but fifty thousand seems a reasonable figure. Cristeros usually operated in their home territory, and they were often accompanied by their entire families. Formed from and sustained by family and village, dedicated to a righteous cause, convinced that any one of them killed in battle was a true martyr, the Cristeros had very high morale, the most important weapon of any guerrilla movement. The rebels operated predominantly in the mountainous areas of western Mexico, which they knew well. But even in open terrain unsuitable for guerrillas, as in much of Jalisco state, the conviction of the Cristeros and the support of the civilian population enabled them to fight with success.

Women were the secret backbone of the movement. Women's Brigades set up and ran rudimentary field hospitals, supplied money, and carried food, intelligence, and ammunition to Cristero units.[45] These brigades enrolled thousands of members, urban and rural, usually between the ages of fifteen and twenty-five.[46] And at the same time, in the mountains of Sonora the Yaqui Indians, long abused by the regime, rose up and cooperated with local Cristero units.

The Cristeros had few weapons except their rifles. Lacking in munitions, but dexterous with machetes, they often engaged in hand-to-hand combat. They blew up bridges and attacked baggage trains and supply columns in the mountainous areas that were their strongholds and refuges. Beyond the mountains Cristeros often proved to be excellent cavalrymen. When they captured a town with a telephone, the Cristeros immediately put in an insulting call to the nearest regime garrison. Some Cristero units shot their prisoners, a practice they copied from the army; sometimes they allowed common soldiers to go free, but not the officers.

Many Cristeros had ample courage, but lacked the most elementary military training and tactical knowledge. This situation improved after August 1927 when a professional officer, Enrique Gorostieta, became commander of the Cristeros in Jalisco, and later in all Mexico.[47] Gorostieta advised Cristero commanders never to fight unless they were sure of victory because of superiority of numbers, advantage of position, exhaustion of the enemy, or achievement of surprise. Most Cristero leaders instinctively knew all this, or soon learned it, and thus their forces suffered far fewer casualties than the regime troops did.[48] By 1928 the Cristeros had learned how to maneuver in large numbers. But in June 1929 regime agents murdered Gorostieta during a parley in which his safety had been guaranteed; his loss was of course a grave blow to Cristero morale.[49]

In all the civil wars and rebellions that followed the Revolution of 1910, tactics were less important than logistics. Lack of ammunition was the principal weakness of the Cristeros: it was the main cause of the failure of their attack on Guadalajara in March 1929, and the root of their tactic of charging well-armed enemies in order to engage in close combat. Working with what little they had, the Cristeros would make many grenades from one unexploded bomb dropped by an army aircraft; they sometimes captured ammunition from enemy troops, or purchased it from regime generals. But there was never nearly enough, and thus in the end they could not win. Although the rebels had plenty of food, provided to them by the villagers of the western states, they simply were not able to obtain adequate ammunition, even if it were available, without money—which could come only from rich Catholics, very few of whom assisted them.

Besides ammunition, another quite vital element was lacking to the Cristeros. If they were to have a serious chance of winning, they would need the backing of the large majority of devout Catholics, and that in turn would require the open support of the Mexican bishops. This was not forthcoming. As a collegial body, the bishops would not condemn the rebellion, but neither would they urge Catholics to embrace it. They would not even appoint chaplains for Cristero units.[50] Some bishops forbade Catholics under their jurisdiction to join the Cristeros. Many of the bishops opposed the rebellion because they were hopeful that persecution would abate in a second Obregón administration. The Cristero failure to win a quick victory further undermined support for them. Some of the bishops were philosophical pacifists; some of them "found martyrdom for the cause glorious."[51] Others believed that violence would be fruitless or even bring about increased persecution; still others thought that engaging in violence would make Catholics morally indistinguishable from the Calles forces. By 1928, the third year of the rebellion, many of the bishops, in fear of their lives, had scattered into several countries, and were deeply divided about what to do. Some lived in comfort across the U.S. border, while Archbishop Orozco y Jimenez of Guadalajara (in pro-Cristero Jalisco) secretly traveled around his state, sheltered by humble folk, eluding the police and the army for years.

The Army

Under the long rule of Porfirio Díaz, the Mexican army's main task was to suppress internal opposition, a task to which it had proved inadequate in the Revolution of 1910. And so it remained.

The regime army fielded around seventy-five thousand soldiers, against fifty thousand Cristeros.[52] By 1928 the army desertion rate may have reached 35 percent annually.[53] Consequently the Calles regime emptied the penitentiaries and forced the inmates into the army. Not surprisingly, army units would come into a disaffected area, rape, loot, kill, and move on. Then the Cristeros would return and receive new recruits into their ranks. The regime also fought the rebellion by population removal, especially in western states. In brief, "it was a colonial war, carried on by a colonial army against its own people."[54]

President Obregón had tamed the ever-restless army leaders in part by allowing them to engage in systematic corruption. Consequently, while the army was conducting itself as a sort of recruiting agency for the rebels, several commanders, especially in Jalisco, not satisfied with looting property, sold arms directly to the Cristeros.[55] Some regime generals falsified reports about the strength of their units so that they could pocket the pay and supplies for phantom soldiers. Generals like Manuel Ávila Camacho made a fortune out of the anti-Cristero campaigns.

Meanwhile, the Calles regime executed suspects without trial, even for non-capital offenses. It also heavily censored press coverage of the rebellion and sought to portray the rebels as backward rural fanatics, a view that resonated among some urban Catholic elements.[56] Others have since tried to paint the Cristeros as small landowners threatened by land reform, or as a White Guard paid by the great landlords. Both portraits are grotesque. "The only 'white guards' in Los Altos were Federal [regime] troops defending the latifundistas [great landlords] against a revolutionary peasantry, the Cristeros."[57]

A Peace, of Sorts

By the end of 1927 the regime was clearly unable to bring the western states under its control. Former President Obregón was declared to have been elected president again on July 1, 1928, after the violent deaths of the opposition candidates. Obregón wanted the religious question settled, but in the midst of peace talks on July 17, 1928, a twenty-six-year-old art teacher named José de Leon Toral fatally shot him. President Calles issued a violent statement accusing the clergy of engineering the killing.[58] A subsequent offensive by regime troops from December 1928 to February 1929 failed.

By then the war had cost the lives of sixty thousand soldiers and forty thousand Cristeros, and unknown numbers of civilians.[59] It was also devouring great chunks of the national budget. The regime feared that the renowned intellectual José Vasconcelos would seek the presidency in 1929; following his inevitable "defeat" at the polls, he would undoubtedly raise a revolt and cooperate with the Cristeros. Moreover, Provisional President Emilio Portes Gil, Calles's handpicked successor,[60] was confronted by dangers from every quarter. Groups of exiled politicians in the U.S., including several who had been on the winning side in previous struggles, were plotting to take advantage of the Cristero revolt. And in March 1929 a new military rebellion was offering cooperation to the Cristeros. In addition, several Obregónist generals, infuriated by their leader's assassination, appeared to believe that President Calles had been involved in the deed. A revolt by them, in combination with the Cristeros, would have smashed the Calles establishment. Besides, President Portes Gil was not a fierce Church-hater like Calles.

But the Cristeros faced mounting problems as well. The rebellion's effectiveness was becoming increasingly hampered by the improved efficiency of army operations, the somewhat more lenient treatment accorded to surrendered Cristeros, the rebels' continuing inability to obtain sufficient quantities of ammunition, the disinclination of Catholics in the U.S. to offer financial assistance, and prominent Catholics' public support for the Mexican government in its disputes with the U.S. Moreover, an open endorsement of the Cristeros by the Mexican bishops, a sine qua non of rebel victory, was clearly not imminent.[61] The rebels had also largely given up any hope of either U.S. intervention or successful anti-Calles revolts within the army. And in April 1928, on the death of the Archbishop of Mexico City, the conciliatory Archbishop Leopoldo Ruiz y Flores, Vatican ambassador to Mexico, emerged as leader of the Mexican episcopate.

Meanwhile, Pope Pius XI believed that passive resistance was the Christian tradition; that war, and especially guerrilla war, was full of moral ambiguities; that the Cristero rebellion might lead to religious schism; and that if the guerrillas were defeated the Mexican Church would pay a terrible price. And—perhaps equally troubling—what if the Cristeros should win, what then? What inappropriate responsibilities for governing Mexico would fall upon the Church? The Pope's formula for peace in Mexico excluded armed revolt; he wanted the Mexican bishops to accept the best settlement available, and to embrace his ideas of social reform. He opposed efforts to seek intervention by the U.S. government for fear that they would make Mexican Catholics seem unpatriotic.[62]

In these circumstances, U.S. Ambassador Dwight Morrow was able to bring President Calles and Mexican Catholic leaders into contact.[63] The war was ended by negotiations among Calles, the Vatican, and Ambassador Morrow, over the heads of the Cristeros and even of the Mexican bishops.[64] On June 21, 1929, an official settlement came in the form of statements issued by Provisional President Portes Gil and Archbishop Ruiz y Flores. Portes Gil acknowledged the right of bishops to appoint priests, and of Catholic citizens to petition for redress of grievances. Still, there was to be no religious instruction in schools, even private ones.

Predictably, many Cristeros expressed great bitterness; thousands of their comrades had suffered death to obtain real constitutional changes, not mere verbal promises by a Calles regime politico.[65] Nevertheless, on June 27, 1929, the Mass was openly celebrated in Mexico City for the first time in three years.

Post-1929 Struggles

Peace had apparently been restored, but only through a verbal agreement, not by a signed document, and at the cost of a deeply divided Catholic community. As it turned out, the criticisms and fears expressed by the Cristeros soon seemed more than justified. Despite President Portes Gil's promise of amnesty, the army shot several hundred surrendered Cristeros without the pretense of a trial. Hunts went on for leaders of the former rebellion; the numbers apprehended and killed may have reached five thousand.[66] Reprisals against the Cristeros provoked further and more desperate rebellious outbreaks, which the bishops publicly disowned. The governor of Vera Cruz state expelled 187 of its 200 priests.[67] In half of the states no priests at all were permitted, despite constitutional guarantees of the free practice of religion.[68] A constitutional amendment in November 1934 forbade the existence of seminaries for training new priests. Since no foreign priests were permitted in the country, this move clearly aimed at the extinction of the priesthood and ultimately of the Church. For good measure, a decree of 1935 prohibited sending religious information through the mail.[69] In that same year in all Mexico there were only 322 priests functioning legally.[70] The Mexican hierarchy allowed Catholics to fulfill their Sunday obligation on any day of the week, because even the vast cathedral in Mexico City was too small to hold all the people crowding in to hear Mass.

By 1934 thirteen states had closed almost all the churches within them. Private homes used for religious services or teaching could be confiscated.[71] The governor of Chihuahua decreed that all places and villages with names of saints must be given new, nonreligious or antireligious names. In Tabasco state, the governor had the churches stripped of all objects of value; police carried off religious images from private homes, removed crosses from graveyards, and compelled unwilling citizens to participate in the destruction of church buildings. Even the traditional term *adios* was forbidden.[72] Political opponents of the Tabasco governor were shot down in the streets of his capital, and a group of paramilitaries from Tabasco fired pistols at civilians coming out of a church in the Coyoacan district of Mexico City, killing and wounding many.[73] In Vera Cruz, police shot women and priests in the streets, and churches were burned.[74] Violence permeated even the inner sancta of the national regime: on September 11, 1935, a fight broke out in the Chamber of Deputies between supporters of President Cárdenas and former president Calles; two deputies were killed and several wounded.[75]

Petitioning the courts for relief, members of the clergy were informed that there was no religious persecution.[76] And Archbishop Ruiz y Flores, who had made the peace agreement with Portes Gil, was deported, despite being a Mexican citizen, because he "owed allegiance to a foreign sovereign," that is, the pope.[77] Pius XI decried the persecution of Mexican Catholics but counseled nonviolence.

The conflict went on. In July 1934 former president Calles announced that "we must enter into and take possession of the minds of the children, the consciences of the young, because they do belong and should belong to the Revolution."[78] He continued in admiration: "and this is what is being done at present in [Stalinist] Russia, [National Socialist] Germany, and [Fascist] Italy."[79] Many public schools were filled with antireligious posters.[80] Meanwhile, for the ordinary Mexican, "conditions [were] worse than those for which the Diaz regime has been so bitterly castigated. The average peon ate measurably less in 1936 than in 1896, and the low real wage paid to him in 1910 would have looked magnificent in 1934."[81]

President Lázaro Cárdenas, inaugurated in 1934, had been a protégé of Calles; it was his "firm intention of achieving the spiritual liberation of the people" from Catholicism.[82] Nevertheless, he did not wish to see another Cristero rebellion. Besides, confrontations with both the U.S. and the machine of ex-president Calles, now an enemy of Cárdenas, were on the horizon.[83] Accordingly, in March 1936 Cárdenas proclaimed that "the government shall not incur the error of previous administrations by treating the religious question as the pre-eminent problem that subordinates other aspects of the program of the Revolution."[84] Most of the clergy supported President Cárdenas in his explosive controversy with the U.S. concerning nationalization of the petroleum industry. Then in May 1937 the Mexican Supreme Court ruled that the law permitting only one priest in the entire state of Chihuahua (for over six hundred thousand inhabitants) was too arbitrary. And when in February 1937 a fourteen-year-old girl in Vera Cruz state was shot dead during a police raid on a private house where Mass was being celebrated, the popular outcry resulted in the reopening of several churches.

Fighting continued sporadically in various states until 1940, when President Cárdenas's chosen successor, General Ávila Camacho, publicly declared that he was "a believer." In 1946, the constitutional article requiring antireligious education was repealed.

Reflection

The Cristero rebellion confronted a regime that had achieved power by armed conquest and that held onto it through rigged elections, financial corruption, press censorship, violations of its own constitution and laws, and totalitarian police practices. For decades after 1910, no peaceful transfer of national power took place; every presidential election was followed (or preceded) by rebellion on the part of those who claimed, with justification, that the ruling clique made elections a total mockery.

The regime failed to defeat the Cristeros. The numerical ratio of the army to the rebels was wholly insufficient; its predatory tactics toward civilians were self-destructive; the political unreliability of many of its officers was notorious. This was a recipe for stalemate, and perhaps for disaster, against an enemy like the Cristeros with broad and only partly mobilized popular support. But the Calles regime had control of the big cities, most of the railways, and the borders, as well as the all-important recognition of the U.S. government.[85] In contrast, the rebels possessed not a single border town or seaport, and consequently could not obtain direct foreign assistance or even purchase foreign ammunition. Against these obstacles, the Cristero rebellion could not have hoped to win unless it could rally a greater proportion of the Catholic population; to do this, it needed the endorsement of the bishops. But, reflecting the urgings of the Vatican, the Mexican bishops declined to support the Cristeros collegially, and few did so individually. Rich Mexican Catholics, and U.S. Catholic leaders, also stood aloof. Ultimately, the Cristeros received the active support of only a minority of Catholics, mainly poor peasants in the western states. But even this was more than the regime could successfully cope with. In any event, what prevented a Cristero victory was the lack of both sufficient arms and the unambiguous endorsement of the episcopate, not the military prowess of the regime.

TIBET

In the 1950s Tibet experienced a massive invasion by its Communist Chinese neighbor. The effort of the Tibetan people to protect their independence and preserve their culture resulted in one of the most protracted and strenuous guerrilla wars in Asian history. That conflict also contributed to a military confrontation between China and India.[86]

One of the remotest of countries, Tibet is also quite extensive, larger in area than Spain, France, and Portugal combined, or Texas plus Oklahoma and New Mexico. Four of Asia's mightiest rivers—the Yangtze, Mekong, Indus, and Brahmaputra—have their sources within its borders. The Plateau of Tibet, twelve thousand feet high, is surrounded by forbidding mountains, notably the Himalayas to the south and west, and the Kunlun Shan to the north. And Tibet comprises, along with Kashmir and Afghanistan, the convergence zone of Russian, Chinese, and Indian aspirations, a zone that has witnessed several major guerrilla insurgencies in recent times.[87]

Tibet's population in 1950 was perhaps three million; the capital, Lhasa, had about twenty-five thousand inhabitants. Religion, in the form of Lamaist Buddhism, was the very essence of Tibetan society. At least one male from every family became a monk; before the Chinese invasion there were three hundred thousand monks of various grades, one-quarter of the entire male population. Since the fourteenth century, the leader of Tibetan society, both temporal and spiritual, had been the Dalai Lama (a term more common outside Tibet than inside). Upon the death of a Dalai Lama, his reincarnated successor was traditionally discovered among the country's humblest classes.

The Tibetans once ruled a great empire stretching from Siberia to India and from Afghanistan to Burma. Parts of Kashmir, Burma, Nepal, and Sinkiang still employ the Tibetan tongue. Tibetan influence in Manchuria and Mongolia has been profound and long lasting: the leader of Mongolian Buddhism, the Grand Lama of Urga, was traditionally selected from Tibet. The country never experienced foreign colonization, until today. Even Genghis Khan did not subdue the fierce Khambas of eastern Tibet.[88] On the contrary, out of Tibet, the strategic heart of Asia, conquering horsemen had several times swept eastward deep into China.

For twenty centuries the Chinese looked upon the Tibetans as a distinct race. Spoken Tibetan is not like Chinese, and its script derives from India, not China.[89] "By the mid-nineteenth century if not earlier, Manchu Chinese influence was minuscule[;] the Tibet-Dogra war of 1841, the Tibet-Nepal War of 1857, the Nyarong War of 1862–1865 and the British invasion of Tibet in 1903–1904 were fought and settled without Chinese assistance."[90] The collapse of the Manchu dynasty in 1911 enabled the Dalai Lama to expel all remaining Chinese officials and troops. Nevertheless, the Nationalist regime of Chiang Kai-shek continued, like the Manchu empire before it, to claim sovereignty over Tibet, a claim the Tibetans explicitly repudiated. As the victory of the Communists in China approached, the isolated Tibetans, without even a radio station, awaited events with foreboding.

The Invasion

The 1949 Maoist victory heralded a new era, and not only for China. For the first time in a century Beijing had a government both willing and able to impose control over far-flung regions like Tibet. In mid-April 1950, thirty thousand Chinese troops crossed the borders of Kham, in eastern Tibet.[91] Beijing informed the government in Lhasa that it must acknowledge Tibet as part of China, with Chinese control over Tibetan defenses as well as diplomatic and trade relations with foreign states. In the face of Tibetan reluctance to accede to these demands, on October 5, 1950, ninety thousand Communist Chinese soldiers invaded eastern Tibet from the east and north. The Tibetan army had only nine thousand poorly trained and meagerly equipped troops.[92] Within two weeks the Chinese invaders had captured most of the members of this army, then sent them to their homes. Chinese troops had received instruction not to mistreat Tibetan civilians, and they proclaimed that they would not injure Tibet's religion or the monastic system.[93]

Throughout the first half of the twentieth century Tibetans had relied on support from British India against Chinese encroachment. But by 1950 the British were gone from India, and in any case they doubted that Tibetan resistance could have any chance of success.[94] Newly independent India did not oppose Chinese occupation of Tibet: the British-trained Indian army had been badly shaken by partition, and had been fighting both the Pakistanis in Kashmir and internal Communist-inspired uprisings.[95] Appealing to the U.N. for help, the Tibetans found sympathy only from El Salvador and Ireland. The U.N. ignored these appeals in part because the Chinese invasion of Tibet had occurred at exactly the same time that world attention was focused on the massive Chinese intervention in the Korean conflict.[96]

In December 1950 the Dalai Lama fled from the Chinese invaders to the Indian border.[97] But after receiving Chinese promises of respect for Tibetan culture he returned, urging his people to submit. The Chinese at first showed restraint, while they brought in more troops and built access roads and fortifications.[98] At the end of 1953 there were three hundred thousand Chinese troops in Tibet, bringing with them venereal diseases hitherto unknown in that isolated country.[99] Once their projects and troop movements were well under way the Chinese felt strong enough to crush any Tibetan resistance. In 1955 they began imposing "reforms," which included moving in large numbers of Chinese immigrants, giving Tibetan land to these immigrants and Chinese officials, and imposing higher taxes on the population.[100] Tibetan schoolchildren now received instruction only in Chinese.[101] The "transition to Socialism" was imposed on the eastern Tibetan areas of Kham and Amdo, provoking revolts there. For the Chinese, transition to Socialism meant collectivization. To the Tibetans, collectivization represented increased Chinese control of Tibetan society, in which environmental and demographic factors had long ago produced "an ideology of individualism unique among the usually densely populated societies of Asia."[102]

Under Chinese occupation Tibetan culture suffered brutal public ridicule. Correctly viewing Tibetan Buddhism as a competing ideology to Maoism, the Chinese moved ferociously against it. Beginning in the mid-1950s, they looted, closed, or destroyed scores of monasteries. They tied elderly lamas to horses and dragged them through the towns; many lamas were beaten to death.[103] The International Commission of Jurists[104] issued a press statement in 1959 condemning Chinese massacres of Tibetan civilians, forced labor, compulsory marriages, and the destruction of monasteries, manuscripts, and art works. Concerning those atrocities the commission wrote: "It would seem difficult to recall a case in which ruthless suppression of man's essential dignity has been more systematically and efficiently carried out."[105]

The Chinese Communists displayed the same sense of their cultural and racial superiority to frontier peoples as the ancient emperors had.[106] Chinese brutality toward Tibetans also reflected "primal fears in the [Chinese Communist Party] of territorial dismemberment of China and [Western] exploitation of national separatist movements."[107] It was the territory and resources of Sinkiang, Inner Mongolia, and Tibet that the Beijing regime desired, not the friendship—or even the presence—of the peoples of those regions.[108]

The Resistance

Armed clashes between Chinese and Tibetans had been occurring since 1952, but a major guerrilla rebellion broke out in the eastern regions of the country (Kham and Amdo) by the turn of 1955–1956. Fresh from their "victory" in Korea, the Chinese leaders tried to deal with this revolt by mere force, which in turn produced more recruits for the guerrillas. By mid-1956 the revolt in Kham had acquired a permanent character. Tens of thousands of guerrillas were in the mountains, while other thousands fled to central Tibet carrying tales of the executions of lamas, the looting and destruction of monasteries, and the most shocking brutalities.[109] The Khamba guerrillas formed the Tibetan Resistance Army (the PTTM), whose symbol was a snow lion on a triangular banner. In July 1956 Chinese Vice-Premier Marshal Chen Yi went to eastern Tibet to see what the trouble was; guerrillas attacked his escort, killing or capturing three hundred Chinese soldiers.[110]

In 1956, the Dalai Lama accepted an invitation to visit Nepal and then crossed into India, where he requested asylum. Chinese Foreign Minister Chou En-Lai promised the Dalai Lama a new policy of moderation in Tibet and urged him to return home; Indian prime minister Jawaharlal Nehru also wished the Dalai Lama to leave his country. Under these circumstances the Dalai Lama reentered Tibet.[111]

The absence of any outside help for the Tibetans, the overwhelming power of the Chinese, and the Dalai Lama's innate pacifism led him to conclude that Tibet could not survive if it resisted. He therefore declined to bless the revolt. In contrast, guerrilla leaders believed they could inflict heavy losses on the Chinese, who would not wish the outside world to view such a sizeable rebellion and hence might make concessions.[112] In 1958 various guerrilla groups formed the National Volunteer Defense Army (NVDA), with headquarters in Lhoka province on the Indian frontier.

The Chinese informed the world that the uprising was the work of a decadent religious aristocracy that sought to maintain its grip on the enslaved Tibetan people.[113] Aside from the obvious question of how such a group could sustain a widespread and vigorous guerrilla war, Nehru himself pointed out that the growing numbers of Tibetan refugees in India were mainly from the humble classes.[114] In fact, "the Tibetan revolt was a national uprising against the Chinese invasion and occupation of Tibet."[115] By the end of 1957 there were at least 150,000 Chinese troops in eastern Tibet trying to suppress the revolt, and Chinese propaganda indirectly admitted the popular character of the resistance.[116]

The Chinese air force attacked the rebels not only with bombs but also with napalm and gas. Most of the guerrillas were Khamba tribesmen of eastern Tibet, "the last cavaliers of the fierce warrior tribes of Central Asia."[117] They had never before been bombed, or even seen bombing aircraft. Their wounds could quickly become gangrenous, because the intense cold prevented frequent or even infrequent bathing, and often monks' urine was applied to wounds as medicine.[118] Inferior in numbers, outclassed in training and equipment, ignored by the outside world, the Tibetans seemed doomed to quick annihilation.

Yet the guerrillas were not without advantages. Four times the size of Italy, ten times the size of Pennsylvania, most of Tibet is covered by the world's most daunting mountains, with its few roads often impassable in winter (in good weather the NVDA closed the road between Kanting and Lhasa with landslides, isolating the Chinese garrison in the capital). The Tibetans of Kham and Amdo provinces were familiar since childhood with guns, animated by religious conviction, and organized into kinship units. They summoned up as well "their fearless fighting qualities, their knowledge of mountain warfare, and their implacable hatred of the Chinese."[119] They were used to a spartan life and had no real supply problems, living on mare's milk and hiding from Chinese aircraft in caves. For allies, they had their excellent horses and fierce mastiffs. And the guerrillas found a sanctuary in the Tibetan-speaking border districts of Nepal (which the Chinese sometimes violated).[120] In Katmandu the NVDA had contact with the CIA and Chiang Kai-shek's Taiwan regime and received training in communication and parachuting from both.[121] And not the least of the guerrillas' advantages was their Buddhist belief in reincarnation; thus death at the hands of Chinese soldiers would be merely an episode, not a finale.

The Chinese invaders in their turn confronted many serious difficulties. In 1956 Khamba bands wiped out Chinese garrisons in Chamdo, Litang, and elsewhere.[122] By 1957 perhaps eighty thousand guerrillas were in the field.[123] The standard formula for counterinsurgency suggests that the Chinese needed eight hundred thousand troops to quell this revolt. But in fact they seem to have had only between two hundred thousand and three hundred thousand, "occupied in an all-out war of extermination in East Tibet."[124] During 1956–1958 alone, forty thousand Chinese died in eastern Tibet. (The Khamba guerrillas, devoid of medical facilities of any kind and constantly on the move, rarely took prisoners and often killed their own wounded to prevent them from falling into Chinese hands.)[125] Besides, in the thin air of Tibet, Chinese soldiers became exhausted after only short marches. And the army had to bring food in from Sinkiang to Lhasa by truck convoys that took sixteen days, costing the Communist regime fifty times as much to feed a Chinese soldier in Tibet as in Beijing.

In July 1958 Beijing withdrew its invitation to Nehru to visit Tibet, fearing large anti-Chinese demonstrations in Lhasa.[126] Then on March 18, 1959, Chinese troops tried to kill the Dalai Lama by shelling the Norbulinka Palace, believing him to be inside.[127] The outraged population of Lhasa, swollen with refugees from the East, rose in revolt. The Dalai Lama fled under NVDA protection to their stronghold in Lhoka province. From there they crossed the border into Bhutan and then decided to go on to India.[128] This escape from Tibet, across some of the most rugged terrain on earth, with at least two hundred thousand Chinese troops in the country (and between thirty thousand and fifty thousand in Lhasa alone) was a remarkable achievement.[129] The Dalai Lama has ever since lived in exile.[130]

India and China Clash

Indian prime minister Nehru had long pursued good relations with Communist China, even at the cost of dissembling about what was happening in Tibet and suppressing Lhasa's efforts to communicate with the outside world.[131] He failed to see at first the strategic implications for India of China's massive occupation of Tibet.[132] Nevertheless, long-standing suspicions between newly independent India and newly Communist China, including Chinese foreign minister Chou En-lai's deep personal distaste for Nehru, helped make a clash between the two Asian giants inevitable. Furthermore, the Dalai Lama's friendly reception in India placed an immediate strain on that country's relations with China.[133]

By 1961–1962 the Chinese held the Tibetan population centers, while the NVDA controlled the mountains and the remote valleys—the classic guerrilla insurgency situation. The only reliable link between Lhasa and Beijing was by air. Along with aircraft and great numbers of troops, the Chinese fought the guerrillas with new roads. One of these strategic roads ran from Sinkiang into northern Tibet through the Aksai Chin area (thirty-three thousand square kilometers), across territory claimed by India. In 1962 Chou En-lai publicly accused India of helping to foment the Tibetan revolt.[134] At the same time Tibetan refugees in India were turning popular and elite opinion there strongly against the Chinese.[135] And it was no longer possible to deny that Chinese occupation of Tibet and the consequent revolt had "converted India's peaceful border with Tibet into a hostile frontier with China."[136] Accordingly, having learned in 1962 of the new invasion road in Aksai Chin, and of the military posts along it, Nehru ordered the Indian army to kick the Chinese out.[137] The results were a rapid and resounding humiliation for the Indian army and for Nehru himself.[138] Close to panic, India turned for support to the British and the Americans, and also to the Soviets (who had been stirring up anti-Chinese rebellion in Sinkiang). The Tibetan resistance benefited from these events: many of the guerrillas had moved into Nepal, with that government's permission, and India now allowed supplies to go across its borders to the Tibetans there.[139] Furthermore, Indian intelligence services organized Unit 22, consisting of ten thousand Tibetans, who received CIA training under supervision of the Indian army.[140] The 1962 Sino-Indian border conflict, precipitated by the Chinese invasion of Tibet, widened the Sino-Soviet split, blasted the superficial diplomatic friendship between Beijing and New Delhi, and moved India closer to the U.S., China's principal adversary in the world.

A few years after the Indo-Chinese border clash, Mao Tse-tung's Great Proletarian Cultural Revolution reached Tibet. Tibetans were now required to cut their hair short in the Chinese style, and Chinese words were added to the Tibetan vocabulary, placing the Tibetan language on the road to extinction. The Chinese even declared that traditional Tibetan decorations and painted cooking utensils were reactionary; everything had to be painted a proletarian blue or green. And many of the remaining religious buildings and monuments in the country were looted and destroyed.[141] By the end of the Cultural Revolution fewer than one thousand monks remained in the eight monasteries that the Chinese had not yet demolished.[142] Of course, the grotesque excesses of the Cultural Revolution had called forth a renewal of armed resistance, the so-called Nemyo revolt in central Tibet in 1969; to quell this latest outbreak the Chinese were forced to move in fresh troops from Sinkiang.[143]

By 1970, the overwhelming power of the Chinese had suppressed any major fighting. The "modernizing reforms" of the Communist occupation, including forced collectivization, compulsory cultivation of wheat, the destruction of art works and monasteries, an influx of Chinese colonists, and the dumping of nuclear waste, had devastated the culture, ecology, and economy of Tibet.[144] Tragically, "the old Tibet was gone."[145] In 1984 the Tibetan government-in-exile estimated that the Chinese invasion and occupation had cost the lives of 1.2 million Tibetans (mainly between 1950 and 1965); of these, 433,000 had perished in various revolts, 73,000 died in prison and labor camps, 93,000 were tortured to death, and 343,000 had starved.[146] In the 1990s, 80,000 Tibetans lived in exile in India, the equivalent of over seven million Americans.

And one has to wonder: what lessons, exactly, did the Beijing oligarchy think its actions in Tibet were teaching to the Taiwanese?

Reflection

In his excellent history of Tibet, Melvin Goldstein contends that much of the blame for the destruction of Tibet as a polity and as a culture must fall upon the leaders of Tibet itself. In his view, those leaders, fearful of contaminating Tibetan and Buddhist values, had neglected to modernize the army, declined to have large numbers of Tibetan army officers trained abroad, and refused to allow sufficient foreign officers into the country to develop the army. Thus "the monastic and religious conservatives [so influential in the government] created a set of conditions whereby the government was unable to defend and preserve those very religious values from the Chinese Communists."[147]

This stark judgment needs some shading. There is no denying the innate conservatism of Tibet's ruling groups. Yet it is hard to imagine that any government could have saved Tibet, even one that was highly in favor of modernization. The new Communist regime in Beijing was determined to set right what it perceived as a long list of historical wrongs; high on this list was the denigration of Chinese sovereign rights in border areas, notably including Tibet. Faced with this determination, Tibet would have needed the steadfast and generous support of the Indian government to have had even a serious chance of preserving its independence. Instead, Tibet received utterly inadequate amounts of assistance from the outside world. (If the West could not save Hungary, how could it have saved Tibet?) This absence of effective help, along with the overwhelming numbers and grim determination of the Chinese, quite negated what would have been the otherwise formidable advantages of a guerrilla movement composed of rugged mountaineers inspired by religious conviction and operating in forbidding terrain against an alien and brutal invader.

Yet the last chapter has not been written. The Dalai Lama received the Nobel Peace Prize in 1989; in the following decade Tibet again became an object of international concern. And "Chinese rule in Tibet was responsible for destroying much, but its primary creation may have been Tibetan nationalism—that which it had devoted its most intense efforts to eradicate."[148]

SUDAN

For the past half century, the Sudan has experienced major guerrilla conflict. Muslim northern Sudan, closely identifying itself with the Arab world, concentrated on the subjugation of a black, largely animist or Christian, southern Sudan. Southerners usually refer to northerners as "Arabs"; approximately half of Sudan's twenty-five million people are Arabic-speaking, and perhaps two-thirds Muslim.[149] Most of the fighting has taken place in the three southernmost provinces, a region of about 250,000 square miles, the size of Texas or Afghanistan. The conflict has become one of the bloodiest and most protracted of the twentieth century.[150]

With an area of one million square miles, Sudan is the biggest country on the African continent, five times the size of Spain, ten times that of Wyoming. Thirteen hundred miles from north to south, Sudan links the Middle East with the heart of Africa. The breakup of Sudan along religious/ethnic lines could thus reverberate throughout world politics.

Islam did not come to Sudan until a thousand years after adherents of that faith had conquered Egypt. Thus, Sudan is marginal in more than one way to the Islamic world. For generations, Arab slavers carried out destructive raids in southern Sudan. Arabs traditionally looked upon black Sudanese as racial inferiors.[151] In the late nineteenth century, the British contemplated erecting southern Sudan as a barrier against Muslim penetration of central Africa.

The regime of the Mahdi (1881–1898) legalized slavery and attempted to force Islam on the blacks. Opposition to Anglo-Egyptian efforts to suppress the slave trade had been a major focus of Mahdism.[152] After the final defeat of the Mahdist state, Sudan became an Anglo-Egyptian condominium, although its southern boundaries with Uganda and Ethiopia were not settled until 1913. The predatory, slave-raiding Mahdist state left important residues in present-day Sudan: the great-grandson of the Mahdi, one Sadiq al-Mahdi, served as prime minister during 1967–1969 and 1986–1989, and the Mahdist movement still possesses a private militia.

The First Sudan War, 1955–1972

As Anglo-Egyptian Sudan approached independence, an overwhelmingly northern constitutional commission rejected federalism, intending instead to make Islam the religion and Arabic the language of a centralized state. In contrast, southerners wanted protection for English and Christianity in their own region. Many southerners, their self-consciousness long sharpened by northern efforts to enslave, Arabize, and Islamize them, perceived that a benevolent British rule was about to be replaced by a malevolent Arab rule.[153] Thus rebellion broke out even before independence, which came in 1956. A military regime soon took power in Khartoum and "adopted a policy of unabashed Islamization and Arabization in the south. Protest was met with violent assertions of government authority."[154] The government closed southern missionary schools, abolished the Sunday holiday, and expelled hundreds of Catholic and Protestant missionaries.

The first anti-Islamist guerrillas called themselves the Land Freedom Army and also Anya-Nya ("snake venom"). Later most of these groups gathered together in the Southern Sudan Liberation Movement (SSLM). They built small base camps deep in the forests or in border regions. In the first days of the rebellion, Anya-Nya mistreated civilians, having no doctrine of organizing the civil population to support the guerrillas. Rival guerrilla groups and self-proclaimed "southern governments" sprang up, mainly based on those tribal divisions that have permitted the conquest and exploitation of the southerners for centuries. The period 1955–1963 was mainly one of guerrilla survival, due in part to the weaknesses of the Khartoum army. Anya-Nya mined the few roads and bridges, so the northern army became dependent on inadequate air transport. By the end of 1964 Anya-Nya counted perhaps five thousand fighters, only a tenth of whom possessed firearms.[155] After 1965, the guerrillas were able to get some good weapons from outside Sudan, especially from defeated rebels in Zaire. By the end of 1968 the guerrillas numbered perhaps ten thousand; nevertheless, equipment, discipline, and coordination remained poor.

In May 1969, Colonel Gafaar Numeiry, commander of the Khartoum garrison, seized power. Declaring that a military solution to the rebellion in the south was impossible, he promised regional autonomy and better treatment of civilians by the army. Still, Numeiry built up his armed forces (to thirty-six thousand), receiving Soviet instructors and arms, and the fighting went on.

Before 1949, there were no secondary schools in the south. The consequent absence of a large southern educated class meant a lack of good political leadership and of effective spokesmen to arouse interest abroad. Thus, when the guerrillas appealed to the U.N. and to the Organization of African Unity to investigate government atrocities, they received no response. (The United States during the 1960s was of course increasingly enmeshed in Vietnam.) But the guerrilla movement benefited from the eventual emergence of Joseph Lagu. Born in Equatoria province in 1931, son of Anglican mission teachers, Lagu received an army commission in 1960. Three years later he joined Anya-Nya and was made a colonel. By 1971, thanks in part to his ability to procure arms from Israel, Lagu had imposed his leadership over almost all of the southern fighting groups, which may have enrolled twenty-five thousand men.

But by far the principal factor operating in favor of the guerrillas was the weakness of the regime's armed forces, which had little or no counterinsurgency training. On the contrary, their Soviet instructors inculcated the doctrine of the Big War.[156] Its numbers were always too small (never more than forty thousand) to control a huge territory with primitive communications. Northern soldiers looked upon assignment to duty in the south as punishment. Northern troops routinely burned missions, schools, clinics, even whole villages, reinforcing the hostility of most southerners to the Khartoum regime.

Over time foreign governments interested themselves in the long conflict: Khartoum received help at various points not only from the USSR but also from Iran, China, and Libya (a Libyan pilot flying a Sudan regime MiG-23 was taken alive by guerrillas in December 1988). The Israelis helped the guerrillas in both conflicts, and trained some of them in Uganda.[157] Ethiopia also aided the guerrillas, in retaliation for Khartoum's assistance to Eritrean rebels.[158] During the second phase of the conflict, elements of the guerrilla forces received training, arms, and sanctuary in Ethiopia.

In March 1972, a ceasefire came into effect mainly through the efforts of the World Council of Churches and Emperor Haile Selassie. According to the so-called Addis Ababa Agreement, the Khartoum regime promised amnesty for insurgents, self-government for the black provinces, equality of all religions, recognition of English as a major language in the south, and incorporation of thousands of guerrillas into the national army. Joseph Lagu received command of all Sudanese government troops in the south.

The Conflict Renewed, 1983–

Eventually it became clear that the Addis Ababa Agreement was not a peace but rather a truce. The Khartoum regime made no distinction between loyal southern army units and groups of bandits or anti-Khartoum guerrillas who were operating in the south in the early 1980s. Indeed, distrusting all southern regular units, the regime tried to disarm and move them into the north. In May 1983 the 103d Battalion under Lt. Col. John Garang mutinied and crossed the border into Ethiopia.[159] This unit and other groups, usually former Anya-Nya men, comprised the nucleus of the Southern People's Liberation Army (SPLA) and the Southern People's Liberation Movement (SPLM), proclaimed in Ethiopia in July 1983. The dictator General Numeiry then imposed the Islamic penal code on the whole country. War would almost certainly have begun again eventually, but "it was Numeiry's unilateral abrogation of the Addis Ababa Agreement . . . that led to the resumption of hostilities in 1983 by the leadership of the [SPLM]."[160]

The regime responded with a conventional military offensive. It captured a dozen towns held by rebels, but this merely forced their defenders back into the impenetrable forests. Meanwhile Khartoum failed to devise any sort of political program to weaken the insurgents.

Since most of the fighting was now being done by troops from the north, regime units suffered many northern casualties—a very important development as Khartoum was not accustomed to losses of this kind. The regime therefore resorted to the formation of local militias, which had first been used in the mid-1960s to fight the Anya-Nya. Because conscription would have been unacceptable in the north, the establishment of local militias was the only option for the Khartoum regime, handicapped as it was with an army that was too small. Eventually several of these militia groups proved quite effective in combating the SPLA units.

The early tactics of the SPLA were to attack small police and army outposts while consolidating its hold in south-central Sudan and working out supply lines from Ethiopia. Civilian sympathy often came to SPLA if only because of the reprehensible behavior of regime troops. SPLA leaders proved immune to bribes, and their military successes humiliated the regime. Partly in consequence of all this, Numeiry was ousted in a coup in 1985. By 1989 SPLA had moved to conventional war, holding three-fourths of the territory of the south including the three southern provincial capitals, plus much of the Ethiopian border (in contrast, the old Anya-Nya had never held an important town).

By 1991 the rebels were besieging the main regime garrison at Juba, which had to be supplied very expensively by air. But in that same year a split, partly tribal-based, developed inside SPLM, when those desiring an independent south broke away from the leadership of John Garang, who advocated not secession but federalism.[161] At the same time the fall of the Mengistu dictatorship in Ethiopia ended the SPLA sanctuary there, a major blow. In December 1991 Iranian president Rafsanjani visited Khartoum after declaring the regime's efforts in the south to be a jihad.

In these circumstances Khartoum planned a final offensive, fueled by Chinese arms and Iranian gold. Proclaiming holy war against the southern rebels, the regime drove four hundred thousand southern refugees out of Khartoum into the desert.[162] The offensive opened in March 1992, with the rebels retreating in the face of overwhelming regime power. The operation ended in July with the capture of the key town of Torit, although fierce guerrilla fighting continued.

The regime purged the judiciary, the civil service, and the teaching profession of non-Muslims. Moreover, the human rights group Africa Watch attested that slavery had reappeared in Sudan, and Secretary of State Warren Christopher declared Sudan to be a sponsor of international terrorism.[163] In February 1993 Pope John Paul II arrived in Khartoum and, in the presence of the dictator Colonel Bashir, deplored forced Islamization.

The non-Muslim Africans of southern Sudan have many historical and contemporary grievances against the Khartoum regime. Their rebellion, over a vast area of very difficult terrain, received assistance from abroad. With its inadequate material resources, Khartoum would have been hard pressed to cope with such a development in the best of circumstances, but the outrages against civilians committed by its troops in the southern areas undercut the possibility of playing on traditional tribal rivalries and guaranteed that the fighting would be protracted and bitter.[164] The war helped produce one of the worst famines in African history. By the mid-1990s the conflict had cost at least one million lives and generated another one and a half million refugees.[165]

SUMMARY

The essentiality of religion in the lives of millions of people around the globe means that when a regime outrages religious sensibilities, it can expect determined, even furious, resistance. The defense of religion against perceived assault legitimizes an insurgency and sustains its morale. The Mexican, Tibetan, and Sudanese conflicts shook their respective regimes; the Vendean and Spanish guerrillas fatally undermined the Napoleonic Empire; and the Afghan insurgency produced fateful consequences for the Soviet Union. Many years ago C.E. Callwell suggested that a well-led insurgency confronts any state with a very grave challenge. Perhaps a religiously motivated insurgency presents the gravest challenge of all.[166]

CHAPTER 5

FOREIGN INVOLVEMENT WITH INSURGENCY

The fundamental method of guerrilla war-making is to attack the enemy's lines of communication. The counterinsurgent equivalent of this is twofold: first, isolating the civilian population from the guerrillas, and, second, preventing outside assistance from reaching the guerrillas. It is the latter effort that this present chapter examines.

Machiavelli observed that "when once the people have taken up arms against you, there will never be lacking foreigners to assist them."[1] During the Cold War, even insurgencies that originated in the most arcane local circumstances became entangled in the schemata of that global ideological struggle. Western and/or Soviet intervention, direct or by proxies, was especially notable in Greece, French Indochina, South Vietnam, Angola, Afghanistan, El Salvador, and Eritrea, among others.

It is very important, however, to recall that outside intervention was not unique to the Cold War era. On the contrary, from the American War of Independence to the anti-Bonapartist struggle in Spain, the British and the French governments each sent notable assistance to rebels against the other power. Indeed in the French view, the American War of Independence was only one more episode in a global contest with the British that stretched from the War of the Grand Alliance (1688–1697) to Waterloo (1815), a struggle whose duration dwarfs that of the Cold War. This in itself is a powerful argument against the proposition that, precisely because of outside interference, lessons derived from insurgencies during the Cold War are of little relevance to the twenty-first century.

THE IMPORTANCE OF OUTSIDE HELP

The presence or absence of outside help for an insurgency can be decisive. The Soviets in Afghanistan learned some "major lessons of modern war in much the same hard way the U.S. learned them in Viet Nam, [notably that] it is virtually impossible to defeat a popular guerrilla army [that has] secure sources of supply and a recovery area."[2] While this statement clearly needs some modification, it contains a good deal of truth. During the American War of Independence and the Spanish *guerrilla* against Napoleon, as well as in French Indochina, South Vietnam,[3] Eritrea,[4] Sudan,[5] and Soviet-occupied Afghanistan, insurgents received outside help that was undoubtedly a necessary condition for their success. Similarly, it is hard to imagine that Tito's Communist resistance in Axis-occupied Yugoslavia would have survived without British aid, despite favorable topography, a regional tradition of guerrilla warfare, and the brutality and inadequate numbers of the Axis invaders.

Because outside assistance is so vital, the geographical location of an insurgency can profoundly influence its outcome. In the Philippines, South Africa, Malaya, and (to a lesser degree) Tibet, geography facilitated cutting off the insurgents from effective external aid; whereas in Spain, French Indochina, South Vietnam, Cambodia, Sudan, Afghanistan, and El Salvador, foreign assistance to the insurgents poured in.

The thirty-year war in Vietnam clearly illustrates that sometimes geography is destiny. Help from neighboring Maoist China enabled the Viet Minh to stalemate the French, and then played a key role in the Battle of Dien Bien Phu.[6] In subsequent years, the Hanoi regime freely acknowledged that the military highway incongruously known as the Ho Chi Minh Trail was decisive in the Communist conquest of South Vietnam.[7] All this is to say that, had South Vietnam been an archipelago, like the Philippines, or a peninsula, like South Korea, it would probably be in existence today.

Or consider the victory of Benito Juárez over the short-lived, French-backed empire in Mexico. Juárez and his followers were certainly tenacious, but they were not a match for the French forces supporting Maximilian of Habsburg. On the other hand, although he was undeniably attractive as a human being, the catalog of Maximilian's political ineptitude is impressive, and includes his failures to build a true indigenous army, rally the peasantry through a program of social reform, and hold the support of the initially enthusiastic Catholic hierarchy. Under these circumstances, outside support became literally matters of life and death for both Juárez and Maximilian. Help for Juárez flowed abundantly across the U.S. border. Meanwhile, confronted by the open hostility of the victorious Union government with its great armies, and the distance between Mexico and France, Napoleon III lost interest in his transoceanic imperial project and left Maximilian to his perhaps undeserved fate. To paraphrase Porfirio Díaz: "Poor Maximilian—so far from France, so close to the United States!"[8]

Geography has not only physical but also political and psychological dimensions. For example, the adherents of the former Rhodesia lost their outside support, their morale, and hence their chances for independence once Portuguese rule in neighboring Mozambique collapsed and South Africa cut off its previous assistance.

Indirect foreign assistance to insurgents can also be vital, and even decisive. The Japanese mauling of Chiang Kai-shek's regime severely weakened it for the coming contest with Mao's Communist guerrillas. In Vietnam, the Japanese humiliation of the French forces during World War II, followed by a massive Chinese Nationalist occupation of the North, made incalculable contributions to the eventual Communist victory there.

It is not always from governments alone that outside support reaches insurgent movements. Diasporas, such as those of the Palestinians and the Tamils, can provide money, recruits, intelligence, and political influence in countries near and far. And in Colombia, the one-time leftist guerrillas of the FARC have evolved into an international criminal organization by enmeshing themselves heavily in the drug trade. Estimates of the money derived from FARC drug activities run into the hundreds of millions of dollars.[9] Riches of that magnitude—and that provenance—can corrupt an insurgent movement and cause internal rifts.[10] What the ultimate effects of becoming more and more dependent on drug money will be for the FARC remain to be seen.

Numerous insurgent movements, some quite famous, did not receive outside assistance or were eventually cut off from such help. All were eventually defeated. They include the Vendeans, the Boers, Aguinaldo's followers, the Cristeros, the Polish Home Army, the Huks, the Malayan Communists, the Algerian FLN (National Liberation Front; see below), and Sendero Luminoso. Indeed, although loudly proclaiming their Maoism, the Senderistas disdainfully refused to ask for help from the world's allegedly backsliding, capitalist-roading Communist states, including the USSR—and China.

A note of caution: while outside help may be a necessary condition for insurgent victory, it does not guarantee it. The Communist-organized insurgencies in Greece and El Salvador[11] received substantial foreign assistance for protracted periods, but were ultimately unsuccessful. Indeed the evidence suggests that outside aid actually hurt the guerrillas in Greece, because it made them believe they did not have to cultivate the good will of the peasant population among which they operated.

Some insurgencies would almost certainly not have been able to achieve their principal aims even if they had been able to obtain outside help. Consider the various Moro (Muslim) rebellions in and around the Philippine island of Mindanao. The Moros, whose economy has historically been based on piracy and slavery, have fought the Spanish, the Americans, and the Philippine Republic. What the Moros claim to want, fundamentally, is an independent Islamic state based on Mindanao. No Philippine government, no matter what its political orientation, could consider such a demand. Hence the only possible winning strategy for the Moros would be to march on Manila, a city inconceivably remote, both geographically and sociologically, from their base.[12] And even on the island of Mindanao, which the media often portray as their stronghold, the Muslims are but a minority of the population.[13]

On the other side of the ledger is outside assistance from one government to another government confronted by insurgency. U.S. aid to the governments of the Philippines and Greece was an important element, and in El Salvador a decisive one, in the defeat of guerrilla insurgencies in those countries. On the other hand, massive American financial assistance to the French in Indochina did not prevent France from ultimately abandoning that region. U.S. assistance to South Vietnam resulted in the defeat of the guerrilla insurgents there, but, deserted by its American ally, South Vietnam later succumbed to a conventional invasion from North Vietnam. The Soviet Union, along with Iran, China, and Libya, assisted the regime in Khartoum against southern rebels, to little avail. Despite massive Soviet aid to both Ethiopia against the Eritrean insurgency after 1974, and to the Kabul regime in Afghanistan after 1979, the insurgents in each of those countries were victorious.

PREVENTING OUTSIDE HELP

Counterinsurgent forces have employed several means to deter, cut off, or diminish supplies coming into a country to help insurgents. One means has been diplomacy, but unambiguous successes under this heading have not been common. Since the 1930s, another primary method has been interdiction of supply routes through air power. This also has met with quite limited success, however, especially the efforts of the Americans in Vietnam and Laos (the Ho Chi Minh Trail) and of the Soviets in Afghanistan (the Pakistan border). In light of the inability of the U.S. Air Force, along with naval airpower, to stem the flow of conventional troops and supplies from China into North Korea, and from North Korea into South Korea, it is a touching testimony to military faith in technology[14] that both the Americans and later the Soviets (with the example of the relative lack of U.S. success before them) should have believed that, even in terrain favorable to guerrillas, air power would be able to disrupt outside aid to them. At any rate, many today would agree with the judgment that "it is extremely difficult—if not impossible—to use modern weapons technology to cut off a guerrilla force from food and other basic supplies."[15]

A more successful, less expensive, and certainly less controversial method of interdiction has been the construction of fortified lines. By A.D. 126, the Romans had finished Hadrian's Wall, very close to the present-day English-Scottish border. The wall was seventy-four miles long from sea to sea, ten feet wide, and twelve feet high in many places, with a ditch in front, a tower every third of a mile, and a fort every seven miles. This was not a static platform from which to fight—its defending troops were trained to fight in the open—but a means of controlling cross-border traffic and impeding incursions by light forces.[16]

A thousand years after the Romans abandoned Britannia, the kings of England wished to incorporate Wales into their domains. They ultimately adopted the method of encastellation—covering the country with a system of small, strong forts—which greatly aided in subduing the warlike and stubborn Welsh who had waged guerrilla war against them for two hundred years.[17]

Other instances of fortified lines will receive examination below, but here it may be helpful to consider briefly some peculiar travails of French fortification in Vietnam.

FRENCH STRONGPOINTS IN VIETNAM

The conflict between the French and the Communist-led Viet Minh was for years a small-scale affair because the latter faced many difficulties in obtaining modern weapons in quantity. But with the triumph of Mao Tse-tung's forces across the mountainous Chinese border, the prospects of the guerrillas improved dramatically. Guarding one of the few good passages between China and northern Vietnam was the French fort at Cao Bang, with excellent natural and man-made defenses. In October 1950 the French Command in Hanoi made the fateful decision to abandon Cao Bang. Thus sixteen hundred French and Vietnamese troops, accompanied by fifteen hundred Indochinese civilians, headed south toward the supposed safety of the city of Lang Son, eighty-five miles away down Colonial Route 4, a miserable track through thick jungle. At about the same time, thirty-five hundred French Moroccan troops headed north out of Lang Son to meet and escort the column coming down from Cao Bang. The two groups linked up, only to be cut to pieces by the swarming Viet Minh. The Cao Bang affair was "the greatest French defeat in the history of colonial warfare," a defeat made possible because the French both lacked air power and underestimated the abilities of the Viet Minh commander, General Vo Nguyen Giap.[18]

The calamity of Cao Bang somehow convinced the French Command that it should also abandon Lang Son, a city of one hundred thousand, France's last remaining major strongpoint along the Chinese border. To avoid alerting the Viet Minh that they were about to evacuate the city, the French did not destroy the great quantities of military supplies within it. Hence the guerrillas obtained ten thousand 75mm shells and thousands of automatic weapons, along with large quantities of gasoline and medicine. According to Bernard Fall, the abandonment of Lang Son was "France's greatest colonial defeat since Montcalm had died at Quebec."[19] The withdrawal of the French from the northern border passes meant that the Viet Minh now had unrestricted access to Communist Chinese supplies, and were free to raid the vital Red River Delta and the Hanoi area almost at will.

These French disasters along the Sino-Vietnamese border suggest that building outposts is a worthless, and even dangerous, pursuit unless they can be reliably supplied. Nevertheless, once such strongpoints are established, the troops within them fare better if they stay and fight the enemy rather than expose themselves to attack by trying to move toward safety over inadequate roads without air cover.[20] Of course, the French would fight one more great outpost battle—at Dien Bien Phu.

BLOCKHOUSE LINES

Any sound counterinsurgent strategy will make a priority of interfering with the guerrillas' mobility, one of their most valuable weapons. A proven, highly effective means for diminishing guerrilla mobility is the blockhouse line. Of the three instances of that tactic examined here, two did not have as their principal purpose the closing off of outside assistance to guerrillas. Nonetheless it became obvious to later counterinsurgents that blockhouse lines can be very effective for achieving that end.

South Africa

The conflict in South Africa of 1899–1902, usually called the Boer War, became "the greatest nineteenth-century partisan war"[21] as well as the "longest, costliest, bloodiest and most humiliating" of Britain's wars between 1815 and 1914.[22] During that conflict, in January 1901, the British began to erect blockhouses to defend railroad lines. The program soon became quite extensive, as the typical earth-and-iron blockhouse cost only £16 to construct.[23] The original purpose of blockhouse cordons was to keep the enemy out; later they turned into an offensive means to hem him in. By May 1902, eight thousand blockhouses extended for thirty-seven hundred miles, manned by fifty thousand white troops and sixteen thousand Africans. Each blockhouse was connected to its neighbors by telephone wire; between the blockhouses also stretched barbed wire and trip-wires rigged with pebble-filled tin cans. Armored patrol trains both protected and were protected by the blockhouses.

By the time the blockhouse program neared completion, the Boers possessed few field guns. During the course of the war, most of their artillery had been lost or captured, or had been depleted of ammunition. Besides, as the Boers turned to guerrilla warfare, cannon hampered their mobility.

Though very effective, the British blockhouse lines were not impenetrable. On more than one occasion the great guerrilla chieftain Christiaan De Wet cut the wires between blockhouses at night and led his men through without a shot being fired. (De Wet called the blockhouse lines, inaccurately but forgivably, "the blockhead system.")[24]

In these circumstances British commander Lord Kitchener began the campaign to flush the guerrillas out of hiding. His great mounted drives—fifty miles across, one man on horseback every ten yards—often rode from blockhouse line to blockhouse line, or from a blockhouse line to a railroad patrolled by armored trains. "[These drives] present perhaps the most remarkable feature of that long drawn-out campaign against the Boer guerrillas."[25] (During the conflict in East

Timor in the 1990s, the Indonesian army often flushed guerrillas out of their hiding places by using a similar method, with long lines of infantry and civilians moving in the same direction, called the "fence of legs.")

Boer advantages included mobility (mounted guerrillas in an extensive, level, and familiar land), civilian sympathy, some really excellent guerrilla tacticians, and the nonexistence of British airpower. For their part the British benefited greatly from their burgeoning blockhouse lines, as well as from great numbers of troops, an improving intelligence system, the services of black and Boer soldiers and scouts, and the absence of any significant outside help for their opponents. The last Boer guerrillas surrendered in 1902.

China

During the mid-1930s, Chinese Nationalist leader Chiang Kai-shek launched several campaigns to exterminate Mao's Communist guerrillas. Blockhouses emerged as a major factor in the struggle.[26] The Nationalist forces erected thousands of small forts, complete with trenches, barbed wire, and interconnecting fields of machine-gun and artillery fire. These blockhouses both protected the Nationalist troops and reduced Communist mobility.[27] (This subject is treated more intensively in chapter 14.)

After their invasion of China proper in 1937, the Japanese built thirty thousand strongpoints in the country, mainly as a protection against small arms fire and grenades, since the guerrillas rarely had artillery.

A Notable Algerian Adaptation

The French developed a variant of the blockhouse tactic during the Algerian war (1954–1962). In Vietnam, the French forces conceded to the enemy free passage across international borders, but not in Algeria. Indeed they determined to limit to the greatest possible degree outside help to the Algerian guerrillas, especially from neighboring Tunisia. To that end the French constructed the famous Morice Line, extending for hundreds of miles along the Tunisian border. The line consisted of an electrified wire barrier, with minefields on both sides and watchtowers at regular intervals. On the Algerian side the French built a constantly patrolled road protected by barbed wire. The whole system involved eighty thousand troops. Attempts to break through the electrified fence set off signals at monitoring stations, to which the

French responded almost immediately with artillery, aircraft, and mobile ground units. Early efforts to break through the line cost the guerrillas so many casualties that serious attempts to infiltrate from Tunisia came to an end.

ISOLATING GUERRILLAS BY SEAPOWER

A variation on blockhouse systems and the Morice Line is using seapower to interdict supplies to guerrillas. Clearly, naval forces can be of great effect in carrying gold and guns to guerrillas, perhaps most famously in the case of the British navy during the Spanish rising against Napoleon. But, less dramatically but no less importantly, naval interdiction of vital supplies has at other times seriously undermined the efforts of guerrillas, as in the case of Aguinaldo's Philippine followers, the Boers, the Huks, and the Malayan Communists, among others.

Regardless of the nature of the conflict, the power of a tight and sustained blockade has deeply impressed many strategic thinkers. Basil Liddell Hart wrote that the British blockade of Germany during World War I was "clearly the decisive agency in the struggle."[28] But perhaps the American Civil War offers the most striking illustration of the power of naval interdiction. The Union blockade of the Confederacy was an essential element of General Winfield Scott's conservative strategy for winning the Civil War. His plan called for pinning down major Confederate forces in Virginia by a constant threat to Richmond, conquering and holding the Mississippi River, and shutting off the Confederacy's contact with Europe through an effective coastal blockade.[29] Scott aimed at exhausting the seceded states rather than subjugating them. Such a strategy would have both been far less expensive in blood and treasure, and avoided forcing the very numerous southern pro-Unionists into the arms of the rebellion. It would also have made postwar reconciliation easier. Scott's critics—the fatuous "On to Richmond" crowd—derided his strategy as the Anaconda Plan (after the snake that slowly crushes its prey). Nevertheless, "events proved the old veteran [Scott] to have been right."[30] The "Anaconda Plan was strategically sound; before the end of the civil war in 1865, the Union would have implemented it in full."[31] The U.S. Navy successfully blockaded the extensive and highly indented coastline (three thousand miles, no less) of the Confederacy—without the aid of radio, radar, or aircraft. The effectiveness of the Union blockade also made it obvious, to anyone who wished to know, that if the defeated Confederates turned to guerrilla war, they could hope for precious little outside help.

The profound impact of the Union blockade on the outcome of the Civil War has received relatively little attention. Nevertheless, the testimony of distinguished observers on the consequences of that naval interdiction is impressive in volume and conviction. As Bern Anderson writes: "[the blockade] was one of the major factors that brought about the ultimate collapse and defeat of the South."[32] E. Merton Coulter: "Without a doubt the blockade was one of the outstanding causes of the strangulation and ultimate collapse of the Confederacy."[33] Albert Bushnell Hart: "The true military reason for the collapse of the Confederacy is to be found, not so much in the hammer blows of Thomas, Sherman and Grant, as in the efforts of an unseen enemy, the ships of the blockading squadrons."[34] Samuel Eliot Morison: "The South showed that she could take care of herself until starved by the blockade and split by the Mississippi."[35] Harold and Margaret Sprout: Victory closely depended upon "that blockade which relentlessly sapped the military strength and morale of the Confederacy."[36] And Allan Nevins: Life in the blockading squadrons was monotonous and confining, "but no service was more important than this strangling hold on the economy of the South"[37] because "the [blockade] had stiffened until near the end it was perhaps the major element in garroting the South."[38]

SUMMARY

An inventory of valid principles regarding foreign intervention in insurgencies across regions and time periods would include the following points. First, insurgencies received outside assistance long before the beginning, and continued to do so after the ending, of the Cold War. Second, foreign help has in almost all cases been a necessary, but not invariably a sufficient, element of insurgent success. Third, some insurgencies are beset by so many strategic disadvantages that probably no amount of outside help, short of conventional invasion, would be decisive. Fourth, methods for preventing foreign assistance for guerrillas have included diplomacy, fortified lines, ground patrols, naval blockade, and air interdiction. Fifth, notable successes at impeding external aid, in both conventional conflicts and insurgencies, include the U.S. Civil War, South Africa, the Philippines, British Malaya, and French Algeria; notable failures include the American War of Independence, Napoleonic Spain, French Indochina, South Vietnam, and Soviet Afghanistan. Sixth, it appears that great quantities of money derived from the drug trade can in some instances substitute for foreign help, and even for domestic support, at least in the intermediate term.

CHAPTER 6

ESTABLISHING CIVILIAN SECURITY

It is an essential thesis of this book that in a guerrilla insurgency the civil population is Clausewitz's "center of gravity."[1] Effective counterinsurgency therefore means establishing secure control over the civilian population, especially in rural areas. The true objective of intelligent counterinsurgency is not to kill guerrillas but to marginalize them, while exacerbating internal guerrilla contradictions. Separating the guerrillas from the population is the crux of counterinsurgency and the government's principal challenge. Without security, the civilians will have no choice but to support the guerrillas. Therefore, "the first reaction to guerrilla warfare must be to protect and control the population."[2]

Insurgents may employ terrorist tactics in the villages in order to demonstrate that the government cannot protect civilians, who will in turn hesitate to cooperate with the government through fear of reprisal. From Malaya to Colombia and Peru, guerrillas flourished where the forces of order failed to offer effective protection.[3] In South Vietnam "the local inhabitants judged the [Saigon government] and the [Communists] above all on their respective ability to provide security."[4] The Viet Cong targeted for assassination the cream of South Vietnam's emerging middle class: officials, social workers, medical personnel, and schoolteachers. Between 1954 and 1958 the terror campaign killed 20 percent of village chiefs. In 1960 alone, terrorists killed fourteen hundred local officials and other civilians. By 1965, assassination had claimed the lives of over twenty-five thousand civilians.[5] Therefore, a central question for the counterinsurgents is how best to protect from retaliation those civilians who side with, or would side with, the government. Two principal methods have dominated counterinsurgent efforts to separate and protect rural civilians from the guerrillas: resettlement and local self-defense. These methods need not be mutually exclusive, as will appear below.

Resettlement

From Manchuria to Mexico, from South Africa to South Vietnam, counterinsurgent forces have employed some form of resettlement in order to move rural populations away from guerrilla areas. The objectives of such a policy are to deprive the guerrillas of their main sources of intelligence and food. Resettlement has always been controversial, and will remain so. Both its exponents and its critics include distinguished and knowledgeable students and practitioners of counterinsurgency.

In the waning years of the nineteenth century, significant guerrilla insurgencies arose in three widely separated localities: South Africa, the Philippines, and Cuba. All these conflicts witnessed resettlement efforts of one kind or another.

In South Africa

The war between the British Empire and the Boer Republics of Transvaal and the Orange Free State began as a conventional war in October 1899. By early summer British forces had beaten the Boer armies and occupied Johannesburg and Pretoria. The war seemed over. But the defeat of the Boer armies and the occupation of their capitals did not bring peace. Instead the war entered a new, guerrilla phase, "the greatest nineteenth century partisan war."[6]

The most notorious feature of the British counterinsurgency effort was the erection of camps in which to concentrate the civilian population of contested areas. These "concentration camps" were intended to serve several purposes. The first camps were to protect Boers and native Africans who had accepted British rule and taken an oath of neutrality. The Boer guerrillas themselves bear a large responsibility for the camps: they left their own families without protection, and very often burned the farms of neutral or surrendered Boers, turning the women and children onto the open veld. Concentration also protected isolated farm families from guerrilla looting or vengeance.

Eventually, however, civilians were brought into the camps against their will, in order to deprive the guerrillas of food and intelligence. All told, between 120,000 and 154,000 Boer and African civilians were inmates of some fifty camps at one time or another.[7] Of these, many thousands, mainly women and children, died of typhoid fever and other diseases. "More Boer boys and girls under the age of 16 died in British concentration camps than all the fighting men on both sides in the course of the entire war."[8] The appallingly unhealthful conditions in the camps were almost invariably the result not of cruelty but of incompetence.[9] There was a severe shortage of medical doctors, and of those available many spoke only English. The camp populations received British army rations and still succumbed to disease in great numbers, an indication of the poor quality of those rations.[10] There was too little discipline in the camps: thus many Boer women, who had lived their entire lives on the spacious veld, had no concept of the hygienic necessities of camp life. Their primitive notions of sanitation, along with their truly ghastly "home remedies," helped to cause and spread illness. Revelations about the high death rates caused a worldwide scandal: in London, Henry Campbell-Bannerman, leader of the opposition Liberal party, declared that British forces in South Africa were employing "methods of barbarism." Eventually most of the camps introduced strict sanitation discipline, and the death rates plummeted.

Boer guerrillas and politicians bitterly criticized conditions in the camps. But the Boer fighting men had left their women and children unprotected. Besides, almost all of the camps were lightly defended and could have been taken by Boer guerrillas. Even when Boers did attack a camp, they carried off supplies, not inmates, for the latter would have been an intolerable burden. And—incredibly—by the conclusion of this long and often bitter struggle, no accusation of torture of prisoners arose on either side.[11]

In the Philippines

Fighting between the Spanish and the Americans in the Philippines had not yet been concluded when tensions developed between U.S. forces and Filipino nationalists under the leadership of Emilio Aguinaldo. The latter had proclaimed himself provisional president of a Philippine Republic, and had expected the Americans to back him. President McKinley, however, rightly judged that Aguinaldo's supporters, mainly of the Tagalog ethnic group, could neither unite the islands nor defend them from Japanese and German imperialism (Wilhelmine Germany had colonies in the area). Actual combat between Aguinaldo's followers and U.S. forces began in February 1899. The Americans soon dispersed Aguinaldo's regular units, and the latter turned to guerrilla tactics. The U.S. government had promised the Filipinos eventual independence; U.S. soldiers were carrying out many fundamental reforms in the judicial and health systems of the islands. Consequently, large numbers of Filipinos either supported temporary U.S. rule, or condemned the methods of the guerrillas. After McKinley's reelection, it was clear that the Americans would not pull out and that Aguinaldo's forces could not possibly win. Nevertheless, fighting continued in certain areas.

American commanders in the islands soon grasped that the most effective way to defeat the guerrillas was to disrupt their food supplies. The food-denial campaign led inevitably to plans to relocate the rural population, especially in those areas where the remaining guerrillas seemed determined to fight on even without hope of success, and even though the Americans repeatedly invited them to accept honorable surrender.

Relocation followed a pattern. The inhabitants of a given area were informed that they must bring their families, animals, foodstuffs, and moveable possessions to a designated town by a particular date. After that date, animals and goods outside the town were subject to confiscation and adult men liable to arrest. Strict controls were imposed on food shipments between towns. The U.S. army strove to provide the relocated civilians with food, medicine (especially vaccination), and employment on public works. Nevertheless, injustices and hardships were many. In some areas poor sanitary conditions contributed to the deaths of at least eleven thousand Filipinos. (At the same time, British efforts to concentrate the Boer population produced a much greater loss of life, mainly from typhoid.)[12] Still, despite all their attendant problems, the concentration of civilians and the regulation of food were highly effective against the guerrillas.[13]

In Cuba

Cuba was the largest of the remnants of Spain's once vast seaborne empire in the Americas. In the waning decades of the nineteenth century, several serious revolts aiming at independence wracked the island. The last of these (as it turned out) began in 1895. The commander of Spanish forces on the island, General Valeriano Weyler y Nicolau (1838–1930), a veteran of campaigns against guerrillas in the Philippines, had two hundred thousand troops under him, of varying quality. Weyler embarked on a mass reconcentration campaign during 1896–1897; his forces herded hundreds of thousands of peasants into camps where great numbers perished, mainly from preventable epidemics. Accompanying the resettlement were the deliberate devastation of the countryside and the slaughter of animals. These policies made many recruits for the insurgents and turned even conservative Cuban opinion against Spain. Weyler's excesses[14] helped prepare U.S.

public opinion for intervention, which became inevitable after the explosion that sank the U.S. battleship *Maine*.

Relocation of civilians continued to be a notable aspect of counterinsurgency strategy into the twentieth century in Latin America, Africa, and Asia. Techniques of relocation ranged from simple expulsion to elaborate efforts to establish entirely new communities.

In Mexico

Mexico's Cristero rebellion had its roots in religious persecution and electoral corruption. The regime fought the insurgency through population removal, especially in western states. The process began in April 1927 in Jalisco state, a particular center of Cristero support. Almost one million villagers were forced from their homes, after their crops and animals had been seized and their houses looted. The presumably emptied rural areas then became free-fire zones. Various epidemics of course followed upon these mass removals. The untold suffering of the persons affected increased the numbers and the determination of the Cristeros. Meanwhile peasant refugees flooded into Leon, Guadalajara, and other cities, bringing the Cristero message and organization with them. Insurgent leaders in flight from the army or the police often found refuge among these displaced people.[15]

In Malaya

In 1950 Malaya's military chief, General Sir Harold Briggs, began to put into action what became known as the Briggs Plan. This consisted of three major elements: (1) clearing the Malayan peninsula of guerrillas methodically, one district at a time, from south to north; (2) uprooting the guerrilla infrastructure in the cleared areas; and (3) resettling the numerous Chinese squatters, the principal source of food for the guerrillas, into secure villages.

This last element became the centerpiece of the entire counterinsurgency; by 1954, 570,000 Chinese squatters had been placed in new communities, where they received title to land. The enterprise stood Mao on his head, draining away the water in which the guerrillas had formerly been swimming. Resettlement was the major component of a general food denial program: controls were placed on all food bought and sold, and rice convoys went heavily guarded. Storekeepers were obliged to puncture cans of food upon sale. Simply getting enough food to stay alive became the primary concern of the guerrillas, who relied more and more on extortion from local peasants.

Of course, the resettlement program was not without its problems, mainly political. The Malayan state governments, under Muslim control, were very reluctant to see Chinese receiving title to good land (or any land). The resettlement areas, called New Villages, were not always situated to provide employment for the inhabitants, and of course many had insurgent spies within them. In addition, tight food control worked hardships on day laborers who had to carry their midday meal with them. Nevertheless, by the summer of 1954 the combination of resettlement and general food denial had become "the most effective planned operation against a guerrilla target and its support organizations."[16] It was "a devastating measure that did more than any other single thing to defeat the Communists in Malaya."[17]

The Korean War greatly facilitated the British victory in Malaya, because the boom in rubber prices helped pay for the war. Nevertheless, the Malayan experience offers probably the most successful plan of resettlement on record.

In Algeria

The problems of counterinsurgency in French Algeria were incomparably more massive than in British Malaya. Algeria is eighteen times the size of Malaya. In fact, Algeria is larger than Germany, France, Britain, Norway, Sweden, Denmark, and Finland combined. In addition, the Algerian guerrillas could count on help from friendly states on the eastern and western borders. In the 1950s Algeria had a population of about ten million, including over a million of European ancestry. Early French counterinsurgency tactics in Algeria were poor: enter a village, question people, and then leave. They consistently violated a most fundamental principle of effective counterinsurgency: *Never* abandon a village after letting civilians rally to your standard. But a successful French counterinsurgency effort eventually emerged, resting on three pillars. The first was the deployment of a great number of troops— 450,000 at its peak, the equivalent of one soldier for every 23 inhabitants of Algeria, and this figure does not include Muslim auxiliaries. The second pillar was a system of effective barriers, notably the Morice Line along the border with Tunisia, to isolate the guerrillas from outside assistance. The third pillar was population resettlement. While the border barriers choked off outside assistance, the army's regrouping of Muslim peasants dried up the insurgents' internal support. Two million Arabs eventually moved, or were moved, out of guerrilla areas. The army settled many of these into new villages and towns, and undertook to provide them with law and order, medical care, schooling, even employment. On the whole, the French army strove to convert hostile or indifferent Muslim peasants into acquiescent French subjects. The army also increased the number of its Muslim auxiliary troops to over 150,000.[18] Most decidedly, the army in Algeria rejected any idea that its main objective was to protect the privileges of the European *colons*, many of whom were not even French. Predictably, taking on responsibility for the care of so many civilians, and enlisting so many Muslims in the armed forces, deepened the commitment of many French officers to victory in the war and the permanence of French control over Algeria. These sentiments lit the fuse for the army mutiny of 1958 that brought the turbulent Fourth Republic to an inglorious end.[19]

In Manchuria

Victory in the war with Russia (1904–1905) had established Japanese influence in southern Manchuria. In 1931 Japan invaded and occupied the region, setting up a puppet state, which it named Manchukuo. Japanese Manchuria became both a protection for Japanese-occupied Korea and a staging area for invasion of China proper. Guerrilla resistance was fairly widespread from the beginning. In 1933, the Japanese began a program of regrouping rural civilians into protected hamlets. By 1937 they had set up about ten thousand of these hamlets, containing a population of five and a half million persons. The hamlets served their principal purpose of isolating the guerrillas from civilians fairly successfully. Nevertheless, the harshly administered program caused much suffering among the affected civilian population, and drove many into the arms of the guerrillas.[20]

In South Vietnam

The so-called strategic hamlets were the centerpiece of counterinsurgency in South Vietnam during the early 1960s. The plan called for creating physical security and social improvement for the peasantry by erecting elementary fortifications around a hamlet (a subsection of a village).[21] Inside, a lightly armed band of local militia would hold off any attacking guerrillas until help arrived in the form of the army or provincial militia. While based on a fundamentally sound concept, the strategic hamlet program collapsed after 1963 for several reasons. First, the basic assumption behind the program was that the only important threat came from outside the fortified hamlet; little attention was paid to the threat from *inside* via the Viet Cong infrastructure—whose members provided intelligence to the guerrillas outside and sometimes assassinated prominent anticommunist villagers. Second, the director of the program under the president's brother, Ngo Dinh Nhu, was himself a Communist.[22] Third, the South Vietnamese Army disliked the strategic hamlets, viewing them as a drain of resources away from the army.[23] Fourth, many aspects of the program alienated the peasantry. While the original concept called for fortifying and defending an existing hamlet, sometimes peasants were unwillingly relocated to new land; the inhabitants were also required to dig ditches and undergo rudimentary military training without compensation.[24] Fifth, instead of fortifying hamlets in relatively controlled areas and then moving outward—a variant of the classic clear-and-hold strategy—the government would often locate a strategic hamlet in a dangerous area, thus inviting instead of deterring attack. Sixth, the program extended too rapidly. While in their Malayan counterinsurgency, the British built five hundred defended villages in three years, the South Vietnamese erected twelve thousand in two years.[25] The consequences of this over-rapid growth were severe. Often the promised social services for the fortified hamlet never materialized. Not infrequently when the exposed hamlet came under attack it was unable to receive the necessary outside support because the radio intended to call for help was useless for lack of replacement parts, or there had been no radio to begin with, or the designated relief force had no means of transportation, and so on.[26] Finally, and above all, the assassination of President Diem brought to power a military regime uninterested in carrying on the effort. Nevertheless, the strategic hamlet program was not without its good effects, and it could have been much more successful had it received more attention, money, and time. On October 23, 1963, (a week before Diem's murder), Secretary McNamara and General Maxwell Taylor told President Kennedy that "we found unanimous agreement that the strategic hamlet program is sound in concept and generally effective in execution."[27] Certainly, the Communists devoted a great deal of effort against it.[28]

In Portuguese Africa

During the 1960s, Portugal faced guerrilla insurgencies in her sprawling and relatively underpopulated African possessions, the last bastions of any European empire on that continent and all that remained of a vast Portuguese colonial enterprise that had once stretched from Brazil through Africa to India, China, and Indonesia.

Out of necessity, the Portuguese pursued an inexpensive, low-technology strategy against the various rebel groups. (See the discussion of their counterinsurgency concepts in chapter 16.) Resettlement became a key piece of that strategy: in Angola alone, the Portuguese eventually regrouped more than one million persons.[29] Not unexpectedly, their "resettlement concept was sound in theory but so often went wrong in execution. Success depended on thorough planning, adequate finance, and knowledgeable people. These ingredients were not always present. . . . Consequently the Portuguese, like their predecessors the British and the French, had both success and failure in the application of this concept."[30]

Relocating the population has been one major arm of counterinsurgency campaigns. Another has been local self-defense through reliance on militia or territorial forces.

LOCAL SELF-DEFENSE: TERRITORIAL FORCES AND MILITIA

Local militia or rural self-defense forces are often a major component of even poorly conceived counterinsurgency efforts. Such organizations can perform several very important functions. First, they separate rural civilians from the guerrillas, while protecting village officials from assassination, a major concern in South Vietnam and Peru. Second, civilians mobilized for local self-defense, along with their family members, become in effect bound to the government. Third, militias release regular government troops for more direct action against the guerrillas. In addition, properly trained and equipped militias possess advantages over regular troops in terms of population defense. For example, local forces tend to be more conservative in their use of firepower, a profoundly important political consideration. And they are of course intimately familiar with the local inhabitants and terrain.

During the Napoleonic occupation of Spain, the French tried to construct civic militias based, as in France, on the middle classes; the Spanish middle class, however, was much smaller than its trans-Pyrenean counterpart. Of at least equal importance, French arrogance toward their Spanish supporters and widespread atrocities all but destroyed the usefulness of any militias that came into existence.[31]

In contrast, militia systems enjoyed notable success in Malaya, Thailand, and Peru, as well as in the Philippines against the New People's Army. In all these countries Maoist-style guerrillas had alienated important civilian strata through terror.[32] The Malayan Home Guard eventually mobilized 250,000 members, including many Chinese; very few defected from the Guard, and hardly any weapons were lost. While their effort to hold onto their centuries-old African empire was eventually unsuccessful, the Portuguese employed local defense quite extensively: by the end of the wars in 1974, there were 30,000 militiamen in Angola alone.

As a result of successful militia programs, by 1982 in Thailand fewer than 4,000 guerrillas were operating in the whole country. In the northeast region, bordering Laos, a center of insurgency where once five thousand guerrillas operated, there were only 800 left.[33] Opposed to these were 170,000 militia in the Northeast alone, along with perhaps 20,000 paramilitary border patrol police.[34] Village militia—*Tahan pran*—defended their own villages and acted as liaisons with the army to obtain local improvements.[35] There were also about 13,000 rangers, recruited from militia and former regular army troops.[36] Backing up these forces was the Royal Thai Army with 141,000 personnel, the air force with 43,000, and the navy with 28,000.[37] The guerrillas were asphyxiated under a mobilized population.

In South Vietnam

By the mid-1960s, the self-defense organization in South Vietnam, called Territorial Forces, consisted of two main elements: the Regional Forces (RF) and the Popular Forces (PF). Members of the Popular Forces were recruited and stationed in their home villages; Regional Forces could be used anywhere in their province (a typical southern province was twelve hundred square miles in area, equal to a circle with a radius of twenty miles).

Before 1968, the Territorials were given cast-off weapons and very little attention. Between 1955 and 1960, almost everything went into building up the conventional ARVN forces. (True enough, the Territorials would have been extremely vulnerable if there had been no shield of regular troops to keep away heavily armed North Vietnamese Army [NVA] and Viet Cong main-force units, but the latter were few before the mid-1960s.) As a result, the situation of the Territorials was deplorable: in the Popular Forces, there were no ranks, no promotions, no decorations, few decent weapons, and very low pay.[38] Consequently, rather than patrol, members developed a tendency to stay inside their flimsy posts at night.[39] A favorite guerrilla tactic against the Territorials was to attack a village or hamlet, and then ambush the rescuing force (if any arrived). Learning to counter this sort of activity must be a main priority for self-defense forces in any country.[40]

The great Tet Offensive of 1968 galvanized South Vietnam and the Territorials. The Saigon government upgraded the weapons of the RF/PF, and also passed out weapons to tens of thousands of civilians. By December 1972, the Regional Forces consisted of 1,800 one-hundred-man companies; the Popular Forces counted 7,500 thirty-man platoons.[41] The previous spring, during the NVA's all-out Easter Offensive, some RF companies had had to face NVA regulars, and on the whole did well.[42]

Throughout most of the conflict, Territorial casualties were higher than those of ARVN, but their desertion rates were lower.[43] Between 1968 and 1972, the regular army lost 36,932 men, while RF/PF lost 69,291.[44] Indeed, "the RF/PF took the brunt of the war, more than any other South Vietnamese armed force."[45] The Territorials received between 2 and 4 percent of the national budget, but accounted for 30 percent of North Vietnamese Army and Viet Cong casualties. The Territorial forces were "the most cost-effective military force employed on the allied side."[46] General Creighton Abrams, successor to Westmoreland, insisted that upgrading the Territorials should become the highest priority.[47] Nevertheless, "their virtues were seldom extolled and their accomplishments usually slighted."[48]

The U.S. Marines developed another type of civilian security system. The Combined Action Platoon program, or CAPs, begun in the summer of 1965, was possibly "the most imaginative strategy to emerge from the Viet Nam conflict."[49] Under that program, a 14-man squad of Marine volunteers would take up permanent residence in a particular village, working with and training a local Popular Forces platoon of 38 men. (Many CAPs in practice had fewer than 14 Marines, and as time went on not all were volunteers.) A typical Vietnamese village consisted of five hamlets with a total population of roughly 3,500 and an area of about four square kilometers. "The Combined Action Program's basic concept was to bring peace to the Vietnamese villages by uniting the local knowledge of the Popular Forces with the professional skill and superior equipment of the Marines."[50] At the end of 1967 there were 79 CAPs, with 114 by early 1970, all of them situated in the very dangerous Military Region 1, just south of the North Vietnamese border. At its peak the program counted 42 Marine officers and 2,050 enlisted Marines, as well as 2 navy officers and 126 navy hospital corpsmen. The permanent Marine presence assured the villagers that they would not be abandoned. It also protected them from excessive American firepower.[51] (The destructiveness of the American way of war is a complex question, but surely few Americans would want to see their families or their neighborhoods "liberated" in the manner of U.S. forces in Vietnam or Korea.)

General Westmoreland did not support the CAPs program. He devotes exactly one paragraph in his memoirs to it, stating, "I simply had not enough numbers to put a squad of Americans in every village and hamlet."[52] It is hard to understand why he said that. To station a rifle squad of Marines in each of two thousand villages would have required twenty-eight thousand troops, which would have amounted to about 5 percent of the total American military presence in Vietnam in 1968. Yet this small fraction of U.S. troops could have provided vastly increased security to seven million peasants—as well as depriving the enemy of their services.

In Peru

One of the most successful experiments in armed rural self-defense occurred in Peru, during the bitter struggle against the Sendero Luminoso insurgency. Peruvian rural defense units were known as *rondas* (members were *ronderos*). By 1990 the proliferation and successes of these rondas produced "the first real defeat of Shining Path since the war had started."[53]

In order to understand the origins and success of the rondas, one needs to appreciate the true nature of the Sendero movement. Abimael Guzman, a philosophy professor at a provincial university, founded Sendero as a splinter of one of Peru's several Communist parties. Sendero Luminoso was never an uprising of oppressed Indians, but rather a movement of the semi-educated middle class, notably provincial professors, graduates, and students. An overexpansion of the provincial university system had produced a large number of unemployed graduates who had hoped to enter the middle class as schoolteachers. Sendero Luminoso represented to such disappointed former students, and other youths as well, the "possibility of social ascent through the new Senderista state."[54]

Since Peru had undergone extensive land reforms in the 1970s, few large landowners remained for Sendero to attack. Hence the insurgents selected Indian "backwardness" as their target. "Instead of eliminating racial sentiment, the Shining Path elite, using ideas of intellectual superiority and party infallibility, justified the racial hierarchies in which it silently believed."[55] The Senderista leadership trivialized peasant values and treated Indians as inert objects with but one dimension, that of social class. In their racist intolerance, Sendero closed Indian markets to starve the cities, removed traditional village authorities, and outlawed Christmas and other major feasts. Real malnutrition plagued Sendero-controlled villages, notable for the absence of salt and meat. Sendero forcibly recruited children as young as eight to be trained as terrorists and soldiers, pitilessly ignoring the entreaties of anguished families. Forcible recruitment also extended to young girls, taken to serve as prostitutes to Sendero fighting men. Predictably, Indian mothers became among the first to openly resist Sendero policies.

But Sendero's most dramatic violation of Indian custom consisted of mass executions, in public, and in macabre ways. By the early 1990s, Sendero was committing numerous massacres of entire families including young children and the elderly. A special target were members of Pentecostal sects, numerous in the highland areas.[56] Sendero also wiped out the membership of the center-left Aprista Party in several regions and killed resistant miners-union leaders as well.[57] Eventually the Shining Path was making war on the poorest peasants, who according to their Maoist theories were supposed to be their firmest supporters.

The Senderistas stood for "an explicit revindication of Stalinism and a clear determination to replicate the Chinese [Cultural Revolutionary] experience in Peru."[58] To the Indians of the Sierra, "they were priests of a god that spoke Chinese."[59]

Sendero's exactions, kidnappings, and mass murders produced a semi-spontaneous mushrooming of rondas.[60] By mid-1993 about four thousand rondas mobilized three hundred thousand peasants. Many Indians willingly moved into consolidated villages, where they erected walls and watchtowers and set up road checkpoints.[61] Usually a rondero had to go out on patrol only once a week or even less. In the early stages, ronderos armed themselves with homemade weapons and farm implements.[62] Eventually they began to receive some good weapons from the government; in 1991, for example, the army distributed ten thousand shotguns to the highland Indians rondas.[63] "These [groups] constitute the state's greatest success in the war."[64]

The rondas had several deep roots. The primary source was of course the growing peasant revulsion toward and fear of Sendero. "Disenchantment with the Shining Path represents a basic cause for the explosive expansion of the rondas."[65] But these self-defense organizations also "grew out of the broad context of the failure of the besieged Peruvian state to guarantee order [to the highland population] in the 1980s and early 1990s."[66] Another stimulus was improved conduct by the military. The armed forces, especially the Peruvian marines, had often imposed mass punishments on the civilian population. As time went on, however, the image and conduct of the army, in particular, improved through its recruitment of more local personnel and engagement in beneficial projects for villages. The army also served as a path of upward mobility.[67] Fostered by these improving ties, the rondas expanded.

In brief, the ronda system of the late 1980s and early 1990s worked because it was the true representative of the peasant community against the university-oriented, peasant-despising Shining Path.

In Guatemala

Various insurgencies smoldered in Guatemala from the early 1960s. By 1982, something on the order of three thousand guerrillas were operating in more than half of the country's twenty-two provinces, with a fairly elaborate infrastructure in the Northwest. The insurgents sometimes mounted operations by as many as two hundred fighters; between 1978 and 1982 they killed over one thousand soldiers, police, and paramilitaries.[68]

Guatemala had one of the best armies in the Caribbean Basin.[69] To multiply its force, the army began to train peasants, mainly northern Indians, as village defense forces.[70] These local Civil Defense Patrols— *Patrullas de autodefensa civil* (individual members were called *patrulleros*)—enrolled between three hundred thousand and four hundred thousand members, out of a 1981 census population of slightly over six million. In addition to peasant mobilization, the army embarked upon fundamental social reforms in the rebellious regions. As a result, the insurgency began to wither. Thus, "the Guatemalan armed forces have demonstrated on two occasions (1966 and 1982) that the mobilization and arming of local populations to fight against guerrillas and the concentration of government services on basic human needs in the areas of conflict are essential elements of a successful counterinsurgency strategy."[71]

In Colombia

The conditions affecting the formation of self-defense forces in Colombia have differed radically from those in neighboring Peru, reflecting peculiarities of Colombian political society and the profound ambivalence of that country's elites toward the question of rural self-defense.

The principal nongovernmental organizations that presently combat the narco-guerrilla Revolutionary Armed Forces of Colombia (FARC) have been known by several names, most often the Autodefensas Unidas de Colombia (United Self-Defense Forces of Colombia), the AUC. Though commentators usually employ the term "paramilitaries" to describe the AUC, its members reject the term. The AUC developed as a loose organization of provincial or local groups, and thus it largely remained.

The absence of the state from much of Colombia has left the rural population exposed to FARC violence (a similar situation once existed in Peru).[72] What insurgent groups often proclaim to be "liberated areas" are usually just regions the government has abandoned or never really tried to control. As of the end of 2002, after many years of FARC excesses, several presidential proclamations of new initiatives, and much wringing of hands and raising of alarms in Washington and elsewhere, the Colombian army still consisted of well under one-half of 1 percent of the total population.[73] With the Colombian elites unwilling to take those steps necessary to provide a semblance of rural security, it was inevitable that local populations would either have to become refugees or else take matters into their own hands. Here is the true genesis of the Colombian paramilitaries; "perhaps there has not been sufficient emphasis on the fact that the accelerated growth of the paramilitary groups coincides with the period following the declaration of the illegality of self-defense and all private justice groups [in April 1989]."[74]

It should not have been difficult to foresee all this. "The FARC's kidnapping campaign and indiscriminant extortions created widespread exasperation . . . and allowed the first paramilitary groups to obtain a firm foothold."[75] These new protagonists functioned as "irregular forces . . . that, in their struggle against the guerrillas, replicate guerrilla methods step by step," especially by "imitating the mobility of the guerrillas and taking advantage of their intimate knowledge of the terrain."[76]

The attitude of governments in Bogotá toward self-defense has been inconsistent and ambiguous. In 1994 President César Gaviria issued a presidential authorization for self-defense groups under the Ministry of Defense. The following year President Samper accepted the creation of the *convivirs*, local militia units. At one time over four hundred of these groups were operative, even though the convivirs were forbidden to have rifles or machine guns, only pistols. President Pastrana then dismantled the convivirs as part of his ill-conceived and unsuccessful peace offering to the FARC. In 2002 newly inaugurated

President Uribe, who had backed the convivirs when governor of the key Department of Antioquia, expressed his determination to once again mobilize the civil population against the guerrillas.

One experienced student of insurgency has written that the Colombian army is hostile to any sort of self-defense system similar to the successful Peruvian rondas because it wishes to preserve its monopoly of legal violence.[77] Nevertheless, army commanders in the field have often cooperated with the AUC—who have been notably successful against the FARC—on the venerable principle that the enemy of my enemy is my friend. These relationships remain extremely difficult to unravel. The inescapable conclusion here appears to be that "paramilitary power is a fact of life in Colombia that will only go away when the force that called them forth, the leftist guerrillas, is also eliminated from the political scene."[78]

SUMMARY

Clearly, a well-executed relocation program can be a very effective weapon of counterinsurgency. Such an undertaking requires money, skilled administrators, and especially, careful planning. In the absence of these components, the affected civilian population may become frustrated and angry, and the relocation centers can turn into recruiting grounds for the insurgents.

The question of the success or failure of resettlement has a great deal to do with who is being resettled. Prosperous farmers may well resent resettlement, whereas tenants and the landless probably will not. In Malaya, the resettled were poor to begin with, and thus had little objection to moving into villages specially set up for them. At any rate, neither the Americans nor their South Vietnamese allies seemed to have learned very much of value from the Malayan experiment.[79]

Earlier studies of resettlement were relatively optimistic. For example, during the 1960s Edgar O'Ballance wrote that the removal of civilians from near guerrilla-controlled areas during the Greek civil war greatly impeded the insurgents, and John J. McCuen stressed resettlement as a valuable tool of counterinsurgency.[80]

Later analyses were less sanguine. A landmark study of Portuguese efforts in sub-Saharan Africa concluded that "the pursuit of [resettlement] is invariably a difficult and chancy policy decision in any counterinsurgency strategy."[81] In the view of a major British study, "empirically the case against resettlement is overwhelming. . . . Resettlement cannot be regarded as a cure but as a symptom—a sign that government control over the people has so evaporated that the destruction of society is contemplated to protect it. . . . Perhaps future counter-revolutionary exponents would be wise to regard Malaya and the New Villages as aberrations rather than examples."[82] The safest conclusion may be that one should undertake any large-scale relocation program only in rare circumstances. In most instances, the authorities should concentrate on bringing security to the civilians, rather than the other way around.

With or without relocation, achieving the supreme objective of security in the countryside requires a system of local self-defense, probably best begun with (1) a variant of the Marine CAPs, until there exist (2) reliable militia units within the villages, supported by (3) a foolproof alert system to summon mobile relief forces who are prepared to deal with ambush, especially at night, (4) effective methods of keeping the guerrillas off-balance and unable to come together in large formations, such as aircraft surveillance and special units to harass the guerrillas in their own areas, and (5) a rigorous program to uproot the guerrilla infrastructure (where it exists) in the defended villages.[83]

Well-conceived and well-founded local self-defense units are major force multipliers. Nevertheless, they clearly need support, or else the guerrillas will overwhelm them one village at a time. To this end, in South Vietnam the Americans established, in addition to the CAPs, a mobile advisory team program. These teams consisted of two officers, three enlisted men, and a Vietnamese interpreter; beginning in late 1967, they paid three-day visits to villages exposed to danger, offering advice and bolstering morale. Recently an interesting proposal has come forth that in Colombia (and presumably other places), rural militia units would have the full-time services of a retired army or marine officer, in the capacity of adviser (not commander).[84]

In this absolutely critical area of civilian security perhaps more than in any other, military operations need to support and supplement clear political objectives. This will require the regular army to maintain (or establish) good relations with the population to be mobilized into militia units, and above all, to employ only conservative military tactics in populated areas.

CHAPTER 7

LOYALISTS: INDIGENOUS ANTI-INSURGENCY

This volume examines many insurgent movements that claimed to fight for national independence against foreign oppression. Almost invariably, however, notable elements in the affected society do not support, or actually oppose, the self-proclaimed independence movement. These elements, referred to here by the general term "loyalists," are often branded as collaborators or traitors. Yet these derogatory labels serve to obscure the fact that numerous anticolonial or secessionist struggles bear striking resemblances to true civil wars. One can acquire insights into the phenomenon of insurgency, as well as into the complex meanings of nationalism by taking a look at indigenous groups that opposed the insurgent movements in the American colonies, Napoleonic Spain, the Confederate States of America, the Philippines, India, Indochina, Algeria, Portuguese Africa, Afghanistan, and Indonesia.[1]

THE AMERICAN LOYALISTS

It is clear that during the American War of Independence the patriotic party comprised the great majority of the politically active population in the former colonies. Nevertheless, it appears that at least one-fifth of the white colonial population remained loyal to the crown, with higher percentages in parts of the South (including perhaps as much as one-third in South Carolina).[2]

The popular image of the American Tories as being all rich and well-born is wide of the mark. In addition to members from the elite class, the ranks of loyalism included many poor backcountry farmers. In the southern colonies, in particular, many frontier smallholders menaced by Indian attacks stayed aloof from the revolutionary cause. Moreover, loyalism tended to be high among the Scots and the Germans of North Carolina, and among settlers who had not been born in the American colonies.[3] Perhaps paradoxically, loyalism seems to have been above average among non-English minorities, especially in New York and Pennsylvania.[4]

After their disaster at Saratoga in October 1777, the British concentrated on the southern colonies in large part because of their belief that the South was swarming with Loyalists. Few in London wished to understand that political loyalty to the crown did not necessarily indicate a willingness, or an ability, to bear arms for it. The exaggerated belief in southern Loyalist strength undermined the British war effort and prepared the road to Yorktown.[5]

In contrast to the patriot party, the Tories never produced any national leaders. In general, they were ineffectual on their own, relying on British direction and seeking protection from British regulars. This lack of initiative was one of the Loyalists' greatest weaknesses. For their part, the British never developed a clear doctrine of how best to use the Loyalists; hence efforts to mobilize them were haphazard and disorganized. British commanders were also hesitant to incorporate Loyalists into their own ranks or to grant them regular commissions. At the same time, the British were very late in raising armed Tory units, and they often treated such units with indifference or contempt.[6] Worst of all, when British forces retreated out of or evacuated an area, they often abandoned those who had revealed their loyalism.[7]

Nevertheless, in spite of all this British mistrust and mismanagement, armed Tory bands were very active. And "altogether there were at times more Loyalists in America who were fighting in the British armies than Washington had in his Continental Army."[8] New York alone furnished fifteen thousand men to the regular British army, and eight thousand militia. All the other colonies furnished as many more, for a total of about fifty thousand American Loyalist regulars and militia.[9] Tories composed a substantial portion of St. Leger's failed expedition on the eve of Saratoga. They made up two-thirds of the British forces in Savannah in 1779.[10] They spread terror in New York's Mohawk Valley for years, and they engaged in plunder and house-burning in the Carolinas. This sort of activity predictably provoked ferocious counterviolence.[11] Thus, a thousand-man Loyalist force suffered annihilation at the battle of King's Mountain, South Carolina, in October 1780.

In the aftermath of the war, many Tories remained in the new United States, especially in the cities, but over sixty thousand left for British territory, mainly Canada.[12] Despite some very good monographs concerning them, the role played by the Tories in the War of Independence has virtually disappeared from view. "The Loyalists in the American Revolution suffered a most abject kind of political failure, losing not only their argument, their war and their place in American society, but even their proper place in history."[13]

THE AFRANCESADOS

Before 1808, the term *Afrancesado* indicated Spaniards who adopted French manners and/or expressions. Afterward it denoted those Spaniards who supported Napoleon's imposition of his brother Joseph as king of Spain. The reasons for such support were varied—geopolitical (the true enemy of Spain was England, not France); ideological (France can bring renewed prosperity and strength to backward Spain); patriotic (resistance to the puissant French will destroy Spain), or self-interested (the anti-French guerrillas will eventually produce social revolution)—and often a mix of these motives were at work. "The core of the Afrancesado position was that collaboration, not resistance, was the best way to protect national independence; allegiance to Joseph [Bonaparte] at least saved Spain from direct military rule from Paris and the division of the kingdom by right of conquest."[14]

No one can be sure of the number of these Afrancesados; undoubtedly it fluctuated according to the perceived chances of French success in Iberia. At any rate, when erstwhile King Joseph Bonaparte retreated across the Pyrenees in 1813, twelve thousand Spanish families followed him.[15]

LINCOLN'S SOUTHERNERS

Americans often refer to their Civil War, the War of Secession, as a struggle between "North" and "South" (or worse, the "war between the states"). These are crude and misleading characterizations, implying that opinion was homogeneous and united on both sides of the Mason-Dixon Line, a far cry from the reality. Scores of thousands of men from seceded states, for example, fought in the Union armies. These included about thirty-two thousand Union soldiers from the western counties of seceded Virginia (these counties later emerged as the state of West Virginia). Another thirty thousand Union troops came from the eastern parts of Tennessee. Each of these figures exceeds the number of troops from several northern states. All told, perhaps one hundred thousand white southerners served in the Union armies. To appreciate these figures, reflect that at Appomattox, Lee surrendered only twenty-eight thousand men, and that when Lee won his great victory at Chancellorsville, he commanded fifty-seven thousand soldiers. If approximately nine hundred thousand men served at various points in the Confederate armies, then this southern Unionist figure of one hundred thousand soldiers is of great consequence, for it not only represents an addition to the Union forces but also a subtraction from the Confederate forces, thus making a real difference of two hundred thousand between the two sides.[16] And of course there is no way of estimating how many men from such states as Alabama, Mississippi, and Georgia might have served in the Union armies, if geography had not prevented them from doing so.

THE PHILIPPINES AFTER 1898

During the Spanish-American War, Manila fell to U.S. forces in August 1898. The self-proclaimed provisional president of the Philippine Republic, Emilio Aguinaldo, expected American recognition of his new government. The McKinley administration had concluded, however, that an independent Philippines was not viable at that time and would dissolve into civil strife and anarchy, thus inviting invasion by the Japanese. Aguinaldo and his followers consequently attacked U.S. forces, initiating what is very misleadingly described as the Philippine-American War. The Americans immediately began successfully recruiting Filipinos to help them against Aguinaldo's forces. Men from the vicinity of the town of Macabebe, with a long tradition of service to Spain and hatred of the dominant Tagalog ethnic group (to which Aguinaldo belonged), became the nucleus of an eventual auxiliary force of fifteen thousand.[17] By mid-1901 thousands (mostly non-Tagalogs) were serving as intelligence agents and scouts for the Americans, and many more joined U.S.-sponsored local police forces. The American-led unit that captured Aguinaldo himself in April 1901 was composed largely of Filipinos.[18]

Predictably, several reasons led Filipinos to support the Americans. Hostility among many ethnic minorities toward the Tagalogs was one. Another was the McKinley administration's published written promise to prepare the Philippines for democratic self-government and eventual independence. Many Filipinos believed the Americans were unbeatable, and thus a lengthy armed resistance would merely result in useless destruction of life and property. Furthermore, as the war wound on, guerrilla units began using terrorist tactics, which alienated many. Not least in importance, the American troops in the islands practiced a policy of attraction, introducing systematic sanitation in the urban areas, providing free smallpox vaccination and other medical services, improving the courts, and—perhaps the most popular measure—setting up free public schools, often with soldiers as teachers.

BRITISH INDIA

If obtaining and holding the loyalty, as well as the obedience, of indigenous troops is "the supreme achievement of a colonial power," then the British in India attained that objective.[19] British regiments recruited peasants from backward areas, where loyalty was first to the clan, and then to the military unit raised among the clan. Bravery and obedience were authentic and fundamental values of those Indians who wore the British Indian Army uniform. During World War I, that army included 740,000 Indians, of whom 136,000 were Punjabi Muslims and 88,000 Sikhs. Over the course of that conflict, British Indian forces suffered 36,000 killed and 70,000 wounded.

Despite widespread and sometimes violent agitation for independence during the 1930s, with 2.5 million members the British Army in India during World War II constituted the largest volunteer army in history. Both the advancing Japanese and the pro-Axis Indian National Army (INA) offered the members of the enormous British Indian Army many inducements to desertion or rebellion. Nevertheless, the Indian Army on the whole remained loyal to Britain (actually, to their British officers), with the approval of nationalist leader and future prime minister Jawaharlal Nehru. British Indian troops beat the Japanese in Burma,[20] and also fought in Malaya, North Africa, East Africa, Greece, Italy, Iraq, Iran, and Syria. In these campaigns they suffered twenty-four thousand dead and sixty-four thousand wounded.[21] Because India attained its independence peacefully, the British Indian Army became, in large part, the army of the Indian Republic.

FRENCH ALGERIA

Despite being a sprawling area larger in size than Western Europe, Algeria has always been sparsely populated, with a total in the 1950s of only 9.5 million people, 8.5 million of whom were Muslim. To combat the Muslim-led rebellion in Algeria which began in 1954, the French utilized the services of 180,000 loyalist Muslim auxiliaries, including 60,000 who belonged to special operational units. Hence more than 2 percent of the Muslim population served with the French, the equivalent of 5.7 million Americans in 2005. Indeed, more Algerian Muslims actively served the French cause than the revolutionary National Liberation Front (FLN): "At no time from 1954 to 1962 did the numbers of those fighting with the FLN for independence match the number of Algerians on the French side."[22]

The French army and its Muslim auxiliaries defeated the rebellion, but President de Gaulle abandoned Algeria anyway.[23] The Algerian Muslims who had fought on the side of the French only to find themselves deserted by them paid a horrific price. Estimates of pro-French Muslims executed by the regimes of independent Algeria after 1962 run from 30,000 to 150,000; the latter figure is almost three times the U.S. losses in the Vietnam War.[24]

PORTUGUESE AFRICA

The Portuguese were employing substantial numbers of native Africans in their armed forces as early as the 1870s. In addition to untold numbers in the militia, fifty-four thousand African soldiers—representing 35 percent of regular Portuguese army units—took part in the independence conflicts in Angola, Mozambique, and Portuguese Guinea between 1961 and 1974. The army paid its African soldiers relatively good wages. But quite beyond that, Africans of different ethnic and religious derivation from the dominant guerrilla groups believed that they would fare better under the Portuguese than under any possible indigenous regime. (The Portuguese were especially assiduous in their cultivation of Muslims in Guinea.)

While the British in Malaya and the French in Algeria had separate European and native units, the Portuguese completely integrated their forces. Apparently not one single mutiny or mass desertion in a regular unit occurred. In the words of one observer, "twelve years after fighting began, in both militia and regular army units blacks and whites served happily together, eating the same food, both officers and men, and sharing the same barracks rooms."[25] The Portuguese often incorporated ex-guerrillas into their service; it was almost certainly some of these who assassinated the well-known independence leader Amilcar Cabral, among others.

These African conflicts were protracted but not intense. Portuguese army combat deaths over a thirteen-year period of struggle, in territories sixteen times the size of the state of New York, totaled four thousand, of which 23 percent were African.[26] After the Portuguese left their African colonies, bloody conflict between indigenous groups continued for more than a quarter of a century.

THE KABUL ARMY

When the Soviets invaded Afghanistan in December 1979, one of their first acts was to disarm most units of the Afghan army. The Soviets deeply distrusted this army, fearing, correctly, that the resistance had thoroughly penetrated it. Among the eighty thousand men in the pre-invasion army, over half either deserted or defected to the resistance. Many of the eight thousand pre-invasion army officers had been killed by the native Communist regime; others found jobs in civilian government agencies, went into exile, or joined the resistance.

In response to this alarming hemorrhage of manpower, the Communist regime in Kabul reduced the training period for officers in its army from three years to two. But even Afghans sent to the USSR for officer training deserted or defected. To control desertion, conscripts were stationed outside of their home areas. Ever more desperate measures followed. Promotions flowed abundantly: one defector said that of four hundred men in his unit, twenty were brigadier generals. Young volunteers received higher pay than pre-invasion deputy ministers. Any tenth grader who volunteered would receive a twelfth grade diploma upon leaving. Any eleventh grader was guaranteed entrance into a university upon completion of his service. All these inducements failed. Hence in 1984 the regime lowered the draft age to sixteen, and later to fourteen, and lengthened the term of conscript service from three years to four. Kabul army outposts and bases were surrounded with thick belts of land mines, not to keep the enemy out but the soldiers in. Such Draconian measures predictably increased the number of mutinies as well as desertions. By the end of 1986, the Kabul army counted thirty thousand, plus ten thousand in the air force and forty thousand in paramilitary units, the secret police, and various militias.[27] These militias normally consisted of ethnic groups different from those supporting the insurgency in a particular province. The regime paid well for militia services, and although of questionable loyalty and lacking centralized organization, these groups often succeeded in keeping guerrilla units out of their immediate territory.

In retrospect, the inability of the Soviets to take better advantage of the abundant ethnic and religious cleavages in Afghanistan is astounding. A main consequence of all this ineptitude was the Soviet discovery that trying to impose a Communist regime over Afghanistan involved incomparably more fighting than they had supposed, and that, for the reasons stated above, most of this fighting had to be borne by the Soviets themselves.

INDONESIA

Indonesia before and during World War II was the scene of a dual collaboration—one of ethnic minorities with the Dutch, and of Indonesian nationalists with the Japanese.

The Ambonese and the Dutch

The island of Ambon, one of the Moluccas in the Banda Sea, has an area of three hundred square miles. The Portuguese arrived in 1512 and made the island their military and religious headquarters. In 1605 the Dutch expelled the Portuguese[28] and established a major naval base near the island's principal town, also called Ambon.

Since those days, if not long before, the Ambonese have considered themselves a people apart. The separateness of the Ambonese had many roots, including their peripheral location in an eastern corner of the Malay Archipelago; a dislike for actual or potential domination of the Indonesian islands by the Javanese (a dislike the Ambonese shared with many other peoples in the area); and admiration for Dutch abilities and methods. Perhaps most important of all was the Ambonese acceptance of Christianity. Conversions to Christianity had begun with the arrival of the Portuguese. When the Dutch replaced the Portuguese, the Dutch East India Company encouraged further conversions among the Ambonese as a means of solidifying their loyalty. It is difficult to say whether it was Ambonese admiration of and loyalty to the Dutch that stimulated conversions, or the other way around, or both. In any event, the education young Ambonese received in Christian schools gave them clear advantages over the Muslim population, who shunned all Dutch schools whether Catholic or Protestant. Educated Christian Ambonese made careers as bureaucrats and soldiers.[29]

The relative lack of economic opportunities on Ambon, along with their religious and emotional affinity for the Dutch, enticed young Ambonese to join the colonial army, the Royal Netherlands Indies Army (KNIL). (In this they differed radically from the Muslims, very few of whom joined the army before 1929.) By the mid-nineteenth century, the Dutch had undertaken a systematic recruitment of Ambonese Christians, and they came to value these recruits highly. In 1876, the commander of the KNIL wrote to the governor general that "the closer binding to us and promotion of the Ambonese soldiers cannot be too highly recommended."[30] Until 1921, Ambonese units enjoyed better food and living conditions than other native units in the KNIL. Dutch policy usually tried to maintain a ratio of one European for every three indigenous soldiers. According to the 1930 census, there were approximately 220,000 Ambonese; of these, 4,300 were serving in the KNIL.[31]

The Dutch recruited the Ambonese primarily for their political reliability; as a result many Ambonese members of the KNIL were stationed outside Ambon, to deter possible rebellion by other ethnic groups. Combined with their differing ethnicity and religion, this role engendered widespread dislike of the Ambonese on the part of other Indonesians. Absent from their own homes and communities, isolated from the populations among whom they were stationed, the Ambonese soldiers developed into a subculture based on loyalty to the Dutch, identification with the KNIL, and a feeling of superiority to other indigenous groups.[32] It became the common practice for Ambonese sons to follow their soldier fathers into the KNIL.

When World War II broke out, the Netherlands East Indies had a population of about 70 million, of whom 1 million were Chinese and about 250,000 Dutch nationals. Japan had long coveted the archipelago for its petroleum,[33] rubber, nickel, quinine, rice, and tea. Units of the Imperial Japanese Army began landing in Indonesia in December 1941 and quickly overwhelmed the poorly-equipped Dutch. The Battle of the Java Sea in February 1942, the first fleet action of the Pacific war, destroyed the small naval squadron of the Dutch and their American, Australian, and British allies. On March 8, 1942, 93,000 men of the KNIL surrendered to the Japanese, as did other Allied units.

The Japanese soon began releasing the native soldiers they had taken prisoner, but not the Ambonese, who had to remain in prison camps along with the Dutch. The Ambonese "were seen both by fellow Indonesians and the Japanese as loyal supporters of the Dutch. Most Ambonese soldiers were proud to be seen as such."[34] During the occupation both the Dutch and the Ambonese suffered much from the Japanese, and also from Muslim Indonesians. These experiences served to bind the Ambonese all the more closely in their loyalty to the Dutch.

With Japanese backing, the nationalist leader Sukarno declared Indonesia an independent republic on August 17, 1945.[35] During the period between the Japanese surrender and the reestablishment of Dutch authority, Ambonese living outside of Ambon were physically attacked. Returnees to Ambon reported widespread anti-Ambonese atrocities, identifying the perpetrators as primarily Indonesian nationalists. In the Javanese capital of Jakarta bitter clashes occurred between Ambonese soldiers and troops of the Indonesian Republic, including attacks on families. A republican guerrilla group declared war on the Dutch, on Eurasians, and on the Ambonese.[36] When Dutch troops returned, reaching Ambon on September 22, 1945, Ambonese everywhere openly rejoiced. In particular, Ambonese KNIL soldiers gave important assistance to the Dutch reoccupation of Jakarta.

Except for a few cases, the returning Dutch did not prosecute those who had collaborated with the Japanese. Instead they entered into negotiations with the republican nationalists for an Indonesian federation united with the Kingdom of the Netherlands. Most Ambonese were alarmed by these developments, viewing federation as the antechamber to a centralized Indonesia dominated by the Javanese; they much preferred a direct union with the Netherlands along the lines of Suriname or Curaçao. Large-scale fighting between the KNIL and republican forces accompanied and sometimes replaced negotiations. Finally the Dutch recognized the federal United States of Indonesia in December 1949.

The outlook for the Ambonese was grim. In 1950 Sukarno and his allies dissolved the federation and proclaimed the consolidated Indonesian Republic. On Ambon, a rebellion against the new centralizing regime flared briefly in the name of the "Republic of the South Moluccas." Indonesian troops destroyed the monument on the island erected by the Dutch in memory of Ambonese soldiers who had suffered for their loyalty to the Netherlands. Early in 1951 about four thousand Ambonese soldiers and their families were evacuated to the Netherlands. Since then many others have followed their example. Most of the emigrants continued to send money home, as Ambonese soldiers had always done. In subsequent years the increasingly centralized and dictatorial regimes in Jakarta have provoked other revolts in various parts of Indonesia.

However wise or unwise their choices may have been along the way, the Ambonese hardly merited the title of "traitors to Indonesia." Such a country did not exist until the end of World War II, and it had required generations of Dutch administration to give it shape and a semblance of reality. It is very revealing that the Indonesian Republic claimed for itself those territories of the archipelago—and only those—that had been part of the former Netherlands East Indies.[37]

The Muslims and the Japanese

A Muslim state flourished in northern Sumatra early in the thirteenth century. Four hundred years later, when the Dutch arrived in what eventually became Indonesia, Islam had taken root in almost all the islands. Indonesian Islam was of a special kind: it had arrived by way of India, not the Middle East, and learned to adapt itself to societies in the archipelago that had already absorbed heavy doses of Hindu culture.[38]

Islam served as a rallying point for resistance to Christian Westerners, both Portuguese and Dutch. For devout Muslims, final acceptance of rule by unbelievers is not possible. While not all Muslim elements in Indonesia manifested permanent hostility to the Dutch, holy wars of liberation broke out in Java throughout the nineteenth century, and on Sumatra as late as 1908.

To counter Islamic resistance, the Dutch colonial administration allied itself with the local aristocracy, which was often quite lukewarm in its devotion to Islam and definitely opposed to the social predominance of religious leaders. Alliance with the aristocracy was a centerpiece of Dutch rule. So was the policy of Christianization, and the colonial governments subsidized both Protestant and Catholic missionary activities. A third fundament of Dutch rule was assimilation: the aim was to bind Indonesia to the Netherlands by creating a pro-Dutch middle class through Western-style education and then admission into the middle and upper ranges of the bureaucracy. There was perhaps more discussion than implementation of this policy; at any rate, in Indonesia as in other colonial areas, Western education had a tendency to create nationalists, not loyalists.[39] Indonesian nationalists of Western education were usually secularist, and certainly not devout Muslims. Consequently, orthodox Muslim elements, which of course rejected secularism whether Dutch or indigenous, sought to counter nationalism with a vision of an Islamic world community. Aside from nationalism, Islam was facing a degree of competition from Communism as well: in the early 1920s the Dutch quickly suppressed a Communist-led uprising and exiled its leaders to New Guinea.

To a large degree, serious Muslims could simply ignore the Dutch presence. No such option existed, however, with the Japanese. The Imperial Japanese Army that arrived in 1941 was very demanding toward the indigenous peoples and extremely punitive toward disobedience. Death, not exile, was their sanction.

The Japanese made clear their intention to incorporate the Netherlands Indies into what they euphemistically called the Greater East Asia Co-Prosperity Sphere. To accomplish this aim, early Japanese occupation policy relied on the ancient principle of divide-and-rule. All over occupied Southeast Asia, the Japanese tried to promote Islam, and throughout the war, most Muslims in Indonesia favored the Axis rather than the Allies.[40] With Japanese favoritism toward Muslims, naturally, came persecution of Christians.

Nationalist groups also flourished under the Japanese, who placed them in the seats of power, greatly augmenting their prestige. Most of the prominent nationalists were of course Dutch-educated. Secular nationalism remained relatively weak among the peasantry, the result partly of the long alliance between the Dutch and the local aristocrats, and partly of police surveillance.

The Japanese soon began building indigenous armed forces. Their original purpose was to assist the Japanese occupation in maintaining order. But after it became clear that Japan was going to lose the war, indigenous forces were seen as a means to continue the struggle against the Allies after the Japanese had left Indonesia.[41] The Japanese-trained officer corps consisted predominantly of Muslim notables and local aristocrats. While they supported the idea, as a rule nationalists—mainly Western-educated and urban—did not join the new army,[42] which was called Peta, the acronym for Defenders of the Homeland. The Peta flag featured a rising sun, with a crescent moon in the center. Later the Japanese set up an Islamic volunteer corps called Hizbu'llah, the Army of God, to serve as a support organization for Peta. By 1944 Peta counted thirty-five thousand members, with another twenty-five thousand military auxiliaries. Thousands of others were enrolled in semi-military organizations armed only with bamboo spears.

The arrogance of the Japanese occupation forces in Southeast Asia eventually proved deeply offensive even to their collaborators.[43] In Indonesia, Japanese insistence on recognition of the divinity of the emperor, and on the necessity to bow deeply toward Tokyo, was of course repugnant to most Muslims. Besides, the relatively rapid Japanese defeat of the Western overlords of Indonesia, soon followed by the looming defeat of the Japanese conquerors themselves, exposed the myth of imperial omnipotence. Thus Japanese-trained armies in Southeast Asia would turn against their Japanese masters late in the war, both because the Japanese were losing and also because they were reneging on their promises to install their collaborators as rulers of independent states. In this context occurred the February 1945 revolt of Peta at Bitar, on Java. Despite such serious problems, hundreds of Japanese soldiers remained behind in Indonesia after the surrender, training guerrillas to continue the struggle against the returning forces of the Western powers.[44]

In summary, the armed forces of the newly proclaimed Indonesian Republic were composed and led to a large degree by those, mainly Javanese, who had collaborated with and been trained by the Japanese. The effects of this fundamental fact on minority groups throughout the archipelago would be profound, and long lasting.

THE SOUTH VIETNAMESE

The history of the state of South Vietnam began with one conflict and ended with another. Consequently the story of its army and the fate of the country were one and the same.

Beginnings of the South Vietnamese Army

The South Vietnamese Army, the ARVN (Army of the Republic of Vietnam), had its roots in the 1946–1954 conflict for control of Vietnam. That struggle is often portrayed as a contest between French colonialism on one side and the Viet Minh organization on the other. Such a depiction is not totally incorrect, but it is misleading. The subsequent nature and record of ARVN, in fact of the entire thirty-year Vietnamese conflict that ended in 1975, must always remain obscure unless one grasps that the Viet Minh were opposed by Emperor Bao Dai's army,[45] along with the indigenous southern religious sects,[46] large sectors of the native Catholic minority, and other important social groupings. Hence the 1946–1954 conflict, whatever its other features, was in fact a Vietnamese civil war.

By 1953, the Communist-dominated Viet Minh, under the leadership of Ho Chi Minh and General Vo Nguyen Giap, mobilized 300,000 conventional troops and guerrillas. As the conflict entered its last and most desperate phase, the forces under the French flag totaled perhaps 265,000. Of this (totally inadequate) number, only 50,000 were French nationals.[47] Another 50,000 were Foreign Legionnaires, Senegalese, and North Africans, including 15,000 in the French naval and air forces. And fully 150,000 of the soldiers in French uniform were Vietnamese. To this last figure one needs to add another 150,000 Vietnamese in Bao Dai's National Army,[48] plus 30,000 more armed personnel mobilized by the sects and the Catholic militias. Thus, out of roughly 450,000 personnel on the anti–Viet Minh side, approximately 330,000, over 73 percent, were Vietnamese.[49]

The French were hesitant to create a Vietnamese armed force that might one day challenge them. Hence neither the Vietnamese in French uniform nor those in Emperor Bao Dai's army had proper training, equipment, or leadership. Further, Vietnamese units were forced to operate with no artillery or heavy armor and inadequate engineering and communications components. Few officers above the rank of lieutenant were Vietnamese.[50]

The Army of the Republic of Vietnam (ARVN) was the heir to those several hundred thousand Vietnamese who, in spite of these conditions, had fought against the Viet Minh. ARVN also enrolled a generous sprinkling of former Viet Minh and (later) Viet Cong who had grown disillusioned with the Communists.[51] When the French army left South Vietnam in 1956, American officers arrived to assist in training and expanding ARVN.[52]

What motivated those hundreds of thousands of Vietnamese to resist, for decades and in great danger, the Viet Minh and later the Viet Cong? No doubt local circumstances influenced the decision of some. But for others, especially Catholics and members of the indigenous sects, it must surely have seemed more patriotic—more Vietnamese—to support Bao Dai and his traditionalist nationalism rather than the local representatives of Euro-Leninism.[53] At any rate, when Vietnam was partitioned in 1954 into a Communist North and a Bao Dai South, nearly a million persons on the Northern side of the line—7 percent of the North's population, equivalent to nineteen million Americans today—migrated from their ancestral homes and property to face the uncertainties of a new life in the South.

In South Vietnam, U.S. military advisers did not develop the type of forces that had proved effective against guerrillas in Malaya and the Philippines. Instead the Americans built an army capable of repelling the North Korean invasion of 1950. Thus ARVN became roadbound like the French and overreliant on heavy firepower like the Americans. U.S. advisers were competent and well-meaning, but generally they served only one-year tours and did not speak the language; consequently they taught and learned little.[54] Further, the equipment ARVN received from the U.S. was inferior to that of the enemy's: ARVN did not get the M-16 rifle in any significant numbers until after the Tet Offensive of 1968; before then it was outgunned by the Communist forces armed with excellent automatic weapons. Many U.S. veterans, moreover, maintain that the M-16 was not as good as the Communists' AK-47. ARVN's American M-41 tanks were inferior to the Soviet-supplied T-54s.[55] And of course for a long time little attention was paid to the police and local militia, crucial elements in any counterinsurgency.

The Romans fielded armies that were small, well trained, and well equipped. ARVN was exactly the opposite. Always short of good officers, and almost always engaged in operations, the average ARVN unit received less than two hours' training a week, with some getting much less than that.[56]

The shortage of officers was a heritage of the French colonial period. The French army required that an officer possess a high school education. Vietnamese pride made it impossible to adopt inferior educational standards for their own officers. ARVN in fact had one of the world's best-educated officer corps: in the mid-1960s, 5 percent of the generals, 13 percent of colonels, and 15 percent of other officers held Ph.D.s. But the high school requirement excluded from the officer corps practically the entire peasant class, the great majority of the population.

There were other problems. Because Catholics were more likely to have attended European-type schools, one-fifth of ARVN officers were Catholics, twice the proportion in the general population.[57] Northern-born officers (very many of them Catholic) comprised fully one-quarter of the officer corps. Worse, President Diem had politicized the army. Under President Nguyen Van Thieu, political considerations for promotion to the highest ranks became even more central, because ARVN was the main institution holding the country together.[58] The keys to advancement were personal connections; as a result competent but unconnected field commanders were left in the field.

Nevertheless, despite all these handicaps, the South Vietnamese Airborne and Marine Divisions outclassed anything in the North Vietnamese Army (NVA).[59] In 1974 an experienced British authority actually ranked ARVN second only to the Israeli army among free-world land forces.[60] During the battle for Quang Tri at the end of 1972, the NVA concentrated overwhelming numbers against ARVN units in that city. Nevertheless, ARVN held on to it, showing that "the South Vietnamese, provided sufficient ammunition, fuel and maintenance, could overcome the traditional advantages enjoyed by the attacker."[61] In the disastrous spring of 1975, when all was collapsing, ARVN would do some of its best fighting. The town of Xuan Loc, for example, was the last obstacle between the conquering Northern armies and Saigon. Xuan Loc was the locale of the 18th ARVN Division, nobody's idea of an elite unit. Yet the 18th's resistance was so ferocious that the NVA was forced to commit four of its best divisions to overcome it.

South Vietnamese Casualties

A persistent, and very puzzling, accusation against ARVN is that it did not do very much fighting. Numbers do not bear out this belief. Between the buildup under President Kennedy and the fall of Saigon, the Americans incurred an average of four thousand military deaths a year. During the Korean War, the comparable figure is eighteen thousand U.S. military deaths per year, and in World War II, one hundred thousand per year. Every year from 1954 to 1975, ARVN combat deaths were higher than those of the Americans in Vietnam.[62] In all, about two hundred thousand ARVN personnel were killed; some authors give higher figures, and these numbers do not include the militia (or civilians).[63] But to say that the South Vietnamese army took higher casualties than the Americans hardly tells the story, because the population of South Vietnam was many times smaller than that of the United States. During the entire Vietnam conflict from 1954 to 1975, fifty-eight thousand Americans lost their lives—a number almost exactly equal to highway fatalities in the United States in 1970 alone. If the U.S. had suffered fatal casualties in the same proportion to its population as ARVN did in relation to the population of South Vietnam, those U.S. military deaths would have numbered not fifty-eight thousand, but 2.6 million.

To grasp the significance of that figure, one must consider that total American military fatalities in all American wars over the past two hundred years—from the American Revolution through Vietnam, including both sides in the Civil War as well as World War I and World War II—amount to less than 1 million. In the long struggle against an armed Communist takeover, ARVN alone (excluding the militia, whose casualty rates were actually higher) suffered, in terms of population, more than forty times as many fatalities as the Americans.

In summary, ARVN had an inappropriate structure, established by its U.S. advisers. It had second-rate weapons and inadequate training. Fighting a war of survival while trying to hold its country together, it was consequently riddled with political interference and financial corruption. With all these burdens, ARVN waged war for twenty years, took enormous casualties, and finally collapsed because, abandoned by its U.S. allies, it lacked adequate supplies to go on, including ammunition, gasoline, or even clean bandages for its wounded and dying.

The Problem of Desertion

ARVN desertion rates were high. Some American journalists concluded from this that the South Vietnamese people did not oppose a Northern victory, indeed that they desired it. But the nexus between political conviction and military valor is not always direct and obvious.

Desertion in ARVN had sociological, not political roots. In rural South Vietnam, there was no social stigma attached to desertion, and the Saigon government did not itself punish deserters with rigor. Much more importantly, ARVN's practice of assigning peasant draftees to units far from their home provinces was incompatible with the values of rural society (a consequence of having an officer corps drawn overwhelmingly from urban areas). "Few steps the [Communist] Party could have taken would have been so effective in crippling the morale and effectiveness of the government's military forces as was the government's own decision to adopt a policy of nonlocal service."[64] This factor accounts for the high desertion rates among first-year soldiers at harvest time and around the family-oriented Tet holidays. In addition, ARVN soldiers served for the duration of the war, in contrast to the Americans' one-year tour of duty. In retrospect, a wiser assignment strategy would have been to give ARVN soldiers a fixed tour and then rotate them to a militia unit near their homes.[65]

Thus desertion within ARVN hardly indicates eagerness for a Communist victory. Indeed, some who deserted ARVN later rejoined. Other deserters joined militia units closer to their homes. Hence to a substantial degree, desertion from ARVN meant a shift of manpower from the army to the militia. Among the militia units defending their native villages or provinces, desertion rates were close to zero, despite casualty rates higher than ARVN's.[66] And it should be noted that Viet Cong desertion rates were as high as ARVN's. A final, crucial point: desertion from ARVN hardly ever meant defection to the Communists, whereas two hundred thousand Viet Cong actually defected to South Vietnamese forces.[67]

To put this question into some comparative perspective, recall that the principal sword and shield of the Union cause during the Civil War was the Army of the Potomac. Recall also that the largest battle ever fought on the continent of North America took place at Gettysburg, Pennsylvania, in July 1863. One month before that battle, newly appointed General George Meade arrived to take command of his Army of the Potomac. He expected to find 160,000 soldiers, but instead found only 85,000 because 75,000 had deserted. During the Civil War, the average Union desertion rate was 33 percent, and for the Confederates, 40 percent.[68]

Popular Opposition to Communist Conquest

Another strange but widespread belief about the South Vietnamese is that there was little opposition to, and considerable longing for, the victory of the Hanoi regime. The evidence usually offered for this proposition is the eventual collapse of the South Vietnamese state and army. Such an argument is like claiming that the defeat of the Confederacy in 1865, or of the Spanish Republic in 1939, proves that the majority of the people who lived under those governments desired the victory of the opponent.

There is no doubt that the French colonial regime in Vietnam carried out, or permitted, many serious abuses. But that statement does not prove that in later years no large social groupings within the population of South Vietnam opposed a Communist conquest. The historical record, patent to anyone who will look, is this: Saigon did not fall to rioting mobs, much less to the pajama-clad guerrillas of American mythology, but rather to a massive conventional invasion by the North Vietnamese Army, one of the world's best land forces. If South Vietnamese society was so apathetic, and the Saigon regime so bereft of support, it is difficult to understand why such a huge military operation was necessary to overcome them.

The South Vietnamese state, based on the Mekong Delta, was no historical anomaly. Long before the partition of 1954, indeed long before the arrival of the French, the people of the southern provinces of Vietnam had become notably different from those of the North, in terms of speech, religion, and social organization. Many factors ac-

counted for and reinforced those differences, the most important being the usual division of Vietnam into a northern and a southern kingdom. Reinforcing southern separateness were the longer-established
French presence in the Saigon–Mekong Delta area ("Cochin China");
the robust membership of indigenous southern religious sects, especially the Cao Dai and Hoa Hao; Japanese wartime administrative policy
that reinforced regionalism; the necessity for the Viet Minh guerrillas
to operate close to the Chinese border, far from the Mekong Delta;
the post–World War II occupation of the North by Chiang Kai-shek's
forces and the South by British troops; the reestablishment of French
control first in the Saigon area; and so on.

While the rural areas were the wellsprings of Communist sympathy
in South Vietnam, their support had been slowly declining for a long
time. Over the course of the conflict, the Communists' popularity suffered severely as they began forcing young men into their ranks to
replace their enormous combat losses. In addition, in the early 1970s
the South Vietnamese government carried out "the most extensive
land reform program yet undertaken in any non-Communist country
in Asia,"[69] thus depriving the Communists of the main source of their
rural attraction.

In the South's large and growing urban areas, neither the Viet
Minh nor the Viet Cong had been able to develop much strength.
Consequently, ardent Communist exhortations for the urban population to carry out a general uprising failed resoundingly during the Tet
and the Easter Offensives. The brutal Viet Cong massacres of civilians
in the city of Hué during the 1968 Tet Offensive confirmed the rejection of the Communist cause by urban Vietnamese.

Many elements in South Vietnam opposed a Northern takeover.
These included close to a million post-partition Northern refugees,
Catholics, ARVN officers and their families, the Southern religious
sects, the urban middle class, the large Chinese minority, non-Viet-
namese mountain tribes, and others. While there was overlapping among
some of these groups, altogether their membership was nonetheless
quite numerous. Together, the ARVN and the Territorials (militia)
numbered over a million men. During the mid-1970s, informed observers estimated that less than one-third of the South Vietnamese
population supported the Communist side.[70]

Clearly, broad strata of the Southern population opposed a Communist takeover. Clearly, ARVN and the Territorials had beaten back
the uttermost Communist military efforts. Nevertheless, the U.S. would

decide to withdraw all its forces from the conflict and, further, to deprive the South Vietnamese of the means to defend themselves.

The U.S. Abandons Its Allies

After years of negotiations, Washington and Hanoi signed peace accords, the Paris Agreements, in January 1973. The accords prohibited U.S. air attacks on North Vietnam and provided that the few remaining U.S. fighting forces would withdraw from South Vietnam. North Vietnam, in contrast, would tacitly be allowed to maintain nearly a quarter of a million troops in South Vietnam, plus another fifty thousand across the Laos border. This stunning asymmetry sealed the fate of the South Vietnamese. President Nixon assured South Vietnam President Thieu in writing that if Hanoi resumed its effort to conquer the South, U.S. military forces would intervene. But the absence of American air strikes allowed the North to ignore the accords completely and greatly increase the number of its troops inside the South.[71]

Simultaneously, South Vietnam's American ally began to turn against it. Congress prohibited any combat by U.S. forces in or over Vietnam for any reason after August 15, 1973. By repudiating President Nixon's written pledges to South Vietnam, Congress gave Hanoi the signal for a new offensive. In addition, in 1973 Congress slashed assistance to the South to but a third of the aid it had received in 1972. By 1974, the United States had spent $150 billion (perhaps $425 billion in 2005 values) on the war. Saigon pleaded for 1 percent of that amount, but Congress begrudgingly granted them only $700 million, a figure totally inadequate to keep ARVN's American equipment working. Between 1976 and 1980, however, Congress managed to find $15 billion for Israel and Egypt. These drastic cuts "seriously undermined South Vietnamese combat power."[72] ARVN radio communications declined by half. Fighter planes stopped flying because they had no replacement parts. Artillery units in heavy combat areas were limited to four shells per day. By summer 1974, each ARVN soldier was allotted eighty-five bullets *per month*. Bandages removed from dead soldiers were washed and used again. Meanwhile large quantities of Soviet ammunition, gasoline, and heavy weapons flowed in to the North.[73]

These drastic reductions in American aid to the South convinced Hanoi that the war had reached "a fundamental turning point."[74] The Easter Offensive of 1972 had shown that regular NVA divisions, with their tanks, were incomparably more vulnerable to air attack than Viet

Cong units had been. Hence the halting of all U.S. air activity was an irresistible invitation for the North to violate the peace accords and take the offensive. In December 1974, North Vietnamese Army units overran Phuoc Long province. To this undeniable repudiation of the peace agreements, the U.S. made no response. President Ford made no mention whatever of Vietnam in his first State of the Union address. The Hanoi politburo now knew it had a green light for all-out invasion.

The Fall

When NVA units seized Ban Me Thuot on March 11, 1975, Congress rejected President Ford's pleas for emergency aid. Thus President Thieu decided on a massive strategic retrenchment: ARVN was to withdraw from northern and central South Vietnam, except for enclaves at Hué and Da Nang, and fall back to Saigon and the Mekong Delta.

Actually, such a strategic retrenchment was long overdue. Most of ARVN's thirteen divisions were in the northern and central provinces, where less than 20 percent of the South's people lived. Halving the amount of territory to be defended would be the equivalent of doubling the size of ARVN. But when President Thieu decided to regroup ARVN southward, he and his staff had done little serious preparation for such a massive operation. Many ARVN officers and government officials received no warning about the retrenchment, and several of the roads and bridges intended for the retreat to the south turned out to be impassable.

As civilians in the northern provinces realized that ARVN was leaving, fears of Communist massacres like those in Hué in 1968 galvanized an exodus of refugees. They clogged the roads to Hué and Da Nang, making movement difficult and defense impossible. North Vietnamese aircraft bombed and strafed the civilian columns thronging the roads. Hanoi agents within the Saigon government spread rumors and panic. Tens of thousands of civilian family members had settled in the areas to which their soldiers had been assigned. Many of those soldiers, desperate to ensure that their families were moving south, left their units to search for them. Here was the final disastrous consequence of assigning draftees far from their home villages.

Thus, within a few days retrenchment turned into collapse. Most ARVN units in the northern and central provinces disintegrated. On March 24, the ancient capital of Hué fell. Six days later the NVA entered Da Nang, amid scenes of indescribable suffering.

But all was not yet lost. The South still held Saigon. It still controlled all sixteen of the provincial capitals of the Mekong Delta. Thirty miles north of Saigon, the 5th ARVN Division was fighting its way toward the capital. ARVN units had broken out of the NVA encirclement of Xuan Loc and were approaching Saigon. Between the capital and the Cambodian border ARVN units were putting up fierce resistance. Within Saigon, all was calm, while military leaders took steps to turn the city into a second Stalingrad.[75] And very soon would come the inundating rains that would mire NVA tanks in a sea of mud. Then, with the NVA conveniently arranged in a circle around Saigon, one single massive B-52 strike could crush Hanoi's military power for a decade.

But on April 30, General Duong Van Minh, assassin of President Diem and last president of the Republic of Vietnam, proclaimed the surrender. As he spoke, rain began to pour down, the torrent that would have stopped the NVA. Thus Saigon fell, exactly twenty-five years after President Truman authorized the first U.S. assistance to the French effort in Vietnam.[76]

Without long-term help from the United States, the South Vietnamese could not have preserved their independence. But for decades the same was true about the West Europeans and the Israelis. Under U.S. protection for more than half a century, independent South Korea today lives in unprecedented prosperity. There is little reason to doubt that the people of South Vietnam, whatever their political frailties, would by today have made similar advances. But they never got that chance.

REFLECTION

One major source of the phenomenon of loyalism is the frequent resemblance of insurgencies and so-called wars of national liberation to civil wars. The identity of loyalist groups is almost invariably linked to ethnicity, religion, kinship and/or venerable tradition. Hence reflexively classifying as traitors those indigenous elements that do not support a self-styled national revolution can obscure important realities. At any rate, loyalism has been a common, and often a salient, feature of such struggles. Yet it has rarely been a decisive one, for several reasons. One is that loyalty to the regime—domestic or imported—or hostility to the insurgents does not necessarily entail willingness to bear arms. Another is that governmental authorities can resoundingly fail to make effective use of loyalist potential, as in the examples of the British in colonial America, the French in Indochina, and the Soviets in Afghanistan.

One of the most prominent and persistent features of the annals of loyalism is also the most disturbing. From the thirteen American colonies to contemporary Algeria, Indonesia, Vietnam, and Afghanistan, the one-time organizers and protectors of loyalist elements have abandoned them to a fate that was predictably cruel and often deadly.

CHAPTER 8

THE CENTRALITY OF INTELLIGENCE

The most effective weapon against an armed insurgency is a good intelligence organization. Sun Tzu observed: "Now the reason the enlightened prince and the wise general conquer the enemy whenever they move and their achievements surpass those of ordinary men is foreknowledge."[1] Machiavelli believed that "nothing is more worthy of the attention of a good general than to endeavor to penetrate the designs of the enemy."[2] On July 26, 1777, General George Washington wrote to Col. Elias Dayton that "the necessity of procuring good intelligence is apparent and need not be further argued. All that remains for me to add is that you keep the whole matter as secret as possible. For upon secrecy success depends in most enterprises of the kind, and for want of it they are generally defeated, however well-planned and promising a favorable issue."

Twentieth-century students and practitioners of counterinsurgency have provided similar testimony. C.E. Callwell observed that "In no class of warfare is a well-organized and well-served intelligence department more essential than in that against guerrillas." Field Marshal Lord Carver wrote: "The importance of timely and accurate intelligence at every level, particularly of the enemy's intentions, cannot be overemphasized." For Lucian W. Pye, "The very essence of counterinsurgency is the collection of intelligence for the government." Frank Kitson argues that "if it is accepted that the problem of defeating the enemy consists very largely of finding him, it is easy to recognize the paramount importance of good information." And John P. Cann concluded that "the centralized flow of intelligence was the key to [the Portuguese] counterinsurgency [in Africa]."[3]

THE USES OF INTELLIGENCE

Clearly, a main purpose of intelligence in counterinsurgency is to facilitate successful operations against both armed enemy units and specific individuals. With some help from the U.S., Peruvian intelligence improved to the point that in September 1992 the authorities were able to apprehend Abimael Guzman, founder of Sendero Luminoso, while he was visiting his girlfriend's house in Lima. This event radically disorganized the Sendero movement.

The quality and quantity of intelligence available to the authorities also serves as a gauge of how the war is going, or at least how people think it is going. Almost invariably, the dominant direction of the intelligence flow is toward the side perceived to be winning. In the Malayan Emergency, the increasingly effective intelligence work of the Police Special Branch heavily depended on the visibly improving level of local security.[4]

Another invaluable benefit of good intelligence is that it can identify internal divisions among the insurgents. Various fissures beset any insurgent movement, sometimes producing violent internal clashes.[5] By revealing the nature and extent of such divisions, good intelligence can be used to drive a wedge between leaders, between leaders and some of their followers, or between different segments of the rank and file along religious, ethnic, tribal, or other cleavage lines. By 1951 at the latest in Malaya, for example, the special privileges of leaders, especially regarding food and women, agitated guerrilla ranks.[6]

On the other hand, neglect of good intelligence can lead to a general underestimating of the enemy—and the disastrous surprises that follow from such an error. This was the experience, for example, of the French in their war with the Viet Minh.

SOURCES OF INTELLIGENCE

Besides cooperative civilians, the most obvious source of intelligence is captured enemy personnel. Therefore a major objective of any well-led counterinsurgency should be to acquire prisoners. This principle is not always self-evident: in the early 1960s, commanders of South Vietnamese Army units gave little attention to interrogating prisoners; indeed, captured Viet Cong were sometimes executed without having been questioned at all. Similarly, during the American Revolution, irregular British forces in the Carolinas often shot captured or surrendered American prisoners on the spot.

Because it can have such lasting effects on intelligence gathering and the potential for future insurgencies, the incarceration of prisoners requires attention. In South Vietnam, captured or surrendered Viet

Cong were frequently confined in ordinary jails along with common criminals. Overcrowded conditions in these places often resulted in the judicial release of enemy prisoners after only two years or less.[7] In other cases, prisons have proven to be schools for revolutionaries; if prisoners are not carefully segregated, incarcerating them will merely produce more sophisticated enemies. This was notably the case with members of Sendero Luminoso, who turned their prison cells into veritable schools of indoctrination. Similarly, during their invasion of Lebanon, the Israelis kept most of their Palestinian prisoners confined in the huge Ansara Prison Camp—a move that inadvertently served to increase the solidarity and cohesion of the prisoners, who later emerged as "the military of the future Palestinian state."[8]

Counterinsurgent forces can augment the flow of intelligence by recruiting among the local population, debriefing amnesty-takers, penetrating insurgent organizations, employing technological means such as aircraft and satellites, and especially by monitoring enemy communications. Observing the great increase in the volume of enemy radio traffic helped U.S. intelligence become aware of the impending Tet Offensive in 1968. Intercepting enemy couriers often provides priceless information; the capture of such persons also disrupts the enemy's internal command system. Thus vigorous and sustained efforts at apprehending couriers should be a high priority in any counterinsurgency strategy. Proactive counterinsurgent tactics also damage the enemy's intelligence capability: "A guerrilla band which is constantly harassed and driven from place to place soon loses contact with its own sources of information; it becomes confused and its intelligence system breaks down."[9]

Sometimes the insurgents cooperate unknowingly (or at least unwillingly) with the counterinsurgent intelligence. In Bolivia, Che Guevara committed the most elementary security blunders, allowing crucial information about the number and condition of his followers, as well as their movements, to fall into the hands of his pursuers. He paid for these errors with his life.[10]

Recall that insurgencies usually display the characteristics of civil wars. Hence local recruits can be a valuable force multiplier for any counterinsurgency. In its efforts to subdue Filipino guerrillas after the Spanish-American War, the U.S. Army recruited scouts from among the many ethnic groups unfriendly to the mainly Tagalog guerrillas. These scouts knew the countryside and the sympathies of its inhabitants. In all, about fifteen thousand Filipinos served in auxiliary units.[11] In the South African war, British intelligence benefited greatly from the use of natives as guides, scouts, and spies.[12] (In addition, hundreds of Cape Colony Boers fought in British uniform. Concerning these, the guerrilla chief De Wet wrote: "The English, we admitted, had a perfect right to hire such sweepings, and to use them against us, but we utterly despised them for allowing themselves to be hired.")[13]

A well-timed and sincere offer of amnesty to the insurgents can not only reduce the number of armed opponents but also provide another lucrative source of intelligence. At the same time, the counterinsurgent side must be very wary of false defectors, whose mission is to sow confusion and error, and gain valuable intelligence for their own side. In Malaya the British effectively weeded out false recruits by requiring self-proclaimed defectors to identify the hideouts of their former comrades.

Counterinsurgent intelligence must also be on guard against insurgents seeking admission into military or militia units. Enemy agents thoroughly penetrated the pro-Soviet Kabul army in Afghanistan and the South Vietnamese ARVN. (In spite of this, ARVN suffered remarkably few defections in the 1968 Tet Offensive, and even during the collapse of 1975.) Additionally, it is important to identify and interrogate local government officials in contested rural areas who seem to take no serious precautions against assassination or kidnapping.

Much information can come from the simple surveillance of suspects, as well as from tips by government well-wishers and the personal enemies of a guerrilla or his family. Usually, such data is best gathered and handled by the police. One authority on the Malayan conflict concluded that the police—whose intelligence often identified targets for operations by the security forces—were "the decisive element" in defeating the insurgents.[14]

But in order for civilians to be willing to provide helpful information to the authorities, they need reassurance about the protection of their identity. Insurgents often succeed in infiltrating the police forces, and informants may consequently risk exposure and severe punishment. "Counterinsurgents seem unaware of how commonly the police of a defending power are penetrated by the revolutionary party and therefore how dangerous it is to an informant to have his name in a police file."[15] A simple and effective method for providing assurance of anonymity to civilian informants is for security forces to enter a village or a neighborhood, distribute paper and pencils to every house, and then collect these items by means of a suitable box.

At the start of the post-1898 Philippine insurgency, U.S. forces in the islands were completely unfamiliar with the local languages and culture (and some remained that way). Nevertheless, American intelligence constantly improved by exploiting several resources. One key technique was surveillance. When army units remained in a given area for an extended period, they learned through close observation to identify supporters of the insurgency. Thus, a relatively small number of soldiers stationed in one place for a long time can be worth more than several units of troops rotating in and out on a fixed, short-term schedule. Money also purchased much information. Local U.S. commanders often paid handsome sums to those who provided knowledge about the insurgent organization in a village or town. (That repository of practical wisdom, the Marines' *Small Wars Manual,* blandly states: "The liberal use of intelligence funds will be of assistance in obtaining information of hostile intentions.")[16] The lure of amnesty was another effective enticement to share information, and guerrillas and prisoners often identified former comrades or locations of hideouts in exchange for their freedom.[17] (Similarly, in Peru during the 1980s, imprisoned Senderista guerrillas sometimes plea-bargained information about former comrades for lenient sentences.) By these means the U.S. Army achieved its greatest intelligence coup: the capture of the Philippines insurgent leader Emilio Aguinaldo himself, on March 23, 1901.[18] Well-treated by his captors, within a few weeks Aguinaldo swore allegiance to the United States. He later wrote his memoirs[19] and even ran for president of the Philippine Commonwealth (he was badly defeated).

In the same country, during the Huk rebellion, the intelligence available to the armed forces greatly improved under Secretary of Defense Ramón Magsaysay. This occurred partly because the image of the soldiers benefited from Magsaysay's insistence that they respect civilian dignity, partly because he offered big rewards for information leading to the capture of guerrillas or the discovery of arms caches, and partly because of the universal rule that intelligence flows more freely to the side that is perceived to be winning.[20] Consequently, in one notable raid, Magsaysay was able to bag most of the members of the Philippine Communist Politburo, along with literally truckloads of documents that provided him and his military commanders with much fascinating reading.[21]

In 1952, General Sir Gerald Templer arrived to take charge of insurgency-torn Malaya. Combining the chief civil and military posts in himself, he was "armed with the greatest powers enjoyed by a British soldier since Cromwell."[22] A former intelligence director, Templer understood the key role of good intelligence in counterinsurgency. Promising that "the emergency [conflict] will be won by our intelligence system," he brought with him the second in command of MI5 (the British equivalent to the FBI) to help build up his intelligence services.[23] Templer wanted prisoners, especially defectors, not corpses; as he expected, the best source of intelligence proved to be surrendered enemy personnel (SEPs). Many if not most of those who had joined the Malayan insurgency had been motivated not by ideology but by a desire to improve their social position. Hence, great numbers of SEPs began to appear in response both to the unmistakably waning prospects for a guerrilla victory and to impressive monetary rewards for information.

Indeed, a continual stream of SEPs came in, despite being warned by the Communists that if taken by the British they would be tortured and shot.[24] Many SEPs led the British straight to their former encampments. At least one student of this conflict expressed amazement at the readiness of these persons to betray former comrades for cash.[25]

During the U.S. involvement in Vietnam, the Viet Cong were very successful in penetrating the South Vietnamese police, army, and civil service. But they also harvested much valuable intelligence in other, quite convenient, ways. South Vietnamese newspapers were always full of information concerning political, financial, and even military affairs. Budget hearings and debates in the South Vietnamese Congress were available to anyone who was interested. The South Vietnamese government was constantly able to prove that North Vietnam was violating agreements, but the evidence offered for these violations frequently allowed the North Vietnamese to identify its origins. High-ranking South Vietnamese commanders often gave wide-ranging interviews to the press.[26]

Despite all this access to open-source intelligence, the Hanoi regime made some serious blunders. For instance, General Giap was convinced, despite every indication, that the U.S. was planning to carry out major amphibious assaults on North Vietnam, and he thus insisted on maintaining a numerous militia there. But the most notable error of Hanoi, and perhaps the most costly, was the belief that the 1968 Tet Offensive would trigger a massive popular uprising throughout the South (see below).

PROBLEMS WITH INTELLIGENCE

Although army staff colleges around the globe stress the vital importance of intelligence in combat, military intelligence branches sometimes find themselves treated like Cinderellas (receiving the same unglamorous status usually accorded to counterintelligence in many national intelligence organizations). Clearly, the importance of intelligence work deserves higher status, reflected in budget allocations and career paths.

Consider the example of pre-1945 Japan. "Intelligence work as a profession was not highly regarded in the Imperial [Japanese] Army. It seemed in many ways the antithesis of action, requiring caution, stealth, patience, forethought—none of these being prized martial virtues."[27] Moreover, the best students in Japanese military academies of the 1930s studied Russian, not English. Thus the Japanese were unprepared for intelligence operations against the Anglo-American Allies in World War II.

Similarly, in South Vietnam ARVN had had little experience with intelligence. During the war with the Viet Minh (1946–1954) intelligence had been the responsibility of the French. Subsequently U.S. military intelligence personnel trained ARVN intelligence for conventional war operations, not counterinsurgency.[28]

Many countries maintain more than one intelligence agency, each with its own special mission or target. Rivalry, sometimes quite intense, often characterizes the relations between these organizations. The effects of interagency hostility on successful counterinsurgency are not difficult to imagine. Under President Diem, the South Vietnamese government did not place a very high priority on intelligence, and in addition it feared creating an uncontrollable power base if all intelligence activities were to be united under one director.[29] One of the most distinguished student-practitioners of counterinsurgency has written: "When I added up the intelligence organizations that were operating in Saigon in 1966 against the Viet Cong there were seventeen, both American and South Vietnamese, and none of them were talking to each other!"[30]

Consequently, "for all the intelligence services it is a valid criticism that the Viet Cong were generally a secondary target, priority being given to surveillance of other enemies of the regime or of one another, partly because the Palace wanted things that way, partly because such targets were easier to deal with and less able to take reprisals when an operation miscarried. While the market places were glutted with spies, the security forces were starved of substantial intelligence."[31]

HOW NOT TO DO INTELLIGENCE: FRENCH ALGERIA

From the beginning of their campaign against the French in 1954, Algerian Muslim insurgents had occasionally employed terror, but they resorted to terrorism much more systematically once it became clear that the French were decisively defeating their guerrilla efforts. Typical terrorist incidents involved planting explosive devices near bus stops where schoolchildren congregated and throwing bombs into crowded restaurants. Appalled by such indiscriminate acts of terrorism that struck both soldiers and civilians, the French army began torturing prisoners to obtain information in order to combat the insurgents' terrorist plans—a move that would eventually disrupt the army itself.

Growing awareness of the army's torture practices had several disastrous effects. First, it provided a weapon for those groups in French politics that for one reason or another wished to undermine the state and/or damage the army. Second, it corroded the morale of many officers, especially younger ones, who had a romantic image of their profession, who saw themselves as knights defending Western civilization against a barbaric and unscrupulous foe; the use of torture was utterly incompatible with this self-image. Third, it set the stage for a collective mutiny against the constitutional authorities of the Fourth Republic by those officers who were participating in, or had long been aware of, the torture of prisoners. The justification for employing torture—that it was not a shameful crime but a grim necessity—had of course been that it was in the service of protecting innocent civilians against maiming or murder, as well as the preservation of French Algeria against its malevolent enemies. But if, by 1958, the politicians in Paris were intending to hand over Algeria to insurgent terrorists, then the torture had been in vain, and many good officers had implicated themselves in illegal and unethical procedures for nothing. This was simply intolerable; the politicians could not be permitted to pull the rug out from under the French army yet again, as they had in Vietnam and at Suez.

Thus in the spring of 1958 the army in Algeria issued a thinly disguised warning to the government in Paris that negotiations with the Algerian rebels were unacceptable. Paratroopers descended upon Corsica and visible preparations were made for a landing on the continent. In the face of these alarming threats, the Fourth Republic collapsed and the retired General de Gaulle accepted the premiership with emergency powers. Eventually hundreds of army officers resigned or were dismissed. Compounding the tragedy of these events is the fact that torture of prisoners in Algeria yielded very little additional information to the army than was being obtained through the usual and much more acceptable methods of surveillance, bribery, informants, and civilian cooperation. Thus, to obtain only a small increment of supplementary information through torture, the French army in Algeria destroyed the Fourth Republic, and eventually itself.

THE TET OFFENSIVE: SURPRISE ALL AROUND

Surprise, including large-scale ("strategic") surprise, is actually not uncommon in war. Consider the unanticipated Japanese attack that opened the Russo-Japanese War in 1904, the Ardennes Offensive of 1940, the German invasion of Russia in 1941, Pearl Harbor, the Doolittle Raid on Tokyo, the landings in Sicily in July 1943,[32] the Normandy invasion, the Battle of the Bulge, the North Korean attack of 1950, MacArthur's landing at Inchon, the Yom Kippur War of 1973, and the Iraqi invasion of Kuwait in 1990, among other examples. The 1968 Tet Offensive in South Vietnam involved a double surprise: to the Americans and their allies, and to the Viet Cong and their Hanoi directors as well.

Many circumstances distracted Americans from the coming Tet Offensive. In January 1968 the enemy launched a major sustained attack against the American base at Khe Sanh; analogies to the fall of the French fortress at Dien Bien Phu in 1954 panicked many in Washington. Hanoi's foreign minister Trinh was proposing peace negotiations. Then the North Koreans seized the USS *Pueblo* on January 23.

But one can make a powerful case that the main surprise, the supreme "intelligence failure" of the Tet Offensive, was on the part of Hanoi. The Hanoi leadership based plans for the Tet Offensive on the double belief that (1) many if not most ARVN units would crumple or defect, and (2) simultaneously with the collapse of the army great strata of the civilian population would rise up against the Saigon government. (Indeed, "the concept of a general uprising represents the major Vietnamese contribution to the theory of people's war.")[33] As it turned out, both these beliefs were disastrously mistaken, and yet leaders in Hanoi held onto them despite clear and repeated warnings from numerous and reliable Communist sources in South Vietnam.

American intelligence analysts knew that no general uprising of the urban population would materialize (as did many local Viet Cong cadres). They also understood that without such a rising no Viet Cong military offensive could possibly succeed. Nevertheless, through December 1967 and January 1968, both the CIA and the South Vietnamese were accumulating much information from prisoners, allied agents, captured documents, and NSA monitoring of enemy radio traffic that indicated strongly that Hanoi was counting on a mass uprising.[34] But American intelligence operatives were simply not able to accept that their Communist enemies really believed in the probability of such an event—it was inconceivable to them that the Communists would make such a gross error. Hence, they interpreted Communist calls for such an uprising as an elaborate deception.

According to an authoritative observer, "for the allies to predict the Tet Offensive, they would have to overcome probably the toughest problem that can confront intelligence analysts: they would have to recognize that the plan for the Tet Offensive rested on a Communist mistake."[35] A highly placed CIA analyst wrote later that "since we did not believe that conditions met the criteria for such a rising, as set forth in the Communists' doctrine for revolutionary war, we dismissed the possibility of an attack on the population centers as not being a viable option."[36] In brief, "a failure to anticipate the possibility of enemy miscalculation had confounded intelligence analysts."[37]

This problem is not new. Clausewitz wrote that "as a rule most men would rather believe bad news than good and rather tend to exaggerate the bad news."[38] Thucydides observed that "in practice we always base our preparations against an enemy on the assumption that his plans are good. Indeed it is right not to rest our hopes on a belief in his blunders."[39] And Machiavelli warned that "the commander of an army should always mistrust any manifest error which he sees the enemy commit, as it invariably conceals some stratagem."[40]

In any event, as Tet approached, decision-makers in both Hanoi and Saigon declined to accept the generally accurate intelligence available to them.

Nevertheless, the CIA had long been warning of some kind of serious Communist move. On January 20, almost two weeks before the outbreak of the Offensive, General Westmoreland told the Joint Chiefs that something big was coming. Consequently, U.S. forces inside Saigon were reinforced, and ARVN units on leave for the Tet holiday were ordered back to station.

But in addition to these military preparations, an essential reason for the failure of the Tet Offensive was that the populations of the large cities, especially Saigon, not only did not rise in support of the Viet Cong but in many instances acted against them. The cities were filled with elements that feared a Communist victory: Catholics, ethnic Chinese, Northern refugees, businessmen and professionals, the ARVN officer corps, soldiers' families, members of indigenous religious sects, employees of South Vietnamese and U.S. government agencies, the politically disengaged, and so on. All together these comprised a dominant majority of the urban population.[41]

Synopsis

The most valuable sources of intelligence are usually prisoners, defectors, and amnesty-takers. In Malaya and South Vietnam, captured guerrillas, when treated well, often changed sides and offered their captors much crucial information.[42] Rectitude on the part of the authorities plays a central role here, as in so many other areas; it was not from humanitarianism that Sun Tzu insisted: "Treat captives well and care for them!"[43] In addition, intercepted enemy communications can provide a rich harvest of information. Police efforts based on systematic surveillance and record keeping, and a reasonable level of security for the civilian population, can also be extremely productive. Last but not least, mistakes on the part of the insurgents, such as Ernesto Guevara's failure in Bolivia to observe the most elementary security measures, and Sendero Luminoso's brutality to Indian peasants, will often produce abundant information for the counterinsurgents.

CHAPTER 9

THE REQUIREMENT OF RECTITUDE

A principal thesis of this book has been that true victory is one that leads to true peace, a peace founded on legitimacy and eventual reconciliation. Obtaining such an outcome requires that the counterinsurgent forces practice rectitude.

THE FOUNDATION FOR LASTING VICTORY

The noted theorist and practitioner of counterinsurgency Sir Robert Thompson defines rectitude as meaning that the forces of order are "acting in accordance with the law of the land, and in accordance with the highest civilized standards."[1] Along the same lines, the U.S. Marines distilled the following sage advice from their experience fighting guerrillas in Central America in the 1920s: "In small wars, tolerance, sympathy and kindliness should be the keynote of our relationship with the mass of the population."[2]

Clearly, rectitude does not mean wearing kid gloves while fighting insurgents and their supporters. Right behavior does not preclude the rigorous punishment either of criminal elements among the insurgents, or of guerrillas who refuse to negotiate even though they are clearly losing, or of civilians who live in secure areas but persist in cooperating with guerrillas. Severity in such cases is acceptable, and often advisable—so long as it is *discriminating*. The harshness of Japanese and German counterinsurgency forces worked against their own aims mainly because of its indiscriminate nature: since the peaceful and law-abiding were punished along with, or instead of, the guilty, many found it safer to abandon normal activities and join the guerrillas.

Counterinsurgent forces ought always to remember that they do not need the active support of the majority of the population. They need merely the support of some and the neutrality of most. A peasant population generally desires security, that is, the ability to live and work according to norms they see as just. If the forces of order behave as they should—specifically, providing the rural population with at least a minimal level of security—they will normally win the acquiescence of that key sector. This is even more true in those instances in which the guerrillas accept the aid or even membership of blatantly antisocial and criminal elements (a phenomenon that severely hurt the Philippine Huks, for but one example). Because they had provided decent administration during their occupation of Manchukuo—in stark contrast to the previous corrupt and arbitrary Chinese regimes—the Japanese won the gratitude of much of the population.[3]

In some cases, numerous civilians in a given area will be supportive of the military and police because they have relatives and friends in those organizations, especially if military units are stationed in areas from which they have been recruited. Both civilian fear of disorder and demonstrations of organizational efficacy by the military will reinforce this friendly predisposition. In these circumstances, right conduct by the military can solidify civilian support and marginalize guerrilla activity.

Writing of Roman campaigns against irregular forces, Machiavelli observed: "Of all the methods that can be taken to gain the hearts of a people, none contribute so much as remarkable examples of continence and justice; such was the example of Scipio in Spain when he returned a most beautiful young lady safe and untouched to her father and her husband; this was a circumstance that was more conducive to the reduction of Spain than force of arms ever could have been. Caesar acquired such reputation for his justice in paying for the wood which he cut down to make palisades for his camps in Gaul that it greatly facilitated the conquest of that province."[4] Intelligence provided to Union forces in Virginia during the American Civil War improved notably after special guerrilla-hunting units learned to deal justly with civilians.[5]

Naturally, quite the contrary result derives from bad behavior by the counterinsurgent forces. Outraging sexual or religious mores and killing prisoners (whether civilian or guerrilla) will nearly always increase recruits for the guerrillas and hence increase casualties among government troops.[6] But even lesser crimes such as "requisitioning" (that is, stealing) from the population only create tension and resentment. Therefore, the entrance of government forces into a district or village should not resemble the descent of a plague of locusts.

THE PRICE OF MISCONDUCT

The strategist Basil Liddell Hart once observed that "the more brutal your methods, the more bitter you will make your opponents, with the natural result of hardening the resistance you are trying to overcome."[7] Insurgents are well aware of this: the Greek and Yugoslavian Communist guerrillas and the Sendero Luminoso constantly sought to provoke the military into harsh reprisals against the civilian population.[8]

Not just insurgencies but even historic continental struggles have been lost because governments either failed to control, or actually encouraged, the bad behavior of their armies. Consider how all Europe, even sincere onetime supporters, eventually turned against Napoleon, in large part because he allowed his wide-ranging armies to "live off the land," a quaint circumlocution for looting civilians. The atrocities of the German army (not, as is often alleged, merely the notorious SS) in Russia forced many anti-Stalinist civilians to join the Soviet army or the partisans, greatly reduced the economic value of the occupied territories, and caused Russian troops to fight to the death rather than be taken prisoner.[9] Indeed one can make a good case that the Nazis' savage treatment of the population of the Ukraine and western Russia cost them victory in World War II.[10]

Besides generating sympathy and recruits for the insurgency, mistreatment of civilians and prisoners erodes military discipline. Robert E. Lee warned his soldiers that "perpetration of barbarous outrages upon the unarmed and the defenseless and the wanton destruction of private property . . . not only degrade the perpetrators and all connected with them, but are subversive of the discipline and efficiency of the army."[11] The enormities committed against civilians by French Revolutionary troops in the Vendée and Brittany, and by German units in Russia and the Ukraine, quite predictably led to insubordination and acts of violence by soldiers against their officers.[12]

Violations of rectitude during insurgencies on the part of the supposed forces of order, and their grave consequences for the latter, are unfortunately not difficult to find. Consider the following examples, some of which have already appeared in earlier sections of this book.

"Wherever the British Army went between 1775 and 1781, it invariably alienated the people whose support it needed, the neutrals. . . . No British commander in chief ever found a way to turn the neutrals into active supporters—or keep his troops from providing endless object lessons in British 'tyranny.'"[13] For one instance, British forces burned down the house of the former South Carolina Revolutionary officer Andrew Pickens, after he had given his parole to remain peacefully at home. The outraged Pickens became a guerrilla chieftain and made his notable contribution to the events that led to Yorktown. The great American insurgent leader Francis Marion, the Swamp Fox himself, wrote: "Had the British officers acted as became a wise and magnanimous enemy, they might easily have recovered the revolted colonies."[14]

In the 1790s the French Revolutionary regime—which had come into power through terror, a strictly limited suffrage, and the support of the army—carried out genocidal policies in the Vendée region, complete with mass drownings and experiments with poison gas. Burned and bludgeoned into submission, the Vendeans nevertheless had their revenge. Rising in revolt against the return of Napoleon in 1815, they compelled him to send into their region thousands of troops that might well have made all the difference at Waterloo.

The atrocities, both systematic and casual, committed by the Napoleonic armies in Spain directly contributed to the huge numbers of French casualties in that country, a higher number even than in the much more sensational Russian campaign.[15]

The excesses of the Mexican regime and the brutality of its armed forces provoked and sustained the Cristero rebellion.

Mao Tse-tung correctly identified Japanese cruelty as a principal justification for his conviction that they would suffer eventual defeat.[16]

At the end of World War II, some of Chiang Kai-shek's Kuomintang (KMT) troops returning to formerly Japanese-occupied areas mistreated Chinese civilians on a vast scale. They thus undermined Chiang in the looming death struggle with Mao's Communists. The great irony here is that before the war, KMT armies benefited from a reputation for not mistreating peasants, at least compared to the warlord armies that the KMT fought against.

The use of torture by certain elements of the French army in Algeria to obtain information from captured terrorists contributed to grave disorders within the army, a constitutional crisis in France, and the destruction of the careers of hundreds of French officers.

The Soviet policy of devastating the Afghan countryside ("migratory genocide") aroused the Afghan resistance to steely determination.[17]

Chinese military atrocities in Tibet have stimulated the independence movement on Taiwan.

In 1989, the murder of six Jesuit priests in El Salvador at the height of a major insurgency nearly caused the U.S. government to cut off aid to that beleaguered country.

The closing off of a peaceful road to change in Kashmir during the 1990s, along with serious failures of the Indian army to maintain military discipline, are among the latest examples of how violations, or wholesale rejection, of right behavior work against the true interests of the violators.

Of course, counterinsurgent forces are not the only ones that violate rectitude. Prolonged guerrilla campaigning can facilitate a coarsening of standards among the most high-minded individuals; in addition, guerrilla war often attracts plain criminals seeking a cover of semi-legitimacy. In the post-1898 Philippines, some of Aguinaldo's followers made assassination of members of the pro-peace Federal Party a specialty; others took up the practice of burning villages that were cooperating with the Americans. During the Greek civil war, as members of the ethnic Macedonian minority came to dominate the ranks of the Communist-led insurgents, they forced young persons to join them; kidnapped children, sending them to be raised in Eastern Europe; and deliberately destroyed villages to create refugees for the hard-pressed government to care for. Luis Taruc, the principal military leader of the Huk insurrection, consistently maintained that the major generative force of that conflict was gross and systematic misconduct by the army of the Philippine Republic; nevertheless, Taruc admitted that during the conflict's latter stages, increasing Huk terrorism and brutality turned many peasants toward the government.[18] In South Vietnam, the Viet Cong bombarded the marketplaces of villages unfriendly to them and attacked columns of helpless refugees. The Peruvian Sendero Luminoso engaged in truly grisly atrocities in the countryside and in Lima, and deliberately provoked reprisals by the Peruvian army against Indian villages. The Salvadoran FMLN caused many civilian casualties during the later stages of the conflict by placing landmines near inhabited areas. In Colombia, the FARC and ELN continue to kidnap and/or murder civilians and deliberately damage the regional ecology. All of these movements flagrantly violated the norms of their own societies; none of them achieved victory.

THE TREATMENT OF PRISONERS

In addition to just treatment of civilians, rectitude toward prisoners on the part of the forces of order is crucial for several reasons. First, as discussed in another chapter, prisoners can be a rich source of intelligence. Second, treating enemy prisoners correctly discourages the enemy from fighting to the death. Third, right behavior toward prisoners is good training for right behavior toward the civilian population. Mao Tse-tung wrote that "the most effective method of propaganda directed at the enemy forces is to release captured soldiers and give the wounded medical treatment."[19] During the struggle between the Fidelistas and the Batista regime, Ernesto Guevara's practice was to give his prisoners a lecture and then turn them loose. Of course, when released prisoners return to their units they are living proof to their comrades that if they surrender they will not be harmed.

Under many circumstances, perhaps, simply releasing prisoners might not be advisable. But it is certain that allowing all to see that prisoners receive humane treatment is a weapon of great value. And in fact, such treatment of prisoners during insurgencies is not uncommon. During the South African war, Boer guerrillas as a rule did not fear to abandon a wounded man to the British.[20] And—incredible as it may seem in our own era—throughout the increasingly fierce conflict, no accusation of torture surfaced against either the Boers or the British.[21] In Manchukuo, Communist political officers told their guerrillas that if they were captured, the Japanese would torture and then kill them. Consequently, when Japanese troops treated their prisoners decently and then released them, guerrilla confidence in their leaders declined.[22] (But in other parts of China, guerrillas rejected Japanese offers of amnesty because they remembered previous Japanese brutality to prisoners.) In South Vietnam, in the early 1960s at least, ARVN commanders gave little attention to the interrogation of prisoners. They assigned POWs to ordinary jails along with common criminals. Conditions in overcrowded prisons often resulted in the judicial release of actual or suspected Viet Cong inmates.[23]

Finally, those who oppose guerrillas must never lose sight of the fact that from Greece to Vietnam, insurgents recruited many of their members by force. Therefore, a policy of easy surrender followed by decent treatment can very effectively drain numbers from the insurgent ranks.

How to Promote Rectitude

"To behave correctly toward civilians is not usually the overriding disposition of armed young men who find themselves in a strange country filled with people who want to kill them; this is especially so because by definition guerrillas seek to look like and hide among the civilian population."[24] Protracted armed conflict loosens the bonds of civilized behavior. The prolonged occupation of foreign territory, where soldiers are forced to perform policing functions, has inevitable corrupting effects on any army. If, on the other hand, a government is confronted by a domestic insurgency, the national army will likely be in poor condition. Unable to defeat, contain, or even locate the guerrillas, its soldiers will often abuse civilians. Hence the essential priority in counterinsurgency is not to increase the size of the army or its ratio to the guerrillas, but to improve its basic skills and its conduct toward civilians.

Yes, but how is this to be done? How can the leadership of counterinsurgent forces promote rectitude?

In the first place, conduct is closely related to morale. Therefore, the government must see to the well-being of the troops. The soldier, especially the conscript, must know that the members of his family are not destitute, and that he will receive opportunities to visit them on an equitable basis. The morale of Portuguese troops in southern Africa greatly benefited from the certainty that if wounded they would receive prompt medical attention via helicopter evacuation. Promotions and decorations need to be distributed fairly. Young men require proper nourishment for morale as well as health; therefore adequate food preparation is very important (Sun Tzu wrote: "Take heed to nourish the troops!").

Another key factor in morale is safety. Hence the size of the counterinsurgent forces must be adequate to their task. Union troops in Civil War Missouri committed many violations of rectitude in large part because their insufficient numbers made them feel constantly vulnerable to guerrilla attacks.[25] Numerical inadequacy led the Japanese army to the "Three alls" campaign ("kill all, burn all, destroy all") that played into the hands of the Communist guerrillas.[26] The inability of the Kremlin to commit sufficient Soviet forces to the war in Afghanistan directly contributed to the self-defeating devastation of wide areas of that country.[27]

It is further essential to control firepower around populated areas.

In their *1940 Small Wars Manual*, the Marines advise that "in small wars, caution must be exercised, and instead of striving to generate the maximum power with forces available, the goal is to gain decisive results with the least application of force and the consequent minimum loss of life."[28] The best way to guard against indiscriminant fire is to station troops in their native area. If there are no local troops available, then whatever troops are at hand need to remain in a given area for an extended period of time. This will not only make them more familiar with and to the inhabitants, but will also allow them to learn the terrain.[29] Every effort should be made to have at least one reliable speaker of the local language accompany the troops in the area, as well as someone who is conversant with local religious practices.

Moreover, rectitude—and the general morale of a fighting force is related to political awareness. Officers and key noncoms need to be able to provide convincing answers to questions their troops ask them about why and against whom they are fighting.

Responsibility aids rectitude. All regional, district, and village commanders must be convinced that they will be held strictly accountable for violations of right conduct. To accomplish this end, commanders will need to leave headquarters and visit the field, an activity they should be performing anyway. When Ramón Magsaysay was Philippine secretary of defense, his practice of making unannounced descents from the sky (a latter-day *diabolus ex machina*) infused local commanders with unaccustomed zeal against the local Huk forces.

The great French colonial commander Lyautey indirectly but effectively taught his soldiers the importance of rectitude by letting the military commander of counterinsurgent operations in a particular area know that, upon the cessation of hostilities, that commander would be appointed governor of that same area.

Finally, there must absolutely never be quotas for enemy dead—no "body counts." Clausewitz wrote: "casualty reports on either side are never accurate, seldom truthful and in most cases deliberately falsified"; "that is why guns and prisoners have always counted as the real trophies of victory."[30]

Certainly no insurgency has been defeated by a display of rectitude alone on the part of its opponents. Many factors must come together to produce a successful counterinsurgency. Nevertheless, Table 1 suggests a very strong relationship between rectitude and counterinsurgent success.

Table 1: Counterinsurgent Rectitude and Victory

	Rectitude Generally Present	Rectitude Generally Absent
YES	Malaya	French Algeria
	Philippines (post-1898)	Tibet
	Huk War (post-1951)	
	Greece	
	South Vietnam	
Counterinsurgent	Vendée (after July 1794)	
Victory?	Peru (Sendero Luminoso)	
	El Salvador (post-1984)	
	Moros (post-1898)	
NO		Soviets in Afghanistan
		Japanese in China
		Germans in Yugoslavia
		British in Carolina
		Napoleonic Spain
		Huk War (to 1951)
		Vendée (to 1794)
		Cuba (Batista)
		El Salvador (pre-1984)

SUMMARY: THE BENEFITS OF RECTITUDE

For the forces combating insurgency, right conduct toward civilians and prisoners has the following principal justifications. First, it depresses the number of their own casualties, by avoiding the creation of new recruits for the guerrillas and by encouraging the surrender of enemy personnel. Second, it increases the likelihood of receiving intelligence from both civilians and prisoners. Third, it promotes morale and discipline within the counterinsurgent forces. Fourth, it helps prepare post-conflict reconciliation with (or at least acquiescence from) those who supported the insurgency. Fifth, it helps prevent the world media from sensationalizing the counterinsurgency and, by implication, legitimizing the guerrillas.

The counterinsurgent side can promote rectitude by committing an adequate number of troops to the struggle; by providing those troops with sufficient means, care, political awareness, and geographical stability; by insisting on a responsible employment of firepower; and by enforcing accountability for violations.

All this is very well worth doing. The long road of warfare is strewn with the wreckage of those who forgot about or sneered at the necessity for right conduct. Rectitude is worth many battalions.

CHAPTER 10

THE UTILITY OF AMNESTY

As Sun Tzu wrote in his *Art of War*, "To subdue the enemy without fighting is the supreme skill." A well-implemented amnesty program can be a very powerful instrument toward this end in the hands of any counterinsurgent force.

EFFECTIVE AMNESTY

To be effective, an amnesty program must be based on a realistic understanding of why people become guerrillas. The reasons for joining a guerrilla band can be complex. Assuming the cause stems always from economic hardship or government brutality can be grossly misleading. Sometimes, especially for very young persons, the real lure is adventure, getting away from a dull routine or a confining family situation. Alternatively, or additionally, the absence of governmental authority—that is, absence of security—can play a main role, opening the way to forced recruitment, a mainstay of the Greek guerrillas of the 1940s and an increasingly common practice of the Viet Cong in the 1960s.

In 1951, at the height of the Communist-dominated Huk insurgency in the Philippine Republic, Ramón Magsaysay became secretary of defense. He would henceforth be the dominant figure in the effort against the guerrillas, placing great stress on reducing the Huk ranks through amnesty. But Magsaysay, himself a former anti-Japanese guerrilla, was well aware that some had joined the Huks a decade before, when they were mere boys. Many of them would have had no place to return to nor life to resume if they left the guerrilla organization, their only home. Magsaysay's solution was to open up virgin lands on some of the southern islands. A guerrilla who accepted amnesty could obtain twenty acres, help from the army to build a house, and a small loan to sustain him until the first crops came in. A house, a piece of land, some cash: a simple concept, an inexpensive program, an effective weapon. Magsaysay's amnesty-plus-resettlement turned people who had been threats to the constitutional order into productive and eventually tax-paying citizens. Besides, the new lives of the amnestied former guerrillas showed the remaining Huks that escape from war to peace was indeed possible.

In his declarations regarding amnesty, Magsaysay carefully avoided the word "surrender." What is essential is that the guerrillas stop fighting, not that they abase themselves. As Michael Howard wrote: "[A] war, fought for whatever reason, that does not aim at a solution which takes into account the fears, the interests, and not least the honour of the defeated peoples, is unlikely to decide anything for very long."[1] In like manner, during the guerrilla conflict following the Spanish-American War, when insurgent Filipino commanders would surrender with their men, American officers would hold impressive ceremonies to honor and reassure their former foes. Indeed it was not unusual for the Americans to immediately appoint a surrendered insurgent chief to some provincial or local office.[2] In Thailand during the 1980s, groups of surrendered guerrillas received an honorable welcome back to society.[3] For counterinsurgents, wisdom consists in making resistance perilous and surrender easy.

The counterinsurgents must of course exercise strict vigilance against false defectors, those who may have been sent by the enemy leadership to accept amnesty in order to deceive or disrupt. In Malaya, the British distinguished carefully between surrendered and captured enemy personnel (SEPs and CEPs, respectively). To prove his good faith, a SEP would have to lead government forces to the hideouts of his former comrades, to arms caches, etc.[4] The South Vietnamese Chieu Hoi program paid well for returnees to lead ARVN soldiers to weapons caches. Also, as a general rule no amnesty should be available to guerrillas accused of personal criminal acts; instead huge cash bounties should be placed on their heads. This can be an excellent means of spreading suspicion and dissension inside the insurgent ranks.

THE CHIEU HOI PROGRAM

In South Vietnam, the major amnesty program was called Chieu Hoi ("Open Arms").

The Communist-dominated Viet Cong (VC) guerrillas attracted ambitious but uneducated young men of low status who saw no future for themselves in Vietnamese society as it then existed. Besides offering such persons promises of an important role in a bright new society, the party assumed in the lives of VC members the functions normally played by the extended family and village.[5]

Generally, a VC guerrilla's motives for "rallying" to the government side were mainly personal, not ideological. Many defectors identified the principal inducements to "return" to allegiance to the government of South Vietnam as loss of faith in ultimate Communist/ Northern victory,[6] revulsion at atrocities against civilians, the greater effectiveness of the allies, and/or the availability of the "Open Arms" program. All Vietnamese have historically considered themselves free (and well-advised) to recognize or follow the "Mandate of Heaven." In practical terms, this meant that switching adherence to the winning side did not amount to treason or dishonor. And especially for the growing numbers of VC whose recruitment had involved coercion, rallying to the government was morally easy, because it involved no change of heart or betrayal of original principles.[7]

Despite its success in attracting rank and file members of the VC, the Chieu Hoi program had little appeal for two particular groups among the enemy. One of those was composed, of course, of high-ranking Communist political or military figures. Upper-level defectors faced loss of status and income, as well as an uncertain future. Recall that opportunities for upward mobility had been a key factor for many— North or South—in joining the Communist side in the first place. In addition, leadership cadres had absorbed very heavy doses of political indoctrination. An amnesty program that aims to attract high-level defectors will therefore need to offer them both political justification for their change of side and some sort of status equivalency. Such a program will not be easy to accomplish, especially in light of the not unreasonable suspicions that will inevitably arise regarding the true motives of high-ranking defectors. Many Southerners, not only in ARVN but also in the civilian government services, were uneasy with Chieu Hoi, especially if it involved the return of civil rights to defectors; they feared that permitting large numbers of former Viet Cong to exercise the functions of citizenship would lead eventually to a coalition government, which would include political representatives of the Viet Cong.[8]

Another group from which amnesty-seekers were rare was the North Vietnamese Army. NVA soldiers were far from home, and so could not be easily integrated into society in the manner of Southern defectors.

Therefore, as Viet Cong units came actually to consist more and more of NVA during the 1970s, the rate of defection decreased.

Chieu Hoi was the beginning of a blueprint for national reconciliation, a program that attempted to address a very important counterinsurgent consideration: How can an insurgency end if the guerrillas are afraid of reprisals and have few certain prospects for reinsertion into society? As in the case of the Huk rebellion, the Vietnamese Hoi Chanh (amnesty-takers) clearly needed some way of earning a living. One solution was to set up Chieu Hoi villages and hamlets. But such settlements for former Viet Cong could not provide the consolations of an extended family; besides, they tended to keep their inhabitants outside the mainstream of Vietnamese society. Moreover, many surrendered Viet Cong were not eager to return to farming, the main occupation in the villages. Finally, and notably, Chieu Hoi settlements provided convenient targets for Communist reprisals.

Approximately 194,000 Viet Cong and NVA personnel accepted amnesty under Chieu Hoi. This clearly represented an intolerable loss to the Communist side, in terms both of manpower and of propaganda.[9] Further, many Hoi Chanh joined ARVN or the various militias, bringing with them rich intelligence regarding the methods and locations of their former comrades. Profoundly alarmed, the Viet Cong leadership and the North Vietnamese Army reacted vigorously against the Hoi Chanh. They ordered heavy increases of counterpropaganda and reindoctrination for their own soldiers. As an even clearer sign of their agitation, the Communist leadership imposed the death penalty on relatives of amnesty-takers; and whoever killed a Hoi Chanh received the same status as one who killed ten enemies.[10] Hence it is not very surprising that even during the great Tet Offensive of 1968, "no Hoi Chanh (of record) went [back] over to the other side."[11]

During the war the cost to process, retrain, and resettle former guerrillas or soldiers who returned to the side of the South Vietnamese government went from $14 to $350 each. Even the higher figure was a risible pittance, however, considering that by 1968 the U.S. was spending $150,000 to kill one guerrilla. Indeed, "Chieu Hoi had the most favorable cost/benefit ratio of any counterinsurgency operation in Viet Nam."[12]

SUMMARY

An amnesty program, properly implemented, can be an effective and inexpensive weapon against insurgents. Successful amnesty campaigns begin with the understanding that certain elements of an insurgent movement may be inclined to desert—either because they were forcibly recruited initially or because they have become disenchanted with their situation and prospects within the movement. To actualize this potential, amnesty programs should avoid any association with humiliation. Finally, the would-be amnesty-taker needs to know that he will have someplace to go, work to do, and protection from reprisals.

CHAPTER 11

THE QUESTION OF SUFFICIENT FORCE LEVELS

Everyone knows that mere numbers do not win wars. Morale, training, leadership, discipline, weapons, supply, and finance are crucial. The Romans fielded armies small in size, generally about twenty thousand men, but excellent in training and discipline. Nevertheless, one cannot successfully wage counterinsurgency on the cheap, that is, without an appropriate commitment of ground forces. The record is replete with examples of disaster descending upon counterinsurgencies that would not or could not observe this fundamental principle.

The ideal situation from the point of view of the counterinsurgents is for the civilian population to support their side; the next-best situation is for the civilian population to believe that the counterinsurgent side is going to win. Appearing to be the winning side is extremely important for both discouraging the enemy and obtaining civilian support and local recruits. Hence the counterinsurgents must give an impression of strength and permanency, and nothing accomplishes that aim quite like an abundance of well-turned-out troops. On the other hand, deploying inadequate numbers of soldiers and police against guerrillas can in fact be extremely expensive, because such parsimony may prolong the conflict and increase friendly casualties. False economy in this area may actually bring about disaster: the low British commitment of troops to the American War of Independence led to the defeat at Saratoga, which in turn magnified the myth of southern loyalism and produced the final blow at Yorktown.[1] This cardinal error of the British in America in 1780 was repeated by, among others, the Soviets in Afghanistan in 1980.

Numerous analysts of insurgency have suggested that, to be successful, the counterinsurgent side needs a ratio of ten-to-one over the guerrillas. The counterinsurgents require such a seemingly great preponderance of manpower for several reasons. First, while the guerrillas are free to come and go, and to fight or not, as they please, the counterinsurgents must garrison cities and key installations and protect roads and railways. They also must set up and maintain patrols to hamper guerrilla movements, hunter units to target specific insurgent leaders or groups, militia groups for local defense, and mobile response forces to go to the aid of militia groups under attack. In the words of the U.S. Marines' inimitable *1940 Small Wars Manual*: "The occupying force must be strong enough to hold all the strategical points of the country, protect its communications, and at the same time furnish an operating force sufficient to overcome the opposition wherever it appears."[2] The Marines derived their concepts largely from their relatively unhappy experiences in Nicaragua, where between 1912 and 1925 their numbers usually consisted of no more than one hundred men, in a country with a population of seven hundred thousand and an area the size of Pennsylvania. Just over 3,300 Marines were in Nicaragua during 1926, down to 1,500 by the end of 1927. Their principal opponent, the guerrilla leader Augusto Sandino, never commanded a force equal to one-tenth of 1 percent of the Nicaraguan population at one time. Between 1928 and 1933, forty-seven Marines died in or as a result of fighting—less than one per month.

INSTANCES OF ADEQUATE COMMITMENT

Revolutionary France in the Vendée

In the early 1790s the radical policies of the Terror provoked widespread popular rebellions across France, especially in the Vendée and Brittany. The regime responded with what amounted to genocide in the Vendée, complete with mass drownings and poison gas.[3] The Revolutionary regime eventually committed great numbers to suppress the uprisings: in October 1794 it had 130,000 troops in the rebellious western provinces, compared to 180,000 fighting major European powers on the northern and eastern frontiers.[4] In December 1795 the Paris regime sent General Lazare Hoche into Brittany with 140,000 soldiers, one for every seven civilian inhabitants of that unhappy province.

The British in the Boer War and Malaya

From 1898 to 1902 the British Empire engaged in a war of conquest against the southern African Boer (Dutch) Republics of the Transvaal and the Orange Free State. To this effort Britain committed 366,000 imperial and 83,000 colonial troops (including 17,000 Australians), along with 53,000 white South Africans. Against these approximately half a million troops, the entire white population of the Orange Free State numbered only 90,000. At the end of the war in spring 1902, 21,000 Boer troops surrendered; 6,000 others had died in combat, and 16,000 had perished from wounds and disease.[5]

The half million British soldiers of various sorts in South Africa absolutely dwarf other British military efforts both before and after. In 1809, after his peninsular victories against Napoleonic forces, Wellington commanded 26,000 British troops, not counting 10,000 sick. At Waterloo, Wellington had 32,000 British soldiers. In 1856, 112,000 British troops went to the Crimea to fight the Russians.[6] In 1914, the British Expeditionary Force that landed in France counted 75,000 men. In 1940, 225,000 British forces were evacuated from Dunkirk. An American comparison: on the eve of Gettysburg, the largest battle ever fought on the continent of North America, General George Meade commanded 85,000 Union soldiers.

About 12,000 guerrillas participated at one time or another in the ill-fated Communist-led attempt to seize control of British Malaya (1948–1960). Against them, by 1954 the authorities were deploying 40,000 regular troops (British, Gurkha, Commonwealth, and Malayan); 24,000 Malayan Federation police; 37,000 special constables; and 250,000 armed militia.[7] In the conflict, 512 British and Commonwealth soldiers lost their lives, less than one per week.

The French in Algeria

The Algerian conflict broke out in October 1954, as 500 insurgents attacked 60 French military posts and police stations across eastern Algeria. At first, the French took the uprising lightly, maintaining only about 50,000 French troops in all Algeria, a territory larger than the combined area of Norway, Sweden, Finland, Denmark, France, Germany, and the United Kingdom. But by April 1956 the army had committed 450,000 men there. In proportion to France's population, this was equal to three times the size of U.S. forces in Vietnam at their numerical height. In 1958 the insurgents numbered perhaps 40,000, fewer than half of whom were actually inside Algeria. The French troops' great numbers allowed them to use *quadrillage* tactics, a variant of those employed against the Vendeans in the 1790s: hold the major towns in strength, station small garrisons in the lesser communities, constantly expand the number of places held, and scour the intervals between garrisoned towns with frequent patrols. These tactics deprived the guerrillas of a secure base and kept them on the move.[8] The French supplemented their ample numbers by constructing the famous Morice Line along the Algeria-Tunisia frontier, a remarkable barrier that effectively isolated those guerrillas inside the country both from their compatriots across the border and from much-needed supplies as well.

INSTANCES OF INADEQUATE COMMITMENT

The French in Spain

In 1808 Napoleon invaded Spain, a move as fateful for his throne as the Russian adventure four years later. The soldiers he initially sent into Spain were second quality at best, "young, impressionable troops, hastily mustered, barely educated or trained, feebly officered, badly equipped, and charged with the invasion of a poor tormented country, whose inhabitants were fanatical, rebellious, and savage [sic]."[9] Worse, the "command was also distinctly second rate, material preparations—as always—more or less non-existent, and that in a country incapable of providing the resources usually presumed to be available on the spot. It was the Emperor who brought disaster upon [the French army in Spain] by despising the rebels and so disbursing [the army] in order to occupy all the provinces at the same time."[10]

But it was quantity at least as much as quality that doomed French efforts in Spain. Confronted by popular fury and Wellington's regulars, the French and their allies never came close to having enough soldiers there. Wellington commanded an Anglo-Portuguese force of 60,000. A very conservative estimate of guerrilla strength in 1812 would place their forces at 35,000 men. Employing the oft-cited ten-to-one ratio of soldiers to guerrillas necessary to achieve counterinsurgent success, the Imperial forces would have had to number 350,000 to combat and hunt the guerrillas, at least 60,000 to contain Wellington, and perhaps another 50,000 to besiege Cádiz, where the Spanish government had taken refuge. This comes to a total of 460,000 men; but in fact the French usually had only between 230,000 and 300,000 troops in Spain.[11] If, however, one accepts the higher estimates of the number of the guerrillas—around 70,000—then the French would have needed over 800,000 men. Such a figure was utterly beyond discussion, even if the French had been able to deploy scores of thousands of allied Polish and Italian troops. And of course the Russian campaign drained regiment after regiment out of Spain. (The notoriously colossal army Napoleon led into Russia actually counted around 500,000 soldiers, fewer than half of them French.) By the spring of 1812, something like 90,000 Imperial troops, a totally inadequate number, were attempting to keep the roads open and the guerrillas scattered between Tarragona and Oviedo.[12] In sum, the French and Imperial forces suffered from "far too low a ratio of force to space to [be able to] dominate the country."[13] Moreover, they had lost their tactical superiority as well, because the fighting skills of the guerrillas were improving all the time.

The French in Vietnam

By 1953 General Giap and the Communist-dominated Viet Minh controlled an estimated 300,000 fighters. Under the standard ratio, the French would have needed 3 million troops to achieve victory. Even to attain the quite insufficient ratio of three to one would have required 900,000. But because French law forbade the sending of draftees to Vietnam, French forces there consisted of only 50,000 soldiers from metropolitan France (out of a population of over 40 million), along with 30,000 colonial troops (mainly North Africans and Senegalese), 20,000 Foreign Legionnaires, and 150,000 Vietnamese in French ranks, plus 15,000 air and naval personnel. Even after adding to these the 150,000 men in Emperor Bao Dai's army, and another 30,000 in the Catholic and Sect militias, the grand total is at most 450,000—precisely half of the quite inadequate three-to-one ratio.[14] French air power was too small to right this imbalance: as late as 1954 there were only ten French helicopters in Vietnam. Besides, the Viet Minh usually operated at night. Thus, in the ominous words of one French officer, "each night the roads were left to the enemy."[15]

The Americans in Vietnam

The U.S. commitment of forces in its Vietnam involvement was massive without being efficacious. When John F. Kennedy entered the White House fewer than 1,000 U.S. service people were in Vietnam; upon his death less than three years later, there were 16,000. By the fall of 1965 President Johnson had sent 184,000, and by the spring of 1968 the number had swollen to well over half a million. (Even at that peak, U.S. forces in Vietnam amounted to less than one-third of 1 percent of the U.S. population.) This growing Americanization of the conflict in Vietnam was just one of the poisoned fruits of the assassination of President Diem.[16]

The presence of this American force in Vietnam was highly problematic. How long could the U.S. maintain such a huge investment of manpower in Southeast Asia, when nearly everybody concurred that Europe was of incomparably greater strategic importance to the U.S.? Besides, since the administration would not permit the closing of the Ho Chi Minh Trail, North Vietnam could negate increases to U.S. forces by infiltrating troops equal to one-fourth or even one-tenth of the American increment. Thus the Americans and their South Vietnamese allies never exceeded the totally inadequate ratio of 1.5 to 1 over their enemies. But with regard to actual fighting troops, the situation was much worse. Of the nearly 600,000 U.S. military personnel in Vietnam in 1968, only 80,000 were combat infantry; most of the others "were busy protecting their own installations, or talking on radio telephones, or compiling questionable statistics, or unloading large crates of canned peaches."[17]

An additional grave problem was that most American military personnel served a one-year tour, and officers even less, so that the American forces constantly experienced an inflow of green troops to replace seasoned soldiers, with a consequent higher casualty rate. As many have noted, the U.S. did not fight a ten-year war in Vietnam; it fought a one-year war ten times.

The Soviets in Afghanistan

When the Soviets invaded Afghanistan in December 1979, they imagined that the troops of the Communist regime in Kabul would do most of what little fighting might need to be done. Thus by January 1980 there were only about 50,000 Soviet soldiers in Afghanistan, many of them recently mobilized Muslim reservists from Soviet Central Asia. The unexpected intensity of popular resistance, as well as the reluctance to fight and the inclination to desert shown by the Kabul troops, made it clear that the Soviets were going to have to do a lot more fighting than originally planned. Yet Moscow never committed adequate numbers of troops to Afghanistan, and the quality of those that were there was often poor, since many Soviet privates arrived in Afghanistan with just one month's training. Five years after the initial invasion, 115,000 Soviet military personnel were in the country, a figure that rose to 120,000 by 1987. Merely maintaining a precarious hold on Kabul required 22,000 of these, however. Soviet troops in Afghanistan never amounted to as much as 4 percent of all Soviet ground forces; only 6 out of 194 Soviet combat divisions were in Afghanistan on a full-time basis. Over 50 percent of these forces were combat troops, a much higher ratio than the Americans ever reached in Vietnam. Still, after subtracting garrison security forces, the Soviets were left with only about one battalion in each province for offensive operations.[18] The grotesquely inadequate numbers of Soviet troops resulted in the adoption of a strategy observers called "migratory genocide": since the Soviets could not control the Afghan population, they would destroy it. Systematic Soviet brutality of course increased the determination of the Mujahideen to rid their land of the invader.

By 1987 the Mujahideen numbered approximately 200,000, of whom perhaps 100,000 were active fighters. To reach the standard ten-to-one ratio, and assuming the ineffective Kabul forces remained at around 80,000 (an optimistic assumption indeed),[19] the Soviets would have had to send at least an additional 800,000 troops into Afghanistan—seven times their actual commitment. Quite aside from the question of where these troops would come from, the challenge of adequately supplying such a huge force in the daunting Afghan terrain swarming with dedicated guerrillas was beyond comprehension.

Because "the Soviet leadership recognized that there could be no military solution in Afghanistan without a massive increase in their military commitment,"[20] and because by the mid-1980s that same leadership had ceased trying to hide the fact that the USSR was facing a profound and systemic economic crisis, Soviet forces withdrew from Afghanistan.

REFLECTION

While the following examples of force commitment deal purely with estimates, they are nonetheless instructive.

In their campaigns against the Boers, the British were able to reach an advantage of at least 21 to 1. In Malaya, Britain and her allies achieved a truly impressive ratio of 28 to 1 over the guerrillas. The French in Algeria, while well below this number, still reached a very comfortable ratio of 20 to 1. It may be superfluous to restate that in these three conflicts, the guerrillas suffered defeat.[21]

By way of contrast, consider the following instances, all of which resulted in either defeat or profound embarrassment for the counterinsurgent side.

During her efforts to subdue sprawling China, Imperial Japan deployed troops only twice as numerous as Mao's guerrillas, all the while having to deal with Kuomintang armies several times the size of the Japanese army in China.

In summer 1943, at the height of World War II in Europe, Axis forces in occupied Yugoslavia included 200,000 Germans along with 160,000 Bulgarians and other allies. Tito's Partisans numbered 110,000 by German estimate. This gave the Axis a mere 3 to 1 advantage, and the Partisans were by no means the only anti-German guerrillas in the country. The Partisans suffered many reverses and heavy casualties, but the Axis forces could never reduce them to the level of a minor threat.[22]

In Vietnam the French would achieve only a 1.5 to 1 ratio over the Viet Minh, which proved totally insufficient.

In Tibet, a massive guerrilla revolt against Chinese Communist occupation broke out at the turn of 1955–1956. By 1957, 200,000 Chinese troops faced perhaps 80,000 guerrillas in the field, a ratio of 2.5 to 1.[23] The Chinese forces experienced grave difficulties for years.

The Soviets in Afghanistan, even with the aid of their unimpressive indigenous allies, were hard-pressed to maintain a simple parity with the guerrillas.

And in the increasingly well-publicized war against the FARC guerrillas, the Colombian government as of 2003 managed to field an army of about 140,000 out of a total population of approximately 36 million, considerably less than one-half of 1 percent of that population.

One may, presumably, be tempted to conclude that successful (or unsuccessful) counterinsurgency is a matter of numerical ratios. But that is too easy. When thinking about numbers, one must recall that (1) even after the Castro guerrilla movement had successfully established itself as a fighting force on the island, the Batista regime enjoyed an advantage in troops of 15 to 1; (2) the French army sent plenty of troops to Algeria and defeated the guerrillas there, but then saw independence granted to that country by the politicians in Paris; (3) the Portuguese, with an unimpressive ratio over the various guerrillas in their African colonies of 6.8 to 1, defeated the guerrillas, but then, following a 1974 coup d'état in Lisbon, hastily granted those colonies independence;[24] (4) the Americans and their South Vietnamese and other allies never had much more than a 1.6 to 1 ratio over their Viet Cong and North Vietnamese adversaries, yet by 1968 the guerrilla movement had clearly suffered strategic defeat; that is why the conquest of Saigon required one of the largest conventional military invasions since World War II.[25] A last cautionary example: as late as 2003, the Russians were maintaining troops in Chechnya equal to one soldier for every six inhabitants—men, women, and children—and still could not control that unhappy land.

CHAPTER 12

DEPLOYING U.S. TROOPS IN A COUNTERINSURGENT ROLE

A POLITICALLY CHARGED QUESTION

If a single point of consensus emerged from the deeply divisive U.S. experience in Vietnam—rightly or wrongly—it seems to be this: the U.S. must be extremely selective in committing its troops to waging counterinsurgency in a foreign environment. When confronting the possibility of involvement in such a conflict, Washington policymakers will need to provide clear answers to questions such as the following:

- What are the origin and nature of the insurgency in question?
- What is the clear and direct U.S. interest in the conflict?
- What evidence exists that U.S. intervention will effectively influence the conflict?
- Why can't the foreign country's government handle the insurgents on its own? An effective government will almost certainly not be faced with a major insurgency. Hence if the U.S. intervenes on the ground against insurgents, sooner or later it will have to address the host country's political situation—always a tricky and often an explosive business. This is not of course to repeat the fatuous insistence by some Americans on instant democracy in South Vietnam. But it is hard to imagine an American ground commitment achieving real—that is, lasting—success in a political rubbish dump. On the other hand, U.S. pressure on El Salvador substantially aided the cleaning up of the regime there.
- Can the necessity for sustained U.S. intervention be persuasively presented to the American electorate and its representatives in Congress, in a post–Cold War environment? Under the

very best of circumstances, most third world conflicts (at least) exhibit extreme moral ambiguities, which will provide sensational pictures for the media and disturb the U.S. electorate.[1] If the reasons for the origin and continuation of the conflict are mainly cultural, then intervention will probably be frustrating and frustrated because cultures are slow to change, especially under foreign pressure, however benign.

- Finally, what is the definition of success for the U.S. intervention under consideration?

Clearly, such a list of questions would prove daunting to any but the most enthusiastic or convinced interventionist. Another persuasive argument against using U.S. combat troops in a faraway insurgency is this: To be effective, any counterinsurgency force needs to obtain useful intelligence, to be familiar with the terrain, and to give proof to the local civilians that the troops will not eventually abandon them. To accomplish all these ends would seem to require locally recruited soldiers, or at least troops designated for long-term service in the same place.

These and other considerations help explain why in some key crises during the Cold War, the U.S. military vigorously and successfully opposed assuming a prominent counterinsurgent role. For example, during the height of the Communist-led Huk rebellion in the Philippines, some policymakers in Washington gave serious consideration to the Manila government's repeated pleas for U.S. ground troops to be dispatched to that country. A memorandum, however, from the Joint Chiefs of Staff to Secretary of Defense Louis Johnson in September 1950 pointed out the nonmilitary roots of the Philippine insurgency. "The basic problem [in the Philippines] is primarily political and economic. Military action should not be an alternative for [erecting] a stable and efficient government based on sound economic and social foundations." The U.S. Armed Forces manifested similar opposition to committing U.S. ground troops during the Greek civil war.[2]

Assuredly, the wisdom of committing U.S. ground troops—or any foreign troops—to a counterinsurgency mission is a complex question. Not infrequently, foreign troops have defeated insurgents: British soldiers held Athens against a Communist uprising in 1945, and they did very well against the Communist insurgency in Malaya. Portuguese forces waged largely successful counterinsurgencies in their African possessions in the 1960s and early 1970s. In contrast, it must be acknowledged that the U.S. committed many errors in South Vietnam (the first direct confrontation between U.S. troops and a Communist insurgency). Yet that does not mean that American troops should never be used against any insurgents anywhere. In fact Americans have achieved some impressive successes in counterinsurgency, notably by the army in the Philippines after the Spanish-American War, and the Marines in Haiti and Nicaragua in the inter-war period.[3] Moreover, the Combined Action Platoons of the U.S. Marines made an impressively successful record in Vietnam. Besides, the Viet Cong did not defeat the Americans in Vietnam—quite the contrary. Governments and armed forces can and do learn from their own and others' mistakes.[4] Thus, the question of whether or not to commit U.S. troops to future counterinsurgent missions requires very careful study and reflection. Much depends on political and geographic factors, as well as how many and what kind of U.S. troops would be involved.

Nevertheless, when an American administration faces an insurgency against a government whose survival is deemed important to the U.S., probably the soundest military and safest political course for it to follow would be to encourage regional powers and/or the former colonial power to shoulder the main responsibility. Countries with extensive counterinsurgent experience include Britain, Colombia, France, India, Indonesia, Israel, Morocco, Peru, the Philippines, Portugal, Thailand, and Turkey.[5] In addition to this course, or instead of it if necessary, the U.S. might confine its counterinsurgency effort to offering advice and support, as it did in both the Greek civil war and the Huk insurgency, achieving its major objectives in each case. Such limited involvement would emphasize U.S. strengths, including money, mobility, intelligence, technology, and the ability to discourage outside aid to the insurgents. If, however, the U.S. decides to commit ground forces, they could assume the operational defensive, occupying key installations and centers in order to free indigenous troops for more offensive operations.[6] In such circumstances, and especially if U.S. ground involvement should widen, great attention would need to be given to such matters as rectitude, civilian-friendly tactics, and securing local personnel as guides, scouts, and auxiliaries. It would almost certainly be of the utmost importance for the U.S. to enter into a counterinsurgency in the company of allies, and especially of at least one ally with key cultural characteristics (language, religion, ethnicity) similar to those of the host country.[7]

U.S. Advisers in Vietnam

It is difficult to isolate specific lessons from the activities of U.S. advisers to South Vietnamese military units, largely because the adviser program was part of a vastly larger U.S. military commitment, one that became and remains profoundly controversial. Nevertheless, certain fundamental aspects of the program merit attention because they may potentially resurface in a future U.S. advisory undertaking.

"Beginning almost unnoticed with a few hundred individuals in 1954, [the U.S. advisory effort] had grown to about ten thousand a decade or so later, representing the largest such commitment in the history of warfare."[8] Many advisers had contradictory feelings toward their own roles. In July 1967 General Creighton Abrams stated that U.S. advisers saw themselves as second-class citizens in the army, and they were treated as such. Despite General William Westmoreland's plans to upgrade their status, many American advisers viewed the assignment as detrimental to their careers, and this seems indeed to have been the case.[9]

Aside from the question of how the U.S. Army evaluated its members serving as advisers, structural aspects of the program interfered with its effective functioning. Most U.S. advisers served with a particular South Vietnamese unit for only six months. Some of them became openly critical of the Vietnamese value system. Relatively few possessed any useful knowledge of the Vietnamese language.[10]

For Americans, learning the language was indeed a challenge; to attain fluency in Vietnamese, a Westerner needs between eight hundred and one thousand hours of intensive study.[11] "Then there was the problem of regional accents and vocabulary which differed to the point of incomprehensibility even among natives."[12] Nevertheless, "experience showed that even with a smattering of conversational Vietnamese, a US adviser could always establish instant rapport and affection. The ability to speak the language, therefore, was a most effective tool for winning the 'hearts and minds'"[13] of the South Vietnamese, and "it was no secret that the most successful and popular advisers were those who came back for a second or third tour and spoke the native language well."[14]

In his memoirs, General Westmoreland wrote this about American advisers in Vietnam: "It can be said that during the crisis days of 1964, when coup followed coup [after the assassination of President Diem] American advisers literally held the country together. The adviser was on duty twenty-four hours a day, seven days a week, often under severe field conditions. Learning to live under the most primitive sanitation conditions was in itself trying."[15] Many advisers even feared to eat Vietnamese food.[16] This last is not surprising. As General Westmoreland observed: "Although advisers drew some American rations, they ate most of their meals with the Vietnamese troops, which took considerable adjusting to when the main course might be rat or dog. Almost all advisers operating with troops had recurrent bouts of amoebic dysentery."[17]

In spite of all these difficulties, large numbers of U.S. advisers fulfilled their assigned roles with dedication and effect. It is truly regrettable that the clouds of controversy and ignorance still surrounding the American experience in Vietnam have obscured the valuable lessons of the U.S. advisory effort in that war.[18]

CHAPTER 13

GUERRILLAS AND CONVENTIONAL TACTICS

Sometimes insurgents have abandoned their guerrilla tactics in favor of conventional warfare. This section considers three major instances of such a fateful change in method: the Greek guerrillas in 1948–1949, the Viet Minh at Dien Bien Phu in 1954, and the Viet Cong during the Tet Offensive of 1968.

THE CIVIL WAR IN GREECE

The Communist-led Greek insurgents passed from guerrilla tactics to conventional tactics more than once. Following the German evacuation of Greece, Communist-led guerrillas attempted in early December 1944 to expel newly arrived British forces from Athens. Churchill himself arrived on Christmas Day 1944 to hearten the defenders of the besieged capital. The attack failed and an uneasy armistice followed.

Fighting soon broke out anew, however. In May 1947, desiring a capital for their "Free Greece," the insurgents attacked the town of Florina, near the Yugoslavian border. After many casualties on both sides, government forces beat off the attack. A major insurgent assault on the town of Konitsa, close to Albania, began on December 25, 1947, but by January 4 this effort had also suffered defeat. It is important to note that these insurgent attacks failed when the Greek National Army was in perhaps its weakest condition.

Under their military commander Markos Vafiades, the insurgents' guerrilla strategy had been reasonably successful: large areas of Greece's rugged terrain were under their control, along with a substantial portion of the civilian population. But Greek Communist Party boss Nikos Zachariades, impatient for victory and jealous of Vafiades, insisted on a permanent turn to conventional war. In November 1948 Zachariades succeeded in ousting Vafiades from military command. In December the insurgents launched major conventional actions, beginning another big siege of Florina in February 1949. Lacking air cover and confronting a much-improved National Army (thanks in part to the effects of the Truman Doctrine), the insurgents suffered heavy casualties and increasing desertions. Nevertheless, in August 1949 Zachariades assembled twelve thousand insurgents in an "impregnable bastion" in the Grammos Mountain area. After heavy fighting and severe casualties, most of the surviving insurgents scuttled over the border of Communist Albania, for the last time. On October 16, 1949, Communist Radio Free Greece announced the suspension of hostilities; on November 28 President Truman informed Congress that the Greek government had been victorious.[1]

Critics of the Greek insurgents maintain that they turned to conventional war too early. But in fact one could argue that the change happened much too late: the Communists' best opportunity to seize power in Greece was probably between late 1944 and the spring of 1945. At any rate, adopting conventional tactics, which had failed previously, against a Greek army much better organized and equipped in 1948 than it had been in 1947, was a grave blunder. Along with U.S. aid to the Greek government, Communist atrocities against civilians, and the closing of the Yugoslavian border against the guerrillas, this miscalculation ranks as a major cause of the total defeat of the insurgency.[2]

DIEN BIEN PHU

The village of Dien Bien Phu lies in northwest Vietnam, near the Laotian border. There in 1954 the French constructed an airstrip, surrounded it with interconnected strongpoints, and parachuted soldiers in to defend them. The main idea behind building this complex was to lure the Communist-led Viet Minh guerrillas into a pitched battle, in which superior French discipline, training, and equipment would grind the enemy down. The fortress became the scene of one of the most famous battles in modern history.

The French Expeditionary Corps in Vietnam included no fewer than seventeen distinct nationalities. At Dien Bien Phu, half of the thirteen-thousand-man garrison consisted of Vietnamese, but the French had to fly six different kinds of food into the fortress: one menu each for the Europeans, Vietnamese, North Africans, sub-Saharan Africans, T'ais, and prisoners. French Muslim troops could not eat the canned pork ration; the Vietnamese needed rice, but Europeans could not subsist indefinitely on it. Planes brought in huge containers of dehydrated wine. The fortress also had a brothel, staffed by Algerians and Vietnamese.

On almost all sides, high ground overlooked Dien Bien Phu. The French Command insisted that the Viet Minh would be unable to position artillery up onto that high ground. Even if they did they would not be able to keep it supplied; and besides, as soon as any Viet Minh guns fired on Dien Bien Phu, French artillery inside the fortress would blow them to pieces. In short, "nobody believed in the strategic mobility and logistics of the Viet Minh."[3] The battle began on March 13, 1954—with a Communist artillery bombardment. Two days later, Col. Charles Piroth, the French gunnery chief, killed himself with a hand grenade.

The besiegers had a four to one advantage in artillery. Further, French aircraft often mistakenly dropped loads of 105mm shells into enemy lines. Without this unanticipated supply, the Viet Minh might well have run out of sufficient shells for their own artillery.[4] "The failure at Dien Bien Phu was due to the fact that this isolated base was attacked by an enemy with artillery and antiaircraft."[5] One noted student of the war observed that antiaircraft fire over Dien Bien Phu was thicker than over Germany in World War II.[6] "If any particular group of enemy soldiers should be considered indispensable to victory, then it must be the Viet Minh anti-aircraft gunners and their Chinese instructors."[7] The French Command considered it impossible to send an overland expedition strong enough to save the fortress, and in all Indochina only about one hundred combat aircraft were available to support Dien Bien Phu, which was at the edge of their flying range. In addition, the Viet Minh usually moved at night, or under cover, so that French pilots could not easily see them. And available French air power was often misused.[8]

On March 17, the fourth day of the siege, the airfield became unusable because of enemy artillery hits. Thus Dien Bien Phu's lifeline was gone. Another of the fundamental assumptions of those who planned the fortress was that the wounded would be evacuated by air. Since this was now impossible, the garrison was left only with its completely inadequate forty-four-bed hospital. As the fighting went on and the casualties mounted, the suffering of the wounded, especially toward the end, transcended description. As one after another of the French defenses collapsed in the rain, the water pumps eventually broke down, the trenches filled up with water, and the wounded lay in that dirty water and in their own waste.

During this drama, somewhere between three thousand and four thousand men in the garrison became "internal deserters"—these were tribesmen, Vietnamese, Foreign Legionnaires, and Frenchmen who threw their weapons aside and literally sat out the siege in remote trenches, in relative safety if not comfort. And back in France, Communists in the labor unions and elsewhere sabotaged shipments of supplies to French forces in Vietnam.[9]

Dien Bien Phu fell on May 8, 1954, the ninth anniversary of VE Day. When Prime Minister Joseph Laniel announced the fall of the fortress in the French National Assembly, all the deputies present rose to their feet, everybody except the Communists.

Dien Bien Phu was a tactical disaster for the French, but hardly a strategic one. The French had committed about one-twentieth of the troops they had in Indochina, of whom 7,800 became casualties. On the other hand, General Giap had gathered together nearly all his available forces, approximately 100,000, of whom over 20,000 became casualties. Yet for orchestrating the collapse of this isolated and hopelessly outnumbered and outgunned French garrison, Giap somehow attained a reputation as a Southeast Asian Napoleon. Nevertheless, if the "primary objective of Giap's military operations was always to weaken the will of the French people to fight," then he was successful.[10] Dien Bien Phu "effectively brought to an end [France's] 200 years as an Asian power."[11] And France's travails in Vietnam laid the groundwork for the revolt in Algeria.

THE TET OFFENSIVE

The Tet Offensive of 1968 was the turning point of U.S. involvement in Vietnam. While there were many reasons behind Hanoi's decision to unleash the Offensive, the primary and decisive one was that the Viet Cong and North Vietnamese forces were suffering casualties at a rate that could not be sustained.

From 1960 to 1967, thirteen thousand Americans lost their lives in Vietnam. In every one of those years, a greater number of Americans died in the U.S. by falling off the roofs of their houses than died in Vietnam.

In contrast, General Giap, victor of Dien Bien Phu, told a journalist that between 1965 and 1968 the Communist side had lost six hundred thousand men. There is no good reason to believe Giap was exaggerating.[12] The North Vietnamese regime was requiring its population to endure casualty rates higher than those sustained by the Japanese during World War II. (In all of World War II, in all theaters, U.S. war deaths numbered four hundred thousand.) Many signs pointed to an approaching general collapse of Communist morale. Clearly, something drastically different had to be done to bring the war to an end on terms favorable to the Communist side.

The decision to carry out the Tet Offensive was a recognition by Hanoi that its guerrilla-based People's War strategy was failing. This was the *genesis* of the Tet Offensive. The *rationale* for the Offensive was Hanoi's insistence that in a crisis ARVN would disintegrate and the oppressed masses of South Vietnamese would rise up against the hated Saigon government.

However, during the Offensive, although the Viet Cong were better armed than the South Vietnamese forces, the great majority of ARVN units neither collapsed nor defected, but held their own. "The professionalism and steadfastness of ARVN during the Tet offensive surprised not only the enemy but the Americans and themselves as well."[13] General Westmoreland declared that "the South Vietnamese had fully vindicated my trust."[14] Even the militia (the Regional Forces and Popular Forces, RF/PF—called Ruff-Puffs by acronym-loving U.S. soldiers) generally did well.[15] The fighting power of ARVN and the militia was not the only shock for the Viet Cong; they were profoundly stunned by the failure of the South Vietnamese people to rise up in support of the Offensive.[16] These disastrous surprises were largely due to the Communist leadership's poor use of available intelligence. Consequently, the Offensive was a military debacle for the Communist side. Of approximately eighty-four thousand Viet Cong involved in Tet, thirty thousand were killed. Some estimates run much higher. No one knows how many were wounded.[17] "In truth, the Tet Offensive for all practical purposes destroyed the Viet Cong."[18] After Tet 1968, the war increasingly became a conventional one with the regular North Vietnamese Army playing an ever more dominant role in place of the broken VC. "Tet was the end of People's War, and essentially of any strategy built on guerrilla warfare and a politically inspired insurgency."[19] Accordingly, "never again was the Tet strategy repeated."[20]

SUMMARY

In each of these cases, the insurgent forces abandoned guerrilla tactics for conventional warfare. Two of the three switchovers culminated in defeat for the insurgents. In all of them, the defeated side had underestimated the enemy: the Greek Communist leadership regarding the National Army, the French regarding the Viet Minh, the Hanoi politburo regarding ARVN.

In the Greek case, the change to conventional war resulted as much from internecine Communist party jealousies as from military analysis. Adopting conventional warfare undeniably hurt the guerrillas. Nevertheless, their error affected the final outcome only marginally, since the insurgents had already been defeated strategically, due to U.S. economic assistance, improvements in the Greek National Army, and the rebels' alienation of much of the rural population. Thus, the outcome of the war was clear *before* the guerrillas changed their tactics.

In 1954, the French set up Dien Bien Phu as an enticement for their guerrilla enemies, whose war-making capabilities they had consistently—and unaccountably—disparaged, to the extent of setting their "trap" for the Viet Minh in a place that was both overlooked by high ground and beyond the effective range of French military power. The Viet Minh, much better informed about their adversaries than vice versa, took the "bait" and overran Dien Bien Phu (with substantial Chinese assistance), breaking the will of the French political classes to continue the war.

In 1968, the Hanoi regime, ignoring intelligence from its own sources and insisting that ARVN would crumble and the civil population would revolt, hurled the Viet Cong into a disastrous conventional confrontation from which it never recovered.[21] After Tet, the conflict in South Vietnam became essentially a conventional war in which North Vietnamese Army regulars increasingly filled the place of the disrupted Viet Cong, even in so-called Viet Cong units. The post-Tet conflict would last another seven years.

CHAPTER 14

THE MYTH OF MAOIST PEOPLE'S WAR

Out of China came one of the great myths of the twentieth century, the myth of guerrilla invincibility. During the 1930s and 1940s, Mao Tse-tung worked out methods of peasant based revolutionary guerrilla warfare, linking guerrilla tactics to political organization. He then wielded this type of warfare to checkmate the Japanese and defeat the Kuomintang. That, at any rate, is the myth, which throughout the second half of the twentieth century exerted incredible power over revolutionaries and counterrevolutionaries alike.[1]

In order to evaluate the Maoist myth, one needs to review both the genesis and nature of Maoist revolutionary guerrilla warfare, and the strategy and tactics it employed against the Chinese Nationalists and the Japanese army.

Contemporary Chinese politics begins with the Revolution of 1911, which overthrew the Sinicized but still foreign Manchu Dynasty. The major catalyst for this event had been the series of humiliations suffered by China during the nineteenth century at the hands of foreigners, especially the notorious Opium Wars. The crowning humiliation was the Sino-Japanese War (1894–1895), in which a small but burgeoning Japan achieved rapid and total victory over a huge but foundering China. The war stunned a whole generation of educated young Chinese, who thereafter searched desperately for leaders with an effective program to lift China out of her backwardness and weakness, and out of the clutches of the encroaching barbarians. One may summarize Chinese politics between the end of the Sino-Japanese War in 1895 and the entry of Mao into Peking in 1949 as the rivalry between the Nationalists and the Communists to establish their identity as the true saviors of China.

It had been easy to overthrow the senile Imperial regime in 1911. It was much harder to establish an effective republican government in its place. The vacuum of legitimate power led to the militarization of Chinese politics; indeed, "the role of the military in shaping twentieth-century Chinese politics and society cannot be overemphasized"[2] because "in no country in the world have soldiers dominated politics so extensively and for so long as in China."[3] A few years after the revolution China descended into the era of warlord politics: provincial military governors exercised semisovereign powers in alliance with or in opposition to the central government in Peking, often under the tutelage of the Russians or the Japanese. Not for the first (or the last) time, China seemed in danger of falling apart into a gaggle of small, squabbling states.

THE KUOMINTANG

The father of modern Chinese nationalism was Sun Yat-sen. Born near Canton in 1866, he was educated at an Anglican school in Honolulu and a medical college in Hong Kong. Active in the 1911 Revolution, Sun founded the National People's Party—the Kuomintang (KMT)—to advance his vision of a reunited and rejuvenated China. The KMT soon became one of the two great contenders for the right to lead China into modernity and unity.

Then, as now, there were two Chinas: heartland (interior) China and maritime (coastal) China.[4] Despite the impositions and invasions of militarily superior foreign states, by the year 1900 the overwhelming majority of Chinese had never even seen a foreigner in the flesh. The great interior heartland, remote, poor, and immobile, had remained relatively untouched by foreign incursion and influence. The impact of Europeans and Japanese had been almost completely limited to the great coastal cities of maritime China. There, the increasing presence of foreign personnel, ideas, and methods had produced a significant number of Chinese with "modern," or at least certainly nontraditional, aspirations. This emerging middle class became the basis of the KMT's support.

The KMT wanted to end warlordism and imperialism—that is, to establish an effective central government. It wanted to modernize the country under the leadership of the educated classes. It wanted, in short, a political revolution, not a social one. The party's base was in Canton, but it received crucial financial support from the great business houses in Shanghai, and also from China's numerous and prosperous diaspora—the Overseas Chinese. "The Kuomintang was the party of the bourgeoisie," the party of maritime China.[5] As such, it never understood the desires of the peasantry. Neither was the KMT the party of the rural elite, the landowners and magistrates of the countryside. Yet the KMT mistook this rural elite for a stabilizing influence, rather than the profoundly destabilizing force that, because of its exploitation and illegitimacy, it actually was.

It is not Sun Yat-sen but rather Chiang Kai-shek who personifies, at least to the West, the aspirations and frailties of the KMT. The militarization of politics in China following the Revolution of 1911 convinced Sun that the KMT could achieve power only if it built its own army. Thus Chiang, graduate of a Japanese military academy and Sun's military adviser, came to the fore. The first director of the KMT military academy at Whampoa (near Canton), he journeyed to Moscow to enlist Soviet help in the coming campaign against the warlords. After breaking violently with the Chinese Communist Party (CCP), Chiang turned to the army of Weimar Germany for advice and equipment.

When Sun died in 1925, Chiang became head of the KMT. He had two key aims: (1) territorial integrity, meaning the expulsion of the imperialists and abolition of the unequal treaties they had imposed on China, and (2) national unification, meaning the destruction of warlordism and communism.[6] Expulsion of the imperialists would be impossible without national unity, that is, the suppression of all internal regional or class struggles. Hence in the KMT program for national salvation, anti-imperialism required anticommunism.[7] China's sprawling size, complex topography, poor communications,[8] teeming and largely uneducated population, and extreme linguistic and provincial diversity were truly daunting obstacles to the achievement of KMT aims.

THE NORTHERN EXPEDITION

The KMT's most immediate priority was eliminating the warlords who controlled northern China. In July 1926 Chiang led the KMT army out of its Canton base on the Northern Expedition. The warlords were no match for the KMT. "The rank and file of warlord armies was made up largely of peasants, recruited by poverty. . . . These armies gave the Chinese military an extremely bad reputation."[9] Within Chiang's Nationalist forces, promotion for merit and combat ability was more common than in warlord armies, or in the former Chinese Imperial armies. KMT party cadres looked after the pay and food of the troops. They taught their men that they were the saviors of China, not social outcasts like traditional soldiers. All this kept up morale and held down depredations against the civilian population. Thus KMT troops benefited from a good reputation among the peasantry; "the [KMT army] proved to be far superior to its military opponents in its fighting spirit and political awareness, which were closely related."[10]

The army of the KMT was but one of many armies in China, and the party's announced program of national unification alerted all its actual and potential enemies. Thus, even to get the Northern Expedition started, Chiang had had to enter into alliances with local warlords in and around the KMT's Canton base in Kwangtung Province. As he progressed north, Chiang offered the warlords in the path of his army a stark choice: resist and be destroyed, or join the KMT. Several warlords prudently chose the latter alternative, bringing their armed followers onto the side of the KMT; in return they were confirmed as being in control of their territories, not as warlords but as official KMT governors.

This policy of co-opting warlords allowed the KMT to present the Northern Expedition as an instrument of unification rather than conquest. More fundamentally, if Chiang had not been willing to accept the conversion of at least some of the warlords, the Northern Expedition might well have suffered military defeat. Besides, if the expedition had fought its way across central and northern China victoriously but too slowly, it could have opened the door to renewed foreign intervention.

Clearly, then, co-opting warlords was not in itself a bad idea; it was the plan's execution that contained the seeds of future trouble. Chiang incorporated several warlord armies into the KMT ranks as whole units, rather than admitting their members on an individual basis. This co-option, along with defection from warlord forces and civilian volunteering, increased the KMT army from one hundred thousand in July 1926 to one million in February 1928.[11] The flood of new soldiers into the KMT overwhelmed and discouraged the competent and sincere party cadres. Consequently these new "allies" received very little political indoctrination. Most of them remained the instruments of former warlords who had donned the KMT colors, for the time being. Additionally, the success of the Northern Expedition brought great numbers of bureaucrats and political careerists into the KMT. Chiang accepted them in wholesale batches, in an effort to establish KMT authority over a unified China as quickly as possible: "Mao purged, Chiang tried to convert."[12]

The Northern Expedition ended in June 1928 when the KMT occupied Peking. Chiang established his capital at Nanking, inaugurating the period of Nationalist rule known as the "Nanking Decade." The tasks facing the new regime were staggering because the multiple pathologies afflicting China were deeply rooted and interconnected. "Thus, though the politically aware looked forward with hope in 1928, progress toward creating a modern nation-state was sure to be slow even under the most favorable conditions. And such were not to be."[13] Clearly, "ten years [would be] too brief a time to establish a completely new national administration and to turn back the tide of political disintegration and national humiliation that for a century and a half had assailed the nation. Even if conditions had been ideal, the new government could have done little more than initiate political, social and economic reforms."[14] Conditions were of course far from ideal, and would become catastrophically worse. Nonetheless, the Nanking Decade witnessed an impressive industrial growth rate of 6 percent per annum.[15] The regime also made serious efforts to abolish concubinage and footbinding, and to introduce marriage choice. Consequently, "although today Nationalist China has become a synonym for corruption and ineptitude, to foreign observers at the time it was a truism that the provinces ruled by Nanking [the KMT] were the heart of an emerging, modern state which was attracting the loyalty of more and more Chinese."[16] During the Nanking Decade "the KMT regime established the foundations of the modern Chinese State and created an incomplete set of political structures which served as a 'rough draft' for the [Communist regime to come]. The reforms since 1976 reestablish this lineage but do not acknowledge it."[17]

THE ENCIRCLEMENT CAMPAIGNS

Since the time of the Ming Dynasty, the southeast province of Kiangsi had been a stronghold of rebellion against central authority. Here the Chinese Communist Party had established its main base. And here Chiang Kai-shek concentrated his efforts on the final destruction of the CCP in the form of the five Encirclement Campaigns, from December 1930 to October 1934. The Communists defeated the first four campaigns. They allowed the Nationalist forces to penetrate deep into their Kiangsi stronghold; then, taking advantage of interior lines, effective communications, and good intelligence, they mobilized their whole strength in surprise night attacks against first one relatively small group of KMT troops, then another. An additional favorite CCP tactic was to surround some vital point and then ambush the rescuing force.

Other factors besides good Communist tactics account for the failures of the first four Encirclement Campaigns. Factional and regional antagonisms among the commanders undermined Nationalist efforts in Kiangsi, as they would in the coming war against the Japanese.[18] In addition, poor communications and logistics, and above all a lack of air power, always hampered KMT counterinsurgency moves.

The First Encirclement Campaign, employing three armies, developed between December 1930 and January 1931, but wound down in the face of superior Communist tactics. The Second Encirclement Campaign, between April and May 1931, deployed 200,000 Nationalist troops. "[W]arlordism and factionalism made cooperation between Nationalist Army units difficult and was the principle reason for their defeat [in that campaign]."[19] The Third Encirclement Campaign occurred between July and September 1931 and deployed 300,000 soldiers. Aware of the factionalism that had hampered the first two campaigns, Chiang took personal charge of the third campaign, but his efforts met with little success owing in large part to a rebellion in Canton by anti-Chiang factionalists and the Japanese invasion of distant Manchuria. The Fourth Encirclement Campaign, from January to May 1933, pitted 153,000 Nationalist troops against 65,000 Communists.[20] Renewed Japanese aggression in north China halted this effort. But Chiang remained profoundly convinced that the Communists were a greater threat to China than the Japanese. His slogan "unification before resistance" encapsulated his desire to defeat the Communists first before dealing with the invading Japanese.

The first four campaigns had been "modern"—employing ideas borrowed from Europe—and their objective had been the annihilation of the enemy forces. The Fifth Encirclement Campaign, in contrast, which lasted from October 1933 to October 1934, was based more heavily on traditional Chinese strategic concepts, especially ones developed during the suppression of the Taiping rebellion in the mid-nineteenth century.[21] This Fifth Campaign sought to take and hold territory, forcing the guerrillas out and away. Chiang deployed about 800,000 troops against 150,000 Communists[22] in a campaign that united strategic offensive with tactical defensive. That is, KMT forces would move massively into Communist territory while employing self-protective tactics to deter enemy attack. Nationalist forces would often end the day's march in mid-afternoon. This allowed the troops time to build a fortified camp in order to discourage night attack (a standard procedure of the ancient Roman army).

Since the end of the Third Campaign in September 1931, the Nationalists had built new roads to help overcome the serious supply problems that had hindered their earlier movements. To the same end they had constructed new airports and set up telephone units. They had also gained another accession of supporters, thanks largely to the radicalization of the CCP program after 1933, which drove the rural elite, hitherto deeply suspicious of the reforming and urban KMT, to support Chiang.

In the Fifth Campaign, the KMT introduced a major new weapon against the Communists: lines of blockhouses.[23] Rural laborers under supervision of the local elite constructed ultimately thousands of small fortifications, surrounded by trenches and barbed wire, with interconnecting fields of machine-gun and artillery fire. Some of the biggest blockhouses were made of brick and stone, three stories high, but simpler ones were put up in from one to three days. After a line of blockhouses had been erected, the troops would advance a few kilometers, and, under the protection of the existing blockhouses, erect a new line of them, then advance again. To support all this building the KMT constructed hundreds of miles of roads.

The blockhouses choked Communist economic activities. They also allowed quick medical care for wounded KMT soldiers, very good for morale. But above all the blockhouse system deprived the Communists of their greatest advantage, the ability to maneuver. At the same time, the Communist forces could not meet the Nationalists in positional warfare, because of the latter's superior weaponry.[24]

So undeniable were the successes of the Fifth Campaign that the CCP leadership decided to abandon Kiangsi completely and embark upon the famous Long March (actually a Long Retreat).[25] The March began in the fall of 1934 and ended with the arrival one year later of the party's tattered remnants in their new home in Shensi Province, in north-central China.

"The Red Army had given a brilliant account of itself [on the Long March]. It is doubtful, however, that it could have continued to maintain itself if Generalissimo Chiang Kai-shek had pursued his policy of military annihilation of the Red forces. . . . At the end of 1936 [Chiang] was preparing a new 'blockhouse-fortress' campaign around the [CCP] base in Shensi along the lines of the Fifth Campaign in Kiangsi. Had he decided to open this campaign, the Communist forces would almost certainly have been either 'exterminated' or forced to begin a new 'Long March,' probably across Mongolia to Soviet Russia."[26]

THE JAPANESE WAR

It has sometimes been claimed that the Chinese Communists were able to expel the Nationalists from the mainland because of the latter's military, political, and moral inferiority. But the "simplistic dichotomy between a 'corrupt KMT' and an 'honest CCP' is far too crude an explanation of modern developments in China to be of much value."[27] Rather, the KMT lost the post–World War II struggle with the Communists as a direct result of the Japanese invasion of 1937. Japan's incursion into China proper had two complementary and decisive effects on the balance of power between the KMT and the CCP. First, it ruined the army, the backbone of the KMT. Second, it rescued the CCP from annihilation and provided an environment for its growth.

Communist guerrillas were quite free to abandon any area that the Imperial Japanese Army (IJA) entered in force; retreating in the face of a superior enemy is exactly what guerrillas are supposed to do. Nationalist troops, in contrast, felt obliged to hold fast and defend key areas. Consequently, although the better-trained and better-equipped IJA troops were never able to destroy the KMT forces, they inflicted tremendous numbers of casualties upon them.[28] For one example, in the eighth year of the war, the IJA launched Operation Ichigo (April–December 1944) with the express purpose of breaking up the Nationalist armed forces. The Japanese advanced to within three hundred kilometers of Chiang's wartime capital at Chungking, forcing Chiang to make a stand. The Japanese eventually withdrew, but Chiang lost seven hundred thousand of his best troops. The battle left the KMT devastated psychologically as well as physically.[29]

These great losses forced the KMT to resort to wholesale conscription. The draft produced large numbers of new soldiers, whom the Nationalist government was hardly ever able to feed, clothe, or pay properly. The efforts to support the enlarged KMT armies became a new and onerous burden to the civilian population. Rapid expansion and heavy casualties in turn required the creation of a huge number of new officers. To meet these demands the training period for officers was reduced from three years to only one, and many candidates were accepted as officers who previously would have been judged unsuitable. Thus the war ruined the KMT officer corps, formerly the essence, the very flower, of the party's hopes.

The war further undermined the Nationalist army by increasing the centrifugal forces within it: the presence or approach of Japanese troops meant that former warlords and provincial military commanders now had the option of switching their allegiance to Japan or to one of the several Chinese collaborationist regimes established by the IJA. These regimes flew the old KMT flag and even used the party name, uniform, and slogans as their own. The resulting confusion made it close to impossible for Chiang's government to carry on effective propaganda in Japanese-occupied areas.[30] Consequently, "the question of what troops would obey whom under what circumstances could not be answered with any certainty."[31] In selecting his commanders and sub-commanders, then, Chiang was compelled to emphasize personal loyalty over professional competence.[32] Clearly, this critical question of loyalty was the poisoned fruit of Chiang's policy of massive co-option of warlord forces during the Northern Expedition. Equally clearly, such issues of loyalty and disloyalty would not have arisen, at least not in the extreme form they did, without the crisis of the Japanese war.

During the Nanking Decade, most of the KMT's efforts at modernization had concentrated on the coastal provinces, which were the most developed areas of the country and the KMT's political base. The Japanese occupation of most of maritime China, including the notorious Rape of Nanking,[33] pushed the KMT into the interior, where it was cut off from its middle-class constituency (as well as its foreign allies) and forced to rely on the predatory rural elites. Thus the Japanese war ravaged the Nationalists not only as an army but as a party as well.

Of at least equal importance, the war also meant a new lease on life for the Communists. "From 1921 to 1937 Communism failed in China because the Chinese people, in general, were indifferent to what the Communist Party had to offer."[34] In fact, thanks to Chiang's Fifth Encirclement Campaign "the [Communist] Party . . . was in its worst straits just before the Japanese invasion."[35] But that invasion "provided the means by which the Communist Partry reentered Chinese political life."[36] The IJA effectively squeezed Nationalist forces out of north China, thus opening that area up to CCP organization and control. At the same time, through their brutal tactics (see below), the Japanese acted as a recruiting agency for the CCP: "peasants who survived the [IJA] mopping-up campaigns were forced to conclude that their only hope lay in resistance, and the Communists were widely regarded as the most competent organizers of resistance."[37] A few numbers quickly tell the tale. On the eve of the 1937 Japanese invasion, the CCP controlled about 35,000 square miles, with 1.5 million inhabitants; by 1945, when Japan surrendered, the CCP ruled 225,000 square miles and 65 million people.[38] In the same period, party membership ballooned from 40,000 to 1.2 million. In 1937 the Red Army had 50,000 members; by 1945 that army, not counting guerrilla units, totalled 900,000 men.

To recapitulate, between 1928 and 1937 the KMT regime had had to confront a legacy of backwardness and decay, a world economic depression, and a Communist insurgency. Against all of these challenges the regime was making visible progress. But then in 1937 came the Japanese invasion, with its concomitants of ex-warlord treachery and wholesale collaborationism.[39] Chiang and his followers could not stand up against these storms. The Japanese war devastated the Nationalist forces, revived the Communist party, and thus changed the history of the world.

MAOIST GUERRILLA WARFARE

In 1936 Mao and his party/army were on the edge of extermination by Chiang's forces. "There is no very good reason to believe that the CCP and the Red Army would have triumphed had it not been for the Japanese invasion of China and the methods of pacification adopted in support of the consolidation of Japanese politico-military power."[40] In short, the Japanese invasion saved Chinese Communism.

During the anti-Japanese war "the Communists . . . eschewed their old slogans of class warfare and violent redistribution of property in their post-1937 propaganda and concentrated solely on national salvation."[41] Mao proclaimed that "we [Communists] must unite the nation without regard to parties or classes and follow our policy of resistance to the end."[42] That is, Mao's basic program began to resemble that of the KMT.

Mao always believed that the Communist conquest of China would require large, well-equipped conventional forces.[43] Guerrillas alone could not deliver victory.[44] "[T]he strategic role of guerrillas is two-fold: to support regular warfare and to transform themselves into regular forces."[45] But in the late 1930s the CCP was by no means strong enough to confront the regular armies of the KMT. It was under these circumstances, and largely because he had no other choice, that Mao developed his theories and techniques of guerrilla warfare. First and foremost among his ideas was the primacy of politics: guerrilla war was a political process. "The fighting capacity of a guerrilla unit," Mao insisted, "is not determined exclusively by military arts, but depends above all on political consciousness."[46] As Cromwell's army was a church in arms, so Mao's army would be a party in arms. Therefore Mao asserted that "every communist must grasp the truth that 'political power grows out of the barrel of a gun,'"[47] but "our principle is that the party commands the gun, and the gun must never be allowed to command the party."[48]

Questions regarding the proper treatment of civilians and enemy prisoners further revealed the political foundations of guerrilla insurgency. Proper behavior toward the civilian population was essential ("Return borrowed articles, be sanitary, be polite"). As for prisoners, Mao wrote that "the most effective method of propaganda directed at the enemy forces is to release captured soldiers and give the wounded medical treatment."[49] Treating captured enemies in this manner would increase the tendency of the opponent to give up rather than fight to the death.

Good morale is essential if the guerrillas are to bear up over a long period under the sacrifices and dangers in their daily lives. Mao maintained that good morale required constant political indoctrination: the insurgents must be assured that their cause is just, their enemy wicked, and their triumph certain. But of course the best morale-builder is victory in combat; if the first duty of the guerrilla is to survive, the second is to win. Hence "if we do not have a 100 percent guarantee of victory, we should not fight a battle."[50] The guarantee of victory lies in concentrating greatly superior numbers at the critical point, and in surprise. Indeed "the peculiar quality of the operations of a guerrilla unit lies in taking the enemy by surprise."[51] All this depends upon the guerrillas moving quickly. Here the guerrillas' light armament becomes an advantage: "the great superiority of a small guerrilla unit lies in its mobility."[52] And hence "the sole habitual tactic of a guerrilla unit is the ambush."[53]

The vastness of the country and its poor communications greatly hampered the counterinsurgency efforts of the KMT. They also allowed Mao to develop his concept of the *secure regional base*: a remote area in which to build up and supply a regular army, and which also served as a laboratory for political and social experimentation.

In strategic terms, Mao envisioned that the anti-Japanese war would consist of three periods or stages. "The first stage covers the period of the enemy's strategic offensive and our strategic defensive. The second stage will be the period of the enemy's strategic consolidation and our preparation for the counter-offensive. The third stage will be the period of our strategic counter-offensive and the enemy's strategic retreat."[54]

How do guerrillas contribute to final victory in Mao's view? "The principal object of the action of a guerrilla unit lies in dealing the enemy the strongest possible blows to his morale, and in creating disorder and agitation in his rear, in drawing off his principal forces to the flanks or to the rear, in stopping or slowing down his operations, and ultimately in dissipating his fighting strength so that the enemy's units are crushed one by one [by conventional forces] and he is precipitated into a situation where, even by rapid and deceptive actions, he can neither advance nor retreat."[55] Or, in an oft-quoted summary: "The enemy advances, we retreat. The enemy encamps, we harass. The enemy tires, we attack. The enemy retreats, we pursue."[56]

Maoist tactics, no matter how intriguing or self-evident on paper, would have had no effect whatsoever without men and women to put them into practice. The golden age of Maoist guerrillas was the struggle against the Japanese during World War II. In that struggle, it was not the attractions of Communist ideology that produced recruits for Mao's guerrilla forces. Rather it was the barbarous behavior of the Imperial Japanese Army—barbarism partly provoked by the operations of Maoist guerrillas.

The activities of CCP guerrillas in north China, especially the famous Hundred Regiments Offensive (in late 1940), brought down the wrath of the Imperial Japanese Army upon the exposed peasantry. In committing their incredible atrocities in the Three-Alls campaign ("kill all, burn all, destroy all"), the IJA did not distinguish between peaceful and hostile peasants. It taught the peasants that there was simply no living with the Japanese, even if the peasants did not help the guerrillas, *even if they opposed the guerrillas.* The IJA thus compelled the peasantry to mobilize, to fight, driving them into the waiting arms of the Communist guerrillas. The Japanese army had been able to push the KMT forces out of vast areas, but in so doing it overextended itself to the point that it could not effectively repress the guerrilla bands behind Japanese lines, which were growing as a direct result of Japanese policy.[57] The annihilation campaigns of the Japanese not only increased hatred for them and made recruits for the Communists; they also severely limited the amount of economic strength the Japanese could derive from the areas they had occupied. Japanese brutality in China resembled German policy in Russia, and had similar consequences.

The IJA countered guerrilla attacks on its lines of communication with massive construction projects. To protect an important road or railway, the Japanese built broad ditches and walls on both sides, reinforced by fortified structures. They also thrust these new fortified roads directly into guerrilla-infested areas, cutting them up into sectors. By the end of 1942 the IJA had constructed over nine thousand miles of roads, thirty thousand blockhouses, and nine thousand forts.[58]

Partly as a response to IJA fortified-road tactics, the guerrillas built tunnels and tunnel complexes under and sometimes between villages, so that they could attack Japanese units from what at first appeared to be deserted villages. The tunnels also aided the guerrillas in escaping from encirclement efforts.

All this digging aside, after the Hundred Regiments Offensive, Communist forces did not engage heavily in fighting against the IJA.[59] This was partly from necessity, as the Communists were often poorly equipped. But the primary rationale for this passivity toward the Japanese was that the Communists were awaiting the end of the war, and the consequent great showdown with the KMT, whose forces they constantly attacked.[60] An IJA report from Kwantung in February 1944 stated that the guerrillas did not present much of a threat because they were intent on conserving their strength.[61] Moreover, as the end of World War II came clearly into view, the CCP began making overtures to the troops of the various Chinese collaborationist regimes. Precisely because the CCP refrained from attacks on areas occupied by such troops, the IJA turned more and more territory over to them, which of course freed Japanese soldiers for other duties.[62]

THE IJA IN CHINA

Mao Tse-tung established his reputation as a great guerrilla strategist mainly in fighting against the Imperial Japanese Army. But what is the actual validity of that criterion? Clearly, the IJA was strong enough to push the Nationalists out of Nanking and Shanghai all the way back to Chungking. But by any account the KMT army was no world-class organization, to say the very least. And yet despite all the shortcomings and mistakes of the KMT forces, the IJA was never able to force them into surrender or accommodation. But why not? What was the actual strength of the Imperial Japanese Army in China proper (excluding Manchukuo[63])? One distinguished study states that in 1937 the IJA totaled less than 1 million men, of whom about two-thirds were in China; by 1941 the IJA had twenty-seven divisions in China, out of a total of fifty-one, for about 1.1 million men.[64] Another authority states that there were only twenty-three divisions in China by late 1941.[65] *The Statesman's Yearbook 1944* estimates fourteen IJA divisions in China in late 1942.[66] Other authoritative sources suggest that Japanese troops in China and Manchukuo numbered between 1 million and 1.2 million, of which many were watching the Soviet border.[67] At the time of the surrender there may have been 950,000 IJA soldiers in China, most of poor quality.[68]

It appears not unreasonable, then, to conclude that the IJA in China proper never had many more than 1 million troops. One million soldiers to subdue and occupy a country of 480 million (85 percent of whom were rural): this would be the statistical equivalent of President Lincoln trying in 1861 to suppress the Confederate rebellion with an army of 19,000 men. Most of the Japanese forces were engaged in operations against the KMT army, not against the Communists. The grotesquely inadequate numbers of Japanese troops allowed space for Communist guerrillas to operate, anarchy to develop, and disillusionment to spread among those conservative Chinese who initially entertained some pro-Japanese sentiments.[69] Confronting these Japanese forces, the KMT began the war in 1937 with 1.5 million men, a number which increased to 5.7 million by 1941. Communist forces numbered about 440,000.

As the quantity of Japanese troops in China was insufficient, so too was their quality uneven. A substantial proportion of IJA forces in China were garrison units, not first-line combat troops. Their levels of training and discipline were, on the average, not impressive; Mao himself commented on the less-than-first-rate condition of his Japanese foes many times.[70] In 1939, the Soviet army was still reeling from the incredibly destructive Stalinist purges of its officer corps; soon that army would make a scandalously poor showing against little Finland. Yet—revealingly—when it clashed with this same Soviet army in Manchuria, during the so-called Nomonhan Incident in the summer of 1939, the IJA came off very badly.[71]

The fighting equipment of the Japanese also left much to be desired.[72] The standard-issue IJA rifle, copied from European models, was too long for the average Japanese soldier. This rifle, along with the IJA field artillery and most of their machine guns, was of World War I design.[73] As to mobility and armor, the Japanese forces on the mainland were no Nazi blitzkrieg force: "the army remained an infantry army, reliant on horses."[74] The standard IJA tank carried a 37mm gun; its armor was so thin that small-arms fire could penetrate it.[75] (In comparison, the Soviet T-34 medium tank carried a 76mm gun and 45mm of armor; the American Sherman tank had a 75mm gun and 75mm of armor.)[76]

Thus in terms of numbers, equipment, quality, and general ability to undertake effective counterinsurgency, the IJA against which Mao would make his reputation was notably inadequate. Nevertheless, the Imperial Japanese Army was able to inflict much damage on Communist forces.[77]

CIVIL WAR, CONTINUED

Soon after the surrender of Japan in August 1945, open civil war between Chiang's KMT regime and Mao's Communists inevitably resumed. Chiang and his associates committed one blunder after another. Desiring to take possession of the former Manchukuo before Mao's forces, Chiang rushed large units there, far from his wartime capital of Chungking. This overextension of the battered Nationalist army exposed it to Mao's favorite tactic: concentrating overwhelming force against a particular enemy unit. Moreover, KMT troops arriving in Manchukuo treated the collaborationist (Japanese puppet) soldiers there so badly that about 75,000 of them went over to the CCP.[78] By the fall of 1948 the protracted fighting in Manchuria had cost Chiang 400,000 soldiers.[79] Previously, as an economy measure, the KMT had demobilized 1.5 million men, including 200,000 officers; jobless and deeply embittered, many of these men also joined the Communists.[80]

The KMT reoccupied all the great cities of China just in time for the renewed civil war to increase food prices dramatically. Desperate, ravenous KMT soldiers engaged in extortion and even looting. The regime tried to pay its mounting costs by inflating the money supply. All this shocked and alienated the urban middle classes, traditional constituency of the KMT.[81] These drastic, even fatal, errors of the KMT had a simple root cause: a dozen years of fighting the warlords, the Japanese, and the Communists had physically and morally exhausted the KMT.

The rest of the story is quickly told: the Communists took Peking in January 1949 and Nanking the following April. Canton, cradle of the KMT, fell in October. The remnants of Chiang's government and army sought refuge on Taiwan.

The ultimate defeat of the Kuomintang resulted from the many burdens under which it labored. The first burden was the legacy of one hundred years of Chinese humiliation and disintegration; no party, no leader, could have healed those deep wounds in one decade. The second was the nature of the party's leading elements: the KMT was a bourgeois party in a peasant country. It was thus vulnerable to a well-organized group that would seek to mobilize the peasantry for revolution. The third burden consisted of the former warlords, careerists, and mercenaries who flocked into the KMT during the Northern Expedition. In his haste to unify the country, Chiang permitted the dilution of the original nationalist and revolutionary KMT to the point that it could no longer serve as an instrument of renewal. But the fourth burden was decisive: the Japanese invasion of 1937. It was not the attractions of Communist ideology or even the KMT's many shortcomings that produced Chiang's final defeat. Rather, it was the clear inability of the Nationalists to carry out their program of unity and independence—their inability to protect China, blindingly revealed and epitomized in the inconceivable savageries perpetrated by the Japanese army upon the men, women, and children of helpless Nanking, Chiang's chosen capital. As the Europeans had stripped the Mandate of Heaven from the Manchu Dynasty, so the Japanese stripped it from the Kuomintang.

SOME CONCLUSIONS

A review of some fundamental but often-ignored facts may sharpen this evaluation of the Maoist model of revolution.

On two occasions—in 1936 and in the early 1940s—the Communists were on the edge of destruction, first at the hands of the KMT and then of the Japanese, both of whom were prematurely diverted from their anti-guerrilla campaigns by developments in international affairs beyond their control.

In 1936 Chiang's forces had Mao and his party/army within their grasp. But then the Japanese invasion, by humiliating the KMT and providing operational space for Mao's guerrillas, saved Chinese Communism. Nevertheless, the Japanese inflicted many casualties on the guerrillas and could well have destroyed them as a serious force. The CCP survived primarily because of limitations on Japanese manpower—limitations severely aggravated when Japan became involved in war against the U.S. and Great Britain. And during the anti-Japanese war Mao all but abandoned his Communist program and stressed national unity. It would be impossible to overemphasize the importance of this latter point: Mao's movement presented itself as one of national resistance, not Leninist revolution.

Certainly, Mao played with consummate skill the cards that had been dealt him. None can deny that he emerged as one of the great guerrilla theorists and chieftains of history. But however sound his basic concepts—establish good relations with the civilian population, explain the political framework of the struggle to the troops, take advantage of interior lines to defeat the enemy piecemeal, treat prisoners humanely—they were neither original[82] nor arcane nor infallible. Since the triumph of the Communists in China, Maoist-style insurgencies have been contained or eliminated in Angola, Cambodia, Peru, Thailand, the Philippines (the New People's Army [NPA]), and elsewhere.[83] These defeats occurred primarily because Mao's would-be imitators in various areas of the world became the victims of a fatally incorrect understanding of why Mao had been able to achieve what he did.[84]

Quite aside from the special geographical, social, and political conditions of China, three aspects of the Maoist victory stand out as both essential and nonreplicable. First, Mao's enemies exhibited peculiar weaknesses that played directly into his strategy; the Japanese, with their alien ways, inadequate numbers, and savage tactics, were the best recruiting agents for the CCP. Second, it was the Americans, not the Chinese—and certainly not the Maoists—who caused the surrender of the Japanese Empire. Third, after the end of World War II, establishing Maoist control over China required years of hard fighting between massive conventional armies, pitting Mao's forces against a regime already devastated militarily and morally by the Japanese invasion and occupation and never fully in command of its own armed forces.

AN ACCOUNTING

No one can know how differently history would have played out if the KMT had defeated or stalemated the CCP after 1945. But, at the very least, without Mao's victory it is difficult to imagine how there would have been a Korean War, with its 900,000 Chinese casualties, or why the Americans would have gone into Vietnam. Certainly the people of China would have escaped Mao's economic Great Leap Forward: "The national catastrophe of the Great Leap Forward in 1958–1960 was directly due to Chairman Mao. In the end some twenty to thirty million people lost their lives through malnutrition and famine because of the policies imposed upon them by the CCP."[85] This figure represents "more Chinese than died in all the famines of the preceding one hundred years."[86] In addition, Maoism brought the Great Proletarian Cultural Revolution, whose "undeniable madness"[87] led to more millions of deaths, the burning down of the British and Indonesian embassies by mobs of young Red Guards, and the irredeemable destruction of much of the priceless patrimony of Chinese culture.[88] On one level, Mao's military victory over the KMT represented the forcible imposition of Leninist/Stalinist concepts and policies, barely thirty years old, on the four thousand-year-old culture of China. On another level, it signaled the victory of rural, heartland China over urban, maritime China. Therein are the keys to understanding why thirty years of Maoist Communism failed to make China a modern country, while Taiwan, South Korea, Singapore, Hong Kong—even Malaysia—surged forward, and Japan became an economic superpower. Mao believed that "only people infected with the evils of bourgeois materialism could want an improved standard of living."[89] In 1989, forty years after Mao proclaimed the People's Republic, Chinese government figures revealed that 100 million people in the western provinces suffered from malnutrition, while 220 million people (70 percent of them women) over the age of fourteen did not know how to read or write.[90]

CHAPTER 15

Two False Starts:
Venezuela and Thailand

During the 1960s, for reasons that may be difficult to comprehend today, the Communist Parties in Venezuela and Thailand decided to launch guerrilla insurgencies against their respective governments. The outcomes of these decisions were quite unexpected, especially to those who had made them.

Venezuela

Venezuela is three times the size of Poland, larger than Texas and Oklahoma combined. In the early 1960s, the population was about 7.5 million. Much of the national territory, especially in the south and east, was sparsely populated.[1]

In 1958, after helping to oust a military dictatorship, the reformer Rómulo Betancourt won the Venezuelan presidency in a free election. According to many analysts (notably Ernesto Guevara),[2] it is not possible to stage a successful popular revolution against a democratic government; nevertheless, the Venezuelan Communist Party, with between 30,000 and 40,000 members (hardly a mass movement), determined that that the time was propitious for a Communist revolution in that country.

Venezuela was a society of ominous social disparities aggravated by high unemployment. The country had a long tradition of successful revolts, but no sustained experience with representative democracy. In return for cooperating with the recently ousted dictator Marcos Perez Jimenez, the Communists had been allowed to take control of many labor unions.[3] They could also count on money, arms, and training from Castro's Cuba. President Betancourt himself was unpopular in Caracas, the nerve center of the nation, as well as in certain conservative army circles. At the same time, Betancourt's insistence on observance of civil rights guaranteed Communists freedom of travel and communication, as well as the right to organize within the precincts of the Central University of Caracas, into which the police were forbidden to go. Neither could the police fingerprint anybody under the age of eighteen. And they lacked cars with radios until late 1963.

Between late 1960 and early 1963, the Communists carried out their "Rapid Victory" campaign, intended to seize control of Caracas and other cities through terror, rioting, robberies, and sniper attacks. Most of the perpetrators of these acts were university and high school students. (Two small, uncoordinated mutinies at military bases were easily put down.) Young Communists went to the countryside to convert the peasants. Instead, the peasants turned them over to the authorities.

The Communists then decided to disrupt the December 1963 presidential elections. Their guerrilla arm, the FALN (Armed Forces of National Liberation), warned that anyone found out of doors on election day, even women, would be shot down.[4] Nevertheless, 91 percent of the registered electorate went to the polls, only two points down from the 1958 turnout.[5]

After this humiliating rebuff, the party turned to rural insurgency, which it undertook in late 1963. The Venezuelan army did not move in sufficient strength against the guerrillas to eradicate them, giving them time to become familiar with terrain and population. However, Betancourt's Democratic Action Party had been organizing the peasantry in most of the countryside for decades; thus the insurgents found little space for recruitment. Moreover, the army had established good relations with the rural population, and on the whole treated prisoners humanely. The Communists' attempts to get a foothold within the rural population were further handicapped by their identification with unpopular foreign states. Finally, and perhaps most importantly, the government gave the coup de grâce to any possibility of a serious guerrilla war by carrying out an extensive land reform.[6] In 1966, Fidel Castro deposited some of his own guerrillas on the Venezuelan coast in an attempt to support the Communists' insurgency. Nothing much came of this move, however, except a further deflation of the myth of the exportable Fidelista revolution. Ultimately, the Venezuelan insurgency faded away, so that by 1969 the country was free of any notable guerrilla activity.

At the same time, an even more impressive failure of Communist insurgency was taking shape literally on the opposite side of the globe, in Southeast Asia.

THAILAND

Thailand has an area of two hundred thousand square miles, the size of Spain, or of Colorado and Wyoming combined. During the 1960s, Thailand looked to some like a good venue for a successful, or at least very troublesome, Communist insurgency, in light of its unique geography and population disparities. The country had long borders with Communist states, and at its nearest point is less than seventy miles from China. Living along extensive segments of these borders were unassimilated ethnic minorities who displayed notable social and economic inequalities with the majority Thai population. During the late 1950s Thai Communists had received training in China, North Vietnam, and Laos, and obtained material aid through offshoots of the famed Ho Chi Minh Trail.[7] At the same time the government in Bangkok did not react with much vigor in the early stages of the Communist insurgency, being habituated to a certain amount of dissidence and even internal violence. The government also found it impossible to believe that the Thai people would find any significant appeal in Communism.[8] In light of all these factors, it is not surprising that an experienced student of Southeast Asian politics should have concluded in the early 1970s that "Thailand's counterinsurgency record to date does not inspire confidence that she will be able to meet this [challenge]."[9]

But as it turned out, the Communist insurgency in Thailand had considerably more weaknesses than strengths. In the first place, the country had never in modern times been colonized; hence the insurgents could not fly the attractive banner of national independence against a foreign overlord. This was extremely significant, because no Communist party had ever come to power on its own without being able to drape itself, however incongruously and uncomfortably, with the robe of nationalism.[10]

Thailand also possessed two powerful and popular institutions: Buddhism and the monarchy. The 1980 census recorded 95 percent of Thais as Buddhists, and 3.8 percent as Muslims.[11] In 1932 young army officers and civil servants, many of whom had studied in Europe, carried out a bloodless coup d'état that transformed the absolute monarchy into a constitutional one. This turned out to be a very fortunate change indeed, for the monarchy and the country both.[12]

Communist popular appeal also encountered severe limitations because, unlike in other countries where insurgencies flourished, 70 percent of Thai farmers owned at least some of the land that they tilled;

partly for this reason "there has been little class friction in the country-side."[13] Yet while the great majority of the population was rural, all the members of the Thai Communist Party politburo came from urban middle-class or elite backgrounds.[14] In addition, the country had relatively few intellectuals whom the Communists could recruit as a membership base; moreover, most intellectuals shared in the national ethos, and they had long since been integrated into government service.[15] Another barrier to Communist appeal was the widely noted disinclination of Thais to entertain abstract schemes and ideas.[16]

Perhaps the biggest albatross around the neck of the Communist Party in Thailand was its association with particular ethnic and racial groups. The earliest Communists in Thailand appear to have been Chinese, sent into the country from China. And Ho Chi Minh himself had lived in Thailand from circa 1928 to 1930.[17] The first efforts to build a Communist Party in Thailand focused on Chinese and Vietnamese living in the country. The party's peculiar ethnic flavor was a significant hindrance to its growth, because "prior to World War II, the most stigmatized ethnic identity in Thailand was that of the Chinese."[18] Ironically, the Chinese minority in Thailand was both economically prosperous and socially vulnerable, and therefore uninterested in supporting a Communist revolution.[19] The Communists also sought, with very limited success, to promote separatism among the eight million Thai of Lao ethnic origin.[20]

Aside from its identification with ethnic minorities and national disintegration, Communism was also linked with foreign enemies in the minds of many Thais: "from the 1954 Geneva Conference onwards Thailand has been fearful that the power obtained by the Viet Minh in North Viet Nam and the Pathet Lao . . . in Laos might be difficult to contain."[21] That is, Communism represented the potential for invasion and/or dismemberment of Thailand at the hands of traditional enemies.[22] Hence the Thai government has consistently taken an anticommunist stance. It supported the French in Indochina and the British in Malaya. It recognized the Nationalist regime on Taiwan, and allowed the KMT to maintain a Chinese-language radio station in Thailand and mount operations into China.[23] Thai troops participated in the Korean War, and in 1954 Thailand vigorously welcomed the Southeast Asia Treaty Organization; indeed Bangkok became the headquarters of SEATO. The presence of the U.S. Air Force at four major Thai air bases unmistakably symbolized Thailand's foreign policy orientation during the 1960s.[24]

The Thai Communist Party Rising

Sometime during 1963 or 1964, the politburo of the Thai Communist Party decided to launch an insurgency by 1965, even though membership in the party was probably less than one thousand.[25] (The decision of the Mao Tse-tung regime to aid the Thai insurgency predates the Thai government's involvement in the Vietnam war.)[26] In addition to foreign assistance, Communist guerrillas obtained money from government officials and road builders in exchange for peace and protection. The first notable armed clash of the insurgency occurred in August 1965 in Thailand's northeast region, along the Mekong River border with Laos.

The Thai Communists adopted a version of classic Maoist strategy, with its fundamental concept that in a successful insurgency "the countryside surrounds the cities." This orientation ruled out expending very much effort in the Bangkok area, which was where millions of Thais lived and the center of everything important. Insurgent activities also displayed considerable decentralization, both because of the difficulty of communications and because the regions of Thailand varied a great deal in ethnic composition and of course in proximity to frontiers, especially Communist ones. The regions of especially notable guerrilla activity were the north, the far south, and the northeast.

The northern region shared mountainous borders with Laos and Burma. Serious fighting broke out there in 1967.[27] Here the guerrillas sometimes operated in battalion size, using weapons they received from the outside.[28]

The southern region, perhaps the most backward in the country, bordered Malaya, scene of a Communist insurgency in the 1940s and 1950s. Most of this region's population were Muslim Malays. The Thai guerrillas in the region received cooperation and guidance from two thousand veteran Malayan guerrillas living illegally in Thai territory.[29]

The Thai government did not establish real control over the northeastern region until the late nineteenth century. Densely populated, one of the poorest areas of the country, and bordering Laos, the region became the center of the Communist insurgency. Combining persuasion and terror, the insurgents gathered recruits in remote villages of this region where a government presence had always been intermittent or nonexistent.

Thai Counterinsurgency

The Thai military's initial response to the insurgency in 1965–1966 was quite heavy-handed, featuring sweep operations supported by artillery. The Thai army responded to ambushes by calling down air and artillery strikes, which often caused casualties among largely non-Thai ethnic minorities. As late as January 1972 the army launched a huge, two-month search-and-destroy operation near the Laos border that accomplished very little except for generating 260 army casualties, mainly from booby traps, while the guerrillas escaped into Laos.[30]

At the same time the government sought to defeat the guerrillas through projects for "economic development," but this expensive program seemed to have little effect. Indeed, those areas that received the most investment were also the areas of the most numerous guerrilla incidents. One problem with economic development efforts apparently lay in the fact that the government would arrive in a province or village and tell the inhabitants what it intended to do for them, rather than ascertaining what the people themselves actually wanted or needed.

The government also tried resettlement among the 260,000 members of the hill tribes, of which 50,000 were Meo (also known as Hmong), mainly in the North.[31] This effort proceeded badly; serious armed clashes occurred with the Meo, and the combination of coercion and resentment predictably resulted in guerrilla reinfiltration among these peoples.[32]

In spite of these initial errors, a sound counterinsurgency program was germinating within the Thai army. To assist the U.S. during the Vietnam conflict, the Thais had maintained in that country a full infantry division, the Black Panthers, along with support troops and naval units. This Black Panther Division returned from Vietnam with its own ideas about what to do and not to do in effective counterinsurgency.[33] Army leaders developed a strategy based on blanketing target areas with troops, uprooting the guerrilla infrastructure, building militia groups, sending out special units to harass the guerrillas, and improving physical conditions in the villages.[34]

The Thai army kept draftees in their home area and in the same unit for the two-year conscription period.[35] Compare the situation in South Vietnam: "Few steps the [Communist] Party could have taken would have been so effective in crippling the morale and effectiveness of the [South Vietnamese] government's military forces as was the government's own decision to adopt a policy of nonlocal service."[36]

The army also rejected American-style body counts as a way of measuring progress in the conflict. Instead of corpses, the army counted the number of surrendered enemy personnel.[37]

A key aspect of Thai counterinsurgency was the realization that great sweep operations accomplish little against guerrillas, who can evade them, but produce much suffering and resentment among civilians, who cannot. The return of the Black Panther Division from Vietnam undoubtedly helped produce the change in emphasis from sweeps to security. The guerrillas clearly were flourishing in areas where there was no state presence; there, villagers had been ignored by the government and were helpless before the insurgents.[38] To counter the guerrillas by increasing security in these areas, the government began to set up village militias (Village Security Teams, or VST), organized around a small group of permanently-stationed police. As the villagers began to see for themselves that the Communists were no longer winning, they became more willing to provide government forces with information. Consequently the Communists turned increasingly to terrorism, further alienating civilians. The government also began settling contested areas with ex-soldiers, many of them veterans of action in Laos, and their families. The Thais were thus evolving a strategy of "counterinsurgency as countermobilization"[39]—strengthening local organization around religious and traditional groups and peasant conservatism.

Concomitantly with these sound military developments, the Thai government strove to coordinate civilian, police, and military efforts in combating the insurgency.[40] It also wisely offered surrendered or captured guerrillas vocational training in its national Open Arms and Rehabilitation program.[41]

The End

In the fall of 1976, the Communists began openly to vilify the person of the monarch, the thirty-nine-year-old King Bhumibol. Previously, the popularity of the king had persuaded the Communists to avoid any serious criticism of him. This new anti-monarchical stance, along with growing party hostility toward Buddhism, seriously damaged the Thai Communists' already limited ability to attract support. By 1979, at the height of their strength, Communist guerrillas numbered perhaps thirteen thousand (with five thousand of these in the northeast), exercising some degree of control over approximately two million people.[42] Things were about to change in a decidedly negative direction.

Students of revolution have pointed out the close connection between the success of a country's revolutionary movement and that country's external relations, especially if they recently involved military defeat and/or foreign occupation. Events in Thailand offer an arresting example of this relationship.[43] By 1976 knowledge about the dreadful events in Pol Pot's Cambodia was becoming widespread. Indeed the northeast, which should have been the best recruiting ground for the Thai Communist insurgency, received the bulk of refugees fleeing the Communist regimes in Laos and Cambodia.[44] In September 1978 Vietnamese premier Pham Van Dong made a five-day visit to Thailand and promised that his government would not support insurgency in that country. Two months later the Vietnamese army invaded Cambodia and brushed aside Pol Pot's army. This move brought to life a basic strategic nightmare of the Thais: Vietnamese military power on their borders. Yet the Vietnamese closed down Thai Communist bases in Cambodia, because the Thai Communist Party took China's side in its growing hostility toward Vietnam (there may have been as many as 1,500 Thai guerrillas inside Cambodia at that time).[45] Then in January 1979 Laos, also under Vietnamese control, expelled most Thai guerrillas within its borders. The Sino-Vietnamese War of 1979 deeply split the Thai Party, but on the whole it publicly supported the Chinese side. Nevertheless, by the late 1970s the Chinese for their own reasons wanted improved relations with Thailand; hence Beijing cut off the aid that had previously been going to the guerrillas. Indeed in November 1978 Deng Xiaoping visited Thailand, and at his own request attended the Buddhist ordination of the crown prince. All this was of course disastrous for Thai Communism, always much more dependent on outside help than other Southeast Asian parties.[46]

The predictable denouement followed fairly quickly. "Early in 1981 the first groups of Communist guerrillas surrendered to Government forces, to be welcomed back into Thai society. That message had its desired effect, and additional larger groups started to surrender, also to be welcomed back with honour and the gift of good farming land."[47] By early 1982, there were fewer than 4,000 guerrillas nationwide, with but 800 in the northeast (down from 5,000 in 1979).[48] Opposed to these were 170,000 militia in the northeast alone, and perhaps 20,000 paramilitary Border Patrol Police.[49] There were also about 13,000 rangers, recruited from militia and former regular army personnel.[50] Backing up these forces was the Royal Thai Army with 141,000 personnel, the air force with 43,000, and the navy with 28,000.[51] In the beginning of 1982 the Communist Party headquarters and main guerrilla base in the Khao Khor mountain area[52] fell to the Thai army. For all practical purposes any serious Communist threat to Thailand had ceased to exist.

REFLECTION

From beginning to end, these two cases of failed insurgency reveal the most serious miscalculations on the most fundamental issues of strategy.

In Venezuela, everything worked against the guerrillas. The army remained cohesive in support of the civilian president. The U.S. provided counterinsurgency training. Oil money paid for land reform. Free and democratic elections provided a peaceful path to change, thereby heading off the alliance of revolutionaries with the middle class that had occurred in Cuba and Nicaragua.

In Thailand, despite having for years enjoyed outside assistance and cross-border sanctuaries, despite the existence of substantial ethnic minorities all to some degree disaffected from mainstream Thai society, the Thai Communists were not able to overcome, or even survive, their fundamental handicaps. Primary among these were, first, the impossibility of the party to assume the mantle of an oppressed Thai nationalism; second, the existence of strong and popularly rooted national institutions, notably the Buddhist religion and the monarchy (which the Communists chose to attack); third, an unavoidably close association in the popular consciousness between Communism and the Chinese minority in Thailand; fourth, the identification of the Thai Communists with foreign powers traditionally deemed dangerous; fifth, the abandonment of Thai Communism by those same foreign powers in the late 1970s; and sixth, certainly by no means least, the sensible and effective counterinsurgency tactics eventually adopted by the Royal Thai Army.

CHAPTER 16

COMPARING NATIONAL APPROACHES TO COUNTERINSURGENCY

This section offers a brief, comparative analytical overview of several general national approaches to, or styles of, counterinsurgency: those of the French, British, Chinese, Japanese, Russians/Soviets, Portuguese, and Americans.

THE FRENCH

During the French Revolutionary and Napoleonic Wars, France faced two major guerrilla conflicts. One of these raged along her own Atlantic coast, in the Vendée and Brittany, the other in Spain.[1] The regime both provoked and protracted these insurgencies, first by outraging the religious sentiments of generally law-abiding peasants, and then by unleashing systematic violence against them.

At first failing to gauge correctly the seriousness of the rebellion in the Vendée, the Revolutionary regime in Paris soon embarked upon a campaign of extermination similar to that of the Soviets in Afghanistan. The government employed overwhelming numbers of troops against the Vendean rebels, who received no substantial foreign assistance. Nevertheless, in return for laying down their arms, the insurgents succeeded in extracting major concessions from the regime. Years later they took their full vengeance on the heirs of the Revolution by contributing notably to Napoleon's defeat at Waterloo.[2]

The French had succeeded in isolating the Vendean rebels from foreign help. In dramatic contrast, Spain became the testing ground of the future Duke of Wellington. British troops and supplies poured into the peninsula, and the conflict became the bleeding ulcer of the Napoleonic system: more French and Imperial troops perished in Spain than in Russia.[3] Again in contrast to the Vendée, the French never employed enough troops in Spain to achieve even superficial pacification. Those forces the French had there, moreover, never received proper operational coordination, nor did they develop effective counterinsurgency tactics. Even with these major differences, the two French counterinsurgency campaigns display certain glaring similarities. These include notable tendencies both to underestimate their opponents and to abuse the civil population—practices that proved extremely costly to the French regime.

During the nineteenth century, France engaged in several sizable colonial conflicts. Out of these wars three major figures emerged in the field of French counterinsurgency: Robert-Thomas Bugeaud (1784–1849), Joseph Gallieni (1849–1916), and Louis Lyautey (1854–1934).

A veteran of the Napoleonic disaster in Spain, Bugeaud became governor-general and commander in chief in Algeria in 1840. The demoralized French forces there had been notably unsuccessful against Muslim insurgents. Bugeaud soon rekindled the offensive spirit of the troops, but he also pursued a policy of punishing civilians for acts committed by guerrillas. Raping at will, burning fields, destroying orchards, killing hundreds of unarmed civilians, his troops indulged in an "orgy of brutality and excess" that both offended public opinion in France and corroded the discipline of the troops.[4]

Joseph Gallieni was the father of the famous "oil stain" metaphor for counterinsurgency, whereby beginning from secure bases the French would slowly extend outward their control over a restless territory. A major element of this oil-stain method was that soon after military occupation came civil administration, with the aim of attracting native support by promoting peace, prosperity, and justice. Gallieni developed and applied these concepts with great success in Senegal, Tonkin, and Madagascar. His already distinguished career reached its culmination when as military governor of Paris in 1914 he played a key role in the crucial French victory on the Marne.

During the earlier phases of his career, Louis Lyautey, conqueror and governor of Morocco, had published some perceptive articles on the subject of colonial pacification and administration. He urged that the person in charge of the military conquest of an area should be designated the future civil governor, in order to inhibit needless damage to the economic life of the area being occupied. He believed that French rule in Africa would liberate the native peoples from interethnic violence and from their oppressive and extortionate traditional rulers, while it respected local customs and forms and especially the Muslim religion. In short, Lyautey was an evangel of *la mission civilisatrice*,

France's mission to bring civilization to less fortunate peoples. Nevertheless, for all his exalted rhetoric, Lyautey eventually showed himself to be quite as prepared as other French colonial commanders to respond to rebellion with brutality. "If [French troops] could not punish the guilty, they would punish whom they could."[5]

It is in light of these experiences that one must view the French effort in Vietnam, a classic, textbook example of an incorrect and unsuccessful approach to counterinsurgency.[6] In Vietnam the French confronted a massive challenge with which neither the Americans in the post-1898 Philippines nor the British in Malaya had had to contend. That challenge was the presence of a newly Communist China right across the frontier, eager to provide substantial and perhaps decisive assistance to the Viet Minh. But the Chinese did not become a direct factor in the Vietnam war until 1949, after the conflict had been going on for almost three years.

To hold onto Vietnam, or at least important parts of it, the French needed either to reach some agreement with the Viet Minh, or show that the Viet Minh could not defeat them. Making peace with the Viet Minh would have involved either cutting a deal to preserve French interests in return for recognizing Vietnamese independence under the Viet Minh, and withdrawing French forces, or offering to share power with the Viet Minh until French withdrawal at some future date.

Since the French opted for war, it was imperative for them (1) to keep the Chinese border shut, through military and/or diplomatic means. To accomplish this essential task, it was necessary either (2) to send substantial reinforcements from France and the Empire, or (3) to raise an authentic indigenous army, properly officered, trained, and equipped, or to do both. A subsidiary but nevertheless very important step would have been (4) to redress some of the main socioeconomic grievances of the peasantry. Finally, if unwilling either to send enough French forces or to build a real native army, and consequently finding themselves unable to hold the northern border, then the only sound recourse for the French would have been (5) to retrench into their base areas in the Red River Delta and Cochin China. As it turned out, the French adopted none of these courses.

To these fundamental failures one must add two venerable practices of French counterinsurgency—easily visible as well in its earlier efforts in the Vendée, in Spain, and in North Africa—that helped make the Viet Minh victory possible. These were, first, collective punishment of the civilian population, as displayed in the scandalous and bloody naval bombardment of the defenseless port of Haiphong, and, second, persistence in underestimating the enemy—the cardinal sin of the soldier—which led to the debacle of Dien Bien Phu.[7]

And so the French lost the war.

Almost immediately after their defeat in Indochina the French faced a new insurgency in Algeria.[8] In contrast to their policies in Vietnam, during the Algerian conflict the French deployed troops in abundance; deprived the rebels of almost all outside aid; and vigorously sought, with significant success, to mobilize popular support among the Arab population. Notwithstanding all the faults of the colonial regime, the French were able to mobilize more Algerians than the insurgent National Liberation Front (FLN) did. Consequently, the French militarily defeated the Algerian insurgents, even though the latter eventually received control of the country through political decisions in Paris. Thus, while not perfectly comparable to the very successful British effort in Malaya and in polar contrast to the experience in Indochina, French counterinsurgency in Algeria provides at least in certain respects a model of effective counterinsurgency.

THE BRITISH

One of the most notable, and unsuccessful, British conflicts with insurgents occurred in the Carolinas during the American War of Independence.[9] But modern British counterinsurgency technique and strategy developed principally during the half-century preceding the outbreak of World War II. Three characteristics of the British Empire were especially relevant to that development. Of first importance, its far-flung territories included peoples of many different races and religions, elements of which rose from time to time in armed rebellion against British control. Second, the standing military forces available to Imperial Britain were never large. (The great exception to this condition was of course the Boer War.)[10] Third, but not least, Britain was in those years transforming itself into a political democracy. Constantly confronted with faraway rebellions, severely limited in the number of troops available to them, reliant on Parliament for both soldiers and supplies, British strategists developed a policy of restricting the use of conventional military force to the minimum level possible. Consequently it was desirable, indeed imperative, to recruit soldiers from among the local peoples, both to augment available manpower and to obtain useful intelligence about the nature of the particular rebellion they faced. In addition, British authorities were often ready to consider that a colonial uprising might derive to some degree from legitimate grievances which they should try to address.[11]

All these factors helped eventually to produce a British style of counterinsurgency consisting of a locally variable mix of the following principles: (1) employ conventional military force sparingly and selectively (in contrast to the French tendency to resort quickly to general punishment and intimidation, and to the American reliance in Vietnam on indiscriminantly destructive technology); (2) emphasize the central role of police measures and civil administration in counterinsurgency; (3) establish the closest cooperation among the military, the police, and the civil government, especially with regard to sharing intelligence; (4) regroup exposed civilian settlements into more secure and defensible areas where feasible; (5) deny the guerrillas a reliable supply of food (the Malayan campaign saw special emphasis on this technique); (6) harass guerrilla base areas with small, highly trained units; and (7) identify and ameliorate major sociocultural irritants.[12]

These principles showed their effectiveness in the Malayan conflict following World War II; indeed Malaya became a textbook example of successful counterinsurgency.[13] Nevertheless, certain peculiarities of that struggle limit to a degree the relevance of its lessons to other conflicts. Perhaps the most salient of those peculiarities was Malayan geography, which made it easy for the British to prevent outside help from reaching the insurgents. Another was the reflex hostility of the ethnic Malay majority to the essentially Chinese insurgency. A third peculiarity of the Malayan conflict was British awareness that retention of Malaya was neither strategically nor psychologically vital to the survival of the British state, so that the authorities could move quickly toward granting Malaya independence.

THE CHINESE

An impressive continuity characterizes Chinese counterinsurgency strategy from 1850 to 1950. During the 1930s, the nationalist/restorationist Kuomintang (KMT) regime under Chiang Kai-shek waged repeated and very damaging campaigns against the Chinese Communists. In these campaigns the KMT deliberately sought to imitate the techniques employed by the Ch'ing Dynasty against the Taiping rebellion (1850–1864) and the Nien rebellion (1853–1868).[14]

In dealing with the Taiping, the Ch'ing retrained their ineffective armies, ruthlessly exterminated rebel leaders, and granted amnesty to most of the others. During the Nien conflict, the Ch'ing also deprived the rebels of food by erecting walls around countless villages, hampered rebel mobility with cordons of fortifications, and weaned civilian support away from the Nien through benevolent administration.

The essence of Ch'ing counterinsurgency strategy thus consisted of conciliation of the population in affected areas, strategic blockades and encirclement, food deprivation, and amnesty. The Ch'ing placed major emphasis on good leadership (Napoleon said there are no bad soldiers, only bad officers). Like the KMT after them, the Ch'ing produced some effective leaders at the highest levels but suffered from a lack of good field-grade officers. Peasants could not become officers, and the cultural values of the upper classes hindered their ability to become effective field commanders.

In its campaigns against the Communists during the 1930s, the KMT employed all the methods developed by the Ch'ing and added to them co-option (often premature and superficial) of warlord troops into the KMT armies, a variant of Ch'ing amnesty policies.[15] The KMT also made use of strategic blockade in the form of extensive lines of blockhouses, which successfully contained the guerrillas and then evicted them from their strongholds.

The great size, widespread poverty, and primitive transportation infrastructure of China, which had limited the counterinsurgent operations of the Ch'ing and the KMT, also affected their Communist successors. During the 1950s the Maoist regime faced a major national uprising in Tibet. In the manner of the Ch'ing and the KMT, the Communists built roads to facilitate the movement and supply of troops into rough and remote terrain. But otherwise, Communist counterinsurgency policies in Tibet contrasted grimly with those of their predecessors. The Beijing regime suffocated Tibet under huge numbers of troops, caused the deaths of countless thousands of civilians, and deliberately sought to destroy the structure and values of Tibetan society.[16]

THE JAPANESE

During the 1930s and 1940s, the Imperial Japanese Army fought guerrillas in Malaya, the Philippines, Burma, and Manchuria, as well as in China proper. In Manchuria (where the guerrillas often cultivated opium), after the initial failure of their wide sweep operations, the Japanese developed effective techniques of counterinsurgency. During the harsh Manchurian winters small groups of around fifty volunteers hunted guerrillas, who possessed no real sanctuary. These Japanese guerrilla-hunters operated out of caves or wooden blockhouses, which they had erected and stocked with supplies during the summer. In wintertime leafless trees offered inadequate shelter to guerrillas. They also suffered increasingly from lack of supplies, owing to Japanese efforts to concentrate the civil population (estimated at 5.5 million in 1938) and restrict the purchase and movement of food.[17] The Japanese built roads and railroads to increase the mobility of their limited numbers, replaced corrupt local officials, and directed propaganda toward the peasantry. Decent treatment of prisoners induced guerrillas to surrender, and sometimes these ex-guerrillas would join counterinsurgent units or act as spies. By such means the Japanese cleared the guerrillas out of large areas of Manchuria, driving many into the USSR, including the future dictator of North Korea, Kim Il Sung.[18] According to Japanese estimates, the number of Manchurian guerrillas fell from 120,000 in 1933 to 20,000 in 1937.

In China proper, Japense operations were seriously hindered by inadequate numbers. Their efforts focused primarily on holding key points and the lines of communications between them, with only an occasional large operation against guerrilla areas. To mitigate their numerical deficiency, the Japanese built thirty thousand strongpoints (reminiscent of British practice during the Boer War), intended mainly to protect troops from small arms fire and grenades, since the guerrillas almost never had artillery.[19] They also relied on the various Chinese puppet regimes to produce armies. But fearing that these puppet troops might one day defect to the KMT, the Japanese strictly limited their numbers, training, and equipment. These conditions resulted in inadequate control in the puppet states and thus provided scope for guerrillas.

The Japanese paid relatively little serious attention to political means of counterinsurgency and imposed group responsibility and collective punishment on peasant communities. Responding to the Communists' so-called Hundred Regiments Campaign in north China, in early 1941 the Japanese launched the infamous Three-Alls (*sanko-seisaku*) operation: Kill all, burn all, destroy all. This was aimed less at the guerrillas than at the peasantry from whom they derived sustenance. Japanese troops would surround a given area and then kill every living thing in it: people, animals, crops, trees. The Three-Alls campaign obliterated the distinction among friend, neutral, and enemy, and thus forced many peasants into the arms of the Communist guerrillas. Only a lack of troops and time prevented the campaign from being even more savagely destructive than it actually was.[20] Nevertheless, "even given their lack of understanding of what was politico-military good sense in northern China, the Japanese and their puppet forces came close in 1941–1942 to breaking the links between the Red Army and the peasantry."[21]

In the end, the subjugation of Manchuria and China was beyond Japan's capacity. China was too big, Japanese numbers too small (as with the Nazis in Russia). The overriding concern to destroy the KMT armies, the need to guard the dangerous Soviet border, and then the all-consuming Pacific War prevented the Japanese from making a priority of counterinsurgency in China. In addition, Japanese aims there were so exploitative and their methods so brutal as to be self-defeating.

THE RUSSIANS AND THE SOVIETS

The Russian/Soviet experience in counterinsurgency probably most familiar to the West is the Afghanistan War of 1979–1988. But for generations before that conflict, long before the Bolshevik Revolution, the Russian state was amassing experience in similar types of struggles. During most of the nineteenth century the Czarist Empire, constantly occupying new territories from the Caucasus to Central Asia, was actively suppressing often very large guerrilla uprisings in those regions. Here the Russians developed their basic formula for defeating guerrillas: (1) deploy great numbers of troops into the disaffected area; (2) isolate that area from outside assistance; (3) establish tight control of central cities or major towns first and then extend domination outward from these (a variation of Gallieni's "oil-stain" doctrine); (4) build successive lines of forts, thus constricting the enemy's movements into an ever-smaller area; and (5) dry up the springs of resistance by the destruction of settlements, livestock, crops, and orchards.[22]

The Soviet regime acquired its own extensive experience with campaigns against insurgencies, which usually took the form of national independence movements. Major instances of these flared in Daghestan and other Caucasian regions, Central Asia, western Siberia, the Ukraine (after World War I and World War II), and Lithuania. Most often, popular hostility to Communist agricultural collectivization and religious persecution ignited these insurgencies. In the 1920s and 1930s, Soviet counterinsurgency technique included systematic assassination of insurgent leaders; the imposition of collective guilt, which sought to discourage resistance through exemplary massacres of local civilians; hostage-taking from among family heads; and permanent mass deportation of civilians. During the counterinsurgency in the Ukraine after 1918, two hundred thousand peasants died and one hundred thousand families were deported.

Mikhail Tukhachevsky (1893–1937), a one-time Czarist officer, has been called the father of Soviet counterinsurgency. During the 1920s his astute prescription for counterinsurgent forces emphasized creating an integrated political-military command, showing respect for local cultures, offering timely amnesties, and recruiting former guerrillas. Soviet ideology nevertheless severely hampered the application of these sound concepts by requiring Tukhachevsky to endorse collective guilt and mass deportation, as well as the position that anti-Bolshevik rebellions must have been fomented by foreign agents and "kulaks." Having attained the rank of marshal, Tukhachevsky died in one of Stalin's purges.[23]

Toward the end of World War II, guerrilla insurgencies confronted Moscow in Lithuania and the Ukraine.[24] Without sanctuaries, isolated from and ignored by the outside world, these uprisings were suffocated by Soviet troops and hordes of the dreaded political police, the successors to Lenin's Cheka. Between 1944 and 1952 the Stalinist regime deported 350,000 Lithuanians. It also deported 600,000 Chechens aboard cattle trains without sanitation, so that many died of typhus, and more died of hunger and exposure in the areas in which they were eventually dumped.[25] But since serious revolts against the Communist regime by Soviet peoples were officially unthinkable, and therefore top secret, the Soviet army and its successors were unable to derive and preserve much of value from the experience of these conflicts.

Up to 1979, the principal aspects of Soviet counterinsurgency style included committing great numbers of soldiers and secret police, shutting off the rebellious area from the outside world, and directing campaigns of mass terror against civilians. Yet, following their invasion of Afghanistan in late 1979, the Soviets deployed troops in numbers quite inadequate to deal with the massive popular uprising that confronted them. At least in part because of this numerical inadequacy, the Soviets failed—in contravention of tried-and-true Czarist and Communist practice—to isolate Afghanistan from the outside world. This failure proved to be fateful, because once the insurgents began receiving sophisticated weapons from outside in some quantity, the Soviets had neither the technological superiority nor the numerical sufficiency to defeat or even contain them. Thus, in the Afghan conflict the Soviets employed only one element of their traditional strategy: the unrestrained devastation of Afghan civilian society, a course of action that inflamed the native populations and also aroused the anger of the Muslim world.[26]

The failure of its counterinsurgency in Afghanistan in the 1980s presaged the collapse of the Soviet Union. In the 1990s the successor Russian Federation confronted "one of the greatest epics of colonial resistance of the past century,"[27] the uprising of the Chechens, who numbered less than three-quarters of a million people and inhabited a territory smaller than New Jersey or Wales. The Russians were unable to achieve victory in Chechnya despite overwhelming numbers and uncontested air supremacy. Clearly, the inadequacy of Soviet counterinsurgency doctrine, so evident in Afghanistan, had combined with a remarkable deterioration in the quality of Russia's armed forces to produce one of the most disastrous counterinsurgency experiences on record, the full implications of which have yet to manifest themselves.[28]

THE PORTUGUESE

Portugal possessed the first, and also the last, European empire in Africa. Her twentieth-century holdings there—Angola, Mozambique, and Guinea-Bissau—were vast (twenty-three times the size of Portugal), far from the metropolitan center of the empire and each other, and sparsely populated. Beginning in 1961, Lisbon had to confront various independence movements in her African colonies.[29] The guerrillas enjoyed sanctuaries across lengthy and remote borders, as well as external aid and Cuban advisers. To deal with such an enormous challenge, Portugal's national resources were quite modest. The country was relatively underdeveloped, with a population smaller than Ohio's, and its army had not engaged in serious combat operations since 1918.

Faced with these far-flung rebellions, Portuguese officers made a thorough examination of the international literature on counterinsurgency. They also sent study missions to the British, French, and U.S. armies. These exercises yielded little that was useful to them, with the notable exceptions of making clear that they needed to avoid both the major mistake of the Americans in Vietnam—substituting weap-

onry for strategy—and the ultimately devastating consequences that
overtook the French army from its use of torture in Algeria. The Portuguese army developed its own sound doctrine of counterinsurgency,
and converted itself almost entirely into a counterinsurgency force.
That is to say, the army adapted itself to the war, instead of trying to do
the reverse. The Portuguese effort came to resemble that of the British
in Malaya—long-term, low-tech, limited casualties. In the thirteen-
year, continent-wide effort, Portuguese forces suffered only four thousand combat deaths, 23 percent of them African.

From the beginnings of their African empire the Portuguese had
recruited large numbers of troops from the indigenous populations.
During the 1961–1974 effort such recruitment was greatly amplified,
both because of the small size of Portugal's own population, and because the Portuguese believed that the willingness of numerous Africans to serve under the flag of Portugal increased the legitimacy of
their African presence. Native Africans served in the Portuguese army
because of the good pay and medical attention, because of the perception that the Portuguese would win, and most of all because of
internecine ethnic conflicts, which the Portuguese intelligence services
deftly exploited. At the end, Africans comprised over 50 percent of
total Portuguese military forces, with all units fully integrated. Eventually Portugal's forces in Africa would equal five times those of the U.S.
in Vietnam, in proportion to population.

In the early 1970s the insurgents in all colonies totaled around
twenty-two thousand, about 0.15 percent of the indigenous populations, roughly one out of every seven hundred. These small numbers
in a combined area of over eight hundred thousand square miles (four
times the size of France), the reluctance of the guerrillas to make contact with troops, and Portugal's limited industrial base combined to
shape these conflicts into low-tech wars of small infantry or cavalry
units. Although they had few helicopters, the Portuguese employed
them with such skill that they provided the government forces' principal mobility advantage over the guerrillas. Immediate medical attention to wounded soldiers, a powerful morale-builder, became a high
priority, while decent treatment of prisoners yielded the predictable
intelligence harvests.

Side by side with sound military tactics, the Portuguese attempted
to address systematically the social problems which they believed constituted some of the roots of the insurgencies. Health care, education,
and the commercial infrastructure received special attention. The Por-

tuguese linked their social and military efforts by establishing a workable village militia system. These policies helped limit the appeal of the guerrillas, which in many areas was not extensive to begin with.

By 1972 the guerrillas had clearly suffered near-total defeat in Angola, and they were being contained in Mozambique and even in Guinea, where the insurgents enjoyed foreign sanctuary, Soviet aid, and Cuban advisers. The Portuguese eventually lost their African colonies, but this was the consequence of domestic upheavals within Portugal and not of any fundamental inadequacy within their counterinsurgency doctrine and practice.[30]

THE AMERICANS

During their War of Independence and War of Secession, Americans gave ample evidence of their ability to effectively assume the guerrilla role.[31] Their experience, however, in conflicts involving counter-guerrilla warfare—including the Philippine rising under Aguinaldo after 1898, the civil war in Greece, the Huk rebellion following World War II, and the conflict in Vietnam—has been mixed.

The American campaign in the post–Spanish War Philippines is a first-rate example of intelligent counterinsurgency culminating in complete victory and enduring peace. The Americans made sure the insurgents received no help from outside. They took pains to isolate the guerrillas from the civilian population. They used heavy weaponry sparingly, relying instead on good small-unit tactics. Perhaps most decisively, the Americans battled the guerrillas with the weapons of political and social reform. They offered sincere and credible promises of self-government and eventual independence. More immediately, they effected notable improvements in the courts and penal institutions, as well as in education, health care, and basic sanitation, all of which made a deeply favorable impression on the Filipinos, including even the insurgents. The end of the conflict was quickly followed by reconciliation and indeed friendship between the Philippine and American peoples that has endured, even through the darkest days of World War II, for a century. The Philippine War was not an immaculate struggle on either side (and how could it have been?), but it was undoubtedly "the most successful counterinsurgency campaign in U.S. history."[32] Some aspects of the American effort make it even more impressive than the British victory in Malaya. For example, the Americans lacked the long and intimate experience of the country that the British enjoyed in

Malaya, and they deployed incomparably fewer troops, both absolutely and proportionately.[33]

After World War II, the United States assisted the governments of Greece and the Philippine Republic against Communist-led insurgencies. Notable aspects of American involvement in these struggles include (1) providing economic assistance that permitted the allied governments to sustain substantial counterinsurgency efforts without unduly dislocating their civilian economies; (2) advocating military and social reforms in the assisted countries, and supporting effective leaders committed to those reforms, such as Ramón Magsaysay; and (3) limiting their military presence to an advisory role, rather than providing ground combat units, even though Washington had pronounced the defeat of the Communist insurgencies in both countries to be vital to its national interest, and despite the fact that until close to the end of the Greek war the insurgents there both enjoyed cross-border sanctuaries and received significant outside assistance.[34] American participation in these Balkan and Southeast Asian conflicts was largely indirect. Nevertheless—or perhaps one could say "therefore"—the Americans achieved their aims.

In its initial involvement in the Vietnam conflicts, the U.S. adopted policies similar to those it successfully pursued in the Greek and Philippine insurgencies.[35] But the Kennedy and Johnson administrations abandoned those policies and Americanized the war against the Viet Cong and Hanoi to an unprecedented degree. Reverting to their World War II model of warfare, the Americans sought to achieve their ends through committing great numbers of U.S. troops and applying devastating technology. They waged a conventional war, defined progress in terms of attrition and "body counts" rather than civilian security, and afflicted friends as well as foes with their destructive firepower. All this was grotesquely inappropriate to sound counterinsurgency. (In the northernmost provinces of the country the Marines and their CAPs program were a notable, if neglected, exception to this distressing picture.)[36] At the same time, and in spite of the massive American military presence, great quantities of enemy personnel and supplies continuously rolled into South Vietnam, because Washington decision-makers failed to grasp the absolute necessity of isolating the battlefield by shutting the Ho Chi Minh Trail. In the entire history of warfare there must be few if any precedents for the combination of unnecessarily aggressive tactics with unnecessarily passive strategy pursued by the Americans in Vietnam.[37]

Nevertheless, despite these grim self-imposed handicaps, the Americans broke the myth of Maoist Revolutionary People's War in South Vietnam by inflicting insupportable numbers of casualties on the Viet Cong. Accordingly, two and a half years after the departure of U.S combat troops, the conquest of South Vietnam required a full-scale conventional invasion by the North Vietnamese Army, at the time one of the largest and best-equipped on the planet.

Under Presidents Carter and Reagan, the U.S. again committed itself to stem an advancing Communist tide, this time in Central America. The conflict in El Salvador witnessed an American return to the fundamental policies of their Greek and Philippine experiences: the provision of financial aid and military advice, and insistence on socio-economic and political reforms. At least in large part because of these policies, a more democratic regime eventually emerged in El Salvador, and the insurgents agreed to lay down their arms.[38]

CHAPTER 17

ELEMENTS OF A
COUNTERINSURGENT STRATEGY

A distinguished student of civil conflict once observed: "The difficulty in generalizing about insurrections arises from the fact that strategies that may be highly successful in one situation may be completely irrelevant in another. As guerrillas must live by their wits, so governments fighting guerrillas must be quick-witted and unencumbered by doctrine."[1]

It is certainly reasonable to caution against a Procrustean approach to a complex set of phenomena. But it is equally reasonable to seek to learn from experience. Careful analysis of failed guerrilla efforts and successful counterinsurgent campaigns may therefore be highly informative in identifying elements for a viable strategy of counterinsurgency.[2]

For present purposes, four successful counterinsurgencies have proven especially instructive. Two unfolded as the nineteenth century turned into the twentieth: the British defeat of Boer guerrillas in South Africa, and the U.S. victory over Aguinaldo in the Philippines, "the most successful counterinsurgency campaign in U.S. history."[3] The other two are episodes from the Cold War: another British victory, this time over Communist-led guerrillas in Malaya, and President Magsaysay's successful, U.S.-backed campaign against the Philippine Huks.

The efforts of the Portuguese in southern Africa and the French in Algeria have also provided some valuable lessons. At least equally instructive are the counterinsurgency errors of the French in the Vendée, in Spain, and in Indochina; the Japanese in China; the Americans in Vietnam; and the Soviets in Afghanistan.

Concerning the question of "learning" (and unlearning) in counterinsurgency, recall that the Filipino Ramón Magsaysay, the Irishman Michael Collins, and the Indonesian Abdul Suharto were successful counterinsurgents who had all been at one time insurgent leaders themselves.[4] On the other side of the ledger were entire regimes, having come to power by means of guerrilla insurgency, that found themselves cast unsuccessfully in the counterinsurgent role, as in Algeria, Angola, Mozambique, and Nicaragua. As an additional example, the Hanoi regime, whose members had waged a successful insurgency against the French and a (militarily) unsuccessful insurgency against the U.S. and its allies, became enmeshed in a very difficult counterinsurgent struggle against the Cambodian Khmer Rouge guerrillas.

Skillfully led guerrillas present a grave challenge even to countries with impressive military power. Under the best of circumstances a counterinsurgency campaign can be protracted, expensive, and filled with moral ambiguity. That type of conflict will be exceedingly difficult for a democratic society, perhaps especially so for the United States. This chapter therefore offers an approach to counterinsurgency that, among other things, should prove least taxing to such a polity. It consists of two main segments. The first presents courses of action that establish the strategic environment for victory: providing a peaceful path to change, committing sufficient forces, and isolating the conflict area. The second segment identifies measures to disrupt and marginalize the guerrilla effort: displaying rectitude, emphasizing intelligence, dividing insurgent leaders and followers, offering amnesty, and reducing the insurgents' access to firearms and food. (Of course, the actions recommended here are clearly interdependent.)

Before proceeding, it would be helpful to keep in mind the observation of Clausewitz that in war everything is simple, but even the simplest thing is very difficult.

FIRST PART: SHAPING THE STRATEGIC ENVIRONMENT

Provide a Peaceful Path to Change

The ultimate method of counterinsurgency is to prevent an insurgency from arising in the first place. And the best preventative is an effective government that offers a peaceful path to change, that is, a recognized method of seeking redress of grievances. A peaceful path for the redress of grievances need not mean Western-style elections. All that is required is a method of representation that the affected society views as legitimate.

While Che Guevara got many important things wrong, he was quite right in his insistence that it is not possible to wage a successful insurgency against a democratic regime, or even against one that merely tries to appear as such. Examples abound to verify the aphorism that "the ballot box is the coffin of insurgency." In the early 1900s the British promised postwar self-government to the Boers, as the Americans did to the Filipinos. The Philippine Huks profited greatly from the "dirty elections of 1949," but as a result of Ramón Magsaysay's decisive actions to clean up the electoral process, "to all intents and purposes the 1951 elections sounded the death knell of the Hukbalahap movement."[5] In Malaya, the 1955 elections gave the coup de grâce to a failing Communist insurgency by providing a legal method to express grievances.[6] In El Salvador, establishing free elections was the foundation of U.S. strategy there, along with rapidly building up the Salvadoran army to forestall an immediate guerrilla victory, and pressuring that army to practice rectitude. In consequence, Napoleon Duarte won election to the presidency, the first time in El Salvador's history that an opposition candidate peacefully attained that office.

In different but highly relevant circumstances, President Lincoln's policies during the closing phase of the Civil War avoided the outbreak of a much-dreaded guerrilla conflagration. Instead of vengeful executions, sweeping confiscations, mass deportations, Vendean drownings, the Gulag Archipelago, the Katyn Forest, instead of all that, Lincoln offered the defeated Confederates quick reentry into the national political community from which they had separated themselves a scant fifty-two months before.

Commit Sufficient Resources

The key idea here is, the more troops, the fewer the casualties—for everybody concerned. Inadequate commitment of forces has often stemmed from underestimating the task at hand, as with the initial British posture toward the Boer Republics, the French toward the Viet Minh, and the U.S. toward North Vietnam.

Guerrilla warfare and counterinsurgency share some important features: both are (or should be), for example, concerned with winning the allegiance, or at least the acquiescence, of the civilian population. But among their essential differences, none is more salient than this: visible, physical control of a given territory, and the people in it, is of quite secondary importance to guerrillas, but it is the heart of a well-planned counterinsurgency.

It is essential that the government side establish and maintain the perception that it is going to win; it must give the appearance of strength, confidence, and unshakable permanency. If this is done, then many who support the insurgents will change sides or become neutral, and many neutrals will shift toward the government. The appearance of being the eventual victor is an incalculable force multiplier. Committing a sufficient number of troops and auxiliaries to a given region does much to convince everybody—insurgents, civilians, even the counterinsurgent forces themselves—that the guerrillas cannot win. Secure control enhances the flow of intelligence, discourages people from joining or supporting the insurgency, and makes easier the practice of rectitude by the counterinsurgent forces.

The historical record is littered with the debris of counterinsurgency efforts that were parsimonious regarding numbers. Nevertheless, *sufficient* numbers do not have to mean *vast* numbers. Students of guerrilla warfare have long maintained that in order to win, the counterinsurgent side needs a ratio of at least ten-to-one over their opponents. Assuming for the time being the desirability of such a ratio, the most obvious way to achieve it—deploying sufficient numbers—may be impossible. But there is another approach to achieving a favorable numerical ratio: reduce or contain the number of insurgents through sound policy. Well-conceived political and economic measures can depress support for the guerrillas, and popular support, however obtained, is the one absolute essential for guerrilla success.

In addition to good governance, timely intelligence and air transport serve as counterinsurgent force multipliers. So does road construction. The Romans held their empire together with a system of excellent roads, some still in use today, yet "surprisingly little attention has been given to roads as a measure of the ability to exert authority."[7] Roads—and railways—are evidence that the government is there, and to stay. They help conventional forces overcome the guerrillas' advantages in mobility and serve to cut up guerrilla territory. The Chinese employed road building as an anti-guerrilla tactic, from Chiang Kai-shek in Kiangsi to Mao Tse-tung in Tibet. The Italians in Ethiopia harassed guerrillas with a road system protected by forts, and the British built military roads and fortified railways from South Africa to Malaya.[8]

Of course, without a well-developed strategy of counterinsurgency based on sound political and military analysis, even great numbers of troops may prove inadequate. Sometimes an apparent insufficiency of government forces is actually the result of trying to do everything at once, instead of proceeding systematically according to an intelligent order of priorities. For example, attempting to hold or take over too much territory was a key mistake of Napoleon in Spain, the Japanese in China, Chiang Kai-shek in Manchuria, and President Thieu in South Vietnam.[9]

Isolate the Conflict Area

This principle is intimately related to the government's level of counterinsurgent commitment. If across-the-border supplies to guerrillas cannot be interdicted, or at least limited, then no level of counterinsurgent commitment on the part of the ruling regime is likely to be adequate. Therefore, all possible diplomatic and military means must be harnessed to this fundamental objective. The failure to cut guerrillas off from supplies coming across international borders, and to prevent the easy passage of guerrillas across those lines, has been the undoing of major counterinsurgencies from Napoleonic Spain to Soviet Afghanistan. The efforts of U.S. forces and their South Vietnamese allies were negated and then obliterated by unwillingness to block the Ho Chi Minh Trail through Laos. A decade later, the Soviets paid a very high price for failing to prevent men and arms passing from Pakistan into Afghanistan. (Notably, in neither Laos nor Afghanistan did air interdiction, however massive, prove sufficiently effective against guerrillas and their supply lines. Specially selected and trained counter-guerrilla units may be needed to more successfully reduce movement across borders.)[10] Conversely, the defeat of the insurgents in South Africa, Malaya, and the Philippines was intimately related to their inability to receive foreign assistance. But perhaps the most impressive example of a counterinsurgent power choking off aid to guerrillas from a neighboring sovereign state arises from the Algerian conflict. In that struggle, the French built the formidable Morice Line, which stopped the passage of supplies and men from Tunisia and hence reduced the guerrillas inside Algeria to impotence.

An insurgency based on an ethnic or religious minority, especially one geographically concentrated in an area away from an international border, is highly vulnerable to a conservative strategy of containment. Consider the Islamic Moros in the Philippines. The Moros have a venerable history of rebellion against non-Islamic authority: first against the Spanish, then the Americans, then the Philippine Republic. Recent Moro insurgencies claiming to fight for an independent Moro state have been notably unsuccessful, for several quite fundamental reasons. In the first place, no government in Manila of any stripe, whatever its origins or composition, could survive if it agreed to a partition of the Philippine Republic's territory. Besides, census figures show that of over eighty-five million Filipinos, fewer than four million are Muslim (Moros), who are overwhelmingly concentrated in thirteen provinces on the island of Mindanao. The world supposes Mindanao to be the Moros' stronghold, yet even there they are a minority of the population. Therefore in any new state containing most of the Moros and ruled by them, the majority of the population would be non-Moro. In addition to these formidable obstacles, the central government in Manila has granted autonomy to certain districts where Moros are very numerous, thus diffusing support for an insurgency in these areas. Moreover, Moro guerrillas are far removed from any potential assistance from presumably sympathetic Arab states. Thus a Moro secessionist insurgency cannot rely on a regional war of exhaustion to attain its aims. Its only hope would be to menace the government by carrying the conflict to the heavily populated areas of Luzon. But by definition a Moro insurgency cannot mobilize popular support in non-Moro areas. Hence the insurgents are self-isolated and strategically defeated. They have few options besides continuing with sabotage, kidnappings, and acts of terrorism, mostly occurring in areas far from the centers of national life.[11] Connections they establish with international terrorist groups are only proofs of their strategic impotence.

(On isolating the battle area in Vietnam, please see the Appendix to this chapter.)

SECOND PART: DEFEATING THE INSURGENTS

Display Rectitude

Rectitude toward civilians and prisoners helps to hold down casualties and keep up morale among the counterinsurgent forces. In country after country, century after century, misbehavior by counterinsurgent forces has played into the hands of rebellion. Here is one area where the record of counterinsurgency "learning" is dismal. Long ago Sun Tzu wrote that the enemy should always be allowed an escape route.[12] Many later conventional-war theorists and practitioners would reject this advice. But with regard to insurgents, Sun Tzu's advice is apt, because the object of the counterinsurgents is not (or ought not to be) to kill or even capture guerrillas, but to occupy territory and to justly administer the civil population, thus marginalizing the guerrillas spatially and morally. And if counterinsurgent forces gain a reputation for rectitude toward prisoners, then even when surrounded or cornered, guerrillas will be disinclined to fight to the death. Stationing soldiers in their home areas is usually an effective means of promoting correct behavior toward civilians.

Like justice, rectitude needs to be *seen* to be done.

Emphasize Intelligence

The necessity of timely intelligence for successful counterinsurgency hardly needs elaboration. The collection of worthwhile intelligence of course depends to a vital degree on the practice of rectitude, and it is in turn essential to the success of the lines of action discussed in the following pages. One of the most important tasks of intelligence is to discern to what degree the insurgency is a truly popular movement as opposed to principally a vehicle for would-be or former elites. Another is to discover the role criminal elements may play in it. Methods that have facilitated the gathering of intelligence by counterinsurgent forces include stationing troops in their home area, or at least in the same particular area for an extended period; recruiting locals as soldiers, scouts, police, and informants; and offering sizable rewards for information, defection, or help in the capture of leaders. It is absolutely vital that the military, police, and civilian intelligence units learn to share their findings with each other. Systematic sharing of information among various services encounters much resistance but produces rich rewards.

Divide Insurgent Leaders from Their Followers

Indonesian general Abdul Nasution, at different times a guerrilla leader and a counterinsurgent commander, wrote that "the guerrilla fighter must be separated from the people. . . . [This is] the essence of anti-guerrilla strategy."[13]

Effective counterinsurgency does not mean killing guerrillas. Even less does it mean killing civilians. Effective counterinsurgency means marginalizing the guerrillas, by providing security to civilians. "The first reaction to guerrilla warfare must be to protect and control the population."[14] U.S. forces proved quite able to do this in the Philippines: "After 1900 the American stress on the isolation of the guerrillas and the protection of townspeople from terrorism and intimidation was an important element in the success of the pacification operations."[15]

Providing security for the civilian population is the diametric opposite of the notorious "body count" approach so disastrously imposed on U.S. forces in Vietnam. In the countryside, the most practical and successful method of separating guerrillas from civilians is the clear-and-hold method, demonstrated by Sir Robert Thompson in Malaya. In relocation, one moves the civilians; in clearing-and-holding, one moves the guerrillas. Clearing-and-holding resembles conventional warfare in slow motion. Its essence is that the counterinsurgent forces secure the government's geographic base areas first (usually urban areas) by saturating them with troops and police, so that the guerrillas are literally crowded out. The process is repeated in one neighboring district and then another, steadily and methodically.

Guerrilla insurgencies are often disguised civil wars, fueled by ethnic conflicts. Moreover, criminal bands can join an insurgency and carry on their usual activities under cover of some political cause. Areas inhabited by ethnic or religious groups hostile to the insurgents, or troubled by criminals posing as insurgents, should therefore be priority targets for clear-and-hold operations.

Once guerrillas have been driven out of a village or district, the counterinsurgents need to erect local militia units, possibly stiffened by a U.S. Combined Action Platoon-type program. This sort of mobilization of the civilian population prevents the reentry of guerrillas into a cleared area. It also acts as a force multiplier, freeing counterinsurgent forces to clear additional areas.

But even with its own militia unit, a village can be very vulnerable. Well-led guerrillas will assemble rapidly in large numbers to attack unsympathetic civilian settlements, as well as small or isolated police stations and army outposts. Protecting the civilian population therefore requires a rapid response capability to counter guerrilla mobility. But guerrilla mining of access roads over which rescue forces were likely to pass was a major problem in Vietnam. Airlift can neutralize this danger and can also serve as an invaluable force multiplier, enabling a relatively few soldiers to do the work of many. In Algeria, "Helicopters, parachutists and special forces made mobility a weapon the French shared with the guerrillas."[16] But there are always caveats in combat. Soviet air mobility was mortally challenged in Afghanistan once the insurgents obtained Stinger-type missiles. Besides, reliance on air superiority to interdict enemy supplies can be gravely disappointing, as the U.S. found out in Korea and Laos, and the Soviets in Afghanistan.[17] Nevertheless, air patrols can reduce or eliminate daytime guerrilla efforts to reenter cleared zones, augmenting both the effectiveness and confidence of local militia units, and the efficacy of fences and block-house lines.

Guerrillas who have been cleared out of a village or district will try to leave behind them an infrastructure there, in the form of civilian sympathizers who supply them with intelligence and food, and who may also terrorize persons of known anti-insurgent views. The infrastructure is to the guerrillas as the root system is to the plant. Even after a village has been cleared of guerrillas and a militia unit established, real security will not exist until every effort has been made, through patient police work, to identify and uproot this infrastructure.

Clear-and-hold procedures, properly executed, will inevitably push the guerrillas into poorer and more remote regions. This is a key consideration: once driven out of their home areas, guerrillas are strangers to the civilians among whom they operate, and their lives can become exceedingly difficult.

Ruling regimes can attain another powerful means of separating guerrilla leaders from their actual and potential followers by addressing the insurgents' legitimate social grievances. In China, statesmen of the Ch'ing monarchy viewed conciliation as an essential element of pacification: "those who cannot win the support of the people cannot permanently suppress a rebellion."[18] An official of the Tung-Chih restoration observed that "if we wish the Empire to have no rebellious people, we must see to it that the Empire has no resentful people."[19] To settle the Vendean insurgency, General Hoche assembled powerful military forces against the insurgents, but he also restored religious worship, removed brutal officials, and punished pillaging soldiers. In the post-1898 Philippines, the American "policy of attraction" through educational and legal reforms had great effect, as did similar policies of the U.S. Marines in Haiti.[20] It is doubtful, however, that youthful guerrillas motivated by religious fanaticism may be easy to reach through reforms and concessions.

A distinguished student of the U.S. effort in Vietnam observed that American development projects in the villages were ineffective measures of counterinsurgency because they benefited everybody. That is, those on the bottom of the social pyramid remained on the bottom, even though their lives were improved, whereas the Communists promised a totally new redistribution of wealth and status.[21] Even granting the truth of this position, it does not follow from it that socioeconomic reforms per se are everywhere of little avail, but rather that the entire social structure of rural Vietnam needed reformation. That indeed was happening by the early 1970s when the South Vietnamese government carried out the most serious land reform in noncommunist Asia.[22]

Finally, relocation of the population in certain areas can effectively separate guerrillas and civilians, but this is an expensive and complicated undertaking, which in the past has had some resounding failures. As such, resettlement probably should be considered only as a last resort or on a limited scale.

Offer Amnesty

In a literal sense, amnesty is a particular method of separating insurgent leaders from their followers. A well-executed amnesty program can also provide a cornucopia of intelligence. Amnesty should be available to almost everyone, except real criminals and longtime insurgent leaders. Ralliers (guerrillas who come over to the government side) can join special guerrilla-hunting units, as in Malaya and Vietnam. Reintegrating amnesty takers into normal society requires education or vocational training, small loans, perhaps grants of land, and the like.

Because maintaining peace was the principal foundation of their claim to legitimate rulership, colonial governments especially were highly intolerant of any type of armed resistance; these governments rarely offered amnesty to insurgents. Yet if a government views guerrillas and those who support them as criminals, it will have to make every effort to stamp them out and punish as many as possible. Under these circumstances, it will be very hard to induce guerrillas to surrender. On the other hand, if the government characterizes the guerrillas as mostly misguided or deceived persons who need to be brought back into society (the Magsaysay approach), the stage is prepared for negotiation and/or surrender.[23] Intelligent amnesty programs save blood and money.

Drain Disturbed Areas of Firearms

If the guerrillas are receiving little or no outside help, reducing the availability of weapons in the zone of conflict can be an especially powerful counterinsurgent device. But attempts to confiscate arms from a large civilian population by house-to-house searches are disruptive and dangerous. In addition to such searches, hostage-taking is another provocative approach to controlling insurgents' access to arms. In the Vendée, General Hoche estimated the male population of a given parish, then demanded that one musket be handed over for every four males, detaining hostages until his demand was met.[24] This practice produced the desired results, but one needs to recall that Hoche was dealing with a profoundly alienated civilian population, and he was also busy removing the original causes of that alienation. It is easy to imagine a whole plethora of ways in which hostage-taking could back-fire destructively. Much less provocative is the offer of cash payment, or the release of a bona fide prisoner, in return for a gun—no questions asked. After 1898 the Philippine insurgents were woefully short of modern weapons, thanks in part to the U.S. Navy. Thus the capture or redemption of rifles became a powerful instrument for reducing the insurgency to helplessness. In addition, amnestied or surrendered guer-rillas often know the location of arms caches.

Disrupt Insurgent Food Supplies

To concentrate on interfering with the enemy's food and water sup-plies may seem unromantic and unheroic, but it is a powerful weapon in any conflict, and in none more so than counterinsurgency. Disci-pline and morale begin to deteriorate after several days without ad-equate food, and the bravest and most disciplined soldiers are reduced to helplessness after only three days without water. A favorite tactic of guerrillas is to harass the enemy's lines of supply; thus, to reduce the guerrillas' access to food and water is to turn one of their main weap-ons against them. Long ago the Roman commentator Vegetius wrote, "The main and principal point in war is to secure plenty of provisions and to weaken or destroy the enemy by hunger."[25] In Machiavelli's view, "It is better to subdue the enemy by famine than by the sword, because in battle *fortuna* plays a greater role than *virtu*."[26] During the Nien rebellion in China, the authorities confined peasants to walled villages and removed all outside food supplies.

To reduce the amount of food going to guerrillas requires security for the civilian population, including protection of the crops and ani-mals of friendly or neutral peasants. Small, specially-trained hunter groups, far-ranging and independently operating, supplied with timely intelligence and aided by observation aircraft, can aggressively seek out guerrilla food-growing areas. This kind of harassment causes guerrillas to break up their bases, adds to their general feeling of insecurity, and tempts them into unwise courses of action.

Operations of this sort worked very well against Aguinaldo, the Huks, and the Malayan Communists. In the latter case, some food did escape British control, coming to the guerrillas from over the Thai border or from discontented elements in some of the resettled villages. Nevertheless, the food deprivation program received high praise from distinguished commentators.[27]

After the Spanish-American War, U.S. forces in the Philippines used food interdiction very effectively. "In the later stages of the conflict, food became as problematical for the insurgents as rifles. The Americans devoted increasingly successful efforts to cutting off food supplies to the guerrillas, scouring a given territory for hidden fields and storehouses. Constant American patrolling kept the guerrillas on the move and uncovered many food caches. Men had to switch their attention and activity from fighting the Americans to getting or growing or stealing food. The food-denial campaign seriously hurt both the guerrillas' morale and their health; guerrilla life, in any country and any conflict, is often filled with hardships; for the Philippine insurgents, no medical facilities and decreasing food supplies meant increasing illness."[28]

The other side of this coin is taking care of one's own troops. Soldiers living under stress need proper food. Sun Tzu's advice on this point is excellent, as usual: "Pay heed to nourishing the troops!"[29]

A Word About Tactics

In guerrilla warfare, tactics are politics, or at least they ought to be. Hence, first and foremost, counterinsurgents should make every effort to abstain from tactics that harm or antagonize civilians. They must also guard against providing guerrillas the opportunity to score victories, even small ones. Therefore they ought to avoid, for example, sweep and encirclement operations, and setting up outposts that are hard to defend or supply.

Sweeps carried out by conventional forces can be heard coming from far away. Thus they provide any guerrillas with ample time to flee (assuming insurgent spies have not already betrayed the sweep plans). Sweeps provide all the circumstances for frustrated soldiers to abuse civilians; they should be avoided except for the most compelling reasons. Encirclements too have a notable record of failure, from Napoleon's Spain to Hitler's Yugoslavia. In Tito's words, "it was vital to impress upon our men that they must never allow the fact of being surrounded to demoralize them, but must regard it as the normal situation in our kind of war. By concentrating our efforts against one point, we could always break out of any encirclement. We were always encircled and always came through."[30]

In Vietnam, a favorite French tactic was to establish outposts far from their Hanoi-Haiphong base. French airpower was weak, and so these outposts depended on convoys for supplies. These convoys, in turn, became a favorite target of Viet Minh ambushes. Between 1952 and 1954 alone, the French lost almost four hundred armored vehicles.[31] To discourage ambushes, the French began building strongpoints at places where ambushes had previously occurred. Of course these strongpoints then needed to be supplied. Hence, convoys went forth to supply outposts that had been erected to protect the convoys.[32] It was to little avail: "the French lived in fear of ambushes to the end of the war."[33] Dien Bien Phu was, literally, the outpost to end all outposts. Failures such as that one illustrate that outposts only make sense if they can be supplied. Nevertheless, in almost every instance, once an outpost has been established, it is less dangerous for the occupants to stay put and defend it rather than try to escape from it.[34]

Of course, conventional counterinsurgent forces must absolutely avoid the use of inappropriate weapons and tactics (especially artillery and bombing aircraft) in populated areas. And they must never leave a village or district undefended after they have entered it and allowed their sympathizers to reveal themselves.

Keeping Pressure on Guerrillas

Some counterinsurgent forces should always be ready to hunt for guerrilla bands. Seasonal conditions can make their search more successful. For example, harsh winter weather cuts down the guerrillas' food supplies and makes them easy to track in the snow (as in Greece) or among the leafless trees (as in Manchuria). Government troops, in contrast, can have the reassurance provided by mobile hospitals and kitchens. Jungle conditions are hard on guerrillas as well. And as the expectation of early victory ebbs, so does the level of guerrilla morale, as in Peru and Malaya.[35]

Quite apart from the danger of capture or death, guerrilla life can hold many hardships. The following are but two examples. During the Boer conflict (as in others) guerrillas were often mere lads.[36] One of these was Deneys Reitz. Son of a former president of the Orange Free State, he entered the fight at the age of seventeen and was part of the guerrilla force that invaded the British Cape Colony under the command of Smuts. The young Reitz left a memorable picture of the difficult early days of this undertaking, and of the less glamorous aspects of guerrilla life: "The night that followed was the most terrible of all. Our guide lost his way; we were floundering ankle-deep in mud and water, our poor weakened horses stumbling and slipping at every turn; the rain beat down on us and the cold was awful. Towards midnight it began to sleet. The grain bag which I wore [from lack of other clothing] froze solid on my body, like a coat of mail, and I believe that if we had not kept moving every one of us would have died."[37]

Half a century later and half a world away, Luis Taruc, principal Huk military commander, recalled that "sickness was our worst enemy and accounted for many times the casualties inflicted by the Japanese and [their] puppets. It was the one problem we were never quite able to overcome. Malaria was the worst cause of death. Our squadrons were often forced to live in the swamps, which were thickly infested by malarial mosquitoes. . . . Dysentery and stomach ulcers from inadequate food were often serious afflictions."[38]

"Flying" Columns

That admirable compendium of good advice, the U.S. Marines' *Small Wars Manual,* states that "the mission of the flying [i.e., fast-moving] column will be to seek out the hostile groups, attack them energetically and then pursue them to the limit. Therefore there should be nothing in its composition or armament that would tend to reduce its mobility or independence of action. . . ." The *Manual* further sagely advises flying columns to carry plenty of cash, in small bills or coin, with which to pay for supplies, guides, interpreters—and information.[39]

Along with their blockhouse system, the British in South Africa developed a new anti-guerrilla tactic, simple and devastating: identify the location of a Boer *laager* (encampment), ride or march to it hard all night, and attack furiously at dawn. Independently operating mobile strike units were increasingly able to locate Boer encampments beyond the blockhouse lines, thanks mainly to greatly improved intelligence, much of which came from native African scouts, guides, and spies.[40] The famous guerrilla leader Christiaan De Wet believed that the British learned their dawn-attack method from the despised National Scouts.[41] The Boers were incredibly lax about posting sentinels, and so the new tactics were often successful, against even the great De Wet. "We soon discovered that these night attacks were the most difficult of the enemy's tactics with which we had to deal."[42] (One might have supposed that both guerrillas and their opponents would always assume the possibility of night or dawn attacks, and site and guard their encampments accordingly. Alas!)

U.S. Marines in Nicaragua developed small hunter groups for long patrols. The purpose of such units was to disrupt the security and rest that guerrillas expect to have in their customary areas. "Nothing upsets a guerrilla band more than to be chased by a compact, fast-moving patrol of soldiers who are familiar with the people and terrain of the area of operations, and are willing to stay in the field until decisive contact is made."[43]

Thus, carrying the conflict to the guerrillas is the work of small units, constantly engaged in long patrols, dependent on the initiative of junior officers, and unable to rely on neatly programmed artillery fire from far away. Such units will not normally have to fear being outnumbered and overwhelmed: "most irregular fighting in thick country takes place at short or point-blank ranges where the accuracy of a military rifle is wasted even in the hands of a well-trained man. Furthermore, much of the fighting takes place in the dark of night when accurate aiming is impossible. Under these circumstances a shotgun blast is likely to be pretty effective."[44] Besides, here as in so many other conflict situations, "weapons and training count far more than mere numbers."[45]

SUMMARY

The aim of true counterinsurgency is to reestablish peace. Real peace means reintegrating into society its disaffected elements. The rate, even the possibility, of such reintegration depends in great part on how the counterinsurgency was conducted. Reintegration becomes incomparably more likely if the counterinsurgents deliberately choose conservative military tactics, undergirded by serious efforts to limit abuses against the civil population, redress salient grievances, make amnesty attractive, and erect a legitimate government.

Such an approach combines sound political initiative with appropriate military actions. Its essence is maximum force with minimum violence. Its goal is to destroy the *will* of the enemy, not their lives, and certainly not the lives of civilians.

APPENDIX: A STRATEGY FOR A VIABLE SOUTH VIETNAM

Out of American involvement in the war to save South Vietnam has emerged a great paradox. The regime in Hanoi had become convinced by the last half of 1967 that People's War, their version of guerrilla insurgency, had failed. From that conviction came the Tet Offensive, then the openly conventional Easter Offensive and finally the conventional 1975 offensive. The latter two campaigns were massive, World War II–style land invasions by the regular North Vietnamese Army, not guerrilla operations. The war ended when North Vietnamese tanks rolled into Saigon. Yet, despite the classically conventional nature of the war after 1968, large numbers of Americans, including many who could be expected to know better, seem to believe to this day that the U.S. was defeated in Vietnam by guerrilla tactics, and they have shrunk from involvement against guerrilla insurgency ever since ("No More Vietnams!"). The myth of the invincible guerrilla clearly affects contemporary U.S. foreign policy, notably in Latin America, but also in the Middle East.

And here is another paradox: one frequently hears critics of the regime in Saigon explain its fall in terms of corruption, military incompetence and cowardice, and a near-total absence of popular support. But if all this is true, then why did the North have to mount a massive conventional invasion—the largest movement of regular troops since the Korean War—to conquer the South? Why didn't the politburo in Hanoi just wait for the overripe fruit to drop into its hands? And why were the huge movements of Vietnamese refugees always southward, even in 1975?[46]

These are just some of the central myths about Vietnam that continue to befog debate in the U.S. on how best to respond to guerrilla insurgency. Perhaps the most influential, as well as pernicious, of the myths regarding Vietnam holds that South Vietnam fell because its citizens were disinclined to fight on their own behalf.

Earlier chapters have offered evidence that these beliefs—these myths—contradict easily ascertainable facts. Perhaps South Vietnam would have fallen to invasion in 1976 or 1980 or 1985, but the reason it fell in 1975 was not because the South Vietnamese were not fighting, but rather because of the disastrous attempt to re-deploy ARVN from the north to the south of the country. And that attempt in turn was provoked by the increasingly open abandonment of the South Vietnamese by the Americans.[47]

Therefore, what was needed was a strategy for fighting the war that would have kept U.S. forces and U.S. casualties in Vietnam at acceptable levels. Of course, any effort to conceive a more viable strategy in South Vietnam has important implications for present and future insurgencies, and any U.S. role in them.

An Alternative Strategy

Clausewitz wrote, "The first, the supreme, the most far-reaching act of judgment that the statesman and commander have to make is to establish the kind of war on which they are embarking; neither mistaking it for, nor trying to turn it into, something that is alien to its nature."[48]

Today no one disputes that the seat of the war in South Vietnam, in terms of inspiration, direction, organization, and supply (of both material and personnel), was in Hanoi. The Johnson administration was unwilling to carry the ground war into the North, mainly for fear of Chinese intervention on the Korean model. Thus the Americans settled on the so-called attrition strategy, which aimed to kill more of the enemy than could be replaced. The Americans and their allies therefore assumed the strategic defensive and the tactical offensive, probably the worst possible stance. Because the Communist side usually controlled both the timing and the scale of combat, and because North Vietnam was able to send great numbers of troops into the South and was willing to accept enormous casualties, the attrition strategy was doomed to failure—if only in the sense that it could not be successful in a time frame and at a cost that the notoriously impatient American public (actually, the American news media) would find acceptable. Attrition ignored the essence of sound counter-guerrilla warfare by concentrating on destroying main-force Viet Cong and North Vietnamese units instead of protecting the population. At the same time, a huge American army went through South Vietnam on one-year tours. This style of warmaking inflated U.S. casualties, devastated friendly civilians, ravaged the environment, and confused the U.S. electorate.

Tragically, in those very years an invaluable critique of and alternative to the Johnson administration's military policies was at hand. In July 1965 the Army Chief of Staff commissioned a study that was completed by March 1966: a nine-hundred-page document titled *A Program for the Pacification and Long-Term Development of South Viet Nam* (PROVN for short).[49] PROVN's officer-authors studied the history and culture of Vietnam and questioned numerous army officers about their experiences in that country. They concluded that "without question, village and hamlet[50] security must be achieved throughout Viet Nam" by means of "effective area saturation tactics in and around populated areas." PROVN correctly identified the cutting of the all-important Ho Chi Minh Trail as a key requirement. It also urged unification of American programs and personnel in South Vietnam under the U.S. ambassador, and direct American involvement with key South Vietnamese governmental functions. Because it criticized attrition and the search-and-destroy tactics underlying it, PROVN got a cool reception from General Westmoreland.[51] Its recommendations received little application until 1969, when General Abrams took over command in South Vietnam. Abrams well understood the essentials of counterinsurgency; by then, however, the war had become largely a conventional one, and the Americans were beginning to pull out.

The Marines had already embarked on their own counterinsurgency program, the Combined Action Platoons (CAPs), "the most imaginative strategy to emerge from the Viet Nam conflict."[52] The emphasis was where it belonged, on civilian security.

PROVN and the CAPs show that there was widespread understanding of the weaknesses of the administration policies in Vietnam. The need for a workable alternative strategy was palpable and urgent. But what would such a strategy have looked like? That is to say, what strategy would have reduced the number of U.S. casualties, optimized U.S. strengths, minimized damage to Vietnamese society, neutralized the Ho Chi Minh Trail, isolated the North Vietnamese/Viet Cong forces from the village population, allocated the principal responsibility for dealing with guerrillas to the South Vietnamese forces, calmed alarms in the American media and Congress about a "wider war," and above all avoided the 1975 ill-organized attempt of the South Vietnamese Army to retrench into the populous areas in the deep south, an attempt that produced the conquest of South Vietnam? How could all this be done?

During and after the conflict, numerous analysts made a convincing case that the key to stopping the invasion[53] of South Vietnam was cutting the Ho Chi Minh Trail. In their plan, U.S. and ARVN forces would have deployed on an east-west axis across Laos to the Thai border, about one hundred miles, roughly the distance between New York City and Philadelphia.[54] But powerful political and military considerations prevented the Johnson administration from committing ground forces to Laos, not to mention the southern provinces of North Vietnam. Primary among these considerations was fear of Chinese intervention. (This fear was unfounded but not unreasonable: by 1968 over three hundred thousand Chinese military personnel were in North Vietnam in engineering and anti-aircraft units.)[55]

Any successful counterinsurgency strategy would employ the kind of clear-and-hold operations that worked so well in Malaya. As set forth by their principal exponent, Sir Robert Thompson,[56] clear-and-hold means systematically driving the guerrillas out of first one designated area and then another, by inundating that area with troops, police, and auxiliaries. In South Vietnam, however, clear-and-hold operations in themselves would not have been sufficient, because the guerrillas were only one aspect of the conflict; the other was the slow-motion invasion of South Vietnam from the North by way of Laos (which became fast-motion in 1972 and 1975).

A successful strategy to save South Vietnam, therefore, would have been rooted in clear thinking about that country's geography, and specifically, how the allies could deal with the Northern troops and supplies coming through Laos, without going into Laos themselves (although a Laotian defense line would certainly have been the optimal choice).[57] Table 2 presents a schematic view of the fundamental choices available to the U.S. in Vietnam.

TABLE 2: Alternative U.S. Approaches to the Vietnam War

| | | TACTICS | |
		Offensive	Defensive
STRATEGIC POSTURE	Offensive	*Invade North Vietnam*	*Close Ho Chi Minh Trail by a Line Across Laos*
	Defensive	*Actual U.S. Approach*	*Approach Proposed Here*

Geographical Realities

The Philippine government had defeated Communist insurgency in no small measure because that country was an archipelago. South Korea had successfully escaped Communist conquest in large part because it was a peninsula. But South Vietnam was neither of these things. Too big, too poorly configured, and too exposed to invasion to be defended in its entirety, South Vietnam's geography would prove to be its doom—unless that geography were altered. That is, it was essential to redefine the shape of South Vietnam: if you can't *isolate* the battlefield, then *redraw* the battlefield.

The population of South Vietnam was heavily concentrated in greater Saigon and the Mekong Delta (Military Regions III and IV), plus a few urban enclaves along the central coast. The northern boundary of Military Region III—roughly 12 degrees north latitude—constituted the demographic frontier between the areas of heavy and sparse population.

The construction of a line across Laos to block the Ho Chi Minh Trail would have been the most effective U.S. choice for holding South Vietnam, but the Johnson administration ruled that strategy out. Therefore the defense of the demographic frontier, plus some coastal enclaves, becomes the next best option, and it is the heart of the strategy proposed here.

In this approach, the allied forces would withdraw from the northern and central provinces of South Vietnam. (Some well-trained South Vietnamese guerrilla units would remain behind in the highlands.) U.S. forces, much reduced in numbers, and some ARVN, would deploy along the demographic frontier and along the border between Military Region III and Cambodia—a total of about 375 miles, the length of the northern border of the state of Colorado. Mobile reserves would be in support of this deployment. All civilians wishing to do so would be free to move south into the defended zone. With allied troops guarding the demographic frontier, ARVN and the Territorials would deal with what Viet Cong elements remained active behind (inside) it. With far fewer U.S. troops in country, the South Vietnamese forces could receive weapons equal in quality to those of the Communists much earlier. CAPs would deploy in highly exposed districts.[58] Ranging over all these forces would be the mighty air power of the allied states.

The ancient capital city of Hué was a tremendously important symbol to all Vietnamese. Allied forces would hold it as an enclave, along with Da Nang, supported by the U.S. Navy. Each place would be a potential launching area for seaborne flanking attacks: Da Nang would be the South Vietnamese Inchon, except that U.S. forces would already be there. The refugees who would flood into those coastal cities could be sealifted south.

These areas altogether—Military Regions III and IV (historic Cochin China) plus the coastal enclaves—would comprise a viable state, twice the size of Switzerland with a population larger than Australia's.

Retrenchment along the demographic frontier would have several major beneficial consequences for the allies. First, it would greatly decrease the size of the U.S. forces in Vietnam and their casualty rates.

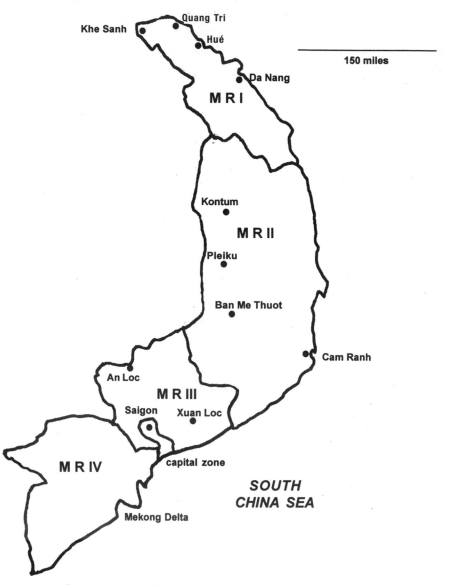

Khe Sanh

Quang Tri

Hué

Da Nang

M R I

Kontum

M R II

Pleiku

Ban Me Thuot

Cam Ranh

An Loc

M R III

Saigon   Xuan Loc

capital zone

M R IV

SOUTH
CHINA SEA

Mekong Delta

150 miles

South Vietnam Military Regions, 1972.
Map by Anne Szewczyk.

The conflict in South Vietnam would now have true front lines. With the enemy on one side and the civilians on the other, American firepower could have free play. Instead of a part-conscript army of more than half a million, American forces in Vietnam would be far fewer, more professional, perhaps completely volunteer—the end of the disastrous one-year tour policy. Employing conservative tactics, those forces would incur far fewer losses: no more hunting the enemy all over the country, no more "search and destroy," no more body counts, no more booby-trap casualties. With the allies retrenched into Military Regions III and IV and the coastal enclaves, the Ho Chi Minh Trail would become irrelevant, and so would the bombing of North Vietnam.

Second, confronted by a true front line, Hanoi would have two choices: either to accept this de facto new partition and abandon the struggle, or else to mount massive assaults in the face of overwhelming allied fire superiority from the land, air, and sea (producing "attrition" to end all attrition).

Third, by creating an authentic rear area, with allied firepower directed toward the enemy and away from civilians, the strategy would have made possible a thorough clear-and-hold operation in the regions of dense population and also have allowed time for serious social and economic improvements to take effect in those same regions.

The fourth advantage of the demographic strategy is perhaps the decisive one: in this strategy the ARVN effort to retrench to the south in 1975, the effort that produced the final disaster, could not have occurred. In January 1975, most of ARVN was in the sparsely populated Central Highlands and the dangerously exposed Military Region I below the 17th parallel. President Thieu's decision to remove the bulk of these forces to positions closer to Saigon was a very good one and should have been carried out years earlier. But the 1975 retrenchment turned into a catastrophe for two main reasons. One was hasty planning. The other, much more important, was the presence of the families of ARVN troops in the areas to be left behind. That ARVN soldiers wished to prevent their families from falling into Communist hands is perfectly understandable, but their attempts to achieve that end resulted in disintegration of many ARVN units and hence the collapse of the South.

For years ARVN had followed a very inadvisable policy of stationing its soldiers far from their home areas and allowing their families to follow them. That was the key to the final debacle. But with the demographic strategy in place, the soldiers' families would stay put in their true homes, with ARVN deployed to defend them. If before 1975 ARVN units had redeployed farther south, in an orderly manner, with their families on one side of them and the Communists on the other, retreat, desertion, or surrender would have become hardly thinkable. Consider the 18th ARVN Division. Nobody had ever imagined that it was worth much in a fight, but in the last days of the war, after its dependents had been evacuated southward, the 18th put up a defense of the city of Xuan Loc that was truly ferocious. (Liddell Hart observed: "So long as their families are safe [men] will defend their country, believing that by their sacrifice they are safeguarding their families also. But even the bonds of patriotism, discipline and comradeship are loosened when the family itself is menaced.")[59]

But, critics will object, a demographic strategy is defensive; it would give the all-important initiative to the enemy. One may respond to this criticism by citing both traditional strategic theory and the actual situation on the ground in Vietnam.

First, the great Clausewitz taught that "the defensive form of warfare is intrinsically stronger than the offensive" and "it is easier to hold ground than to take it."[60] In his *The Art of War*, Sun Tzu wrote, "invincibility lies in the defense." Lee won perhaps his greatest victory at Fredericksburg, on the defensive. If the North Vietnamese took the offensive against the demographic frontier, so much the worse for them. They would not only hurl themselves against entrenched positions, but also bring down on themselves everything from B-52s to the sixteen-inch guns of the USS *New Jersey*. That would have been Clausewitz's defensive with a vengeance.

Besides, in actual fact General Westmoreland was on the defensive anyway. The Communists primarily dictated the time, place, and intensity of the fighting, thanks mainly to their sanctuaries in Laos and Cambodia. How to reduce or eliminate the effects of those sanctuaries is the real question.

While agreeing with this assessment, other critics might find fault with the plan's call for giving up territory in Military Regions I and II. After all, is that what the Americans were in Vietnam to do, hand over territory to the enemy? Yet consider the case of the territory in North Vietnam, over which the Saigon government always claimed to be the sole legitimate authority. In 1954 Washington had acquiesced in giving up the northern half of Vietnam to the Communists, against the will of the U.S.-recognized government of Bao Dai. The borders of

South Vietnam had been created by an agreement between the French Army and Ho Chi Minh. South Vietnam was under no obligation to defend every inch of the territory within those borders; neither was the U.S. By fighting in the Central Highlands, outflanked by the Ho Chi Minh Trail, the Americans were allowing the enemy to choose the battlefield, and their casualty lists showed it.[61] Besides, a strategic regroupment is not equivalent to a political/diplomatic cession. Trading territory for time is a venerable strategy: the Russians retreated before Napoleon and Hitler; the Chinese before the Japanese; Lee defended Virginia, not Arkansas. Even the clear-and-hold strategy has as a fundamental operating principal that one concentrates on solidifying the base areas first, allowing the enemy to run loose in other areas for the time being. And the South Vietnamese did indeed eventually see the wisdom of retrenchment, of trading space for time—only too late.

In short, blocking the Ho Chi Minh Trail—drawing a defensive line across Laos—would have been the best strategic option to ensure a viable South Vietnam, but it was considered politically unacceptable at the time. Retrenching to the southern demographic frontier—drawing that defensive line farther south, across Military Region III—while only a second-best option, would nonetheless most likely have preserved a viable South Vietnamese state, like the South Korean state the U.S. has been defending for more than half a century.

CONFLICT IN IRAQ

In 2003, having swiftly toppled the regime of Saddam Hussein, the victorious coalition—more than thirty countries—pledged to establish a democratic government in Iraq. Almost immediately, however, the situation began to darken. The predictable postwar outbreak of terrorism struck at "soft" targets, including United Nations and Red Cross personnel, foreign civilians in general, even children. Then terrorism elided into guerrilla insurgency as assaults on coalition military units became frequent. Rising U.S. casualties in the second year after the end of the conventional war alarmed many Americans. As the problems in Iraq became grist (or rather chaff) for partisan mills, widespread and indignant comparisons of Iraq to Vietnam showed how inadequately the Americans understand what happened in Vietnam, how ill-served they are by their news media, and, consequently, how vulnerable they are to an Iraqi version of the Tet Offensive.

In what comparative contexts might one realistically view U.S. casualties in Iraq? For one, consider the size of the country. With 173,000 square miles, Iraq is larger than Germany and Austria combined, larger than New York, Pennsylvania, Ohio, and Indiana together. Iraq is twenty-nine times the size of Chechnya (called for good reason the "tombstone of Russian Power"), thirty-two times the size of Northern Ireland, and forty-three times the size of Kosovo. Iraq's population of twenty-three million is twenty-five times that of Chechnya, and fifteen times that of Northern Ireland. The latter province is smaller than Aroostook County in the state of Maine; yet within its constricted space, for almost three decades beginning in 1972, a very few hundred terrorists were able to operate in the presence of twenty-five thousand British troops, who had the support of a majority of the local population and were close to their home bases.

It is, moreover, a regrettable fact that some of the Americans who have lost their lives in Iraq would have died even if they had been serving in the U.S., or elsewhere, in conditions of peace. Between 1980 and 2004, nearly 20,000 American military personnel died in accidents—an average of 833 deaths every year.[1] (Violent death also strikes American civilians in distressing numbers: in an average year in the U.S., nearly 16,000 persons are murdered, over 29,000 commit suicide, and 43,000 die in motor vehicle accidents.)

Nevertheless, the question legitimately arises: American casualties in Iraq to achieve what? U.S. aims in Iraq are tremendous: to construct a democratic order—with honest elections,[2] and constitutional guarantees for ethnic and religious minorities and women—in a country riven by internecine conflict, where the vast majority of the population has had no experience of democracy, or even of decent government.[3] Whether or not the U.S. vision for the peoples of Iraq is truly achievable, it certainly represents core Western values. There is the essence of the problem: influential elements in Iraq, with potentially broad support, reject such values, far more fundamentally and violently than the Soviets ever did. Here is an instance of that "clash of civilizations" identified years ago by Samuel P. Huntington.[4] Nothing is going to fix that situation in the short term.

Clearly, a peaceful Iraq under a civilized government would be in almost everybody's interest. Conversely, an Iraq dominated by vengeful Islamists, or consumed by civil wars—another, much larger Lebanon—would destabilize the entire Middle East and menace the interests of what many call, rather hopefully, "the international community." But the U.S. electorate will not indefinitely support an effort in Iraq in which over three–quarters of the foreign troops, and of the foreign casualties, are American. The international community, such as it is, must therefore accept its proper share of responsibility for maintaining a reasonable order in Iraq. Nevertheless, to attain that goal, the U.S. will have to remain a primary actor there for at least the intermediate term. In the difficult days that lie ahead, "perseverance may be the most formidable weapon in the counterinsurgency arsenal."[5]

NOTES

PROLOGUE: GUERRILLA INSURGENCY AS A POLITICAL PROBLEM

1. It is not always easy to differentiate guerrilla acts from terrorist acts *in practice*. The general distinction, however, is valid. In this volume, guerrillas are irregular troops who conduct military operations against conventional government forces. Terrorists are those who perpetrate premeditated, politically motivated violence against noncombatants. Guerrillas have the ability to do whatever terrorists can, but the reverse is not true. Consult Jane's *World Insurgency and Terrorism* (Surrey, UK: Jane's, May-August 2002).

2. C.E. Callwell, *Small Wars* (London: Greenhill, 1990 [orig. 1896]), p. 126. One might add: "With help from outside."

3. Antoine-Henri Jomini, *The Art of War*, trans. G.H. Mendell and W.P. Craighill (Westport, CT: Greenwood, n.d. [orig. 1838]), p. 46.

4. See Anthony James Joes, *America and Guerrilla Warfare* (Lexington, KY: University Press of Kentucky, 2000), chapter 1, "American Guerrillas: The War of Independence."

5. The Russian campaign cost the French 210,000 soldiers; this figure includes prisoners and missing, but does not include losses among Napoleon's allies, such as the Poles. Estimates of French and allied casualties during the Spanish occupation run from 200,000 to 400,000. J. Tranie and J.-C. Carmigniani tend to favor the lower figure; see *Napoleon's War in Spain*, trans. Janet Mallender and J. Clements. (London: Arms and Armour, 1982), p. 10. Owen Connelly leans toward the higher number; see *Blundering to Glory: Napoleon's Military Campaigns* (Wilmington, DE: Scholarly Resources, 1987), p.112n. French General Bigarre wrote that guerrillas killed 180,000 Imperial troops; see Gabriel H. Lovett, *Napoleon and the Birth of Modern Spain* (New York: New York University, 1975), p. 683. For comparison, Union battle deaths during the American Civil War totaled 138,000; U.S. deaths from all causes in Vietnam were 58,000.

6. On the eve of Waterloo Napoleon had to send over 30,000 troops to contain the royalist insurgency in the Vendée, leaving him but 72,000 soldiers with whom to meet Wellington. Georges Lefebvre, *Napoleon from Tilsit to Waterloo* (New York: Columbia University, 1969), p. 363.

7. Neil Bruce, *Portugal: The Last Empire* (New York: Wiley, 1975); Antonio Rangel Bandiera, "The Portuguese Armed Forces Movement: Historical Antecedents, Demands, and Class Conflict," *Politics and Society* 6 (1976); G.W. Grayson, "Portugal and the Armed Forces Movement," *Orbis* 19 (Summer 1975); Philippe S. Schmitter, "Liberation by Golpe," *Armed Forces and Society* 2 (Fall 1975).

8. *New York Times*, March 4, 2003, p. A8; *Statesman's Yearbook 2002* (New York: Palgrave, 2002).

9. Machiavelli, *The Prince*, Chapter XXI.

10. C.H.V. Sutherland, *The Romans in Spain* (Westport, CT: Greenwood, 1982 [orig. 1939]), p. 70.

11. "In terms of revolutionary strategy, communism has succeeded only when it has been able to co-opt a national liberation struggle, and it has failed whenever it was opposed to or isolated from a national liberation struggle, such as those in Israel, Algeria, Indonesia, and Burma. Needless to add, even when supporting a war of national liberation, the communists have occasionally been defeated, as in Greece, Malaya, the Philippines, and Venezuela." Chalmers Johnson, *Autopsy on People's War* (Berkeley, CA: University of California, 1973), p. 10.

12. Lucian Pye in Harry Eckstein, ed., *Internal War* (Glencoe, IL: Free Press, 1964), p. 163.

13. Indra de Soysa, "The Resource Curse: Are Civil Wars Driven by Rapacity or Paucity," in Mats Berdal and D.M. Malone, eds., *Greed and Grievance: Economic Agendas in Civil Wars* (Boulder, CO: Lynne Rienner, 2000), p. 114.

14. Close to four decades ago, a distinguished American political scientist wrote: "The most important political distinction among countries concerns not their form of government but their degree of government." Samuel P. Huntington, *Political Order in Changing Societies* (New Haven, CT: Yale University, 1968), p. 1.

15. See Thomas R. Mockaitis, "From Counterinsurgency to Peacemaking: New Applications for an Old Approach," in Anthony James Joes, ed., *Saving Democracies: U.S. Intervention in Threatened Democratic States* (Westport, CT: Praeger, 1999).

16. Bertrand Russell, *Power* (London: Allen and Unwin, 1962), p. 82.

17. Lucien Pye, in Harry Eckstein, ed., *Internal War* (Glencoe, IL: Free Press, 1964), p. 162; my italics.

18. Eliot Cohen, "The Strategy of Innocence? The United States, 1920–1945" in Williamson Murray, MacGregor Knox and Alvin Bernstein, eds. *The Making of Strategy: Rulers, States and War* (Cambridge: Cambridge University Press, 1994), p. 464.

19. Colin Gray, "Strategy in the Nuclear Age: The United States, 1945–1991" in Murray et al., *Making of Strategy*, p. 603.

20. Ralph Peters, "Heavy Peace," *Parameters*, v. 29, no. 1 (Spring 1999).

21. Charles Tilly, "Does Modernization Breed Revolution?" *Comparative Politics*, vol. 5 (April 1973), p. 447. My italics. Tilly continues: "Population growth, industrialization, urbanization, and other large-scale structural changes, to be sure, affect the probabilities of revolution. But they do so indirectly, by shaping the potential contenders for power, transforming the techniques of governmental control, and shifting the resources available to contenders and governments."

22. Charles W. Freeman, Jr., *Arts of Power: Statecraft and Diplomacy* (Washington, DC: United States Institute of Peace, 1997), p. 67.

23. Carl von Clausewitz, *On War*. Edited and translated by Michael Howard and Peter Paret (Princeton, NJ: Princeton University, 1976), pp. 87, 605, 607.

24. Sun Tzu, *The Art of War*, trans. Samuel B. Griffith (New York: Oxford University Press, 1963), p. 77.

25. Caesar, *The Civil War*, in *The Gallic War and Other Writings of Julius Caesar*, trans. Moses Hadas (New York: Modern Library, 1957), p. 247.

26. Callwell, *Small Wars*, pp. 41–42.

27. Quoted in B.H. Liddell Hart, *Scipio Africanus* (New York: Da Capo, 1994), p. 153.
Compare Polybius: "Those who know how to win are much more numerous than those who know how to make proper use of their victories." *The Histories*, Chapter X.
28. Quoted in John Cloake, *Templer: Tiger of Malaya* (London: Harrap, 1985), p. 262. Templer, victor over the Communist insurgents in Malaya, probably invented the phrase "winning hearts and minds."
29. Michael Howard, "When are Wars Decisive?" *Survival*, vol. 41 (Spring 1999), p. 135.
30. Gene Z. Hanrahan, *Japanese Operations Against Guerrilla Forces* (Chevy Chase, MD: Operations Research Office, Johns Hopkins University, 1954), p. 15.
31. Freeman, *Arts of Power*, p. 67.
32. Basil H. Liddell Hart, *Strategy* (London: Faber and Faber, 1967), p. 353.
33. Basil H. Liddell Hart, *Thoughts on War* (London: Faber and Faber, 1944).

CHAPTER 1: GUERRILLA STRATEGY AND TACTICS

1. Callwell, *Small Wars*, p. 85.
2. Sir Robert Thompson, "Regular Armies and Insurgency," in Ronald Haycock, ed., *Regular Armies and Insurgency* (London: Croom Helm, 1979), pp.9–10. But in fact well-led guerrillas will most certainly not be "losing every battle."
3. In today's world, however, so many states are such in name only that it may not be necessary or even advisable for guerrilla insurgents to seek a protracted war, but rather a fast dash into the capital city. See Victor Young, "The Victors and the Vanquished: The Role of Military Factors in the Outcome of Modern African Insurgencies," *Small Wars and Insurgencies*, vol. 7 (1996).
4. For much of the American War of Independence, General George Washington employed tactics similar to those of guerrilla warfare. See Russell F. Weigley, "A Strategy of Attrition: George Washington," in *The American Way of War* (Bloomington, IN: Indiana University press, 1977).
5. "A commander can more easily shape and direct the popular insurrection by supporting the insurgents with small units of the regular army." Clausewitz, *On War*, Chapter XXVI.
6. On the fruitful symbiotic relationship between Marion the Swamp Fox and General Nathanael Greene against General Lord Cornwallis, see no less an authority than Sir John Fortescue, *A History of the British Army* (London: Macmillan, 1899–1930), vol. III, p. 409.
7. Douglas Pike, *PAVN: People's Army of Viet Nam* (Novato, CA: Presidio Press, 1986), chapter 9, first line.
8. "People's War, as a banner that had led the Party through a generation of trials, was finished." Timothy J. Lomperis, *From People's War to People's Rule: Insurgency, Intervention, and the Lessons of Viet Nam* (Chapel Hill, NC: University of North Carolina Press, 1996); both quotations on p. 341.
9. Jomini's first principle of war is "to obtain by free and rapid movements the advantage of bringing the mass of the troops against fractions of the enemy": Antoine-Henri Jomini, *Art of War*, p. 299.
10. "A small but highly trained force striking 'out of the blue' at a vital spot can produce a strategical effect out of all proportion to its slight numbers." Basil Liddell Hart, *The Real War 1914–1918* (Boston: Little Brown, 1930), p. 42.

11. Liddell Hart, *Real War*, p. 324. "The enemy must not know where I intend to give battle; for if he does not know where I intend to give battle, he must prepare in a great many places. And when he prepares in a great many places, those I have to fight in any one place will be few." Sun Tzu, *Art of War*, VI.14

12. "Operations directed against an opponent's communications represent the most effective weapon in the armoury of strategy." Callwell, *Small Wars*, p. 87.

13. Viet Cong guerrilla units sometimes lay in wait at an ambush site for as long as ten days.

14. Caesar, *The Gallic Wars*, VI, 34. Vercingetorix also used these tactics after he could no longer meet the Romans in open combat; *Gallic Wars*, VII, 14–16; General J.F.C. Fuller among others has pointed out that the organization and tactics of the Roman armies made them unwieldy against guerrilla tactics; see his *Julius Caesar: Man, Soldier and Tyrant* (New Brunswick, NJ: Rutgers University, 1965).

15. Jan Christian Smuts, *Selections from the Smuts Papers*, W.K. Hancock and Jean van der Poel, eds. (Cambridge: Cambridge University Press, 1966), vol. 1, p. 609.

16. "The two factors that produce surprise are secrecy and speed." Clausewitz, *On War*, Book III, Chapter 9.

17. Perhaps 20,000 Communist agents were ARVN officers and NCOs. Others had penetrated U.S. armed forces intelligence services and the CIA, as well as South Vietnamese intelligence and police. Edgar O'Ballance, *The War in Viet Nam* (New York: Hippocrene, 1981), pp. 144–45.

18. Mao Tse-tung, *Selected Military Writings* (Peking: Foreign Languages Press, 1966), p. 33.

19. Raul Castro said to one group of captured Batista soldiers: "We took you this time. We can take you again. And when we do we will not frighten or torture or kill you, anymore than we are doing to you at this moment. If you are captured a second time or even a third time by us, we will again return you exactly as we are doing now." Hugh Thomas, *The Cuban Revolution* (New York: Harper and Row, 1977), pp. 217–18.

20. "We sought to instill in our units the strictest possible discipline, not by extra drills but by ceaseless political instruction with the object of improving both individual and collective morale and of securing a proper attitude toward the population." Tito to author, Fitzroy Maclean, *Disputed Barricade* (London: Jonathan Cape, 1957), p. 235.

21. "It is not spectacular victories and territories that count, but the annihilation of small units and the preservation of one's own vital force." Milovan Djilas, *Wartime: With Tito and the Partisans*, trans. M.B. Petrovich (London: Secker and Warburg, 1977), p. 32.

22. "It was particularly important for us to look after our wounded and never to relax our care for them whatever the difficulties. That had a very great effect on the morale of our troops, though very often to save one wounded man cost us the lives of three or four [of our] soldiers." Tito to author, Maclean, *Disputed Barricade*, p. 236. See also John P. Cann, *Counterinsurgency in Africa: The Portuguese Way of War 1961–1973* (Westport, CT: Greenwood, 1997).

23. Cao Van Vien and Dong Van Khuyen, *Reflections on the Viet Nam War* (Washington, DC: US Army Center of Military History, 1980), p. 149. See also Douglas Pike, *Viet Cong: The Organization and Techniques of the National Liberation Front of South Viet Nam* (Cambridge, MA: M.I.T. Press, 1966), especially chapters 10 and 20; and the works of Sir Robert Thompson, especially *Defeating Communist Insurgency: The Lessons of Malaya and Viet Nam* (New York: Praeger, 1966).

24. Thomas Gray, "Elegy Written in a Country Churchyard."

25. John Lawrence Tone, *The Fatal Knot: The Guerrilla War in Navarre and the Defeat of Napoleon in Spain* (Chapel Hill, NC: University of North Carolina, 1994), p. 95.

26. Gabriel H. Lovett, *Napoleon and the Birth of Modern Spain* (New York: New York University, 1965), v. 2, p. 709.

27. Charles Oman, *A History of the Peninsular War* (Oxford: Clarendon Press, 1902–1930), v. 3, p. 489.

28. Nasty habits persist. While on campaign in December 1862, Mosby wrote his wife to send him his copies of Macauley, Scott, Plutarch, Shakespeare, and Byron.

29. Jeb Stuart, quoted in *The Memoirs of Col. John S. Mosby* (Nashville: J.S. Sanders, 1995), p. 270.

30. Mosby, *Memoirs,* p. 267

31. Mosby, *Memoirs,* p. 285.

32. Jeffrey D. Wert, *Mosby's Rangers* (New York: Simon and Schuster, 1990), p. 83. See also Kevin H. Siepel, *Rebel: The Life and Times of John Singleton Mosby* (New York: St. Martin's, 1983).

33. Becoming a proponent of cooperation with the British, Smuts served as prime minister of the Union of South Africa from 1919 to 1924, and again from 1939 to 1948. He was active in organizing the United Nations. The Nationalist Party finally drove him from office.

34. Byron Farwell, *The Great Anglo-Boer War* (New York: Norton, 1976), p. 332.

35. G.W. Greene, *Life of Nathanael Greene* (Cambridge, MA: Hurd and Houghton, 1871), vol. 2, p. 167.

36. Christopher Ward, *War of the Revolution* (New York: Macmillan, 1962), vol. 2, p. 661.

37. Robert D. Bass, *Swamp Fox* (New York: Henry Holt, 1959), p. 126.

38. Sun Tzu, *Art of War*, X, 20.

39. In 1928, Mao wrote: "The existence of a regular Red Army of adequate strength is a necessary condition for the existence of Red political power. . . . Unless we have regular armed forces of adequate strength, even though we have won the mass support of the workers and peasants, we certainly cannot create an independent regime, let alone an independent regime that lasts long and develops daily." Geoffrey Fairbairn, *Revolutionary Guerrilla Warfare: The Countryside Version* (Harmondsworth, England: Penguin, 1974), p. 92n.

40. The vast sums available to Colombian guerrillas through the international narcotics trade are an important and ominous variation on this theme of outside help to insurgents. See Rensselaer Lee, *The White Labyrinth: Cocaine and Political Power* (New Brunswick, NJ: Transaction, 1989); Francisco Thoumi, *Political Economy and Illegal Drugs in Colombia* (Boulder, CO: L. Rienner, 1995); and annual reports of the U.S. DEA.

41. Compare the well-known advice of Clausewitz to guerrillas: "The following are the only conditions under which a general uprising can be effective: (1) The war must be fought in the interior of the country; (2) It must not be decided by a single stroke; (3) The theater of operations must be fairly large; (4) The national character must be suited to that type of war; (5) The country must be rough and inaccessible, because of mountains, or forests, or marshes, or the local methods of cultivation." *On War*, Book Six, Chapter XXVI. In Jomini's words, "In mountainous countries the people are always most formidable; next to these are countries covered with extensive forests." *Art of War*, p. 27.

42. Michael L. Smith, "Taking the High Ground: Shining Path and the Andes," in David Scott Palmer, ed., *Shining Path of Peru* (New York: St. Martin's, 1994), p. 47. "Sendero is often able to mobilize population in many parts of the sierra because there is no one to stop them." Gordon H. McCormick, *From the Sierra to the Cities: The Urban Campaign of the Shining Path* (Santa Monica, CA: RAND, 1992).

43. This was a major error of the Greek guerrillas in 1948. During the 1968 Tet Offensive, the Viet Cong abandoned guerrilla for conventional tactics, to its great cost.

44. "Small countries like Belgium which lack this [territorial] condition have little or no such possibility" of waging successful guerrilla warfare. Mao Tse-tung, *Selected Military Writings*, p. 171.

45. It is reasonable to suspect that modern airpower and armored desert vehicles have made a repetition of a Lawrence-of-Arabia campaign impossible.

46. Sometimes the inhabitants of the sanctuary can be unwilling hosts, like the Cambodians to the Viet Cong.

47. See Anthony James Joes, *America and Guerrilla Warfare* (Lexington, KY: University Press of Kentucky, 2000).

48. Brian McAlister Linn, *The Philippine War, 1899–1902* (Lawrence, KS: University Press of Kansas, 2000), p. 268.

49. Paul-Marie De La Gorce, *The French Army: A Military-Political History* (New York: George Braziller, 1963), p. 448.

50. Anthony James Joes, *From the Barrel of a Gun: Armies and Revolution* (Washington, DC: Pergamon-Brassey's, 1986).

51. "FARC's kidnapping campaigns and indiscriminant exactions created widespread exasperation . . . and allowed the first paramilitary groups to gain a firm foothold"; Fernando Cubides, "From Private to Public Violence: The Paramilitaries"; "The guerrillas' use of tactics such as extortion, kidnapping and terror brought forth a ruthless paramilitary right that . . . is now contending for control of some of the rural areas long dominated by the guerrillas"; Charles Bergquist, "Waging War and Negotiating Peace: The Contemporary Crisis in Historical perspective"; both articles in Charles Bergquist, R. Penaranda and G. Sanchez, *Violence in Colombia, 1990–2000* (Wilmington, DE: Scholarly Resources, 2001).

52. See Tom Marks, *Colombian Army Adaptation to FARC Insurgency* (Carlisle, PA: Strategic Studies Institute, 2002).

53. "Colombians Petition for Force against Kidnappers," *Washington Post*, November 25, 2000, p. A13; "Rightist Squads in Colombia Beating the Rebels," *New York Times*, December 5, 2000, p. 1; "Colombia's Other Army," *Washington Post*, March 12, 2001, p. A1.

54. Joseph Buttinger, *Viet Nam: A Dragon Embattled* (New York: Praeger, 1967), p. 408.

55. Buttinger, *Viet Nam: A Dragon Embattled*, pp. 408–12; Bernard Fall, *The Two Viet Nams* (New York: Praeger, 1967, 2d ed.), p. 281; Jeffrey Race, *War Comes to Long An* (Berkeley, CA: University of California, 1972), p. 83; William J. Duiker, *The Communist Road to Power in Viet Nam* (Boulder, CO: Westview, 1981), p. 180; Eric M. Bergerud, *The Dynamics of Defeat* (Boulder, CO: Westview, 1991), pp. 67–68; Stephen T. Hosmer, *Viet Cong Repression [Assassinations] and its Implications for the Future* (Santa Monica: RAND, May 1970); Douglas Pike, *The Viet Cong Strategy of Terror* (Monograph, Saigon, 1970).

56. Douglas Blaufarb, *The Counterinsurgency Era: United States Doctrine and Performance 1950 to the Present* (New York: Free Press, 1977), pp. 12–13.

57. See Michael Desch, ed., *Soldiers in Cities: Military Operations on Urban Terrain* (Carlisle, PA: Strategic Studies Institute, 2001), and Ralph Peters, "Our Soldiers, Their Cities," *Parameters*, XXVI, no. 1 (Spring 1996).

58. Before the rising, the Home Army had been committing sabotage, gathering intelligence, publishing a clandestine press, and assassinating particularly brutal Nazis officials. The rising was provoked by the announcement of an imminent Nazi dragnet of all young persons in Warsaw and the approach of the Red Army (which halted when the rising began). Of the 25,000 Home Army personnel involved, only 2,500 had firearms. Before their inevitable surrender, they suffered 22,000 casualties and inflicted 20,000 casualties on the German forces. Bor [T. Komorowski], *The Secret Army* (New York: Macmillan, 1951), p. 378; Richard Lukas, *The Forgotten Holocaust: The Poles under German Occupation, 1939–1945* (Lexington, KY: University Press of Kentucky, 1986), p. 219.

59. Besides, during its operations in Chechnya in 1994–1996, the Russian army displayed such incredible disorganization and incompetence that, even if one insists on calling the resistance forces "guerrillas," the fighting was hardly a fair test of whether sustained urban guerrilla warfare is possible. See Pavel Baev, *The Russian Army in a Time of Troubles* (London: Sage, 1996); Raymond C. Finch, "Why the Russian Military Failed in Chechnya," Fort Leavenworth, KS: U.S. Army Foreign Military Studies Office, 1998; Olga Oliker, *Russia's Chechen Wars 1994–2000: Lessons for Urban Combat* (Santa Monica, CA: RAND, 2001); Rajan Menon and Graham E. Fuller, "Russia's Ruinous Chechen War," *Foreign Affairs*, vol. 79 (March/April, 2000); John R. Pilloni, "Burning Corpses in the Streets: Russia's Doctrinal Flaws in the 1995 Fight for Grozny," *Journal of Slavic Military Studies*, vol. 13 (2000); and Timothy Thomas, "The Battle for Grozny: Deadly Classroom for Urban Combat," *Parameters*, vol. xxix (1999).

60. Chalmers Johnson, *Autopsy on People's War* (Berkeley, CA: University of California, 1973).

61. Thomas, *Cuban Revolution*, p. 215.

62. Henry Butterfield Ryan, *The Fall of Che Guevara: A Story of Soldiers, Spies and Diplomats* (New York: Oxford University Press, 1998); *The Complete Bolivian Diaries of Che Guevara and Other Captured Documents*, Daniel James, ed. (New York: Cooper Square Press, 2000).

63. Timothy Wickham-Crowley, *Guerrillas and Revolutions in Latin America: A Comparative Study of Insurgents and Regimes since 1956* (Princeton, NJ: Princeton University, 1991), p. 287.

64. For a shorter analysis of the conflict in El Salvador, see Anthony James Joes, *America and Guerrilla Warfare*, "El Salvador: A Long War in a Small Country." See also José Napoleon Duarte, *Duarte: My Story* (New York: Putnam's, 1986); Henry Kissinger et al., *Report of the Bipartisan Commission on Central America* (Washington, DC: U.S. Government Printing Office, 1984); Cynthia McClintock, *Revolutionary Movements in Latin America: El Salvador's FMLN and Peru's Shining Path* (Washington, DC: U.S. Institute of Peace, 1998); Benjamin Schwarz, *American Counterinsurgency Doctrine and El Salvador: The Frustrations of Reform and the Illusions of Nation Building* (Santa Monica, CA: Rand, 1991).

65. Mark Galeotti, *Afghanistan: The Soviet Union's Last War* (Portland, OR: Frank Cass, 1995), pp. 28, 30.

66. Anthony Arnold, *The Fateful Pebble: Afghanistan's Role in the Fall of the Soviet Empire* (Novato, CA: Presidio Press, 1993).

CHAPTER 2: SOME WELLSPRINGS OF INSURGENCY

1. This status is not always deserved. In states afflicted with deep ethnic or religious divisions, the most democratic and honest elections can be the occasion for exacerbating cleavages. Where one well-defined group comprises a permanent majority, and another a permanent minority, free elections can lead to civil war, as in Northern Ireland. See Donald L. Horowitz, *Ethnic Groups in Conflict* (Berkeley, CA: University of California, 1985).

2. Samuel P. Huntington, *Political Order in Changing Societies* (New Haven, CT: Yale University, 1968), p. 275.

3. Ernesto Guevara, *Guerrilla Warfare* (New York: Vintage, 1960). Then he forgot his insight, and went to Bolivia to be killed trying to overthrow a government that pretended to be democratic.

4. William Doyle, *The Oxford History of the French Revolution* (Oxford: Oxford University Press, 1989), p. 193. Simon Schama writes that only 6 percent of those eligible (who were, it must be remembered, only a small minority to begin with) actually voted; *Citizens: A Chronicle of the French Revolution* (New York: Knopf, 1989), pp. 644–46. See also Georges Lefebvre, *The Coming of the French Revolution* (Princeton, NJ: Princeton University, 1947), vol. 1, p. 241, and Albert Soboul, *The French Revolution 1788–1799*, translated by A. Forrest and C. Jones (New York: Random House, 1975), p. 267.

5. For sources on the Vendean revolt, see footnotes in chapter 3 of this book.

6. Robert E. Quirk, *The Mexican Revolution and the Catholic Church* (Bloomington, IN: Indiana University, 1973), p. 177.

7. John W.F. Dulles, *Yesterday in Mexico: A Chronicle of the Revolution, 1919–1936* (Austin, TX: University of Texas, 1961), p. 86.

8. Dulles, *Yesterday in Mexico*, p. 265.

9. Ibid., pp. 342ff.

10. The fate of the other principal demand of the Maderistas—clean elections—is well known.

11. Dulles, *Yesterday in Mexico*, p. 351.

12. See Jean A. Meyer, *The Cristero Rebellion* (New York: Cambridge University, 1976); James W. Wilkie, "The Meaning of the Cristero Religious War Against the Mexican Revolution," *Journal of Church and State*, vol. 8 (1966); Jim Tuck, *Holy War in Los Altos: A Regional Analysis of Mexico's Cristero Rebellion* (Tucson, AZ: University of Arizona, 1982); J. Lloyd Mecham, *Church and State in Latin America* (Chapel Hill, NC: University of North Carolina, 1966, rev. ed.); David Bailey, *Viva Cristo Rey!* (Austin, TX: University of Texas, 1974); Robert E. Quirk, *The Mexican Revolution and the Catholic Church* (Bloomington, IN: Indiana University, 1973); Brian Kelly, *The Cristero Rebellion* (Ph.D. dissertation, University of New Mexico, 1973).

13. William Manchester, *American Caesar: Douglas MacArthur, 1880–1964* (Boston, MA: Little, Brown, 1978), pp. 421–22, 525–26.

14. Benedict J. Kerkvliet, *The Huk Rebellion: A Study of Peasant Revolt in the Philippines* (Berkeley, CA: University of California, 1977), p. 238; see also Napoleon Valeriano and Charles T.P. Bohannan, *Counter-Guerrilla Operations: The Philippine Experience* (New York: Praeger, 1962); Carlos P. Romulo and Marvin M. Gray, *The Magsaysay Story* (New York: John Day, 1956); Edward Lansdale, *In the Midst of Wars: An American's Mission to Southeast Asia* (New York: Harper and Row, 1972); Carlos P. Romulo, *Crusade in Asia* (New York: John Day, 1955).

15. For analysis of the 1953 campaign and results, see Frances Lucille Starner, *Magsaysay and the Philippine Peasantry* (Berkeley, CA: University of California, 1961), chapters 3, 4 and appendix 1.
16. See the very interesting works by Taruc, *Born of the People* (Westport, CT: Greenwood, 1973 [orig. 1953]), and *He Who Rides the Tiger* (New York: Praeger, 1967).
17. Balraj Puri, *Kashmir Toward Insurgency* (New Delhi: Orient Longman, 1993), p. 89.
18. See *The Christian Science Monitor*, April 5, 2000.
19. Sumir Ganguly, *The Crisis in Kashmir: Portents of War, Hopes of Peace* (New York: Cambridge University Press, 1997), pp. 15–16, 98–99.
20. Paula R. Newberg, *Double Betrayal: Repression and Insurgency in Kashmir* (Washington: Carnegie Endowment for International Peace, 1995), p. 42.
21. On Kashmir, see Eric S. Margolis, *War at the Top of the World: The Struggle for Afghanistan, Kashmir and Tibet* (NY: Routledge, 2000); Alexander Evans, "The Kashmir Insurgency: As bad as it gets," *Small Wars and Insurgencies*, vol. 11, no. 1 (Spring 2000); R. Rajagopalan, "Restoring Normalcy: The Evolution of the Indian Army's Counterinsurgency Doctrine," *Small Wars and Insurgencies*, vol. 11, no. 1 (Spring 2000); Manoj Joshi, *The Lost Rebellion* (New Delhi: Penguin, 1999); Victoria Schofield *Kashmir in Conflict* (London: Tauris, 2000).
22. On the relationship between poverty and the system of landownership in El Salvador, see John Sheahan, *Patterns of Development in Latin America: Poverty, Repression, and Economic Strategy* (Princeton, NJ: Princeton University, 1987). For historical background on Central America, see Ralph Lee Woodward, *Central America: A Nation Divided* (New York: Oxford University, 1976), and Thomas L. Karnes, *The Failure of Union: Central America, 1824–1975* (Chapel Hill, NC: University of North Carolina, 1976).
23. Cynthia McClintock places great stress on the stolen 1972 elections as an explanation for the emergence of the FMLN several years later; *Revolutionary Movements in Latin America: El Salvador's FMLN and Peru's Shining Path* (Washington, DC: United States Institute of Peace, 1998). In a similar fashion, the M-19 insurgent effort arose in Colombia in large measure because of the widespread belief that former President Rojas Pinilla had been cheated out of his victory in the presidential election of 1970. Jorge G. Castañeda, *Utopia Unarmed: The Latin American Left after the Cold War* (New York: Vintage, 1993). See also Timothy Wickham-Crowley, *Guerrillas and Revolutions in Latin America: A Comparative Study of Insurgents and Regimes since 1956* (Princeton, NJ: Princeton University, 1991), p. 224 and passim.
24. Henry Kissinger et al., *Report of the Bipartisan Commission on Central America* (Washington, DC: U.S. Government Printing Office, 1984), p. 104.
25. Most observers believed that Duarte had won the presidential election of 1972 but had been counted out.
26. See José Napoleon Duarte, *Duarte: My Story* (New York: Putnam's 1986); Stephen Webre, *José Napoleon Duarte and the Christian Democratic Party in Salvadoran Politics 1960–1972* (Baton Rouge, LA: Louisiana State University, 1979); James Dunkerly, *Power in the Isthmus: A Political History of Modern Central America* (New York: Verso, 1988), pp. 409 and 424n; José Garcia, "El Salvador: Recent Elections in Historical Perspective," in John Booth and Michael Seligson, eds., *Elections and Democracy in Central America* (Chapel Hill, NC: University of North Carolina, 1989).
27. See Jeff Goodwin and Theda Skocpol, "Explaining Revolutions in the Contemporary Third World," *Politics and Society* 17, no. 4 (1989).

28. In his State of the Union Address of January 27, 2000, President Clinton asked Congress for a two-year, $1.6 billion program for Colombia.

29. Michael Shifter, "Colombia on the Brink: There Goes the Neighborhood," *Foreign Affairs*, vol. 78 (July/August, 1999), p. 17.

30. See Miguel Angel Centeno, *Blood and Debt: War and the Nation-State in Latin America* (University Park, PA: Pennsylvania State University Press, 2002), p. 8 and passim.

31. On the long, sad story of internecine violence in Colombia, see the classic study by Robert H. Dix, *Colombia: The Political Dimensions of Change* (New Haven: Yale University, 1967). And see Charles Bergquist et al., *Violence in Colombia: The Contemporary Crisis in Historical Perspective* (Wilmington: Scholarly Resources, 1992); Gonzalo Sanchez, "La Violencia in Colombia: New Research, New Questions," *Hispanic American Historical Review*, vol. 65, no. 4 (November, 1985); Paul Oquist, *Violence, Conflict and Politics in Colombia* (New York: Academic Press, 1980); Richard Maullin, *Soldiers, Guerrillas and Politics in Colombia* (Lexington, MA: Lexington, 1973); Herbert Braun, *Our Guerrillas, Our Sidewalks: A Journey into the Violence of Colombia* (Niwot, CO: University Press of Colorado, 1994). See also Russell W. Ramsey, "Critical Bibliography on the Violence in Colombia," *Latin American Research Review* (Spring 1973).

32. *Statesman's Yearbook 1953* (New York: St. Martin's, 1953).

33. Shifter, "Colombia on the Brink," p. 17.

34. Nazih Richani, "The Political Economy of Violence: The War System in Colombia," *Journal of Interamerican Studies and World Affairs*, v. 39 (Summer 1996). See also Wolfgang Heinz, "Guerrillas, Political Violence, and the Peace Process in Colombia," *Latin American Research Review*, vol. 24, n. 3 (1989).

35. David Passage, *The United States and Colombia: Untying the Gordian Knot* (Carlisle Barracks, PA: U.S. Army War College, March 2000), p. 22.

36. Shifter, "Colombia on the Brink," p. 18. Christopher Abel, "Colombia and the Drug Barons: Conflict and Containment," *World Today*, vol. 49 (May 1993).

37. Shifter, "Colombia on the Brink," p. 15; Gabriel Marcella and David Schulz, *Colombia's Three Wars: U.S. Strategy at the Crossroads* (Carlisle Barracks, PA: U.S. Army War College, March, 1999), say $600 million.

38. The inability of the Colombian state to govern the country is not unique in South America; see Centeno, *Blood and Debt*.

39. The size of the Colombian army in 1945 was 11,000; in 1947, 15,000; in 1957, 21,000; in 1961, 21,000; in 1966: 53,000; in 1968: 64,000. (Source: *Statesman's Yearbook*, indicated years).

40. See Thomas Marks, *Colombian Army Adaptation to FARC Insurgency* (Carlisle Barracks, PA: Strategic Studies Institute, 2002).

41. Marcella and Shulz, *Colombia's Three Wars*; Max Manwaring, *Implementing Plan Colombia* (Carlisle Barracks, PA: Strategic Studies Institute, 2000), *U.S. Security Policy in the Western Hemisphere* (Carlisle Barracks, PA: Strategic Studies Institute, 2001), and *Nonstate Actors in Colombia* (Carlisle Barracks, PA: Strategic Studies Institute, 2002); Charles Bergquist et al., *Violence in Colombia: Waging War and Negotiating Peace* (Wilmington, DE: SR Books, 2001); David E. Spencer, *Colombia's Paramilitaries: Criminals or Political Force?* (Carlisle Barracks, PA: Strategic Studies Institute, 2001).

42. See Judith A. Gentleman, *The Regional Security Crisis in the Andes: Patterns of State Response* (Carlisle Barracks, PA: U.S. Army War College, July 2001).

43. Richard L. Millett, *Colombia's Conflicts: The Spillover Effects of a Wider War* (Carlisle Barracks, PA: Strategic Studies Institute Oct 2002); Judith A. Gentleman, *The Re-*

gional Security Crisis in the Andes (Carlisle Barracks, PA: Strategic Studies Institute, 2001); see also Christopher Abel, "Colombia and the Drug Barons: Conflict and Containment," *The World Today*, May 1993; Charles Bergquist et al., *Violence in Colombia: The Contemporary Crisis in Historical Perspective* (Wilmington, DE: Scholarly Resources, 1992); and Jorge Osterling, *Democracy in Colombia: Clientelist Politics and Guerrilla Warfare* (New Brunswick, NJ: Transaction, 1989). See also the valuable series of articles in *Small Wars and Insurgencies* by Dennis M. Rempe, "Guerrillas, Bandits and Independent Republics: U.S. Counterinsurgency Efforts in Colombia 1955–1965," vol. 6 (Winter 1995); "An American Trojan Horse? Eisenhower, Latin America, and the Development of U.S. Internal Security Policy, 1954–1960," vol. 10, no. 1 (Spring 1999); "The Origin of Internal Security in Colombia", vol. 10, no. 3, (Winter 1999); and Dennis M. Rempe, *The Past as Prologue? A History of U.S. Counterinsurgency Policy in Colombia, 1958–1966* (Carlisle Barracks, PA: Strategic Studies Institute, 2002).

44. Chalmers Johnson, *Autopsy on People's War* (Berkeley, CA: University of California, 1973), p. 5. See Also Robert Thompson, *Revolutionary War in World Strategy 1945–1969* (New York: Taplinger, 1970), pp. 24–25.

45. Geoffrey Fairbairn, *Revolutionary Guerrilla Warfare: The Countryside Version* (Harmondsworth, England: Penguin, 1974), p. 71.

46. Timothy Wickham-Crowley, *Guerrillas and Revolution in Latin America: A Comparative Study of Insurgents and Regimes Since 1956* (Princeton, NJ: Princeton University, 1991), p. 41. The reference is to Theda Skocpol, "France, Russia and China: A Structural Analysis of Social Revolutions," in *Comparative Studies in Society and History*, v. 18 (April 1976). Samuel Huntington had offered a similar suggestion in the 1960s; see his *Political Order in Changing Societies* (New Haven: Yale University, 1968).

47. Yvon Grenier, "From Causes to Causers: The Etiology of Salvadoran Internal War Revisited," *Journal of Conflict Studies*, v. XVI (Fall 1996); this is also a major thesis of Timothy Wickham-Crowley, *Guerrillas and Revolutions in Latin America*. See also Jeff Goodwin and Theda Skocpol, "Explaining Revolutions in the Contemporary Third World," *Politics and Society*, vol. XVII (1989).

48. See especially Wickham-Crowley, *Guerrillas and Revolutions in Latin America*, and Cynthia McClintock, *Revolutionary Movements in Latin America* (Washington, DC: U.S. Institute of Peace, 1998).

49. Max G. Manwaring and Court Prisk, *A Strategic View of Insurgencies: Insights from El Salvador* (Washington, DC: Institute for National Strategic Studies, 1990). In 1990, the incumbent President Ortega received 41 percent of the total vote; in 1996, attempting a return to power, he received 38 percent.

50. Vilfredo Pareto, *Sociological Writings* (New York: Praeger, 1966), p, 135. He continues: "This illusion operates also on the [incumbent] elite, many among them betray the interests of their class, believing they are fighting for the realization of these fine principles all to help the unfortunate masses, whereas in reality the sole effect of their action is to fasten onto the masses a yoke which may be more severe than that of the [displaced] elite."

51. "The archetype of the new warrior class is a male who has no stake in peace, a loser with little education, no legal earning power, no abiding attractiveness to women, and no future. . . . For the new warrior class, many of whose members possess no skills marketable in peace, the end of fighting means the end of the good times." Ralph Peters, "The New Warrior Class," *Parameters*, XXIV, no. 2 (Summer 1994), p. 17.

See also his "The Culture of Future Conflicts," *Parameters* XXV, no. 4 (Winter 1995–96), and "Our Old New Enemies," *Parameters* XXVII, no. 2 (Summer 1997). Another class of "insurgents" is comprised of what can perhaps be best described as pirates; see Mats Berdal and David Malone, eds. *Greed And Grievance: Economic Agendas in Civil Wars* (Boulder, CO: Lynne Rienner, 2000), especially Paul Collier, "Doing Well Out of Civil War."

52. One example is Crane Brinton's classic, *The Anatomy of Revolution* (New York: Vintage, 1965); see especially chapter 6, "The Accession of the Extremists."

53. Jacques Solé, *Questions of the French Revolution* (New York: Pantheon, 1989), pp. 241–42, my italics. Donald Sutherland writes: "By 1795 at the latest, an enormous proportion of the population in the west and south supported movements that demanded nothing less than a return to the old regime." *The Chouans: The Social Origins of Popular Counterrevolution in Upper Brittany, 1770–1798* (Oxford: Oxford University, 1982). Albert Mathiez writes of "the opposition and discontent which were seething among the mass of the populace throughout the whole of France." *The French Revolution* (New York: Russell and Russell, 1962 [orig. 1928]), p. 304. For more on the minority nature of the French Revolutionary regimes, see Simon Schama, *Citizens: A Chronicle of the French Revolution* (New York: Knopf, 1989), pp. 644–46 and passim; William Doyle, *The Oxford History of the French Revolution* (New York: Oxford University Press, 1989), pp. 193, 406, and passim.

54. V.I. Lenin, *Collected Works* (Moscow: Progress Publishers, 1966), v. 31, p. 87n.

55. Hannah Arendt, *On Revolution* (New York: Viking, 1965).

56. This is a theme running throughout John T. McAlister, *Viet Nam: The Origins of Revolution* (Garden City: Doubleday Anchor, 1971).

57. Bernard Fall, *The Two Viet Nams: A Political and Military Analysis*, 2d rev. ed. (New York: Praeger, 1967), p. 35.

58. Dennis J. Duncanson *Government and Revolution in Viet Nam* (New York: Oxford University Press, 1968), p. 103.

59. Fall, *Two Viet Nams*, p. 35.

60. Duncanson, *Government and Revolution*, p. 103.

61. Ellen J. Hammer, *The Struggle for Indochina, 1940–1955* (Stanford, CA: Stanford University, 1966), p. 73.

62. McAlister, *Viet Nam*, pp. 300–1. For a Vietnamese with a European education, "to be a Marxist represented a grand gesture of contempt for the corrupt past as well as the humiliating present." William J. Duiker, *The Communist Road to Power in Viet Nam* (Boulder, CO: Westview, 1981), p. 26. The theme of frustrated upward mobility is prominent in Eric M. Bergerud, *The Dynamics of Defeat: The Viet Nam War in Hau Nghia Province* (Boulder, CO: Westview, 1991).

63. See Bui Tin, *Following Ho Chi Minh: Memoirs of a North Vietnamese Colonel* (Honolulu, HI: University of Hawaii, 1995), pp. 6–9.

64. Joseph Buttinger, *Viet Nam: A Political History* (New York: Praeger, 1968), chapter 3.

65. Samuel Popkin, *The Rational Peasant* (Berkeley, CA: University of California, 1979), p. 242.

66. Gabriel Kolko, *Anatomy of a War* (New York: Pantheon, 1985), p. 482.

67. Robert Scalapino, "We Cannot Accept a Communist Seizure of Viet Nam," the *New York Times Magazine*, December 11, 1966; Wesley Fishel, ed., *Viet Nam: Anatomy of a Conflict* (Itasca, IL: Peacock, 1968), pp. 653, 659; Gabriel Kolko, *Anatomy of a War: Viet Nam, the United Sates, and the Modern Historical Experience* (New York:

Pantheon, 1985), p. 250; Robert Thompson, *No Exit from Viet Nam* (New York: David McKay, 1969), p. 65; Robert Thompson, *Peace Is Not at Hand* (New York: David McKay, 1974), p. 169; Jeffrey Race, *War Comes to Long An*, p. 188; Howard R. Penniman, *Elections in South Viet Nam* (Washington, DC: American Enterprise Institute, 1972), p. 199; Dennis J. Duncanson, *Government and Revolution in Viet Nam* (New York: Oxford University, 1968), p. 13.

68. See Anthony James Joes, *America and Guerrilla Warfare*, chapter 7, "Viet Nam: A Case of Multiple Pathologies," pp. 224–25.

69. Thompson, *Peace Is Not at Hand*, p. 169. See Anthony James Joes, *The War for South Viet Nam 1954–1975* (Westport, CT: Praeger, rev. ed., 2001), pp. 133–34.

70. Malcolm Salmon, "After Revolution, Evolution," *Far Eastern Economic Review*, December 12, 1975, pp. 32–34.

71. Bergerud, *Dynamics of Defeat*, p. 4.

72. Ibid., p. 23.

73. Douglas Blaufarb, *The Counterinsurgency Era: United States Doctrine and Performance 1950 to the Present* (New York: Free Press, 1977), p. 8.

74. Bergcrud, *Dynamics of Defeat*, p. 326.

75. Robin Kirk, "The Deadly Women of the Shining Path," *San Francisco Examiner*, March 22, 1992, quoted in Jorge G. Castañeda, *Utopia Unarmed: The Latin American Left After the Cold War* (New York: Vintage, 1994), p. 121n. And see Carlos Ivan DeGregori, "Harvesting Storms," in Steve J. Stern, ed., *Shining and Other Paths: War and Society in Peru, 1980–1995* (Durham, NC: Duke University, 1998), p. 130.

76. Aristotle, *The Politics*, II, 7.

77. George Orwell, *1984.*

78. Lenin, "Left-Wing Communism," in *Selected Works*, v. 3, p. 343, my emphasis.

79. Edwin Lieuwin quoted Lenin approvingly in *Arms and Politics in Latin America* (New York: Praeger, 1960), p. 134.

80. Arendt, *On Revolution*, p. 112.

81. Katherine Chorley, *Armies and the Art of Revolution* (Boston, MA: Beacon, 1973), p. 23. "So long as the government retains the loyalty of the armed forces no revolt can succeed." Stanislav Andreski, *Military Organization and Society* (Berkeley, CA: University of California, 1968). And see Leon Trotsky, *History of the Russian Revolution* (Ann Arbor, MI: University of Michigan Press, 1957).

82. William Henry Chamberlin, *The Russian Revolution, 1917–1921*, vol. 1 (New York: MacMillan, 1935), p. 87.

83. Theda Skocpol, *States and Social Revolutions: A Comparative Analysis of France, Russia and China* (New York: Cambridge University Press, 1979), pp. 14, 23.

84. "Revolutions always appear to succeed with amazing ease in their initial stage, and the reason is that the men who make them first only pick up the power of a regime in plain disintegration; they are the consequences but never the causes of the downfall of political authority." Hannah Arendt, *On Revolution* (New York: Viking, 1965), p. 112.

85. Samuel Huntington, *Political Order in Changing Societies* (New Haven, CT: Yale University, 1969), p. 335.

86. Martin Malia, *The Soviet Tragedy* (New York: Free Press, 1994), p. 50. Chalmers Johnson noted correctly that no Communist regime ever came to power on its own except under the banner of nationalism; Chalmers Johnson, *Autopsy on People's War* (Berkeley, CA: University of California, 1973), p. 10.

87. Chalmers Johnson, *Peasant Nationalism and Communist Power* (Stanford, CA: Stanford University, 1961), p. 155.

88. In Nicaragua, the army of the Somoza regime was not defeated; rather, the Carter administration negotiated an agreement between that army and the Sandinista insurgents. See *New York Times*, July 12, 1979. President Carter's memoirs are silent on this episode.

89. Malaya, along with some other formerly British territories in the area, became the Federation of Malaysia in 1963.

90. Winston Churchill, *The Hinge of Fate* (Boston, MA: Houghton Mifflin, 1950), p. 92.

91. B.H. Liddell Hart, *History of the Second World War* (New York: Da Capo, 1999 [orig. 1970]), p. 233.

92. S. Woodburn Kirby, *Singapore: The Chain of Disaster* (New York: Macmillan, 1971).

93. See W.H. Elsbree, *Japan's Role in Southeast Asian Nationalist Movements 1940–1945* (Cambridge, MA, 1953); Joyce Lebra, *Japanese-Trained Armies in Southeast Asia: Independence and Volunteer Forces in World War II* (New York: Columbia University, 1977).

94. For serious irregularities in the behavior of returning British forces toward the Chinese in Malaya, see Richard Stubbs, *Hearts and Minds in Guerrilla Warfare: The Malayan Emergency, 1948–1960* (New York: Oxford University, 1989), pp. 73–74, and Anthony Short, The *Communist Insurrection in Malaya, 1948–1960* (New York: Crane, Russak, 1975), p. 160.

95. The genocidal policies of the French revolutionary government in the Vendée developed after the insurgency had broken out.

96. Anatol Lieven, *Chechnya: Tombstone of Russian Power* (New Haven, CT: Yale University, 1998), p. 324.

97. John B. Dunlop, *Russia Confronts Chechnya: Roots of a Separatist Conflict* (Oxford: Clarendon Press, 1998), pp. 58–69.

98. Lieven, *Chechnya*, 321; see also Carlotta Gall and Thomas de Waal, *Chechnya: Calamity in the Caucasus* (New York: New York University Press, 1998).

99. "It is hard to believe that the Russian Army has found it so difficult to overwhelm and defeat the Chechen rebels." Steven J. Blank and Earl H. Tilford, *Russia's Invasion of Chechnya: A Preliminary Assessment* (Carlisle Barracks, PA: Strategic Studies Institute, 1995), p. 4. "The victory of the Chechen separatist forces over Russia has been one of the greatest epics of colonial resistance of the past century." Lieven, *Chechnya*, p.3. The Chechen campaigns exposed the "demoralization, corruption, and rampant inefficiency of the Russian military." Dunlop, *Russia Confronts Chechnya*, p. 213. See also Anne Aldis, ed., *The Second Chechen War* (Camberley, England: Conflict Studies Research Center, 2000); and Carl Van Dyke, "Kabul to Grozny: A Critique of Soviet (Russian) Counterinsurgency Doctrine," *Journal of Slavic Military Studies*, v. 9 (1996).

100. This conflict is not the rising of the Warsaw Ghetto, which occurred in 1943, after most of the Ghetto's population had been expelled by the Nazis. On the Ghetto rising see Dan Kurzman, *The Bravest Battle: The 28 Days of the Warsaw Ghetto Uprising* (New York: Da Capo 1993 [orig. 1976]); Shmuel Krakowski, *The War of the Doomed: Jewish Armed Resistance in Poland 1942–1944* (New York: Holmes and Meier 1984}; Israel Gutman, *Resistance: The Warsaw Ghetto Uprising* (New York: Houghton Mifflin, 1994).

101. Timothy Garton Ash, *The Uses of Adversity* (New York: Vintage, 1990), p. 134. See also Jan Gross, *Polish Society Under German Occupation* (Princeton, NJ: Princeton University Press, 1979).

102. Richard C. Lukas, *The Forgotten Holocaust* (Lexington, KY: University Press of

Kentucky, 1986), p. 127. Nechama Tec reproduces a German poster announcing the execution on one day in December 1943 of eight Poles for the crime of "sheltering Jews." *When Light Pierced the Darkness: Righteous Christians and the Polish Jews* (New York: Oxford University Press, 1988).

103. J.K. Zawodny, *Nothing But Honor* (Stanford, CA: Hoover Institution, 1978), p. 118. Another 170,000 Poles were organized into military units by the Soviets. See illuminating comments on Polish forces in John Keegan, *Six Armies in Normandy* (New York: Viking, 1982), pp. 262ff.

104. Tadeusz Bor-Komorowski, *The Secret Army* (New York: Macmillan, 1951), p. 142.

105. Zawodny, *Nothing But Honor*, p. 45.

106. Bor-Komorowski, *Secret Army*, p. 30.

107. F.H. Hinsley et al., *British Intelligence in the Second World War*, 5 vols. (London: Her Majesty's Stationery Office, 1979–1990), vol. 1, pp. 488–95.

108. Bor-Komorowski, *Secret Army*, p. 151.

109. Stefan Korbonski, *Fighting Warsaw* (New York: Funk and Wagnalls, 1968), p. 219.

110. Ibid., p. 127.

111. Bor-Komorowski, *Secret Army*, p. 156; Lukas, *Forgotten Holocaust*, p. 91–92.

112. Bor-Komorowski, *Secret Army*, p. 195.

113. Ibid., p. 196.

114. Prior to the Warsaw Rising, approximately 62,000 AK throughout occupied Poland had been killed. Lukas, *Forgotten Holocaust*, p. 93.

115. Korbonski, *Fighting Warsaw*, p.183.

116. Ibid., p. 374.

117. Jan M. Ciechanowski, *The Warsaw Rising of 1944* (London: Cambridge University,1974), pp.261 and 256.

118. Ciechanowski, *Warsaw Rising*, p. 258.

119. Lukas, *Forgotten Holocaust*, p. 219; Bor-Komorowski, *Secret Army*, p. 378.

120. The place near Smolensk where in 1940, under direct orders from Stalin and the Politburo, the NKVD massacred 15,000 Polish officer-prisoners. See J.K. Zawodny, *Death in the Forest* (South Bend, IN: University of Notre Dame, 1962).

121. Korbonski, *Fighting Warsaw*, p. 388. See Winston Churchill, "The Martyrdom of Warsaw" in *Triumph and Tragedy*, volume 6 of his classic history of the Second World War.

CHAPTER 3: RELIGION AND INSURGENCY IN THE 18TH AND 19TH CENTURIES

1. Jean-Clement Martin, *La Vendée et la France* (Paris: Editions du Seuil, 1987), p. 25; Simon Schama, *Citizens: A Chronicle of the French Revolution* (New York: Alfred A. Knopf, 1989), p. 693.

2. On the Chouans of Brittany, see Donald Sutherland, *The Chouans: The Social Origins of Popular Counterrevolution in Upper Brittany, 1770–1798* (Oxford: Oxford University Press, 1982); Maurice Hutt, *Chouannerie and Counter-Revolution* (Cambridge: Cambridge University, 1993); Peter Paret, *Internal War and Pacification* (Princeton, NJ: Princeton University Center of International Studies, 1961); Walter Laqueur, *Guerrilla, A Historical and Critical Study* (Boston: Little, Brown, 1977); Schama, *Citizens*; Ramsay Weston Phipps, *The Armies of the First French Republic and the Rise of the Marshals of Napoleon I* (Westport, CT: Greenwood, 1980).

3. Schama, *Citizens*, pp. 349–50; Jacques Solé, *Questions of the French Revolution*

(New York Pantheon, 1989), p. 160.

4. Schama, *Citizens*, p. 350.

5. Both quotations are from Albert Mathiez, *The French Revolution* (New York: Russell and Russell, 1962 [orig. 1928], translated by Catherine A. Phillips), p. 191. See also Tilly, *The Vendée*, p. 233.

6. King Louis was ignorant of this papal rejection at the time he gave his assent to the documents; see inter alia Lefebvre, *The French Revolution*, p. 169.

7. Brinton, *Anatomy of Revolution*, p. 143; my emphasis.

8. John McManners, *The French Church and the Revolution* (Westport, CT: Greenwood, 1982), p. 38, my emphasis.

9. McManners, *The French Church*, p. 46.

10. Solé, *Questions of the French Revolution*, p. 97.

11. Doyle, *Oxford History of the French Revolution*, p. 144.

12. Louis Adolphe Thiers, *The History of the French Revolution* (Philadelphia: Lippincott, 1894; translated by Frederick Shoberl), vol. 1, p. 187.

13. Mathiez, *The French Revolution*, p. 115.

14. Sutherland, *The Chouans*, pp. 296–97 and passim.

15. Ibid., p. 250; Tilly, *The Vendée*, p. 257.

16. Schama, *Citizens*, p. 700.

17. Sutherland, *The Chouans*, p. 256.

18. Peter Paret, *Internal War and Pacification: The Vendée, 1789–1796* (Princeton, NJ: Princeton University, 1961), p. 69.

19. Paret, *Internal War and Pacification*, p. 22.

20. Doyle, *Oxford History of the French Revolution*, p. 224.

21. A. Aulard, *The French Revolution: A Political History 1789–1804* (New York: Scribner's, 1910, translated by Bernard Miall),vol. 2, p. 307.

22. Émile Gabory, *La Révolution et la Vendée*, vol. 1: Les deux parties (Paris, Perrin, 1925), p. 216.

23. See the interesting discussion of the tendency of revolutionary regimes to provoke foreign wars in Stephen Walt, *Revolution and War* (Ithaca, NY: Cornell University, 1997). And of course T.C.W. Blanning, *Origins of the French Revolutionary Wars* (New York: Longman, 1986).

24. Tilly, *The Vendée*, pp. 305, 320; Paret, *Internal War and Pacification*, p. 13.

25. Sutherland, *The Chouans*, p. 269. Richard Cobb refers to "the town dwellers who made up the revolutionary battalions." *The People's Armies*, translated by Marianne Elliott (New Haven: Yale University, 1987; original French edition 1961), p. 446.

26. Paret, *Internal War and Pacification*, p. 18.

27. Gabory, *La Révolution et la Vendée*, vol. 2, p. vi. And see Gabory, *La Révolution et la Vendée*, vol. 1, chapter XI.

28. Schama, *Citizens*, p. 697.

29. Paret, *Internal War and Pacification*, p. 28; Aulard, *The French Revolution*, vol. 2, p. 308; Paret, *Internal War and Pacification*, p. 18

30. Gabory, *La Révolution et la Vendée*, vol. 2, p. 19.

31. Paret, *Internal War and Pacification*, p. 2.

32. Ibid., p. 34.

33. Ramsey Weston Phipps, *The Armies of the First French Revolution* (Westport, CT: Greenwood, 1980 [orig. 1921]), p. 8.

34. Gabory, *La Révolution et la Vendée*, vol. 2, pp. 12–13.

35. Tilly, *The Vendée*, p. 334.

36. Gabory, *La Révolution et la Vendée*, vol. 1, p. 311.

37. Tilly, *The Vendée*, p. 324.

38. Thiers, *History of the French Revolution*, vol. 3, p. 117.

39. Andre Montagnon, *Une Guerre subversive: La guerre de Vendée* (Paris: La Colombe, 1959), p. 58; Thiers, *History of the French Revolution*, vol. 1, p. 310, and vol. 3, p. 73. See also André Montagnon, *Les guerres de Vendée, 1794–1832* (Paris: Perrin, 1974).

40. Phipps, *Armies of the First French Revolution*, p. 9.

41. Ibid., p. 7.

42. François-Athanase Charette de La Contrie, a naval officer, born in 1763. Pardoned in the general peace of February 1795, he joined the descent at Quiberon, was captured, and executed on March 29, 1796. Montagnon, *Une Guerre subversive*, p. 13.

43. Tilly, *The Vendée*, p. 338.

44. Gabory, *La Révolution et La Vendée*, vol. 1, p. 261.

45. Gabory, *La Révolution et La Vendée*, vol. 2, p. 14.

46. Montagnon, *Une Guerre subversive*, pp. 55–56.

47. Paret, *Internal War and Pacification*, p. 27.

48. Ibid., pp. 24–25.

49. Lefebvre, *The French Revolution*, vol. 2, p. 46.

50. Montagnon, *Une Guerre subversive*, p. 66.

51. Paret, *Internal War and Pacification*, p. 40.

52. Ibid., p. 30.

53. Montagnon, *Une Guerre subversive*, p. 67; see also Tilly, *The Vendée*, p. 333.

54. Montagnon, *Une Guerre subversive*, p. 75.

55. Thiers, *History of the French Revolution*, vol. 3, pp. 282–83.

56. Montagnon, *Une Guerre subversive*, p. 84.

57. Doyle, *Oxford History of the French Revolution*, p. 256.

58. Montagnon, *Une Guerre subversive*, p. 87; see the description of the massacre of the Vendeans in Gabory, *La Révolution et la Vendée*, vol. 2, chapter IX.

59. Thiers, *History of the French Revolution*, vol. 3, p. 292.

60. Martin, *La Vendée et la France*, p. 226.

61. Paret, *Internal War and Pacification*, p. 1.

62. Pierre Chaunu, in Reynald Secher, *Le Génocide franco-français: La Vendée-Vengé*. (Paris: Presses universitaires de France, 1988, 2d ed.), p. 24.

63. Secher, *Génocide franco-français*, p. 151.

64. Paret, *Internal War and Pacification*, p. 55.

65. Secher, *Génocide franco-français*, p. 136.

66. Ibid., pp. 155 and 164; on the grisly work of the infernal columns see also Henri de Malleray, *Les Cinq Vendées* (Paris: Plon-Nourrit, 1924), p. 97.

67. Montagnon, *Une Guerre subversive*, p. 123.

68. Martin, *La Vendée et la France*, p. 232.

69. Paret, *Internal War and Pacification*, p. 37.

70. Lefebvre, *The French Revolution*, vol. 2, p. 84.

71. Paret, *Internal War and Pacification*, p. 57.

72. Ibid., p. 54.

73. Secher, *Génocide franco-français*, p. 296.

74. Ibid., p. 159.

75. Paret, *Internal War and Pacification*, p. 54.

76. Ibid.

77. Ibid., p. 56.

78. Martin, *La Vendée et la France*, p. 230.

79. Schama, *Citizens*, p. 792.

80. The following event was typical: "A peasant woman about to give birth had concealed herself in a hovel near her village. Some soldiers found her. They cut out her tongue, slit open her stomach, and hoisted the infant on their bayonets. Neighbors a quarter mile away heard the screams of this unfortunate woman, but when they arrived to help her she was dead." Secher, *Génocide franco-français*, p. 297 (my translation).

81. Cobb, *The People's Armies*, p. 442.

82. See the connection between dechristianization and antifeminism pointed out by Cobb, *The People's Armies*, pp. 450–54.

83. Martin, *La Vendée et la France*, p. 232.

84. Secher, *Génocide franco-français*, p. 164.

85. Ibid., p. 172.

86. Paret, *Internal War and Pacification*, p. 58.

87. Thiers, *History of the French Revolution*, vol. 3, p. 71.

88. See for example Secher, *Génocide franco-français*, p. 166.

89. Gabory, *La Révolution et la Vendée*, vol. 2, p. 212.

90. Tilly, *The Vendée*, p. 339.

91. Thiers, *History of the French Revolution*, vol. 3, p. 453; Schama, *Citizens*, p. 789.

92. Martin, *La Vendée et la France*, p. 221.

93. Schama, *Citizens*, p. 789; Secher, *Génocide franco-français*, p. 155.

94. Schama, *Citizens*, p. 790.

95. Secher, *Génocide franco-français*, p. 186.

96. Ibid., p. 150.

97. Tilly, *The Vendée*, p. 333; Gabory, *La Révolution et la Vendée*, vol. 2, p. 38.

98. Montagnon, *Une Guerre subversive*, p. 119.

99. Doyle, *Oxford History of the French Revolution*, p. 424.

100. Solé, *Questions of the French Revolution*, chapter 12.

101. Doyle, *Oxford History of the French Revolution*, p. 193; Schama says only 6 percent of the eligibles actually voted, *Citizens*, pp. 644–46; for more on this crucial point of political minorities controlling elections, see Lefebvre, *French Revolution*, vol. 1, p. 241, and Albert Soboul, *The French Revolution 1787–1799*, translated by A. Forrest and C. Jones (New York: Random House, 1962), p. 267.

102. Schama, *Citizens*, p. 637.

103. Skocpol, *States and Revolutions*, p. 189.

104. Doyle, *Oxford History of the French Revolution*, p. 406.

105. Sutherland, *The Chouans*, p. 5.

106. Mathiez, *The French Revolution*, p. 304.

107. Montagnon, *Une Guerre subversive*, p. 97.

108. Hutt, *Chouannerie and Counter-Revolution*, p. 358.

109. Paret, *Internal War and Pacification*, p. 55.

110. Thiers, *History of the French Revolution*, vol. 4, pp. 352–54.

111. Thiers, *History of the French Revolution*, vol. 4, p. 352.

112. Ch.-L. Chassin, *Les pacifications de l'ouest, 1794–1801* (Mayenne: Floch, 1973 [orig. 1896]), vol. 1, p. 36.

113. Paret, *Internal War and Pacification*, p. 63.

114. Thiers, *History of the French Revolution*, vol. 4, p. 353.

115. Hutt, *Chouannerie and Counter-Revolution*, p. 448.

116. Martin, *La Vendée et la France*, p. 278; for his efforts see Chassin, *Pacification*, vol. 1, pp. 45ff.

117. Martin, *La Vendée et la France*, pp. 276–79.

118. Montagnon, *Une Guerre subversive*, p. 98.

119. Sutherland, *The Chouans*, p. 292; Christophe Roguet, *De la Vendée militaire* (Paris: J. Coreard, 1834), pp. 105–7.

120. Solé, *Questions of the French Revolution*, p. 144.

121. Secher, *Génocide franco-français*, pp. 265, 243; Martin, *La Vendée et La France*, p. 312.

122. Solé, *Questions of the French Revolution*, p. 144.

123. Laqueuer, *Guerrilla*, p. 23.

124. Pierre Chaunu in Secher, *Génocide franco-français*, p. 23.

125. By 1815, an additional one million lives would be lost. Doyle, *Oxford History of the French Revolution*, p. 425.

126. Phipps, *Armies of the First French Revolution*, p. 45.

127. It was not the brutality of the regime, but its overwhelming numbers of troops, plus the sagacity of Hoche, that finally defeated the rebels.

128. From the American Revolution and Napoleonic Spain to the Viet Minh and the Viet Cong, guerrillas have benefited greatly from symbiotic operations with regular units. True, the Afghan insurgency did well enough without the presence of friendly troops, but unlike the Vendeans they received substantial foreign aid and operated in close to ideal terrain.

129. See Lefebvre, *Napoleon from Tilsit to Waterloo*, vol. 2, p. 363; Alan Schom, *One Hundred Days: Napoleon's Road to Waterloo* (Oxford University Press, 1993), pp. 149–54, 201.

130. As the British ships drew near the enemy fleet, Nelson sent his captains the signal that has come down to us through two centuries: "England expects that every man will do his duty."

131. Lefebvre, *Napoleon*, p. 21

132. For the French disaster in Haiti, which led to the sale of Louisiana to the United States, see Thomas R. Ott, *The Haitian Revolution* (Knoxville, TN: University of Tennessee, 1973), and C.L.R. James, *Black Jacobins: Toussaint L'Ouverture and the San Domingo Revolution*, 2d edition (New York: Vintage, 1963).

133. Charles Oman, *A History of the Peninsular War*, 7 vols. (Oxford: Clarendon Press, 1902–1930), vol. 6, pp. 273ff; John M. Sherwig, *Guineas and Gunpowder: British Foreign Aid in the Wars with France, 1793–1815* (Cambridge, MA: Harvard University, 1969), esp. pp. 219–21 and 227–29.

134. J.W. Fortescue, *History of the British Army* (London: Macmillan, 1919–1920), vol. 8, p. 435, vol. 9, p. 36; Archer Jones, *The Art of War in the Western World* (New York: Oxford University, 1987), p. 359.

135. For example, see Gabriel H. Lovett, *Napoleon and the Birth of Modern Spain*. 2 vols. (New York: New York University, 1965), vol. 2, pp. 725–28.

136. Lefebvre, *Napoleon*, 19.

137. Lovett, *Napoleon*; Don W. Alexander, *Rod of Iron: French Counterinsurgency Policy in Aragon During the Peninsular War* (Wilmington, DE: Scholarly Resources, 1985); John Lawrence Tone, *The Fatal Knot: The Guerrilla War in Navarre and the Defeat of Napoleon in Spain* (Chapel Hill, NC: University of North Carolina, 1994).

138. A.G. Macdonnell, *Napoleon and his Marshals* (New York: Macmillan, 1934), p. 213.

139. Dezydery Chlapowski, *Memoirs of a Polish Lancer*, trans. Tim Simmons (Chicago: The Emperor's Press, 1992 [orig. 1837]), p. 47.
140. Lefebvre, *Napoleon*, vol. 1, pp. 226–27
141. Macdonnell, *Napoleon*, p. 213; W.F.P. Napier, *History of the War in the Peninsula and in the South of France*, 6 vols. (London: Frederick Warne, 1890–1892), vol. 4, p. 171,
142. Oman, *History*, vol. 4, p. 363
143. Lovett, *Napoleon*, v. 2, p. 688
144. J. Tranie and J.C. Carmigniani, *Napoleon's War in Spain*, trans. J. Mallender and J. Clements (London: Arms and Armour, 1982), p. 116
145. Felix Markham, *Napoleon* (New York: New American Library, 1963), p. 203. The Russian losses seem more dramatic to us because they occurred over a short period of time, whereas the Spanish ulcer bled for six years.
146. Tranie and Carmigniani say that there were 200,000 Imperial casualties in Spain, half of them inflicted by the guerrillas. *Napoleon's War in Spain*, p. 10. Owen Connelly estimates 260,000 French killed and wounded, plus another 40,000 allied casualties. *Blundering to Glory: Napoleon's Military Campaigns* (Wilmington, DE: Scholarly Resources, 1987), p. 132. The French general Bigarre wrote that guerrillas had killed 180,000 Imperial troops, not counting wounded and missing. Lovett, *Napoleon*, vol. 2, p. 683. Consider that the Vietnam conflict cost 58,000 U.S. lives.
147. Connelly, *Blundering to Glory*, p. 117

CHAPTER 4: RELIGION AND INSURGENCY IN THE 20TH CENTURY

1. Henry S. Bradsher, *Afghanistan and the Soviet Union* (Durham, NC: Duke University, 1985), chapter 5. See also Olivier Roy, *Islam and Resistance in Afghanistan* (Cambridge: Cambridge University Press, 1986), and Anthony Hyman, *Afghanistan under Soviet Domination* (London: Macmillan, 1984).
2. Amin Saikal and William Maley, Introduction to *The Soviet Withdrawal from Afghanistan*, ed. Amin Saikal and William Maley (Cambridge: Cambridge University Press, 1989), p. 5.
3. David C. Isby, "Soviet Strategy and Tactics in Low Intensity Conflict," in *Guerrilla Warfare and Counterinsurgency: U.S.-Soviet Policy in the Third World*, ed. Richard H. Shultz, Jr., et al. (Lexington, MA: Lexington Books, 1989).
4. A more common version: "The road to Paris lies through Peking."
5. See Joes, *America and Guerrilla Warfare*, chapter 9, "Afghanistan: Cracking the Red Empire."
6. Jean A. Meyer, *The Cristero Rebellion* (Cambridge: Cambridge University, 1976), p. 216.
7. Meyer, *Cristero Rebellion*, p. 219.
8. Charles C. Cumberland, *Mexico: The Struggle for Modernity* (New York: Oxford University, 1968), p. 174.
9. J. Lloyd Mecham, *Church and State in Latin America* (Chapel Hill, NC: University of North Carolina, 1966, rev. ed.), p. 366.
10. The reader interested in the Maximilian affair might wish to consult Ralph Roeder, *Juárez and His Mexico* (New York: Viking, 1947, 2 vols.); Jack Autrey Dabbs, *The French Army in Mexico, 1861–1867* (The Hague: Mouton, 1963); Jasper Ridley, *Maximilian and Juárez* (New York: Ticknor and Fields, 1992); Percy F. Martin, *Maximilian in Mexico* (New York: Scribner's, 1914); Egon Graf Corti, *Maximilian*

and Charlotte of Mexico (New York: Knopf, 1928), 2 vols; and José Luis Blasio, *Maximilian Emperor of Mexico: Memoirs of his Private Secretary* (New Haven, CT: Yale University, 1934).

11. Porfirio Díaz (1830–1915), a lieutenant of Juárez, assumed the presidency after a civil war in 1876 and held it with a brief interruption until overthrown by the Madero revolution in 1911. His regime was notable for domestic peace, financial stability, rising material prosperity, correct relations with the U.S., systematic injustice toward the peasantry, and thoroughgoing electoral corruption.

12. In April 1914, American and Mexican lives were lost when U.S. Marines, in an anti-Huerta move, landed in Vera Cruz; but two years later Wilson sent forces under General Pershing into northern Mexico against the protests of President Carranza.

13. Robert E. Quirk, *The Mexican Revolution and the Catholic Church* (Bloomington, IN: Indiana University, 1973), p. 177.

14. The fate of the other principal demand of the Maderistas—clean elections—is well known.

15. Dulles, *Yesterday in Mexico*, p. 351.

16. Quirk, *Mexican Revolution*, p. 112.

17. Mecham, *Church and State*, p. 384.

18. Ibid., p. 389.

19. Cumberland, *Mexico*, p. 270.

20. Quirk, *Mexican Revolution*, p. 96.

21. Mecham, *Church and State*, p. 388.

22. Carranza came from Coahuila, Obregón and Calles from Sonora, Villa from Chihuahua.

23. Quirk, *Mexican Revolution*, p. 149.

24. Meyer, *Cristero Rebellion*, pp. 26 and 31.

25. Meyer, *Cristero Rebellion*, p. 25.

26. See the discussion of the "psychopathology of the Catholic [sic] in Mexico," in Frank Brandenburg, *The Making of Modern Mexico* (Englewood Cliffs, NJ: Prentice-Hall), pp. 171–77. And the well-done if controversial study by Anita Brenner, *Idols Behind Altars* (New York: Harcourt, Brace, 1929).

27. See the excellent study of Zapata and his movement by John Womack, *Zapata and the Mexican Revolution* (New York: Vintage, 1969).

28. Meyer, *Cristero Rebellion*, p. 37.

29. See, for examples, Quirk, *Mexican Revolution*, pp. 154 and 176.

30. Meyer, *Cristero Rebellion*, p. 41. And see Dulles, *Yesterday in Mexico*, p. 301.

31. Mecham, *Church and State*, p. 403.

32. Quirk, *Mexican Revolution*, p. 182.

33. Even Obregón had said that "it is preferable that [Mexican children] receive any instruction rather than grow illiterate." Mecham, *Church and State*, p. 389.

34. Ibid., p. 394.

35. Ibid., p. 407.

36. Dulles, *Yesterday in Mexico*, p. 302.

37. Meyer, *Cristero Rebellion*, pp. 74–75.

38. Mecham, *Church and State*, p. 395. For instances of the repressive, even totalitarian, nature of the Calles regime, consult the following works by pro-regime observers: Ernest Gruening, *Mexico and Its Heritage* (New York: Century, 1928), and Carlton Beals, *Mexican Maze* (Philadelphia, PA: Lippincott, 1931).

39. According to the 1921 census, of Mexico's 14 million inhabitants Jalisco had 1.2 million.

40. Meyer, *Cristero Rebellion*, p. 79.

41. Ibid., p. 128.

42. James W. Wilkie, "The Meaning of the Cristero Religious War Against the Mexican Revolution," *Journal of Church and State*, vol. 8 (1966).

43. Meyer, *Cristero Rebellion*, p. 187.

44. Jim Tuck, *Holy War in Los Altos: A Regional Analysis of Mexico's Cristero Rebellion* (Tucson, AZ: University of Arizona, 1982), p. x.

45. Meyer, *Cristero Rebellion*, pp. 95–98. Unsurprisingly, the man who became commander of all the Cristeros called for votes for women.

46. Meyer, *Cristero Rebellion*, p. 135 and passim.

47. Gorostieta was a northerner and possibly at one time a Freemason; he had his own reasons for joining the Cristeros, but eventually he became devoutly religious.

48. Meyer, *Cristero Rebellion*, pp. 170–73 and passim.

49. Dulles, *Yesterday in Mexico*, p. 472.

50. Meyer, *Cristero Rebellion*, p. 73.

51. Wilkie, "Meaning of the Cristero Religious War," p. 227.

52. Meyer, *Cristero Rebellion*, p. 52. Meyer estimates 35,000 Cristeros in January 1928 and 50,000 in June 1929; *Cristero Rebellion*, pp. 58–59.

53. Meyer, *Cristero Rebellion*, p. 161.

54. Ibid., p. 51.

55. Cumberland, *Mexico*, p. 280; Dulles, *Yesterday in Mexico*, p. 311.

56. The peasant often appears to the city man as stupid, because he is taciturn and suspicious, with good reason. In *The Old Regime and the French Revolution*, Tocqueville observed that "it is only with difficulty that men of the better classes come to a clear understanding of what goes on in the souls of the people and especially of the peasants."

57. Tuck, *Holy War in Los Altos*, p. 14.

58. Calles's statement was premature, untrue, and ill-considered. Mecham, *Church and State*, p. 400.

59. See estimates in Meyer, *Cristero Rebellion*, p. 65 and passim.

60. A meeting of Calles and leading generals had decided on Minister of the Interior Portes Gil to be provisional president.

61. "There is little doubt that the [bishops] were sincerely laboring in support of a policy of conciliation and cooperation." Mecham, *Church and State*, p. 403.

62. Ibid., p. 398.

63. See Quirk, *Mexican Revolution*, chapter 8; Walter Lippmann, "The Church and State in Mexico: The American Mediation," *Foreign Affairs*, vol. viii (1930).

64. See Harold Nicolson, *Dwight Morrow* (New York: Harcourt, Brace, 1935).

65. Besides, the Mexican Congress had refused countless times before to accept Catholic petitions. See Wilkie, "Meaning of the Cristero Religious War," pp. 230–31.

66. Meyer, *Cristero Rebellion*, pp. 201–2; Quirk, *Mexican Revolution*, p. 245; David Bailey, *Viva Cristo Rey!* (Austin, TX: University of Texas, 1974), pp. 293–94; Tuck, *Holy War in Los Altos*, pp. 181ff.

67. These events provided the inspiration for Graham Greene's *The Power and the Glory* (1940), later made into a John Ford film, *The Fugitive*, starring Henry Fonda.

68. Mecham, *Church and State*, pp. 404–5.

69. Ibid., p. 408.

70. James W. Wilkie, "Statistical Indicators of the Impact of the National Revolution

on the Catholic Church in Mexico 1910–1967," *Journal of Church and State*, XII (1970), n.1, p. 98; Meyer, *Cristero Rebellion*, p. 205.
71. Guenter Lewy, *Religion and Revolution* (New York: Oxford University, 1974), p. 409.
72. Dulles, *Yesterday in Mexico*, pp. 619–21.
73. Ibid., p. 623.
74. Ibid., pp. 530–31.
75. Ibid., p. 646.
76. Mecham, *Church and State*, p. 405.
77. Ibid., p. 405.
78. Ibid., p. 406; Lyle C. Brown, "Mexican Church-State Relations," *Journal of Church and State*, vol. VI (1964), p. 205.
79. Meyer, *Cristero Rebellion*, p. 204.
80. Brown, "Mexican Church-State Relations," p. 213.
81. Cumberland, *Mexico*, p. 275. For an equation of the Calles clique to the Díaz dictatorship, see Edwin Lieuwen, *Mexican Militarism: The Political Rise and Fall of the Revolutionary Army, 1910–1940* (Westport, CT: Greenwood, 1981 [orig. 1968]), p. 92.
82. Brown, "Mexican Church-State Relations," p. 211.
83. Cárdenas had Calles expelled from Mexico in April 1936.
84. Brown, "Mexican Church-State Relations," p. 214.
85. The U.S. State Department desired above all a stable Mexico, and thus backed the likely winners. Bailey, *Viva Cristo Rey!*, pp. 307–8.
86. Neville Maxwell, *India's China War* (New York: Anchor, 1972); Michael Carver, *War Since 1945* (New York: Putnam's, 1981).
87. China has not aided the anti-India uprising in Kashmir at least in part because it fears repercussions in Tibet. Ahmed Rashid, "The China Factor," *Far Eastern Economic Review*, January 13, 1994. See Eric S. Margolis, *War at the Top of the World: The Struggle for Afghanistan, Kashmir and Tibet* (NY: Routledge, 2000).
88. In 1270, Kublai Khan was converted to Lamaist Buddhism.
89. H.E. Richardson, *A Short History of Tibet* (New York: E.P. Dutton, 1962), chapter 1. To Tibetans, "the Chinese were foreigners as much as the British or the Indians." Tsering Shakya, *The Dragon in the Land of Snows* (New York: Columbia University, 1999), p. 250.
90. Melvin C. Goldstein, *A History of Modern Tibet, 1913–1951* (Berkeley, CA: University of California Press, 1989), p. 44. For more background see Sir Charles Bell, *The People of Tibet* (Oxford: Clarendon Press, 1928); T. Shakabpa, *Tibet: A Political History* (New Haven, CT: Yale University Press, 1967); and Shakya, *Dragon in the Land of Snows*.
91. Warren W. Smith, *Tibetan Nation: A History of Tibetan Nationalism and Sino-Tibetan Relations* (Boulder, CO: Westview, 1996), p. 272.
92. "Tibetans made excellent troops when properly led and armed, but the political implications of a modern and efficient army continued to threaten the religious elite and precluded the development of such a force. The Tibetan government continued purposely to maintain [during the 1930s] an ineffective army." Goldstein, *Modern Tibet*, p. 288.
93. Ibid., pp. 683ff.
94. Ibid., pp. 667, 718, 791.
95. B.N. Mullik, *My Years with Nehru: The Chinese Betrayal* (Bombay: Allied Publish-

ers, 1971), pp. 79–80. Nevertheless, on October 26, 1950, the Indian government declared that the "invasion by Chinese troops of Tibet cannot but be regarded as deplorable." *The Question of Tibet and the Rule of Law* (Geneva: International Commission of Jurists, 1959), p.132.

96. The U.S. watched events in Tibet with interest. As early as July 11, 1950, the State Department inquired of the U.S. Embassy in New Delhi if arms should be sent to Tibet. A secret Aide-Memoire from the Department to the British Embassy in Washington dated December 30, 1950, stated that "consideration could be given to recognition of Tibet as an independent State." A week later Secretary of State Dean Acheson informed the U.S. Ambassador in New Delhi that the "US Govt still stands ready [to] extend some material assistance if appropriate means can be found for expression Tibetan resistance to aggression." U.S. Department of State, *Foreign Relations of the United States 1950,* Vol. VI: *East Asia and the Pacific* (Washington, DC: USGPO, 1976), pp. 377, 613 and 618. The Dalai Lama correctly noted that the U.S. was less interested in helping Tibet than in promoting anticommunism; see his *Freedom in Exile* (New York: Harper Perennial, 1990), pp. 121–22.

97. For an account of this journey, see Heinrich Harrar, *Seven Years in Tibet* (New York: Dutton, 1954).

98. According to one hostile but well-informed Indian observer, all this was "to hoodwink the United Nations and give China the excuse to induct an unlimited number of troops into Tibet." Mullik, *My Years,* p. 599.

99. George N. Patterson, *Requiem for Tibet* (London: Aurum, 1990), p. 136.

100. Mullik, *My Years,* pp. 597–98.

101. Patterson, *Requiem,* p. 136; Smith, *Tibetan Nation,* p. 402.

102. Smith, *Tibetan Nation,* p. xxvii.

103. "The great monasteries of Tibet were attacked and looted and unspeakable sacrileges were committed. . . . Many monks were beaten to death. . . ." Mullik, *My Years,* p. 220. Michel Peissel says that 250 monasteries were destroyed; *The Secret War in Tibet* (Boston: Litle, Brown, 1973), p. 86. On the public torture and killing of monks see Smith, *Tibetan Nation,* pp. 404 and passim. The Chinese betrayed "a prima facie case of a systematic intention by such acts and other acts to destroy in whole or in part the Tibetans as a separate nation and the Buddhist religion in Tibet." *The Question of Tibet and the Rule of Law* (Geneva: The International Commission of Jurists, 1959), p. 71.

104. This International Commission was headed by P. Trikamdas, General Secretary of the Indian Commission of Jurists. The International Commission of Jurists is a non-governmental organization with 35,000 members in 53 countries, and has consultative status to the United Nations.

105. *The Question of Tibet and the Rule of Law,* p. 59.

106. Smith, *Tibetan Nation,* Chapter 10 and passim.

107. Smith, *Tibetan Nation,* p. 426.

108. Ibid., p. 450. On Chinese desire for the land and resources of neighboring areas, consult June T. Dreyer, *China's Forty Millions: Minority Nationalities and National Integration in the People's Republic of China* (Cambridge, MA: Harvard University, 1976).

109. Smith, *Tibetan Nation,* pp. 421–22. And see the Dalai Lama, *My Land and My People* (New York: McGraw-Hill, 1962), pp. 156–58.

110. Peissel, *Secret War,* p. 92.

111. Smith, *Tibetan Nation*, pp. 412–15. See also the Dalai Lama, *Freedom in Exile*, p. 122.

112. George N. Patterson, *Tibet in Revolt* (London: Faber and Faber, 1960), p. 120.

113. As a matter of fact, the majority of the agricultural population owned land. Peissel, *Secret War*, p. 54.

114. Mullik, *My Years*, p. 222.

115. Smith, *Tibetan Nation*, p. 447. "The revolt was essentially in defense of the value system of the ordinary men and women, to which the Dalai lama was central." Shakya, *Dragon in the Land of Snows*, p. 210.

116. Smith, *Tibetan Nation*, pp. 395, 443 and passim.

117. Peissel, *Secret War*, p. 4.

118. Patterson, *Requiem*, p. 67.

119. Patterson, *Requiem*, p. 150. See also Frank Moraes, *The Revolt in Tibet* (New York: Macmillan, 1960), and Jamyang Norbu, *Warriors of Tibet* (London: Wisdom, 1986).

120. Peissel, *Secret War*, p. 219.

121. The CIA recruited Tibetans in Darjeeling and Kalimpong and trained them on Saipan and at a camp near Leadville, Colorado, in the techniques of guerrilla warfare. The Agency also supported NVDA raids with their Civil Air Transport company. But the increasing hopelessness of the situation, and growing U.S. involvement in Vietnam caused U.S. commitment to the Titans to wane; John Ranelaugh, *The Agency: The Rise and Decline of the CIA* (New York: Simon and Schuster, 1987), pp. 335–36; Smith, *Tibetan Nation*, p. 507; Kenneth Conboy and James Morrison, *The CIA's Secret War in Tibet* (Lawrence, KS: University Press of Kansas, 2002); John Kenneth Knaus, *Orphans of the Cold War: Americans and the Tibetan Struggle for Survival* (New York: Public Affairs, 1999). And see discussions as to the possible repercussions of U.S. recognition of a Free Tibet in *Foreign Relations of the United States*, vol. XIX, 1958–1960 (Washington, DC: USGPO, 1996), pp. 751–801.

122. Patterson, *Requiem*, p. 154; Peissel, *Secret War*, p. 105.

123. Peissel, *Secret War*, p. 105.

124. Patterson, *Tibet in Revolt*, p. 152; Patterson, *Requiem*, p. 136; Peissel, *Secret War*, p. 170. Mullik agrees with these figures; see *My Years*, p. 216.

125. Patterson, *Requiem*, p. 164. In June 1959 a press statement issued by the International Commission of Jurists estimated that at least 65,000 Tibetans, mostly civilians, had died in the fighting; See *The Question of Tibet and the Rule of Law*, p. 60, and Patterson, *Requiem*, p. 187.

126. Mullik, *My Years*, p. 213.

127. Patterson, *Tibet in Revolt*, p. 173.

128. Peissel, *Secret War*, chapter 10. There may have been 5,000 guerrillas in the Lhoka district; Smith, *Tibetan Nation*, p. 444.

129. This epic drama has been well captured in the film masterpiece *Kundun*.

130. See the Dalai Lama, *My Land and My People* (New York: McGraw-Hill, 1962); John F. Avedon, *In Exile From the Land of Snows* (New York: Knopf, 1984); and Chanakya Sen, ed., *Tibet Disappears: A Documentary History of Tibet's International Status, the Great Rebellion and its Aftermath* (New Delhi: Asia Publishing House 1960).

131. Peissel, *Secret War*, pp. 139ff.

132. The one-time head of India's Intelligence Bureau wrote that "India's security is seriously threatened by the Chinese presence on the Himalaya frontier. . . . To guaran-

tee effectively the security of the Himalayas, it is essential to restore Tibetan independence." Mullik, *My Years*, p. 630.

133. Neville Maxwell, *India's China War* (New York: Anchor, 1972), pp. 99ff.

134. Smith, *Tibetan Nation*, p. 519.

135. The Indian Government stated in August 1961 that there were 33,000 Tibetan refugees in India. Smith, *Tibetan Nation*, p. 538n.

136. Ibid., pp. 492–93.

137. There had already been a rather bloody clash between Indian and Chinese troops at Kingka Pass in October 1959; see Maxwell, *India's China War*, pp. 107ff.

138. See Maxwell, *India's China War*, for a briefer account, see Sir Michael Carver, *War Since 1945* (New York: G.P. Putnam's Sons, 1981), chapter 11, "India's Wars." See also George N. Patterson, *Peking Versus Delhi* (New York: Praeger, 1964).

139. Smith, *Tibetan Nation*, p. 508.

140. Unit 22 still existed as of 1996; Smith, *Tibetan Nation*, p. 509. Shakya says that 150 Tibetans were flown to the U.S. for training; *Dragon in the Land of Snows*, p. 284. CIA assistance to the Tibetans apparently ended in 1972 at the time of the Sino-U.S. rapprochement.

141. Smith, *Tibetan Nation*, pp. 544–46.

142. Ibid., p. 561.

143. Ibid., pp. 548–51.

144. By 1980 only 10 out of the former 2,500 monasteries were still open, with fewer than 1,000 monks; A. Tom Grunfeld, *The Making of Modern Tibet* (London: Zed, 1987), p. 211 (Grunfeld is a tireless apologist for the Chinese). For the destruction of Tibetan culture by Chinese Red Guards, see Patterson, *Requiem*, pp. 210–11; people were attacked on the streets even for wearing traditional Tibetan hair-styles; Grunfeld, *Modern Tibet*, p. 181. For continuing Chinese hostility to Tibetan Buddhism, and plans to assassinate the Dalai Lama, see the *New York Times*, March 6, 1996, p. A8.

145. Patterson, *Requiem*, p. 149. "Tibet is dead"; Moraes, *Revolt*, p. 219. And see Mary Craig, *Tears of Blood: A Cry for Tibet* (Washington, DC: Counterpoint, 1999).

146. Smith, *Tibetan Nation*, p. 488.

147. Goldstein, *Modern History*, "Conclusions," pp. 815–24.

148. Smith, *Tibetan Nation*, p. 562.

149. According to the 1994–1995 *Statesman's Year-Book*, in 1992 there were 21.9 million Sunni Muslims, mostly in the North, and 2.4 million Christians plus 5 million "traditionalist animists" in the South.

150. "The magnitude of the human destruction in Sudan since independence makes the conflict one of the most savage of our time." J. Millard Burr and Robert O. Collins, *Requiem for the Sudan* (Boulder, CO: Westview, 1995), p. 2.

151. Northerners display "racial and religious animosity toward the Southern Sudanese, long regarded as inferior or heretical." Burr and Collins, *Requiem for the Sudan*, p. 4.

152. P.M. Holt, *The Mahdist State in Sudan* (Oxford: Oxford University Press, 1958), pp. 24, 34, 117; A.B. Theobald, *The Mahdiya* (London: Longmans, 1962); Gerard Prunier, "Le Sud-Soudan depuis l'indépendence (1956–1989)" in Marc Lavergne, ed., *Soudan Contemporain* (Paris: Karthala, 1989), p. 383.

153. Milton Viorst, "Sudan's Islamic Experiment," *Foreign Affairs*, v. 74 (May-June, 1995), p. 50

154. "Au Sud, la politique d'arabisation et d'islamisation forcée accompagnant la domination politique et economique du Nord provoqua la guerre civile et l'éclatement de la societé sudiste." Catherine Miller in Lavergne, *Soudan Contemporain*, p. 106; M.W.

Daly, "Broken Bridges and Empty Baskets: The Political and Economic Background of the Sudanese Civil War," in M.W. Daly and A.A. Sikainga, eds., *Civil War in the Sudan* (New York: British Academic Press, 1993), p. 14.

155. Edgar O'Ballance, *The Secret War in the Sudan* (Hamden, CT: Archon, 1977), p. 79.

156. "Trained as a regular army to fight conventional wars, the Sudanese army was ill-equipped to combat the highly mobile and elusive insurgents." Burr and Collins, *Requiem*, p. 18.

157. O'Ballance, *Secret War*, chapter 10.

158. Douglas H. Johnson and Gerard Prunier, "The Foundation and Expansion of the Sudan People's Liberation Army," in Daly and Sikainga, eds., *Civil War in the Sudan*, p. 122.

159. Born 1945, a Dinka, Ph.D. agriculture, Iowa State University.

160. Francis Mading Deng, "War of Visions for the Middle East," *Middle East Journal*, v. 44 (August, 1990), p. 596.

161. See M. Khalid, ed., *John Garang Speaks* (London: KPI, 1987).

162. *New York Times*, February 22, 1992, and June 3, 1992.

163. Perhaps as many as 75,000 Dinka children were sold into northern slavery. Burr and Collins, *Requiem*, p. 257.

164. In 1993 Amnesty International accused the Khartoum regime of "ethnic cleansing" in the South.

165. Viorst, "Sudan's Islamic Experiment," p. 50; Prunier, "Le Sud-Soudan," p. 25.

166. Callwell, *Small Wars*.

CHAPTER 5: FOREIGN INVOLVEMENT WITH INSURGENCY

1. *The Prince*, Chapter XX.

2. Anthony H. Cordesman and Abraham Wagner, *The Lessons of Modern War*, vol. 3, *The Afghan and Falklands Conflicts* (Boulder, CO: Westview, 1990), p. 95.

3. The guerrillas were of course defeated in South Vietnam.

4. The Eritrean insurgents first received help from the Soviets, but later from the Americans. See J. Bowyer Bell, "Endemic Insurgency and International Order: The Eritrean Experience," *Orbis* (Summer 1974); Roy Pateman, *Eritrea: Even the Stones Are Burning* (Trenton, NJ: Red Sea Press, 1990), and "The Eritrean War," *Armed Forces and Society*, vol. 17 (Fall 1990); Richard F. Sherman, *Eritrea in Revolution* (doctoral dissertation, Brandeis University, 1980).

5. Southern Sudanese insurgents at various times received help and training from Israel and Ethiopia, among others.

6. Chen Jian, "China and the First Indo-China War, 1950–1954," *China Quarterly*, no. 133, March 1983, pp. 85–110. "Chinese military assistance was critical to the Viet Minh in their war against the French." John Lewis Gaddis, Foreword to Qiang Zhai, *China and the Viet Nam Wars 1950–1975* (Chapel Hill, NC: University of North Carolina, 2000), p. ix. See also Xiaoming Zhang, "The Viet Nam War, 1964–1969: A Chinese Perspective," *Journal of Military History*, 60, 4 (October, 1996).

7. The failure of the Johnson administration to block the Trail is in the opinion of many the key to the fall of South Vietnam. The distance across Laos from South Vietnam to Thailand is less than that between Philadelphia and Washington, DC. General Westmoreland believed a line across Laos could be held by three divisions (*A Soldier Reports*, p. 148), a position endorsed by Harry Summers (*On Strategy: A Critical*

Analysis of the Viet Nam War (Novato, CA: Presidio 1982). For a broader discussion of the issue of the Trail, see Joes, *America and Guerrilla Warfare*, pp. 240–42. See also C. Dale Walton, *The Myth of Inevitable U.S. Defeat in Viet Nam* (London: Frank Cass, 2002), and Bui Tin, *From Enemy to Friend* (Annapolis: Naval Institute Press, 2002), pp. 74–80.

8. The reader interested in the Maximilian affair might wish to consult Ralph Roeder, *Juárez and his Mexico* (New York: Viking, 1947, 2 vols.); Jack Autrey Dabbs, *The French Army in Mexico, 1861–1867* (The Hague: Mouton 1963); Jasper Ridley, *Maximilian and Juárez* (New York: Ticknor and Fields, 1992); Percy F. Martin, *Maximilian in Mexico* (New York: Scribner's, 1914); Egon C. Corti, *Maximilian and Charlotte of Mexico* (New York: Knopf, 1928, 2 vols.); and José Luis Blasio, *Maximilian Emperor of Mexico: Memoirs of his Private Secretary* (New Haven, CT: Yale University, 1934).

9. Gabriel Marcella and David Shulz, *Colombia's Three Wars: U.S. Strategy at the Crossroads* (Carlisle Barracks, PA: Strategic Studies Institute, 1999).

10. Daniel Byman et al., *Trends in Outside Support for Insurgent Movements* (Santa Monica, CA: RAND, 2001).

11. On help to the Salvadoran guerrillas see James LeMoyne, "El Salvador's Forgotten War," *Foreign Affairs,* v. 66 (Summer 1989); José Moroni Bracamonte and David E. Spencer, *Strategy and Tactics of the Salvadoran FMLN Guerrillas* (Westport, CT: Praeger, 1995); David E. Spencer, *From Viet Nam to El Salvador: The Saga of the FMLN Sappers and Other Guerrilla Special Forces in Latin America* (Westport, CT: Praeger, 1996).

12. Even if Moro units were able to reach the outskirts of Manila, it would not guarantee them success, as the Huks discovered in the 1940s.

13. On the Moros, past and present, see George W. Jornacion, "Time of the Eagles: United States Army Officers and the Pacification of the Philippine Moros," Ph.D. dissertation, University of California, Los Angeles, 1973; Frank E. Vandiver, *Black Jack: The Life and Times of General John J. Pershing* (College Station, TX: Texas A&M University, 1977); Donald Smythe, *Guerrilla Warrior: The Early Life of John J. Pershing* (New York: Scribner's, 1973); T.J. George, *Revolt on Mindanao: The Rise of Islam in Philippine Politics* (Kuala Lumpur: Oxford University, 1980); Herman Hagedorn, *Leonard Wood* (New York: Harper, 1931, 2 vols.); Andrew J. Bacevich, "Disagreeable Work: Pacifying the Moros 1903–1906," *Military Review,* v. 62 (June 1982).

14. And to the ability of intelligent human beings not to see what they do not wish to see.

15. Cordesman and Wagner, *Lessons,* vol. III, p. 95. Granted, U.S. air power operated under many politically imposed restraints both in Korea and in Vietnam (at least until 1972 in the latter case), and technologies exist today that were not available in Korea or Vietnam. See Eduard Mark, *Aerial Interdiction: Air Power and the Land Battle in Three American Wars* (Washington, DC: Center for Air Force History, 1994); Richard Hallion, *The Naval Air War in Korea* (Baltimore, MD: Nautical and Aviation Publishing, 1986); *The Pentagon Papers,* Gravel Edition (Boston: Beacon Press, 1971), vol. IV, pp. 1–276; James S. Corum and Wray R. Johnson, *Air Power in Small Wars: Fighting Insurgents and Terrorists* (Lawrence, KS: University Press of Kansas, 2003).

16. See Graham Webster, *The Roman Imperial Army* (Totowa, NJ: Barnes and Noble, 1985, 3d ed.), pp. 66–73; David J. Breeze and B. Dobson, *Hadrian's Wall* (London: Allen Lane, 1976); Eric Birley, *Research on Hadrian's Wall* (Kendal, England: T. Wilson, 1961); David J. Breeze, *The Northern Frontiers of Roman Britain* (New York: St.

Martin's, 1982); David Divine, *The North-west Frontier of Rome: A Military Study of Hadrian's Wall* (London: Macdonald, 1969); Edward N. Luttwak, *The Grand Strategy of the Roman Empire* (Baltimore: Johns Hopkins University, 1976), chapter 2.
17. See, for example, Glanmor Williams, *Owen Glendower* (London: Oxford University Press, 1966).
18. Donald Lancaster, *The Emancipation of French Indochina* (London: Oxford University, 1961), p. 218.
19. Bernard Fall, *Street Without Joy* (Harrisburg, PA: Stackpole, 1964), p. 30.
20. See Joes, *Modern Guerrilla Warfare*, pp. 103–4.
21. Lewis H. Gann, *Guerrillas in History* (Stanford, CA: Hoover Institution on War, Revolution and Peace, 1971), p. 36.
22. Thomas Pakenham, *The Boer War* (New York: Random House, 1979), p. xix.
23. Ibid., p. 569.
24. Christiaan Rudolf De Wet, *Three Years' War* (New York: Scribner's, 1903), p. 260.
25. Callwell, *Small Wars*, p. 143.
26. See William Wei, *Counterrevolution in China: The Nationalists in Jiangxi During the Soviet Period* (Ann Arbor, MI: University of Michigan, 1985), pp. 108ff.
27. The Japanese also employed lines of blockhouses; see below. See the discussion of similar strategies in the Vendean and Boer conflicts.
28. *The Real War* (Boston: Little Brown, 1963 [orig. 1930]), p. 472.
29. Scott outlined his Anaconda Plan in letters to General George McClellan, May 3 and May 21, 1861. *War of the Rebellion: A Compilation of the Official Records of the Union and Confederate Armies,* Series 1, vol. 51, Part 1(Washington, DC: Government Printing Office, 1897), pp.369–70 and 386–87.
30. Samuel Eliot Morison, *The Oxford History of the American People* (New York: Oxford University Press, 1965), p. 626.
31. John S.D. Eisenhower, *Agent of Destiny: The Life and Times of General Winfield Scott* (New York: Free Press, 1997), p. 386.
32. *By Sea and by River: The Naval History of the Civil War* (New York: Knopf, 1962), p. 232.
33. *The Confederate States of America, 1861–1865* (Baton Rouge, LA: Louisiana State University, 1950), p. 294.
34. "Why the South was Defeated in the Civil War," in *Practical Essays on American Government* (New York: Longmans, Green, 1893), p. 277.
35. Morison, *Oxford History of the American People*, p. 626; see also "Sea Power and the War," Ibid., pp. 642–45.
36. Harold and Margaret Sprout, *The Rise of American Naval Power, 1776–1918* (Princeton, NJ: Princeton University Press, 1967), p. 164.
37. Allan Nevins, *The War for the Union: The Improvised War 1861–1862* (New York: Scribner's, 1959), p. 290.
38. *The War for the Union: The Organized War to Victory 1864–1865* (New York: Scribner's, 1971), p. 272.

CHAPTER 6: ESTABLISHING CIVILIAN SECURITY

1. Clausewitz, *On War*, Book Eight, Chapter Four.
2. Richard L. Clutterbuck, *The Long, Long War: Counterinsurgency in Malaya and Viet Nam* (New York: Praeger, 1966). "The guerrilla fighter must be separated from the people. The guerrilla must be fought with his own tactics. These are the essence of

anti-guerrilla strategy." General Abdul H. Nasution, *Fundamentals of Guerrilla War-fare* (New York: Praeger, 1965 [orig. 1953]), p. 64.

3. John Coates, *Suppressing Insurgency: An Analysis of the Malayan Emergency, 1948–1954* (Boulder, CO: Westview, 1992), p. 82.

4. Eric Bergerud, *The Dynamics of Defeat: The Vietnam War in Hau Nghia Province* (Boulder, CO: Westview, 1991), p. 83.

5. Stuart A. Herrington, *Silence Was a Weapon: The Viet Nam War in the Villages* (Novato, CA: Presidio, 1982), p. 137; Fall, *Two Viet Nams*, p. 281; Race, *War Comes to Long An*, p. 83; Robert Shaplen, quoted in *The Pentagon Papers* (Boston: Beacon Hill, 1971), vol. I, p. 334; Bergerud, *Dynamics of Defeat*, pp. 67–68; Robert Scigliano, *South Viet Nam: Nation Under Stress* (Boston: Houghton Mifflin, 1964), p. 140; Robert Thompson, *Defeating Communist Insurgency: The Lessons of Malaya and Viet Nam* (New York: Praeger, 1966), p. 27; Stephen T. Hosmer, *Viet Cong Repression and Its Implications for the Future* (Santa Monica, CA: Rand, 1970).

6. Lewis H. Gann, *Guerrillas in History* (Stanford, CA: Hoover Institution, 1971), p. 36.

7. Thomas Pakenham, *The Boer War* (New York: Random House, 1979), p. 549.

8. Byron Farwell, *The Great Anglo-Boer War* (New York: Norton, 1976), p. 392.

9. Conditions in British camps for their Boer prisoners of war were much better, disproving any intent to commit genocide. And some civilian camps were better than others.

10. Farwell describes Army rations as "execrable." *Great Anglo-Boer War*, p. 400.

11. Ibid., p. 349.

12. Joes, *America and Guerrilla Warfare*, pp. 110–11.

13. Brian McAlister Linn, *The Philippine War 1899–1902* (Lawrence, KS: University Press of Kansas, 2000), p. 304.

14. Granted, many of the guerrillas were no less brutal than Weyler's men.

15. The best source on the Cristeros is Jean A. Meyer, *The Cristero Rebellion* (New York: Cambridge University, 1976). See also Brian Kelly, *The Cristero Rebellion* (Ph.D. dissertation, University of New Mexico, 1973).

16. Anthony Short, *The Communist Insurrection in Malaya, 1948–1960* (London: Frederick Muller, 1975), p. 378.

17. Edgar O'Ballance, *Malaya: The Communist Insurgent War* (Hamden, CT: Archon, 1966), p.108.

18. Peter Paret, *French Revolutionary Warfare from Indochina to Algeria* (New York: Praeger, 1964), p. 41.

19. See Anthony James Joes, *From the Barrel of a Gun: Armies and Revolutions,* Chapter 7, "French Algeria: The Victory and Crucifixion of an Army" (Washington, DC: Pergamon-Brassey's, 1986).

20. Chong Sik Lee, *Counterinsurgency in Manchuria: The Japanese Experience 1921–1940* (Santa Monica, CA: RAND, 1967).

21. A typical village included five hamlets, with a population of about 3,500 over an area of approximately four square kilometers.

22. Bergerud, *Dynamics of Defeat*, p. 35.

23. James W. Dunn, "Province Advisers in Viet Nam, 1962–1965" in Richard A. Hunt and Richard H. Shultz, Jr., eds., *Lessons from an Unconventional War* (NY: Pergamon, 1982), pp. 1–23.

24. "When the relocated people are then left without adequate assistance by the GVN, their enmity is further increased. . . . the GVN is bringing groups of the enemy into its

midst and hardening their hostility by the callous treatment it accords them. This is a good recipe for losing the war." Quoted in Richard A. Hunt, *Pacification: America's Struggle for Viet Nam's Hearts and Minds* (Boulder, CO: Westview, 1995), p. 230.

25. Sir Robert Thompson, *Defeating Communist Insurgency: The Lessons of Malaya and Viet Nam* (New York: Praeger, 1966), chapter 12.

26. Cao Van Vien and Dong Van Khuyen, *Reflections on the Vietnam War* (Washington, DC: U.S. Army Center of Military History, 1980), p. 27n.

27. *The Pentagon Papers* (Boston: Beacon Press, 1971), vol. II, p. 756.

28. Ibid., p. 686; Dennis Duncanson, *Government and Revolution in Viet Nam* (New York: Oxford University Press, 1968), p. 319. For veiled but repeated suggestions of how much the Communists feared and hated the strategic hamlet program, see *Victory in Viet Nam: The Official History of the People's Army of Viet Nam, 1954–1975*, trans. Merle Pribbenow (Lawrence, KS: University Press of Kansas, 2002), passim.

29. R. Marston, "Resettlement as a Counter-revolutionary Technique," in *Journal of the Royal United Services Institute for Defence Studies*, vol. 124, no. 4 (1979), p. 48.

30. John P. Cann, *Counterinsurgency in Africa: The Portuguese Way of War, 1961–1974* (Westport, CT: Greenwood, 1997), p. 145.

31. Gabriel H. Lovett, *Napoleon and the Birth of Modern Spain* (New York: New York University, 1965), vol. 2, p. 573.

32. See Thomas A. Marks, *Maoist Insurgency Since Viet Nam* (Portland, OR: Frank Cass, 1996).

33. John S. Girling, *Thailand: Society and Politics* (Ithaca, NY: Cornell University, 1981), p. 257 and passim; Charles F. Keyes, *Thailand: Buddhist Kingdom as Modern Nation-State* (Boulder, CO: Westview 1987), p. 109.

34. Girling, *Thailand*, p. 258.

35. Stuart Slade, "Successful Counterinsurgency: How the Thais burnt the books and beat the Guerrillas," *International Defense Review*, v. 22 (October 1989), p. 24.

36. Marks, *Maoist Insurgency Since Viet Nam*, pp. 68, 109.

37. John McBeth, "Counting on Nearby Friends," *Far Eastern Economic Review*, July 13, 1979, p. 13.

38. Cao Van Vien and Dong Van Khuyen, *Reflections*, p. 42–43; Ngo Quang Truong, *Territorial Forces* (Washington, DC: U.S. Army Center of Military History, 1981), p. 53.

39. Ngo Quang Truong, *Territorial Forces*, pp. 75ff.

40. For the use of these tactics by the Viet Cong, see George K. Tanham, *Communist Revolutionary Warfare: From the Viet Minh to the Viet Cong*, 2d ed. (New York: Praeger, 1967), pp. 159–60.

41. W. Scott Thompson and Donaldson D. Frizzell, *The Lessons of Viet Nam* (New York: Crane, Russak, 1977), p. 257.

42. Thompson and Frizzell, *Lessons of Viet Nam*, pp. 256–61; Ngo Quang Truong, *Territorial Forces*, p. 77.

43. Guenter Lewy, *America in Viet Nam* (New York: Oxford University Press, 1978), p. 173.

44. Ngo Quang Truong, *Territorial Forces*, p. 128. RF/PF losses were usually twice those of ARVN, yet the RF/PF desertion rate was only a small percentage of that of ARVN, with almost no defections. Ngo Quang Truong, *Territorial Forces*, p. 128.

45. Thomas C. Thayer, "Territorial Forces," in Thompson and Frizzell, *Lessons of Viet Nam*, p. 258.

46. Ibid., 258–60.

47. Lewis Sorley, *A Better War: The Unexamined Victories and Final Tragedy of America's Last Years in Viet Nam* (New York: Harcourt, Brace, 1999), pp. 72–73.

48. Ngo Quang Truong, *Territorial Forces*, p. 133.

49. Al Hemingway, *Our War Was Different: Marine Combined Action Platoons in Viet Nam* (Annapolis, MD: Naval Institute Press, 1994), p. 178. But see also William R. Corson, *The Betrayal* (New York: Norton, 1968).

50. Hemingway, *Our War*, p. x.

51. Lewy, *America in Viet Nam*, p. 116. See also Michael E. Peterson, *Combined Action Platoons: The U.S. Marines' Other War in Viet Nam* (New York: Praeger, 1989).

52. William Westmoreland, *A Soldier Reports* (Garden City, NY: Doubleday, 1976), p.166.

53. Carlos Ivan DeGregori, "Harvesting Storms: Peasant Rondas and the Defeat of Sendero Luminoso," in Steve J. Stern, ed., *Shining and Other Paths* (Durham, NC: Duke University, 1998), p. 146.

54. Cynthia McClintock, *Revolutionary Movements in Latin America: El Salvador's FMLN and Peru's Shining Path* (Washington, DC: U.S. Institute of Peace, 1998), pp. 185ff; DeGregori, "Harvesting Storms," p. 130.

55. Marisol de la Cadena, "From Race to Class: Insurgent Intellectuals *de provincia* in Peru 1910–1970," in Stern, *Shining and Other Paths*, p. 53.

56. Ponciano del Pino, "Family, Culture, and 'Revolution': Everyday Life with Sendero Luminoso," in Stern, *Shining and Other Paths*.

57. David Scott Palmer, "The Revolutionary Terrorism of Peru's Shining Path," in Martha Crenshaw, ed., *Terrorism in Context* (University Park, PA: Pennsylvania State University Press, 1995).

58. Ivan Hinojosa, "On Poor Relations and the Nouveau Riche: Shining Path and the Radical Peruvian Left," in Stern, *Shining and Other Paths*, p.76.

59. DeGregori, "Harvesting Storms," p. 138.

60. Carlos Ivan DeGregori, "Shining Path and Counterinsurgency Strategy Since the Arrest of Abimael Guzman" in Joseph S. Tulchin and Gary Bland, eds., *Peru in Crisis* (Boulder, CO: Lynne Rienner, 1994), p. 83. President Garcia had launched the rondas in the latter part of his administration, and President Fujimori reestablished them.

61. Orin Starn, "Villagers at Arms: War and Counterrevolution in the Central-South Andes," in Stern, *Shining and Other Paths*, pp. 231–32.

62. Nelson Manrique, "The War for the Central Sierra," in Stern, *Shining and Other Paths*, p. 222, n. 9

63. Starn, "Villagers at Arms," p. 232.

64. DeGregori, "Shining Path and Counterinsurgency Strategy," p. 89. For further study, consult Gustavo Gorriti, *The Shining Path*, trans. Robin Kirk (Chapel Hill, NC: University of North Carolina, 1999); Enrique Obando, "Defeating Shining Path: Strategic Lessons for the Future," in Anthony James Joes, ed., *Saving Democracies: U.S. Intervention in Threatened Democratic States* (Westport, CT: Praeger, 1999).

65. Starn, "Villagers at Arms," p. 236.

66. Ibid., p. 253, n.5

67. Ibid., p. 237.

68. Caesar Sereseres, "The Highlands War in Guatemala," in Georges Fauriol, ed., *Latin American Insurgencies* (Washington, DC: Georgetown University, 1985), p. 112.

69. Sereseres, "Highlands War in Guatemala," p. 104.

70. Alfred R. Barr and Caesar Sereseres estimate the number of patrulleros at "several

hundred thousand." "US Unconventional Warfare Operations and Lessons from Central America, 1980–1990: A Successful Economy of Force Engagement Strategy," *in Low Intensity Conflict and Law Enforcement,* vol. 8, no. 2 (Summer 1999), p. 20.

71. Sereseres, "Highlands War in Guatemala," p. 121.

72. The absence of government authority over large territories is an old problem: See Stanley J. Stein and B.H. Stein, *The Colonial Heritage of Latin America* (New York: Oxford University Press, 1970).

73. *Jane's Intelligence Review* placed the number of professional soldiers at 50,000 in early 2002. There are additional thousands of ill-trained and ill-motivated conscripts.

74. Fernando Cubides, "From Private to Public Violence: The Paramilitaries," in Charles Bergquist, Ricardo Penaranda, and Gonzalo Sanchez, eds., *Violence in Colombia 1990–2000* (Wilmington, DE: Scholarly Resources, 2001), p. 132.

75. Cubides, "From Private to Public Violence", pp. 134–35.

76. Ibid., pp. 130, 132.

77. Thomas Marks, *Colombian Army Adaptation to FARC Insurgency* (Carlisle Barracks, PA: Strategic Studies Institute, January 2002). This is a vigorous defense of the much-criticized "paramilitaries," elements of which have become involved in the ubiquitous drug miasma. But see also Dennis M. Rempe, "Guerrillas, Bandits and Independent Republics: US Counterinsurgency Efforts in Colombia 1959–1965," *Small Wars and Insurgencies,* vol. 6 (Winter 1995).

78. Cubides, "From Private to Public Violence," p. 127.

79. Christopher Harmon, "Illustrations of Learning in Counterinsurgency Warfare," *Comparative Strategy,* vol. 11 (1992), p. 39.

80. Edgar O'Ballance, *The Greek Civil War* (London: Faber and Faber, 1966), p. 214; John J. McCuen, *The Art of Counter-Revolutionary Warfare* (Harrisburg, PA: Stackpole, 1966), pp. 231ff. And see also D. George Kousoulas, *Revolution and Defeat: The Story of the Greek Communist Party* (New York: Oxford University Press, 1965), pp. 258–59.

81. Cann, *Counterinsurgency in Africa,* p. 163.

82. Marston, "Resettlement," p. 49.

83. Anthony James Joes, *The War for South Viet Nam 1954–1975,* 2d revised edition (Westport, CT: Praeger, 2001), pp. 61–70; Hunt, *Pacification,* p. 230 and passim.

84. See Joseph R. Nunez, *Fighting the Hobbesian Trinity in Colombia: A New Strategy for Peace* (Carlisle Barracks, PA: Strategic Studies Institute, April 2000).

CHAPTER 7. LOYALISTS: INDIGENOUS ANTI-INSURGENCY

1. The literature on ethnic struggle is very extensive. Two exceptionally useful treatments, from different approaches, are Donald L. Horowitz, *Ethnic Groups in Conflict* (Berkeley, CA: University of California, 1985), and Walker Connor, *Ethnonationalism: The Quest for Understanding* (Princeton, NJ: Princeton University, 1994).

2. Of course all such figures are estimates.

3. Robert O. DeMond, *The Loyalists in North Carolina During the Revolution* (Hamden, CT: Archon, 1964 [orig. 1940]), pp. 50–52. C.H. Van Tyne, *The Loyalists in the American Revolution* (New York: Peter Smith, 1929), p. 303.

4. William H. Nelson, *The American Tory* (Oxford: Clarendon Press, 1961), p. 89.

5. Paul H. Smith, *Loyalists and Redcoats: A Study in British Revolutionary Policy* (Chapel Hill, NC: University of North Carolina, 1964), pp. ix and ff., 10, 98.

6. Smith, *Loyalists and Redcoats,* pp. 62, 169; Van Tyne, *Loyalists,* p. 246.

7. Piers Mackesy, *The War for America 1775–1783* (Cambridge, MA: Harvard University, 1965), p. 112; Robert Stansbury Lambert, *South Carolina Loyalists in the American Revolution* (Columbia, SC: University of South Carolina, 1987), p. 203; Smith, *Loyalists and Redcoats,* p. 102 and passim.

8. DeMond, *Loyalists in North Carolina,* p. 61; Van Tyne, *The Loyalists,* p. 172.

9. Van Tyne, *The Loyalists,* pp. 182–83.

10. Ibid., p. 185.

11. Christopher Ward, *The War of the Revolution* (New York: Macmillan, 1952), vol. 2, chapter 62; John Shy, "American Society and Its War for Independence" in Don Higginbotham, ed., *Reconsiderations on the Revolutionary War* (Westport, CT: Greenwood, 1978); Demond, *Loyalists in North Carolina,* pp. 138–40 and passim.

12. Van Tyne, *The Loyalists,* p. 299.

13. Nelson, *The American Tory,* p. v.

14. Raymond Carr, *Spain, 1808–1939* (London: Oxford University Press, 1966), p. 112.

15. Gabriel H. Lovett, *Napoleon and the Birth of Modern Spain* (New York: New York University, 1965), vol. 1, ch. xiii, and vol. 2, p. 573. Carr, *Spain, 1808–1939,* p. 105.

16. Albert B. Moore, *Conscription and Conflict in the Confederacy* (New York: Macmillan, 1924), pp. 357–58; James M. McPherson, *Battle Cry of Freedom* (New York: Oxford University, 1988), pp. 306–7n. These figures do not of course include or take account of the roughly 180,000 blacks, almost all southerners, who served in Union uniform.

17. Brian McAlister Linn, *The Philippine War, 1899–1902* (Lawrence, KS: University Press of Kansas, 2000), p. 128; see also Brian McAlister Linn, *The U.S. Army and Counterinsurgency in the Philippine War, 1899–1902* (Chapel Hill, NC: University of North Carolina, 1989).

18. See intriguing details of this famous capture in Frederick Funston, *Memories of Two Wars: Cuban and Philippine Experiences* (New York: Scribner's, 1911), chapter vii.

19. Stephen P. Cohen, *The Indian Army* (Berkeley, CA: University of California, 1971), p. 32

20. See the classic account of the Burma war by Field Marshall Viscount William Slim, *Defeat into Victory* (London: Cassell, 1956). Slim's ultimately victorious forces included Burmans, Chinese, Karens, Gurkhas, sub-Saharan Africans, and others.

21. See V. Longer, *Red Coats to Olive Green: A History of the Indian Army 1600–1974* (Bombay: Allied Publications 1974) and Roger Beaumont, *Sword of the Raj: The British Army in India 1747–1947* (Indianapolis, IN: Bobbs Merrill, 1977).

22. Alistair Horne, *A Savage War of Peace: Algeria 1954–1962* (Harmondsworth, England: Penguin, 1987), p. 255. Peter Paret says 150,000 Muslims fought with the French; whatever the exact number, "the presence of tens of thousands of armed Muslims under the tricolor gave credence to the French claim to fight for Algeria rather than against it." *French Revolutionary Warfare from Indochina to Algeria: The Analysis of a Political and Military Doctrine* (New York: Praeger, 1964), p. 41. See also Alf Andrew Heggoy, *Insurgency and Counterinsurgency in Algeria* (Bloomington: Indiana University Press, 1972), p. 179; Edgar O'Ballance, *The Algerian Insurrection, 1954–1962* (Hamden, CT: Archon, 1967); Bachaga Boualam, *Les Harkis au service de la France* (Paris: Editions France Empire, 1963); J.C. Guillebaud, "Les harkis oubliés par l'histoire" *Le Monde,* July 3, 1979, p. 9.

23. For a brief treatment of the conflict and its ending, see Joes, *From the Barrel of a Gun*, chapter 7, "French Algeria: The Victory and Crucifixion of an Army."

24. Michael Carver, *War Since 1945* (New York: Putnam's, 1981), chapter 8.

25. Neil Bruce, *Portugal: The Last Empire* (New York: Wiley, 1975), p. 73.

26. See Thomas H. Hendriksen, "Lessons from Portugal's Counterinsurgency Operations in Africa," *Journal of The Royal United Services Institute for Defence Studies,* vol. 123 (1978); Douglas L. Wheeler, "African Elements in Portugal's Armies in Africa, 1961–1974," in *Armed Forces and Society* 2 (February 1976); John P. Cann, *Counterinsurgency in Africa: The Portuguese Way of War, 1961–1974* (Westport, CT: Greenwood, 1997), pp. 103–4.

27. J. Bruce Amstutz, *Afghanistan: The First Five Years of Soviet Occupation* (Washington, DC: National Defense University, 1986); Mark Urban, *War in Afghanistan* (New York: St. Martin's, 1988); Gérard Chaliand, "The Bargain War in Afghanistan," in *Guerrilla Strategies*, ed. Gérard Chaliand (Berkeley, CA: University of California, 1982); Eliza Van Hollen, *Afghanistan: Three Years of Occupation* (Washington, DC: U.S. Department of State, 1982); Edward Girardet, *Afghanistan: The Soviet War* (New York: St. Martin's, 1985); Craig Karp, *Afghanistan: Seven Years of Soviet Occupation* (Washington, DC: U.S. Department of State, 1986).

28. The Portuguese retained control of the eastern part of Timor until late in the twentieth century.

29. For scathing remarks on the effects of Dutch rule in Indonesia, see K.M. Panikkar, *Asia and Western Dominance* (London: Allen and Unwin, 1959).

30. Richard Chauvel, *Nationalists, Soldiers and Separatists: The Ambonese Islands from Colonialism to Revolt* (Leiden: KITLV, 1990), p. 44.

31. Ibid., p. 32n. In addition to Ambonese, the KNIL recruited well among the Menadonese and Timorese.

32. Ibid., p. 39. Consult also Gerke Teitler, *The Dutch Colonial Army in Transition* (Rotterdam: Erasmus University, 1980).

33. Fifty-nine million barrels in 1940.

34. Chauvel, *Nationalists*, p. 70.

35. Consult G.M. Kahin, *Nationalism and Revolution in Indonesia* (Ithaca, NY: Cornell University, 1959).

36. Chauvel, *Nationalists*, p. 201.

37. Consult Rupert Emerson, *From Empire to Nation* (Cambridge, MA: Harvard University, 1960), pp. 124–25.

38. To this day the people of the island of Bali have retained their Hindu religion.

39. See Harry J. Benda, *The Crescent and the Rising Sun* (The Hague: Van Hoeve, 1958). For comparative examples of this process, see John T. McAlister, *Viet Nam: Origins of Revolution* (Garden City, NY: Doubleday Anchor, 1971), and Emerson, *From Empire to Nation*.

40. Joyce Lebra, *Japanese-Trained Armies in Southeast Asia* (New York: Columbia University, 1977), p. 111.

41. See Theodore Friend, *The Blue-Eyed Enemy: Japan Against the West in Java and Luzon 1942–1945* (Princeton, NJ: Princeton University, 1988). In Burma, the British recruited Karens, Kachins, and Shans, while the Japanese occupation relied on ethnic Burmans. See Lebra, *Japanese-Trained Armies*, and also Dorothy Guyot, "The Burman Independence Army: A Political Movement in Military Garb," in Josef Silverstein, ed., *Southeast Asia in World War II* (New Haven, CT: Yale University, 1966); and John Furnivall, *Colonial Policy and Practice: A Comparative Study of Burma and Neth-*

erlands India [sic] (Cambridge: Cambridge University, 1948), pp. 178–85, on the Burma Independence Army.

42. Benda, *Crescent and the Rising Sun,* pp. 138ff.

43. See Lebra, *Japanese-Trained Armies.*

44. Ibid., p. 170.

45. The French Republic recognized Emperor Bao Dai as head of state of independent Vietnam on June 5, 1948, confirmed by the Élysée Agreement of March 1949. By 1954 thirty-five countries maintained diplomatic relations with Bao Dai's government.

46. Between them the Cao Dai and the Hoa Hao sects numbered millions of adherents in the southern provinces. Assassinations of their leaders by the Viet Minh turned them into bitter opponents.

47. The population of metropolitan France at that time was over 40 million.

48. The number may have reached 400,000 by June 1954.

49. Estimates of the number of French and allied forces in Vietnam vary. I have derived these figures mainly from Edgar O'Ballance, *The Indo-China War, 1945–1954* (London: Faber and Faber, 1964), and Henri Navarre, *Agonie de l'Indochine* (Paris: Plon, 1956), p. 46.

50. See Pierre Boyer de Latour, *Le Martyre de l'Armée française: de l'Indochine a l'Algérie* (Paris: Presses du Mail, 1962); Philippe Devillers, *Histoire du Viet-Nam de 1940 à 1952* (Paris: Editions du Seuil, 1952), 3d edition; Paul Ely, *L'Indochine dans la tourmente* (Paris: Plon, 1964); Henri Marc and Pierre Cony, *Indochine française* (Paris: Editions France-Empire, 1946); Jean Marchand, *L'Indochine en guerre* (Paris: Pouzet, 1955); Navarre, *Agonie de L'Indochine.*

51. Ronald Spector, *Advice and Support: The Early Years, 1941–1960* (Washington: U.S. Army Center of Military History, 1983), p. 131; Ellen J. Hammer, *The Struggle for Indochina 1945–1955* (Stanford, CA: Stanford University, 1966), p. 287; Henri Navarre, *Agonie de l'Indochine,* p. 46; Douglas Pike, *PAVN: People's Army of Vietnam* (Novato, CA: Presidio, 1986), p. 5.

52. Spector, *Advice and Support.*

53. Hammer, *Struggle for Indochina,* p. 321; Bui Diem, *In the Jaws of History* (Boston: Houghton-Mifflin, 1987).

54. Well into the 1960s, the U.S. Army picked advisers on the basis of their ability to speak *French,* not Vietnamese. American officers tended to shun assignment as advisers to ARVN because they believed such service did not enhance their prospects for promotion, despite official assurances; Richard A. Hunt, *Pacification: The American Struggle for Viet Nam's Hearts and Minds* (Boulder, CO: Westview, 1995). The number of U.S. advisers peaked at around 16,000, with many of them in administrative, not combat, roles; Robert W. Komer, *Bureaucracy at War: U.S. Performance in the Viet Nam Conflict* (Boulder, CO: Westview, 1986), p. 128. And see R.D. Parrish, *Combat Recon: My Year with the ARVN* (New York: St. Martin's, 1991).

55. Phillip B. Davidson, *Viet Nam at War: The History, 1946–1975* (Novato, CA: Presidio, 1988), p. 660; James Lawton Collins, *The Development and Training of the South Vietnamese Army, 1950–1972* (Washington, DC: Department of the Army, 1975), pp. 47, 101. See William Westmoreland, *A Soldier Reports* (Garden City, NY: Doubleday, 1976), p. 159. Every upgrade of weapons sent to ARVN was in response to a previous superiority on the side of the enemy; hence ARVN was almost always outclassed in equipment; Davidson, *Viet Nam at War,* p. 660. "On the military side we simply did not do the job with the South Vietnamese that we did with the South Koreans because

we had always assumed that we would win the war for them." Thomas C. Thayer, *War Without Fronts: The American Experience in Viet Nam* (Boulder, CO: Westview, 1985), p. 257.

56. Thayer, *War Without Fronts,* p. 71.

57. Allan E. Goodman, *An Institutional Profile of the South Vietnamese Officer Corps* (Santa Monica, CA: RAND, 1970). Nevertheless, Buddhists, who comprised 59 percent of the general population, were 62 percent of the ARVN officer corps; Goodman, *Institutional Profile,* p. 9.

58. "ARVN at the same time held a politically troubled country together in the face of ever-increasing enemy strength. Few organizations in the world could have done so well." Westmoreland, *Soldier Reports,* p. 250.

59. Olivier Todd, *Cruel April: The Fall of Saigon* (New York: Norton, 1990), p. 438.

60. Sir Robert Thompson, *Peace Is Not at Hand* (New York: David McKay, 1974), p. 169.

61. William E. Le Gro, *Viet Nam from Ceasefire to Capitulation* (Washington, DC: U.S. Army Center of Military History, 1981), p. 60.

62. Thayer, *War Without Fronts,* p. 106.

63. Todd, *Cruel April,* says 250,000 ARVN were killed from 1960 to 1974 (p. 234). Of allied (American, South Vietnamese, and other countries) combat deaths from 1965 to 1972, 77 percent were South Vietnamese from all branches; Thayer, *War Without Fronts,* p. 105.

64. Race, *War Comes to Long An,* p. 164n.

65. Thayer, *War Without Fronts,* p. 171.

66. Ibid., 163.

67. Ibid., p. 202; Douglas Pike, *PAVN: People's Army of Viet Nam* (Novato, CA: Presidio, 1986), p. 244; Westmoreland, *A Soldier Reports,* p. 252.

68. Bruce Catton, *Glory Road* (Garden, City, NJ: Doubleday, 1952), pp. 102, 255; Allan Nevins, *The War for the Union: The Organized War to Victory, 1864–1865* (New York: Scribner's, 1971), p. 131.

69. Charles Stuart Callison, *Land to the Tiller in the Mekong Delta* (Lanham, MD: University Press of America, 1983), p. 111.

70. Dennis J. Duncanson, *Government and Revolution in Viet Nam* (New York: Oxford University, 1968), p. 13, estimates that only one-fourth of the Southern population supported the Communists. This is a crucial and decisive point. Consult Robert A. Scalapino, "We Cannot Accept a Communist Seizure of Viet Nam," in the *New York Times Magazine,* December 11, 1966, p. 46; the CBS survey is quoted in Wesley Fishel, *Viet Nam: Anatomy of a Conflict* (Itasca, IL: Peacock, 1968), pp. 653, 659; Howard R. Penniman, *Elections in South Viet Nam* (Washington, DC: American Enterprise Institute, 1972), p. 199; Kolko, *Anatomy of a War,* p. 250; Thompson, *No Exit from Viet Nam,* p. 65; Race, *War Comes to Long An,* p. 188.

71. See G. Tien Hung Nguyen and Jerrold Schechter, *The Palace File* (New York: Harper and Row, 1986).

72. Le Gro, *Viet Nam from Ceasefire to Capitulation,* p. 88.

73. Guenter Lewy, *America in Viet Nam* (New York: Oxford University, 1978), p. 208; Van Tien Dung, *Our Great Spring Victory* (New York: Monthly Review, 1977), pp. 17–18; General Dong Van Khuyen, *The RVNAF* (Washington, DC: U.S. Army Center of Military History, 1980), pp. 287–88; Le Gro, *Viet Nam from Ceasefire to Capitulation,* pp. 84–87; Timothy J. Lomperis, *The War Everyone Lost—and Won* (Baton Rouge, LA: Louisiana State University, 1984), p. 75.

74. General Vo Nguyen Giap, *How We Won the War* (Philadelphia: Recon, 1976), p. 24.

75. The successful defense of Stalingrad against a furious Nazi assault (August 1942–January 1943) was the turning point of World War II in Europe.

76. Cao Van Vien, *The Final Collapse* (Washington, DC: U.S. Army Center of Military History, 1983); Alan Dawson, *55 Days: The Fall of South Viet Nam* (Englewood Cliffs, N.J.: Prentice-Hall, 1977); Stephen T. Hosmer, K. Kellen, and B.M. Jenkins, *The Fall of South Viet Nam* (New York: Crane, Russak, 1980); Todd, *Cruel April*; Larry Englemann, *Tears Before the Rain: An Oral History of the Fall of South Viet Nam* (New York: Oxford University, 1990); Van Tien Dung, *Our Great Spring Victory*.

CHAPTER 8: THE CENTRALITY OF INTELLIGENCE

1. Sun Tzu, *Art of War*, chapter 13. Conversely, "One who confronts his enemy for many years in order to struggle for victory in a decisive battle yet who, because he begrudges rank, honors, and a few hundred pieces of gold, remains ignorant of his enemy's situation, is completely devoid of humanity." *The Arthashastra* of Kautilya, composed probably in the fourth century BC, is also full of acute and practical observations and advice. See also N.J.E. Austin and N.B. Rankov, *Exploratio: Military and political intelligence in the Roman world from the Second Punic War to the battle of Adrianople* (London: Routledge, 1995).

2. Machiavelli, *The Discourses*, chapter 18.

3. Callwell, *Small Wars*, p. 143; Field Marshal Lord Carver, *War Since 1945* (New York: G.P. Putnam's Sons, 1981), p. 281; Lucian W. Pye, "The Roots of Insurgency," in Harry Eckstein, ed., *Internal War* (New York: Free Press, 1964), p. 177; Frank Kitson, *Low Intensity Operations* (London: Faber and Faber, 1971), p. 95; John P. Cann, *Counterinsurgency in Africa: The Portuguese Way of War, 1961–1974* (Westport, CT: Greenwood, 1997), p. 124. For a rather different view, see John Keegan, *Intelligence in War* (New York: Knopf, 2003).

4. R.W. Komer, *The Malayan Emergency in Retrospect: Organization of a Successful Counterinsurgency Effort* (Santa Monica, CA: RAND, 1972), p. 76.

5. See, for example, Timothy P. Wickham-Crowley, *Guerrillas and Revolution in Latin America: A Comparative Study of Insurgents and Regimes since 1956* (Princeton, NJ: Princeton University, 1962), p. 224–28 and passim.

6. Anthony Short, *Communist Insurrection in Malaya 1948–1960* (London: Muller, 1975), p. 309.

7. Jeffrey J. Clarke, *Advice and Support: The Final Years, 1965–1973* (Washington, DC: U.S. Army Center of Military History, 1988), pp. 118–19.

8. Dov Tamari, "Military Operations in Urban Environments: The Case of Lebanon, 1982," in Michael C. Desch, ed., *Soldiers in Cities: Military Operations on Urban Terrain* (Carlisle Barracks, PA: Strategic Studies Institute, 2001), p. 45.

9. U.S. Marine Corps, *Small Wars Manual* (Washington, DC: U.S. Government Printing Office, 1940), paragraph 2.3.

10. See chapter 1 above, "Guerrilla Strategy and Tactics," note 62.

11. Brian McAlister Linn, *The U.S. Army and Counterinsurgency in the Philippine War, 1899–1902* (Chapel Hill, NC: University of North Carolina, 1989), pp. 128, 216.

12. Victor Sampson and Ian Hamilton, *Anti-Commando* (London: Faber and Faber, 1931), pp. 148–51.

13. Christian Rudolf De Wet, *The Three Years' War* (London: Constable, 1902), pp. 78–79.

14. Richard L. Clutterbuck, *The Long, Long War: Counterinsurgency in Malaya and Viet Nam* (New York: Praeger, 1966), p. 178.

15. Chalmers Johnson, *Autopsy on People's War* (Berkeley, CA: University of California, 1973), p. 41.

16. U.S. Marine Corps, *Small Wars Manual,* paragraph 2.3.

17. Linn, *The U.S. Army and Counterinsurgency,* p. 43.

18. See the interesting story of this key event in Frederick Funston, *Memories of Two Wars Cuban and Philippine Experiences* (New York: Scribner's, 1911).

19. Emilio Aguinaldo, *A Second Look at America* (New York: Robert Speller, 1957).

20. Luis Taruc, *He Who Rides the Tiger* (New York: Praeger, 1967), p. 97; Fairbairn, *Revolutionary Guerrilla Warfare.*

21. Carlos P. Romulo, *Crusade in Asia: Philippine Victory* (Westport, CT: Greenwood, 1973 [orig. 1955]), p. 135. For a description of this great catch, see Carlos P. Romulo and Marvin M. Gray, *The Magsaysay Story* (New York: J. Day, 1956), pp. 113–19.

22. Fairbairn, *Revolutionary Guerrilla Warfare,* p. 151.

23. John Cloake, *Templer, Tiger of Malaya* (London: Harrap, 1985), p. 227.

24. Richard Stubbs, *Hearts and Minds in Guerrilla Warfare: The Malayan Emergency of 1948–1960* (Singapore: Oxford University, 1989), p. 183.

25. Edgar O'Ballance, *Malaya: The Communist Insurgent War, 1948–1960* (Hamden, CT: Archon, 1966), p. 174.

26. Hoang Ngoc Lung, *Intelligence* (Washington, DC: U.S. Army Center of Military History, 1982), p. 222.

27. Meirion and Susie Harries, *Soldiers of the Sun: The Rise and Fall of the Imperial Japanese Army* (New York: Random House, 1991), p. 376.

28. Hoang Ngoc Lung, *Intelligence,* p. 12.

29. Ibid., pp. 13 and 233.

30. Sir Robert Thompson, *Lessons from the Viet Nam War* (London: Royal United Services Institute, February 1966).

31. Duncanson, *Government and Revolution in Viet Nam,* p. 256. For the inter-organizational competition and sabotage, low pay, long hours, and inadequate institutional resources of Peru's intelligence apparatus against the Senderistas, see Gustavo Gorriti, *The Shining Path: A History of the Millenarian War in Peru* (Chapel Hill, NC: University of North Carolina Press, 1999), esp. chapter 17. Note that the author singles out the DIRCOTE as an exception to this dismal picture, the group that captured Guzman in September 1992 (other high-ranking leaders were also captured that year).

32. This was the largest Allied landing in Europe next to Normandy. The Allied success in achieving surprise in Sicily was partly the result of the intelligence deception known to Americans as "The Man Who Never Was."

33. James J. Wirtz, *The Tet Offensive: Intelligence Failure in War* (Ithaca, NY: Cornell University, 1991), p. 23.

34. Ibid., pp. 256–58.

35. Ibid., p. 84.

36. George W. Allen, *None So Blind: A Personal Account of the Intelligence Failure in Viet Nam* (Chicago: Ivan R. Dee, 2001), p. 257.

37. Wirtz, *Tet Offensive,* p. 128. See also Hoang Ngoc Lung, *Intelligence;* Bruce Palmer

Jr., *U.S. Intelligence in Viet Nam*, a special issue of the CIA's *Studies in Intelligence*, vol. 28, no. 5 (1984); John F. Sullivan, *Of Spies and Lies: A CIA Lie Detector Remembers Viet Nam* (Lawrence, KS: University of Kansas, 2000); Joseph A. McChristian, *The Role of Military Intelligence 1965–1967* (Washington, DC: Department of the Army, 1974).

38. Clausewitz, *On War*, Book One, Chapter vi.
39. Thucydides, *The Peloponnesian Wars*, in *The Landmark Thucydides*, ed. Robert B. Strassler (New York: The Free Press, 1996) I, 84.
40. Machiavelli, *The Discourses*, chapter 48.
41. See Chapter 7 of this volume, "Loyalists."
42. Lucian Pye, *Guerrilla Communism in Malaya* (Princeton, NJ: Princeton University, 1956); Fairbairn, *Revolutionary Guerrilla Warfare*, p. 298.
43. Sun Tzu, *On War*, II, 19.

CHAPTER 9: THE REQUIREMENT OF RECTITUDE

1. Sir Robert Thompson, "Regular Armies and Insurgency," in Ronald Haycock, ed., *Regular Armies and Insurgency* (London: Croom Helm, 1979), p.10.
2. U.S. Marine Corps, *Small Wars Manual*, p. 1–16d.
3. Chong Sik Lee, *Counterinsurgency in Manchuria: The Japanese Experience 1931–1940* (Santa Monica, CA: RAND, 1967), passim.
4. Machiavelli, *Art of War*. Tiberius Sempronius Gracchus also achieved much through honest negotiation and displays of honor; see C.H.V. Sutherland, *The Romans in Spain* (Boulder, CO: Westview, 1989 [orig. 1939]).
5. Jeffrey D. Wert, *Mosby's Rangers* (New York: Simon and Schuster, 1990) p. 251–52. See also the excellent work of James Ramage, *Gray Ghost: The Life of Colonel John Singleton Mosby* (Lexington, KY: University Press of Kentucky, 1999).
6. "Members of the United States forces should avoid any attitude that tends to indicate criticism or lack of respect for the religious beliefs and practices observed by the native inhabitants." U.S. Marine Corps, *Small Wars Manual*, p. 1–31d.
7. Basil Liddell Hart, *Strategy* (New York: Praeger, 1967), p. 357.
8. See for example Carlos Ivan DeGregori, "Shining Path and Counterinsurgency Strategy Since the Arrest of Abimael Guzman" in Joseph S. Tulchin and Gary Bland, eds., *Peru in Crisis* (Boulder, CO: Lynne Rienner, 1994), p. 94.
9. See Omer Bartov, *Hitler's Army* (New York: Oxford University Press, 1991), esp. chapter 3, "The Perversion of Discipline."
10. See for example Ronald Lewin, *Hitler's Mistakes* (New York: William Morrow, 1984), chapter. 8.
11. General Orders No. 73, June 27, 1863. Tito as a guerrilla leader said that "we sought to instill in our units the strictest possible discipline, not by extra drills but by ceaseless political instruction with the object of improving both individual and collective morale and of securing a proper attitude toward the population." Fitzroy Maclean, *Disputed Barricade* (London: Jonathan Cape, 1957), p. 235.
12. "The criminalisation of warfare produced a growing indiscipline and demoralization among German forces themselves. The Germans shot fifteen thousand of their own number, the equivalent [sic] of a whole division." Richard Overy, *Why the Allies Won* (New York: Norton, 1995), p. 304 and passim.
13. Fred Anderson, in J.W. Chambers, ed., *The Oxford Companion to American Military History* (New York: Oxford University Press, 1999), p. 609.

14. Robert D. Bass, *Swamp Fox* (New York: Henry Holt, 1959), p. 112.

15. Owen Connelly, *Blundering to Glory: Napoleon's Military Campaigns* (Wilmington, DE: Scholarly Resources, 1987), p. 112n; Gabriel H. Lovett, *Napoleon and the Birth of Modern Spain*, 2 vols. (New York: New York University, 1965), p. 683; J.Tranie and J-C. Carmigniani, *Napoleon's War in Spain*, trans. J. Mallender and J. Clements (London: Arms and Armour, 1982), p. 10.

16. "On the Protracted War" in *Selected Works of Mao Tse-tung* (Peking: People's Publishing House, 1952).

17. Anthony James Joes, *Modern Guerrilla Insurgency* (Westport, CT: Praeger, 1992), pp. 180–83.

18. Luis Taruc, *He Who Rides the Tiger* (New York: Praeger, 1967), pp. 38, 144. See also Benedict J. Kerkvliet, *The Huk Rebellion: A Study of Peasant Revolt in the Philippines* (Berkeley, CA: University of California, 1977), p. 217.

19. Mao Tse-tung, *Selected Military Writings* (Peking: Foreign Languages Press, 1966), p. 33.

20. Deneys Reitz, *Commando* (London: Faber and Faber, 1929), p. 169.

21. Byron Farwell, *The Great Anglo-Boer War* (New York: Norton, 1976), p. 349.

22. Lee, *Counterinsurgency in Manchuria*, pp. 67–68.

23. Jeffrey J. Clarke, *Advice and Support: Final Years, 1965–1973* (Washington, DC: U.S. Army Center of Military History, 1988), pp. 118–19.

24. Joes, *America and Guerrilla Warfare*, p. 331.

25. Anthony James Joes, *Guerrilla Conflict before the Cold War* (Westport, CT: Praeger, 2000), p. 141.

26. Lincoln Li, *The Japanese Army in North China 1937–1941* (Tokyo: Oxford University Press, 1975) p.13.

27. This is not to say that more troops would have led to a Soviet success. The Soviet forces in Afghanistan also lacked valid guerrilla-fighting concepts, and indeed knew amazingly little about the country and peoples against whom they were struggling. See, e.g., The Russian General Staff, *The Soviet-Afghan War*, trans. and ed. Lester W. Grau and Michael A. Gress (Lawrence, KS: University Press of Kansas, 2002).

28. U.S. Marines, *Small Wars Manual*, p. 1–16c.

29. Brian McAlister Linn, *The U.S. Army and Counterinsurgency in the Philippine War, 1899–1902* (Chapel Hill, NC: University of North Carolina, 1989), p. 22; Glenn Anthony May, *Battle for Batangas: A Philippine Province at War* (New Haven, CT: Yale University, 1991), pp. 138, 158.

30. Carl von Clausewitz, *On War*, ed. and trans. Michael Howard and Peter Paret (Princeton, NJ: Princeton University, 1976), Book 4, Chapter 4.

CHAPTER 10: THE UTILITY OF AMNESTY

1. Michael Howard, "When are Wars Decisive?" *Survival*, vol. 41 (Spring 1999), p. 135.

2. Brian McAlister Linn, *The Philippine War, 1899–1902* (Lawrence, KS: University Press of Kansas, 2000), pp. 285, 297.

3. Stuart Slade, "Successful Counter-insurgency," *International Defence Review*, v. 22 (October, 1989), p. 25.

4. Lucian Pye, *Guerrilla Communism in Malaya* (Princeton, NJ: Princeton University Press, 1956).

5. On Viet Cong recruits, see Jeannette A. Koch, *The Chieu Hoi Program in South Viet*

Nam, 1963–1971 (Santa Monica, CA: RAND, January 1973); see also Eric Bergerud, *Dynamics of Defeat*; John C. Donnell, *Viet Cong Recruitment: Why and How Men Join* (Santa Monica, CA: RAND, 1975); Gerald C. Hickey, *Village in Viet Nam* (New Haven, CT: Yale University, 1964), pp. 233–47; Nathan Leites, *The Viet Cong Style of Politics* (Santa Monica, CA: RAND, 1969); Truong Nhu Tang, *A Viet Cong Memoir* (New York: Harcourt, 1987); Thomas C. Thayer, *War Without Fronts: The American Experience in Viet Nam* (Boulder, CO: Westview, 1985).

6. Receding hopes of victory also deeply affected guerrillas in Malaya; see Pye, *Guerrilla Communism*, passim.

7. Koch, *Chieu Hoi*, pp. 6–7.

8. Ibid., p. vii and passim. For ARVN skepticism about ralliers, see Richard A. Hunt, *Pacification: The American Struggle for Viet Nam's Hearts and Minds* (Boulder, CO: Westview, 1995), pp. 101–2.

9. Koch, *Chieu Hoi*, p. 107.

10. Ibid., p. 5.

11. Ibid., p. 16.

12. Ibid., p. vi.

CHAPTER 11: THE QUESTION OF SUFFICIENT FORCE LEVELS

1. The British ruling class did not want to spend much money on subduing the American rebels. This was the real root of the convenient belief in London that the war, at least in the southern colonies, could be won by mobilizing the allegedly quite numerous native Loyalists, aided by small numbers of British troops. Out of these woeful misconceptions arose the fierce and protracted struggle in the Carolinas, in which guerrilla chieftains such as the Swamp Fox (Francis Marion) and the Game Cock (Thomas Sumter) achieved deserved fame. Thus, the Battle of Saratoga was one of the most decisive in history, because it convinced the French to give open aid to the Americans; nevertheless, when British General Burgoyne surrendered there, he commanded only 3,500 troops (all that was left of the 7,700 he started the campaign with). The surrender at Yorktown convinced the British government to end the war, even though Cornwallis's trapped army numbered but 7,100 (500 casualties). See Joes, *America and Guerrilla Warfare*, chapter 1, "American Guerrillas: The War of Independence."

2. U.S. Marine Corps, *Small Wars Manual*, paragraph 1.9.

3. See Joes, *Guerrilla Conflict Before the Cold War*, chapter two, "Genocide in La Vendée."

4. Ramsay Weston Phipps, *The Armies of the First French Republic and the Rise of the Marshals of Napoleon I* (Westport, CT: Greenwood, 1980), p. 5

5. Thomas Pakenham, *The Boer War* (New York: Random House 1979), p. 607; Byron Farwell *The Great Anglo-Boer War* (New York: Norton, 1976), p. 452.

6. Philip Warner, *The Crimean War: A Reappraisal* (New York: Taplinger, 1972), p. 341. See also C.E. Vulliamy, *Crimea: The Campaign of 1854–1856* (London: Jonathan Cape, 1939).

7. Edgar O'Ballance, *Malaya: The Communist Insurgent War* (Hamden, CT: Archon, 1966), p. 154. The reduction of the British commitment in India freed large numbers of troops and other personnel for service in Malaya.

8. See a brief but incisive description of these tactics in Paul-Marie De la Gorce, *The French Army* (New York: George Braziller, 1963), pp. 442–43.

9. Tranie and Carmigniani, *Napoleon's War in Spain*, p. 33. See also Charles Oman,

History of the Peninsular War, vol. 1 (Oxford, England: Clarendon Press, 1902), pp. 103–7.

10. Lefebvre, *Napoleon,* vol. II, p. 21.

11. David Chandler, Foreword, in Tranie and Carmigniani, *Napoleon's War in Spain,* p. 10.

12. J.W. Fortescue, *History of the British Army,* vol. 8 (London: Macmillan, 1919), p. 435.

13. Archer Jones, *The Art of War in the Western World* (New York: Oxford University Press, 1987), p. 359.

14. Figures vary from year to year and from source to source; see, for example, Henri Navarre, *Agonie de l'Indochine* (Paris: Plon, 1954, revised ed.), p. 46; Edgar O'Ballance, *The Indo-China War 1945–1954* (London: Faber and Faber, 1964), pp. 195–96; and Ian Beckett et al., *War in Peace: Conventional and Guerrilla Warfare since 1945* (New York: Harmony, 1982), p. 67.

15. Paul Ely, *Lessons of the War in Indochina,* vol. II (Santa Monica, CA: RAND, 1967), p. 76. These figures have been computed from Ely, *Lessons*; Henri Navarre, *Agonie de l'Indochine*; Edgar O'Ballance, *The Indochina War, 1945–1954,* Bernard Fall, *Street Without Joy* (Harrisburg, PA: Stackpole, 1964); and Thayer, *War Without Fronts.*

16. See Joes, *America and Guerrilla Warfare,* pp. 218–23.

17. Joes, *The War for South Viet Nam, 1954–1975* (Westport, CT: Praeger, 2001, rev. ed.), p.116. See also "Cincinnatus," *Self-Destruction: The Disintegration and Decay of the United States Army During the Viet Nam Era* (New York: Norton, 1981); James R. Ebert, *A Life in a Year: The American Infantryman in Viet Nam, 1965–1972* (Novato, CA: Presidio, 1993); Herman Kahn, "If Negotiations Fail," *Foreign Affairs* vol. 46, no. 4 (July 1968); Andrew Krepinevich, *The Army and Viet Nam* (Baltimore, MD: Johns Hopkins, 1986), p. 197; Thayer, *War Without Fronts,* p.114; Thompson, *No Exit from Viet Nam,* p. 53; Westmoreland, *A Soldier Reports,* pp. 296–97, 417.

18. Craig Karp, *Afghanistan: Eight Years of Soviet Occupation* (Washington, DC: U.S. Department of State, 1987), p. 2. "Most Western estimates put Soviet troop strength at about 120,000 men." From U.S. Department of State, *Afghanistan: Soviet Occupation and Withdrawal* (Washington, DC: Department of State, 1988), p. 5; Mark Urban, *War in Afghanistan* (New York: St. Martin's, 1988), p.129; J. Bruce Amstutz, *Afghanistan: The First Five Years of Soviet Occupation* (Washington, DC: National Defense University, 1986), pp. 168, 196; Stephen Blank, "Soviet Forces in Afghanistan: Unlearning the Lessons of Viet Nam," in Stephen Blank et al., eds., *Responding to Low-Intensity Conflict Challenges* (Maxwell AFB, AL: Air University Press, 1990).

19. Assisting the Americans in South Vietnam was an indigenous force eventually numbering 1 million regulars and militia, out of a population of about 17 million; compare this to the 80,000 men and boys the pro-Soviet Kabul regime was able to scrape together out of a population of 15 million.

20. U.S. Department of State, *Afghanistan: Soviet Occupation and Withdrawal,* p. 2.

21. The guerrillas were defeated in Algeria, but had their independence given to them in Paris.

22. Fitzroy Maclean, *Disputed Barricade* (London: Jonathan Cape, 1957), p. 248.

23. Peissel, *Secret War in Tibet,* pp. 105, 170; George N. Patterson, *Tibet in Revolt* (London: Faber and Faber, 1960), p. 152; B.N. Mullik, *My Years with Nehru* (Bombay: Allied Publishers, 1971), p. 216.

24. See the very good study of the Portuguese counterinsugent efforts in John P.

Cann. *Counterinsurgency in Africa: The Portuguese Way of War 1961–1974* (Westport, CT: Greenwood, 1997).

25. Joes, *War for South Viet Nam,* and *America and Guerrilla Warfare,* chapter seven, "Viet Nam: A Case of Multiple Pathologies."

CHAPTER 12: DEPLOYING U.S. TROOPS IN A COUNTERINSURGENT ROLE

1. In 1994, then-U.S. Senate Majority Leader George Mitchell (Dem-Maine) stated that the American news industry was "more destructive than constructive than ever." Representative Barney Frank (Dem-Mass.) declared that "You people [the media] celebrate failure and ignore success. Nothing about government is done as incompetently as the reporting of it." *New York Times,* October 1, 1994. There is something close to a consensus today that the major media misreported the 1968 Tet offensive in South Vietnam and thereby changed the course of that conflict.

2. U.S. Department of State, *Foreign Relations of the United States 1950: vol. 6, East Asia and the Pacific* (Washington, DC: U.S. Government Printing Office, 1976), pp. 1485–89. For opposition on the part of U.S. military leaders to large-scale American ground commitment in the Greek civil war, see Joes, *America and Guerrilla Warfare,* pp. 169–70.

3. See Joes, *America and Guerrilla Warfare,* chapter 4, "Nicaragua: A Training Ground"; Allan R. Millet, *Semper Fidelis: The History of the United States Marine Corps* (New York: Macmillan, 1980).

4. See Christopher Harmon, "Illustrations of Learning in Counterinsurgency Warfare," *Comparative Strategy* 11 (1992); John P. Cann, *Counterinsurgency in Africa: The Portuguese Way of War 1961–1974* (Westport, CT: Greenwood, 1997).

5. On Indian counterinsurgency, see Rajesh Rajagopalan, "'Restoring Normalcy': The Evolution of the Indian Army's Counterinsurgency Doctrine," *Small Wars and Insurgencies,* vol. 11, no. 1 (Spring 2000).

6. U.S. Army Field Manual 100–20, pp. 2–45 and 2–47.

7. Long-term occupation of a foreign land and a foreign people can have a profoundly corrupting effect on any army. For the damage done to the readiness, reputation, and morale of the Israeli army by its protracted occupation of Lebanon and the "Territories," see Martin Van Creveld, *The Sword and the Olive: A Critical History of the Israeli Defense Force* (New York: Public Affairs, 1998).

8. Jeffrey J. Clarke, *Advice and Support: The Final Years* (Washington, DC: U.S. Army Center of Military History, 1988), p. 497. Also consult Stephen T. Hosmer, *The Army's Role in Counterinsurgency and Insurgency* (Santa Monica, CA: RAND, 1990).

9. Clarke, *Advice and Support,* pp. 237, 239, 511.

10. Ibid., p. 510

11. Gerald C. Hickey, *The American Military Advisor and His Foreign Counterpart: The Case of Viet Nam* (Santa Monica, CA: RAND, 1965), p. 39.

12. Cao Van Vien et al., *The U.S. Adviser* (Washington, DC: U.S. Army Center of Military History, 1980), p. 195.

13. Ibid., p.155.

14. Ibid., p.193.

15. Westmoreland, *A Soldier Reports,* p. 294.

16. See Hickey, *The American Military Advisor.*

17. Westmoreland, *A Soldier Reports,* p. 294.

18. See James L. Collins, *The Development and Training of the South Vietnamese Army,*

1950–1972 (Washington, DC: Department of the Army, 1975), pp.120–30; Ronald Spector, *Advice and Support: The Early Years, 1941–1960* (Washington, DC: U.S. Army Center of Military History, 1983), pp. 291–93. For another view, see Tobias Wolff, *In Pharaoh's Army: Memories of a Lost War* (London: Picador, 1994).

CHAPTER 13: GUERRILLAS AND CONVENTIONAL TACTICS

1. Some of the best studies of the Greek civil war include: Evangelos Averoff-Tossizza, *By Fire and Axe: The Communist Party and the Civil War in Greece, 1944–1949* (New Rochelle, NY: Caratzas, 1978); Doris M. Condit, *Case Study in Guerrilla War: Greece During World War II* (Washington, DC: Department of the Army, 1961); Howard Jones, *"A New Kind of War": American Global Strategy and the Truman Doctrine in Greece* (New York: Oxford University, 1989); D. George Kousoulas, *Revolution and Defeat: The Story of the Greek Communist Party* (London: Oxford University, 1965); Edgar O'Ballance, *The Greek Civil War* (London: Faber and Faber, 1966); Field Marshal Alexander Papagos, "Guerrilla Warfare," *Foreign Affairs* 30 (January 1952); Stefanos Serafis, *Greek Resistance Army: The Story of ELAS* (London: Birch Books, 1951); Edward R. Wainhouse, "Guerrilla War in Greece, 1946–1949: A Case Study," *Military Review* 37(June 1957); C.M. Woodhouse, *The Struggle for Greece 1941–1949* (London: Hart-Davis, MacGibbon, 1976).

2. For a short analysis, see Joes, "Greece: Civil War into Cold War," in *America and Guerrilla Warfare.*

3. Jules Roy, *The Battle of Dien Bien Phu* (New York: Harper and Row, 1965), p. 60.

4. Bernard Fall, *Hell in a Very Small Place* (Philadelphia: Lippincott, 1967), p. 473, n2.

5. Gen. Paul Ely, *Lessons of the War in Indochina*, 2 vols. (Santa Monica, CA: RAND, 1967), p. 154.

6. Fall, *Hell in a Very Small Place*, p. 337.

7. Ibid., p. 455. See Chen Jian, "China and the First Indo-China War, 1950–1954," *China Quarterly*, no. 133, March 1983, pp. 85–110. From 1956 to1963 Chinese aid to North Vietnam included 10,000 artillery pieces and 28 naval vessels. Chinese antiaircraft troops defended important sites in the North; a total of 320,000 Chinese engineer and other troops served in North Vietnam. "Without that support, the history, even the outcome, of the Viet Nam War might have been different." Chen Jian, "China's involvement in the Viet Nam War, 1964–1969," *China Quarterly*, no. 142 (June 1995), pp. 356–88, quotation on p. 380.

8. Fall, *Hell in a Very Small Place*, pp. 255, 455; Denis Warner, *Certain Victory: How Hanoi Won the War* (Kansas City, KS: Sheed, Andrews, and McMeel, 1978), p. 89.

9. John Keegan, *Dien Bien Phu* (New York: Ballantine, 1974), p. 63.

10. Jean Pouget, *Nous étions à Dien Bien Phu* (Paris: Presses de la Cite, 1964), p. 86. See also Howard R. Simpson, *Dien Bien Phu: The Epic Battle America Forgot* (Washington, DC: Brassey's, 1996), and P. Rocelle, *Pourquoi Dien Bien Phu?* (Paris: Flammarion, 1968).

11. Keegan, *Dien Bien Phu*, p. 169. General Vo Nguyen Giap's book, *Dien Bien Phu* (Hanoi: Foreign Languages Publishing House, 1964) is a poor translation and filled with asphyxiating Communist phraseology.

12. *Washington Post*, April 6, 1969.

13. Philip B. Davidson, *Viet Nam at War: The History, 1946–1975* (Novato, CA: Presidio, 1988), p. 546.

14. Westmoreland, *A Solder Reports*, p. 332.
15. Hoang Ngoc Lung, *The General Offensives of 1968–1969* (Washington, DC: U.S. Army Center of Military History, 1981), pp. 138, 150; Wirtz, *Tet Offensive*, p. 224; Palmer, *Summons of the Trumpet*, p. 210; Lewis Sorley, *A Better War: The Unexamined Victories and Final Tragedy of America's Last Years in Viet Nam* (New York: Harcourt, Brace, 1999), p. 164.
16. Palmer, *Summons*, p. 246; Wirtz, *Tet Offensive*, p. 224; Hoang, *General Offensives*, pp. 22–23.
17. Maxwell Taylor, *Swords and Plowshares* (New York: Norton, 1972), p. 383; Robert S. Shaplen estimates 92,000 were killed; see his *The Road from War: Viet Nam, 1965–1971* (New York: Harper and Row, 1970), p. 219.
18. Davidson, *Viet Nam at War*, p. 475.
19. Timothy J. Lomperis, *From People's War to People's Rule: Insurgency, Intervention and the Lessons of Viet Nam* (Chapel Hill, NC: University of North Carolina, 1996), p. 341.
20. Gabriel Kolko, *Anatomy of a War: Viet Nam, The United States, and the Modern Historical Experience* (New York: Pantheon, 1985), p. 334.
21. Accusations arose in several quarters that Hanoi had deliberately exposed the Viet Cong to destruction; see for example Truong Nhu Tang, *A Viet Cong Memoir* (New York: Harcourt, 1987).

CHAPTER 14: THE MYTH OF MAOIST PEOPLE'S WAR

1. A distinguished student of these matters wrote that the Vietnamese Communist version of Maoist Revolutionary War was "a strategy for which there is no known, proven counterstrategy." Douglas Pike, *PAVN* (Novato, CA: Presidio, 1986), p. 213.
2. Chi Hsi-Sheng, *Nationalist China at War* (Ann Arbor, MI: University of Michigan, 1982), p. 1.
3. Lucian Pye, *Warlord Politics* (New York: Praeger, 1971), p. 3.
4. See John K. Fairbank, "Introduction: Maritime and Continental in China's History," in John K. Fairbank, ed., *The Cambridge History of China*, vol. 12, *Republican China 1912–1949*, part one. (Cambridge: Cambridge University Press, 1983).
5. James E. Sheridan, *China in Disintegration: The Republican Era in China 1912–1949* (New York: Free Press, 1975), p. 230. Canton was the first Chinese port regularly visited by Europeans; the far-sailing Portuguese secured a foreign trade monopoly there in 1511. Canton is ninety miles from Hong Kong and sixty-five miles from Macau. The Overseas Chinese, very numerous in Singapore, Indonesia, the Philippines and elsewhere, wanted a strong Chinese state to protect them from persecution and exploitation in the lands of their residence.
6. "The target of the Nationalist Revolution is imperialism and the warlords." Chiang Kai-shek, *China's Destiny*, (New York: Roy Publishers, 1947), p. 111.
7. Chiang held the imperialists responsible for Chinese economic backwardness, as well as civil conflict, drug abuse, and warlord strife. *China's Destiny*, pp. 78, 84, 92, and 111.
8. In 1937, China had 7,500 miles of railroads, less than in the state of Illinois, which was one-sixty-fourth its size.
9. James E. Sheridan, "The Warlord Era: Politics and Militarism under the Peking Government 1916–1928," in *Cambridge History of China* (Cambridge: Cambridge University, 1983), v. 12, *Republican China, 1912–1949*, pp. 288–89. See also Pye,

Warlord Politics. On the value of mercenary troops, see Machiavelli's *Prince*, chapter XII.

10. Donald A. Jordan, *The Northern Expedition: China's National Revolution 1926–1928* (Honolulu, HI: University of Hawaii, 1976), pp. 231, 234 and passim.

11. Jordan, *The Northern Expedition*, p. 277. See also Hu Pu-yu, *A Brief History of the Chinese National Revolutionary Forces* (Taipei: Chung Wu Publishing Co., 1971).

12. Thomas A. Marks, *Counterrevolution in China* (London: Frank Cass, 1998), p. 80. Chiang of course had quite given up trying to convert the members of the CCP.

13. C. Martin Wilbur, "The Nationalist Revolution: From Canton to Nanking, 1923–1928," in *The Cambridge History of China*, vol. 12, *Republican China, 1912–1947*, part one (Cambridge: Cambridge University, 1983), vol. 12, p. 720.

14. Lloyd Eastman, "Nationalist China during the Nanking Decade," *Cambridge History of China* (Cambridge: Cambridge University, 1983), vol. 13, *Republican China, 1912–1947*, part two, p. 163. See Tien Hung-Mao, *Government and Politics in Kuomintang China, 1927–1937* (Stanford, CA: Stanford University, 1972), chapter 1; and Hsieh Jan-Chih, *The Kuomintang: Selected Historical Documents 1894–1969* (New York: St. John's University, 1970).

15. See Arthur N. Young, *China and the Helping Hand, 1937–1945* (Cambridge, MA: Harvard University, 1963).

16. Henry MacAleavy, *The Modern History of China* (London: Weidenfeld and Nicolson, 1968), p. 267.

17. Robert Bedeski, *State-Building in Modern China: The Kuomintang in the Prewar Period* (Berkeley, CA: University of California Center for Chinese Studies, China Research Monograph #18, 1981), p. ix. See also Jordan, *The Northern Expedition*, p. 67 and passim.

18. William W. Whitson, *Lessons from China* (n.p., n.d.), p. 7.

19. Edwin Leung, ed., *Historical Dictionary of Revolutionary China 1839–1976* (Westport, CT: Greenwood, 1992), p. 122.

20. William Wei, *Counterrevolution in China: The Nationalists in Jiangxi during the Soviet Period* (Ann Arbor, MI: University of Michigan, 1985), p. 121.

21. See Franz H. Michael, *The Taiping Rebellion: History and Documents*, 3 vols. (Seattle, WA: University of Washington, 1966–1971); and Mary C. Wright, *The Last Stand of Chinese Conservatism* (Stanford, CA: Stanford University, 1967).

22. Whitson, *Lessons*.

23. Credit for this new tactic should go to the KMT itself, not to visiting German officers, as is sometimes alleged. See Wei, *Counterrevolution*, pp. 108ff.

24. The Japanese also employed lines of blockhouses; see below, as well as the discussion of similar strategies in other chapters of this volume.

25. Of the Fifth Encirclement Campaign, Mao wrote: "The Red Army was greatly weakened, and all the base areas in the south were lost." *Selected Military Writings*, p. 98. See also Mao Tse-tung, *Selected Works* (New York: International Publishers, 1957), vol. 1, chapters 4 and 5, pp. 198–254.

26. Lyman P. Van Slyke, *The Chinese Communist Movement: A Report of the U.S. War Department July 1945* (Stanford, CA: Stanford University, 1968), p. 33.

27. Bedeski, *State-Building*, p. 170.

28. Van Slyke, *The Chinese Communist Movement*, p. 114.

29. Chi Hsi-sheng, *Nationalist China at War*, chapter 2.

30. Johnson, *Peasant Nationalism and Communist Power*, pp. 47–48. On the complexities of Chinese collaborationism, see the illuminating study by John Hunter Boyle,

China and Japan at War: The Politics of Collaboration (Stanford, CA: Stanford University, 1972).

31. Tang Tsou, *America's Failure in China, 1940–1950* (Chicago, IL: University of Chicago, 1963), p. 50.

32. Ironically, years later a variation of this phenomenon would appear in Mao's insistence that ideological purity was more desirable than technical expertise: "Red rather than Expert."

33. Iris Chang, *The Rape of Nanking: The Forgotten Holocaust* (New York: Basic Books, 1997); Joshua A. Fogel, ed., *The Nanjing Massacre* (Berkeley, CA: University of California, 2000).

34. Johnson, *Peasant Nationalism and Communist Power*, p. 7.

35. Ibid.

36. Ibid., p. 10.

37. Ibid., p. 5.

38. Tang Tsou, *America's Failure in China*, p. 51.

39. Warlord troops flying Chiang's colors often defected to the Japanese, and these provided the bulk of Japanese puppet troops in China.

40. Geoffrey Fairbairn, *Revolutionary Guerrilla Warfare: The Countryside Version* (Harmondsworth, England: Penguin, 1974), p. 118.

41. Johnson, *Peasant Nationalism and Communist Power*, p. 4.

42. Samuel B. Griffith, *Mao Tse-tung on Guerrilla War* (New York: Praeger, 1961), p. 69.

43. "The existence of a regular Red Army of adequate strength is a necessary condition for the existence of Red political power." Mao Tse-tung, *Selected Military Writings*, (Peking: Foreign Languages Press, 1963), p. 14.

44. Colin Gray, *Modern Strategy* (New York: Oxford University Press, 1999), pp. 292–93.

45. Mao Tse-tung, *Selected Military Writings*, p. 246.

46. Mao Tse-tung *Basic Tactics*, trans. Stuart Schram (New York: Praeger, 1966 [orig. 1938]), p. 130. Compare: "Weapons are an important factor in war, but not the decisive factor: it is people, not things, that are decisive." Mao Tse-tung, *Selected Military Writings*, p. 217.

47. Mao Tse-tung, *Selected Military Writings*, p. 274.

48. Ibid., p. 274.

49. Ibid., p. 33.

50. Mao Tse-tung, *Basic Tactics*, p. 56. Confer: "We should resolutely fight a decisive engagement in every campaign or battle in which we are sure of victory; we should avoid a decisive engagement in every campaign or battle in which we are not sure of victory; and we should absolutely avoid a strategically decisive engagement on which the fate of the whole nation is staked" because "we are not gamblers who risk everything on a single throw." *Selected Military Writings*, pp. 254 and 257.

51. Mao Tse-tung, *Basic Tactics*, p. 86.

52. Ibid., p. 73.

53. Ibid., p. 102.

54. Mao Tse-tung, *Selected Military Writings*, pp. 210–11. "The second stage may be termed one of strategic stalemate." *Selected Military Writings*, p. 212.

55. Mao Tse-tung, *Basic Tactics*, p. 81.

56. Mao Tse-tung, *Selected Military Writings*, p. 72.

57. Johnson, *Peasant Nationalism and Communist Power*, chapter 2.

58. Van Slyke, *Chinese Communist Movement*, pp. 111–12.

59. Marks, *Counterrevolution*, p. 83.

60. Van Slyke, *Chinese Communist Movement*, pp. 6 and 104.

61. Ibid., p. 120.

62. Ibid., pp. 120–21.

63. The Japanese puppet state established in Manchuria after 1931.

64. F.F. Liu, *Military History of Modern China, 1924–1949* (Princeton, NJ: Princeton University Press, 1956), p. 205.

65. Colin S. Gray, *The Leverage of Seapower: The Strategic Advantage of Navies in War* (New York: Free Press, 1992), p. 256.

66. *The Statesman's Yearbook 1944*, p. 1067.

67. Lyman P. Van Slyke, "China Incident," in *The Oxford Companion to World War II*, ed. I.C.B. Dear (New York: Oxford University Press, 1995), pp. 232–33. See Lincoln Li, *The Japanese Army in North China, 1937–1941: Problems of Political and Economic Control* (Tokyo: Oxford University Press, 1975), p. 12; and *A Dictionary of the Second World War*, ed. Elizabeth-Anne Wheal et al. (New York: Peter Bedrick, 1990), p. 244.

68. See Hsu Long-Hsuen and Chang Ming-Kai, eds., *History of the Sino-Japanese War 1937–1945* (Taipei: Chung Wu Publishers, 1971), p. 565; and Stanley Woodburn Kirby, *The War Against Japan*, vol. v (London: H.M. Stationery Office, 1969), p.196.

69. Chalmers Johnson, *Peasant Nationalism and Communist Power*, chapter 2; M. Harries and S. Harries, *Soldiers of the Sun: The Rise and Fall of the Imperial Japanese Army* (New York: Random House, 1991). See also *Oxford Companion*, p. 221, and E.F. Carlson, *The Chinese Army* (New York: Institute of Pacific Relations, 1940), pp. 27–28.

70. See Griffith, *Mao Tse-tung*, pp. 67, 94. See also Harries and Harries, *Soldiers of the Sun*, pp. 260–62, 320–21, 348.

71. Nomonhan was the name of the border post where the Soviet army entered western Manchukuo. See A.D. Coox, *Nomonhan: Russia Against Japan, 1939* (Stanford, CA: Stanford University, 1985), and P. Snow, "Nomonhan—the Unknown Victory," *History Today*, July 1990.

72. Harries and Harries, *Soldiers of the Sun*, pp. 348–54.

73. Richard Overy, *Why the Allies Won* (New York: Norton, 1995), p. 222. See also Lincoln Li, *The Japanese Army in North China*.

74. Overy, *Why the Allies Won*, p. 221.

75. Ibid.

76. Not to mention the American Pershing tank, a late entrant into the war, with a 100mm gun and 105mm of armor, or the German Panther tank, with a 75mm gun and 120mm of armor.

77. See Nigel de Lee, "The Far Eastern Experience," in Ian F.W. Becket, *The Roots of Counterinsurgency* (London: Blandford, 1988); Harries and Harries, *Soldiers of the Sun*, pp. 253–54. By 1940 the IJA had severely defeated Communist guerrillas in Manchukuo; see Chong Sik Lee, *Counterinsurgency in Manchuria: The Japanese Experience 1931–1940* (Santa Monica, CA: RAND, 1967), p. 65 and passim; see also Gene Z. Hanrahan, *Japanese Operations Against Guerrilla Forces* (Chevy Chase, MD: Operations Research Office, Johns Hopkins University, 1954), p.8.

78. Liu, *Military History*, p. 229.

79. O. Edmund Clubb, *Twentieth Century China*, 2d ed. (New York: Oxford University Press, 1972), pp. 289–90.

80. Liu, *Military History*, p. 229.

81. Suzanne Pepper, *Civil War in China: The Political Struggle 1945–1949* (Berkeley, CA: University of California, 1978), chapter 1. See also George T. Yu, *Politics in Republican China: The Kuomintang 1913–1924* (Berkeley, CA: University of California, 1966), and Hsieh Jan-chih, *The Kuomintang: Selected Historical Documents 1899–1969* (New York: St John's University, 1970).

82. "The strategic theory of Mao Tse-tung . . . is massively derivative from Chinese classical military writings." Colin S. Gray, *Modern Strategy* (Oxford, England: Oxford University Press, 1999), p. 289.

83. See Tom Marks, *Maoist Insurgency Since Viet Nam* (London: Frank Cass, 1995).

84. See Chalmers Johnson, *Autopsy on People's War* (Berkeley, CA: University of California, 1973).

85. John K. Fairbank, *The Great Chinese Revolution 1800–1985* (New York: Harper and Row, 1986), p. 296.

86. Lucian W. Pye, *China*, 4th ed. (New York: HarperCollins, 1991), p. 250.

87. Ibid., 307.

88. "In his last years Mao was as much a wreck as the country and party he had twice led to disaster. The GPCR is now seen, especially by its many victims, as ten lost years in China's modern development." Fairbank, *Great Chinese Revolution*, p. 335.

89. Pye, *China*, p. 271.

90. Pye, *China*, chapter 17.

CHAPTER 15. TWO FALSE STARTS: VENEZUELA AND THAILAND

1. Much of the following discussion derives from *Castro-Communist Insurgency in Venezuela* (Alexandria, VA: Georgetown Research Project, Atlantic Research Corp, n d [1964?]), and Winfield J. Burggraaff, *The Venezuelan Armed Forces in Politics 1935–1959* (Columbia, MO: University of Missouri, 1972.

2. Ernesto Guevara, *Guerrilla Warfare* (New York: Vintage, 1961).

3. Robert J. Alexander, *Communism in Latin America* (New Brunswick, NJ: Rutgers University, 1960).

4. Timothy Wickham-Crowley, *Guerrillas and Revolution in Latin America: A Comparative Study of Insurgents and Regimes Since 1956* (Princeton, NJ: Princeton University, 1991), p. 38.

5. Raúl Leoni and John D. Martz, *The Venezuelan Elections of December 1, 1963* (Washington, DC: Institute for the Comparative Study of Political Systems, 1964).

6. See Castañeda, *Utopia Unarmed*, passim, and John D. Martz and David Meyers, "Venezuelan Democracy and the Future" in Martz and Meyers, eds., *The Democratic Experience* (New York: Praeger, 1977).

7. See Daniel D. Lovelace, *China and "People's War" in Thailand 1964–1969* (Berkeley, CA: University of California Center for Chinese Studies, 1971).

8. George K. Tanham, *Trial in Thailand* (New York: Crane, Russak, 1974), p. 110.

9. Justus Van der Kroef, "Guerrilla Communism and Counterinsurgency in Thailand," *Orbis*, v. 18 (Spring 1974), p. 139. But John S. Girling took a more optimistic (and as it turned out more accurate) view; see his "Northeast Thailand: Tomorrow's Viet Nam?" in *Foreign Affairs*, January 1968.

10. Johnson, *Autopsy on People's War*.

11. Charles F. Keyes, *Thailand, Buddhist Kingdom as Modern Nation-State* (Boulder, CO: Westview, 1987), p. 14.

12. Tanham, *Trial in Thailand*, p. 15. "The reasons for Thailand's relative immunity to Communism lie in its traditional independence from European colonialism and in the long history of monarchy and respect for authority which form an important part of Thai psychology." Donald E. Nuechterlein, *Thailand and the Struggle for Southeast Asia* (Ithaca, NY: Cornell University, 1965), p. 103.

13. Lovelace, *China and "People's War,"* p. 18.

14. Thomas A. Marks, *Maoist Insurgency Since Viet Nam* (London: Frank Cass, 1996), p. 8.

15. Lovelace, *China and "People's War,"* p. 17.

16. Tanham, *Trial in Thailand*, p. 36.

17. See Peter A. Poole, *The Vietnamese in Thailand: A Historical Perspective* (Ithaca, NY: Cornell University, 1970), p. 29.

18. Keyes, *Thailand*, p. 204. Perhaps half of Bangkok's population in the mid-1960s was of Chinese origin; Lovelace, *China and "People's War,"* p. 51.

19. Lovelace, *China and "People's War,"* p. 21.

20. Wit, *Thailand: Another Viet Nam?*, p. 6.

21. Charles F. Keyes, *Isan: Regionalism in Northeast Thailand* (Ithaca, NY: Cornell University, 1967), p. 52.

22. "Peking's ultimate goal is that Burma, Thailand, Laos, Cambodia and Malaysia—like North Viet Nam—come under the rule of Communist parties which pursue domestic and foreign policies consonant with those of China. Peking also expects that these Communist governments will come to power using the techniques of armed struggle developed in China's own Communist revolution." *Neutralization in Southeast Asia: Problems and Prospects*, a special report to the U.S. Senate by C.E. Black et al (Washington, DC: US Government Printing Office, 1966), p. 14.

23. Jay Taylor, *China and Southeast Asia: Peking's Relations with Revolutionary Movements* (New York: Praeger, 1976, 2d ed.), p. 290.

24. For Thai foreign policy during these years, see Wit, *Thailand*. In 1966, 80 percent of U.S. air strikes against North Vietnam flew from Thai bases; Lovelace, *China and "People's War,"* p. 151.

25. Tanham, *Trial in Thailand*, p. 42. See also Thomas A. Marks, *Making Revolution: The Insurgency of the Communist Party of Thailand in Structural Perspective* (Bangkok: White Lotus, 1994).

26. Van der Kroef, "Guerrilla Communism," p. 13n.

27. Jeffrey Race, "War in Northern Thailand," *Modern Asian Studies*, v. 8 (1974).

28. Tanham, *Trial in Thailand*, p. 62. Race estimated there were 2,000 guerrillas in 1970; "War in Northern Thailand," p. 109.

29. John S. Girling, *Thailand: Society and Politics* (Ithaca, NY: Cornell University, 1981), p. 267.

30. Marks, *Maoist Insurgency*, p. 37. And see Race, "War in Northern Thailand," pp. 103–4 and 107–8.

31. There were between two million and four million Meo living in China, and some hundred thousands in Vietnam, Laos, and Burma. Race, "War in Northern Thailand," p. 93n. And see Peter Kunstadter, ed., *Southeast Asian Tribes, Minorities and Nations* (Princeton, NJ: Princeton University, 1967).

32. Girling, *Thailand*, pp. 264–65.

33. Stuart Slade, "Successful Counterinsurgency: How the Thais Burned the Books and Beat the Guerrillas," *International Defence Review*, v. 22 (1989), p. 23. Several thousand Thai troops had also operated clandestinely in Laos in the 1960s.

34. Marks, *Maoist Insurgency*, pp. 60–61. Anonymous, "Reflections on Counterinsurgency in Thailand," *World Affairs*, vol. 146 (Winter 1984–1985), p. 81.
35. Tanham, *Trial in Thailand*, p. 81.
36. Race, *War Comes to Long An*, p. 164n.
37. Anonymous, "Reflections on Counterinsurgency," p. 260.
38. "In the early fifties there was no government presence in the rugged forests which form Thailand's northern border with Laos and Burma." Race, "The War in Northern Thailand," p. 90.
39. Marks, *Maoist Insurgency*, pp. 68 and 72.
40. Tanham, *Trial in Thailand*, p. 85 and passim. See also Richard Lee Hough, "Development and Security in Thailand: Lessons from Other Asian Countries," *Asian Survey*, March 1969, pp. 178–88.
41. Tanham, *Trial in Thailand*, p. 77; Race, "War in Northern Thailand," pp. .104–5.
42. Keyes, *Thailand*, p. 109. Government forces had suffered 4,400 fatal casualties between 1969 and 1977; in 1977 the Communists had killed 582 military and civilian officials, and in 1978 another 646; Girling, *Thailand*, p. 257n.
43. See Theda Skocpol, *States and Social Revolutions* (New York: Cambridge University Press, 1979); Samuel P. Huntington, *Political Order in Changing Societies* (New Haven, CT: Yale University Press, 1968), chapter 5; Johnson, *Autopsy on People's War*; Joes, *From the Barrel of a Gun.*
44. Girling, *Thailand*, pp. 282–83; David K. Wyatt, *Thailand: A Short History* (New Haven, CT: Yale University Press), pp. 304–5.
45. John McBeth, "A Battle for Loyalty in the Jungles," *Far Eastern Economic Review*, June 8, 1979.
46. Zimmerman, "Insurgency in Thailand."
47. Slade, "Successful Counterinsurgency," p. 25.
48. Girling, *Thailand*, p. 257 and passim; Keyes, *Thailand*, p. 109.
49. Girling, *Thailand*, p. 258.
50. Marks, *Maoist Insurgency*, p. 68.
51. John McBeth, "Counting on Nearby Friends," *Far Eastern Economic Review*, July 13, 1979, p. 13.
52. On the border between the north and northeast regions.

CHAPTER 16: COMPARING NATIONAL APPROACHES TO COUNTERINSURGENCY

1. On the Vendée, see Peter Paret, *Internal War and Pacification: The Vendée, 1789–1796* (Princeton, NJ: Princeton University Center of International Studies, 1961), and Harvey Mitchell, "The Vendée and Counterrevolution: A Review Essay," *French Historical Studies*, vol. 5 (Fall 1968); on Spain, Don W. Alexander, *Rod of Iron: French Counterinsurgency Policy in Aragon during the Peninsular War* (Wilmington, DE: Scholarly Resources, 1985); John L. Tone, *The Fatal Knot: The Guerrilla War in Navarre and the Defeat of Napoleon in Spain* (Chapel Hill: University of North Carolina, 1994); William F. Lewis, *Francisco Xavier Mina: Guerrilla Warrior for Romantic Liberalism* (Doctoral dissertation, University of California, Santa Barbara, 1968).
2. See Lefebvre, *Napoleon*, p. 363.
3. See Joes, *Guerrilla Conflict before the Cold War*, pp. 115–16.
4. Douglas Porch, "Bugeaud, Gallieni, Lyautey: The Development of French Colo-

nial Warfare," in Peter Paret, ed., *Makers of Modern Strategy: From Machiavelli to the Nuclear Age* (Princeton: Princeton University, 1986), p. 381.

5. Porch, "Bugeaud, Gallieni, Lyautey," p. 393. See also Douglas Porch, *The Conquest of Morocco* (New York: Fromm, 1982); Alan Scham, *Lyautey in Morocco* (Berkeley, CA: University of California, 1970); Andre Maurois, *Lyautey* (New York: Appleton, 1931); and Sonia Howe, *Lyautey of Morocco* (London: Hodder and Stoughton, 1931).

6. Lucien Bodard, *The Quicksand War* (Boston: Little, Brown, 1967); Paul Ely, *Lessons of the War in Indochina*, vol. 2 (Santa Monica, CA: Rand Corporation, 1967); Bernard Fall, *Street Without Joy* (Harrisburg, PA: Stackpole, 1964).

7. See the classic studies by Fall, *Hell in a Very Small Place*, and Jules Roy, *Battle of Dien Bien Phu*. See also Vo Nguyen Giap, *Dien Bien Phu* (Hanoi: Foreign Languages Publishing House, 1964). And see chapter 13, note 10.

8. Alf A. Heggoy, *Insurgency and Counterinsurgency in Algeria* (Bloomington, IN: Indiana University, 1972); George Kelly, *Lost Soldiers: The French Army and Empire in Crisis* (Cambridge, MA: MIT, 1965); Edgar O'Ballance, *The Algerian Insurrection, 1954–1962* (Hamden, CT: Archon, 1967); Alistair Horne, *A Savage War of Peace: Algeria 1954–1962* (New York: Viking, 1967); Peter Paret, *French Revolutionary Warfare from Indochina to Algeria: An Analysis of a Political and Military Doctrine* (New York: Praeger, 1964); David C. Gordon, *The Passing of French Algeria* (New York: Oxford University, 1966).

9. Piers Mackesy, *The War for America 1775–1783* (Cambridge, MA: Harvard University, 1965); Edward E. Curtis, *The Organization of the British Army in America* (New Haven, CT: Yale University, 1926); R. Arthur Bowler, *Logistics and the Failure of the British Army in America, 1775–1783* (Princeton University, 1975); John S. Pancake, *This Destructive War: The British Campaign in the Carolinas, 1780–1782* (University, AL: University of Alabama, 1985); Paul H. Smith, *Loyalists and Redcoats: A Study in British Revolutionary Policy* (Chapel Hill, NC: University of North Carolina, 1964).

10. See especially the excellent studies by Byron Farwell, *The Great Anglo-Boer War* (New York: Norton, 1976), and Thomas Pakenham, *The Boer War* (New York: Avon, 1979).

11. See John Pimlott, "The British Experience," in Ian F.W. Beckett, ed., *The Roots of Counter-Insurgency: Armies and Guerrilla Warfare, 1900–1945*; Callwell's *Small Wars* is full of practical wisdom.

12. See the good discussion of these points in Thomas R. Mockaitis, *British Counterinsurgency 1919–1960* (New York: St. Martin's, 1990).

13. There is an extensive and high-quality literature on this conflict, including Edgar O'Ballance, *Malaya: The Communist Insurgent War, 1948–1960* (Hamden, CT: Archon, 1966); Anthony Short, *The Communist Insurrection in Malaya, 1948–1960* (London: Frederick Muller, 1975); Richard Stubbs, *Hearts and Minds in Guerrilla Warfare: The Malayan Emergency of 1948–1960* (Singapore: Oxford University, 1989).

14. Franz H. Michael, *The Taiping Rebellion: History and Politics*, 3 vols. (Seattle: University of Washington, 1966–1971); Mary C. Wright, *The Last Stand of Chinese Conservatism* (Stanford, CA: Stanford University Press, 1957). S.Y. Teng, *The Nien Army and Their Guerrilla Warfare* (Westport, CT: Greenwood, 1984 [orig. Paris, 1961]).

15. Tien Hung-mao, *Government and Politics in Kuomintang China, 1927–1937* (Stanford: Stanford University, 1972); F.F. Liu, *Military History of Modern China, 1924–1949* (Princeton: Princeton University, 1956); William Wei, *Counterrevolution in China* (Ann Arbor: University of Michigan, 1985).

16. George N. Patterson, *Requiem for Tibet* (London: Aurum, 1990); Peissel, *Secret War in Tibet*; Shakya, *Dragon in the Land of Snows* ; Warren W. Smith, *Tibetan Nation: A History of Tibetan Nationalism and Sino-Tibetan Relations* (Boulder, CO: Westview, 1996).

17. Chong-Sik Lee, *Counterinsurgency in Manchuria: The Japanese Experience, 1931–1940* (Santa Monica, CA: Rand Corporation, 1967).

18. Nigel de Lee, "The Far Eastern Experience" in Beckett, *Roots*, p. 141.

19. Gene Z. Hanrahan, *Japanese Operations Against Guerrilla Forces* (Chevy Chase, MD: Operations Research Office, Johns Hopkins University, 1954), pp. 8, 20.

20. Chalmers Johnson, *Peasant Nationalism and Communist Power* (Stanford, CA: Stanford University, 1961).

21. Geoffrey Fairbairn, *Revolutionary Guerrilla Warfare: The Countryside Version* (Harmondsworth, UK: Penguin, 1974), p. 118.

22. See W.E.D. Allen and Paul Muratoff, *Caucasian Battlefields* (Cambridge: Cambridge University, 1953); John F. Baddeley, *The Russian Conquest of the Caucasus* (New York: Russell and Russell, 1969 [orig 1908]); Marie Broxup, ed., *The North Caucasus Barrier: The Russian Advance towards the Muslim World* (New York: St. Martin's, 1992); Moshe Gammer, *Muslim Resistance to the Tsar: Shamil and the Conquest of Chechnya and Daghestan* (London: Frank Cass, 1994).

23. Thomas G. Butson, *The Tsar's Lieutenant: The Soviet Marshal* (New York: Praeger, 1984); Sally W. Stoecker, *Forging Stalin's Army: Marshal Tukhachevsky and the Politics of Military Innovation* (Boulder, CO: Westview, 1998).

24. John Armstrong, *Ukrainian Nationalism* (New York: Columbia University, 1955); Alexander Buchsbajew, *Toward a Theory of Guerrilla Warfare: A Case Study of the Ukrainian Nationalist Underground in the Soviet Union and Communist Poland* (Doctoral dissertation, City University of New York, 1984).

25. Ian F.W. Beckett, "The Soviet Experience," in Beckett, *Roots of Counter-Insurgency*; Anatol Lieven, *Chechnya: Tombstone of Russian Power* (New Haven: Yale University Press, 1998), p. 321; John B. Dunlop, *Russia Confronts Chechnya: Roots of a Separatist Conflict* (Oxford: Clarendon, 1998), pp. 58–69.

26. Alexander Alexiev, *Inside the Soviet Army in Afghanistan* (Santa Monica, CA: Rand Corporation, 1988); Mark Galeotti, *Afghanistan: The Soviet Union's Last War* (Portland, OR: Frank Cass, 1994); James S. Robbins, *Soviet Counterinsurgency Strategy in Afghanistan1979–1989* (Doctoral dissertation, Tufts University, 1991).

27. Anatol Lieven, *Chechnya: Tombstone of Russian Power* (New Haven, CT: Yale University Press, 1998), p. 3.

28. Stephen J. Blank and Earl H. Tilford, *Russia's Invasion of Chechnya: A Preliminary Assessment* (Carlisle Barracks, PA: U.S. Army War College, January 1995); Dunlop, *Russia Confronts Chechnya*; Carl Van Dyke, "Kabul to Grozny: A Critique of Soviet (Russian) Counterinsurgency Doctrine," *Journal of Slavic Military Studies*, vol. 9, no. 4 (1996); Matthew Evangelista, *The Chechen Wars* (Washington, DC: Brookings, 2003). Some of the implications have to do with perhaps grave Western overestimates of Soviet military capabilities, especially (but not exclusively) during the 1980s.

29. John P. Cann, *Counterinsurgency in Africa: The Portuguese Way of War, 1961–1974* (Westport, CT: Greenwood, 1997); Neil Bruce, *Portugal: The Last Empire* (New York: Wiley, 1975); Ian F.W. Beckett, "The Portuguese Army: The Campaign in Mozambique, 1964–1974," in *Armed Forces and Modern Counter-Insurgency*, ed. Ian F.W. Beckett and John Pimlott (London: Croom Helm, 1985); Gerald J. Bender, "The Limits of Counterinsurgency: An African Case," *Comparative Politics*, vol. 4

(April 1972); Michael Calvert, "Counter-Insurgency in Mozambique," *Journal of the Royal United Services Institute for Defence Studies* (March 1973); Thomas H. Hendrikson, "Portugal in Africa: Comparative Notes on Counter-Insurgency," *Orbis* (Summer 1977).

30. On the 1974 overthrow of the Portuguese government by the armed forces, see the following: Neil Bruce, *Portugal: The Last Empire;* G.W. Grayson, "Portugal and the Armed Forces Movement," *Orbis* 19 (Summer 1975); Douglas Porch, *The Portuguese Armed Forces and the Revolution* (Stanford, CA: Hoover Institution, 1977); Philippe C. Schmitter, "Liberation by Golpe," *Armed Forces and Society* 2 (Fall 1975).

31. On guerrillas in the American War of Independence, see Russell F. Weigley, *The Partisan War: The South Carolina Campaign of 1780–1782* (Columbia, SC: University of South Carolina, 1970); Noel B. Gerson, *The Swamp Fox: Francis Marion* (Garden City, NY: Doubleday, 1967); Hugh F. Rankin, *Francis Marion: The Swamp Fox* (New York: Crowell, 1973); Robert D. Bass, *Swamp Fox* (New York: Henry Holt, 1959); Robert D. Bass, *Gamecock: The Life and Times of General Thomas Sumter* (New York: Holt, Rinehart, Winston, 1961); Robert Stansbury Lambert, *South Carolina Loyalists in the American Revolution* (Columbia, SC: University of South Carolina, 1987); Robert O. DeMond, *The Loyalists in North Carolina During the Revolution* (Hamden, CT: Archon, 1964 [orig. 1940]). For the Civil War, see John S. Mosby, *The Memoirs of Colonel John S. Mosby* (New York: Kraus Reprint, 1969); Ramage, *Gray Ghost*; Michael Fellman, *Inside War: The Guerrilla Conflict in Missouri during the American Civil War* (New York: Oxford University, 1989); Albert Castel, *William Clarke Quantrill: His Life and Times* (New York: Frederick Fell, 1962); William Elsey Connelley, *Quantrill and the Border Wars* (New York: Pageant, 1956 [orig. 1909]); Duane Schultz, *Quantrill's War* (New York: St. Martin's, 1996).

32. Brian McAlister Linn, *The Philippine War, 1899–1902* (Lawrence, KS: University of Kansas, 2000), p. 328.

33. See the following excellent studies: John Morgan Gates, *Schoolbooks and Krags: The United States Army in the Philippines, 1898–1902* (Westport, CT: Greenwood, 1973); Brian McAlister Linn, *The U.S. Army and Counterinsurgency in the Philippine War, 1899–1902* (Chapel Hill: University of North Carolina, 1989); Glenn A. May, *Battle for Batangas: A Philippine Province at War* (New Haven, CT: Yale University, 1991).

34. D. George Kousoulas, *Revolution and Defeat: The Story of the Greek Communist Party* (London: Oxford University, 1965); O'Ballance, *Greek Civil War*; C.M. Woodhouse, *The Struggle for Greece, 1941–1949* (London: Hart-Davis, MacGibbon, 1976).

35. The literature on the U.S. involvement in Vietnam is voluminous and growing. In contrast, therefore, to the other sections of this essay, no attempt is made to identify even a sampling of the best works.

36. Andrew F. Krepinevich, *The Army and Viet Nam* (Baltimore: Johns Hopkins University, 1986).

37. General Westmoreland's successor, Creighton Abrams, introduced less destructive tactics, but by then the Americans were pulling out. See the excellent study by Lewis Sorley, *A Better War: The Unexamined Victories and Final Tragedy of America's Last Years in Viet Nam* (New York: Harcourt, Brace, 1999).

38. Soviet loss of interest in the struggle was of course another important factor. Consult John Waghelstein, *El Salvador: Observations and Experiences in Counterinsurgency* (Carlisle Barracks, PA: U.S. Army War College, 1985); Max G. Manwaring and

Courtney Prisk, eds., *El Salvador at War: An Oral History* (Washington, DC: National Defense University, 1988); Caesar Sereseres, "Lessons from Central America's Revolutionary Wars, 1972–1984," in *The Lessons of Recent Wars in the Third World,* ed. Robert E. Harkavy and Stephanie G. Newman (Lexington, MA: Lexington Books, 1985); Ernest Evans, "El Salvador's Lessons for Future U.S. Interventions," *World Affairs,* Vol. 160 (Summer 1997); A.J. Bacevich et al., *American Military Policy in Small Wars: The Case of El Salvador* (Washington, DC: Brassey's, 1988); Benjamin Schwarz, *American Counterinsurgency Doctrine and El Salvador: The Frustrations of Reform and the Illusions of Nation-Building* (Santa Monica, CA: Rand, 1991); Timothy Wickham-Crowley, *Guerrillas and Revolution in Latin America: A Comparative Study of Movements and Regimes since 1956* (Princeton, NJ: Princeton University, 1992); Cynthia McClintock, *Revolutionary Movements in Latin America: El Salvador's FMLN and Peru's Shining Path* (Washington, DC: U.S. Institute Peace, 1998); A.J. Bacevich et al., *American Military Policy in Small Wars: The Case of El Salvador* (Washington: Pergamon-Brassey's, 1988); Anthony James Joes, "El Salvador: A Long War in a Small Country," in *America and Guerrilla Warfare.*

CHAPTER 17: ELEMENTS OF A COUNTERINSURGENT STRATEGY

1. Lucian Pye, "The Roots of Insurgency," in Harry Eckstein, ed., *Internal War* (Glencoe, IL: Free Press, 1964), p. 162.
2. Christopher Harmon, "Illustrations of Learning in Counterinsurgency Warfare," *Comparative Strategy,* vol. 11 (1992); and see John P. Cann, *Counterinsurgency in Africa: The Portuguese Way of War, 1961–1974* (Westport, CT: Greenwood, 1997), on how the Portuguese deliberately framed their counterinsurgent efforts to avoid the kinds of mistakes the U.S. made in Vietnam. See also Max G. Manwaring, *Internal Wars: Rethinking Problem and Response* (Carlisle Barracks, PA: Strategic Studies Institute, 2001).
3. Linn, *Philippine War*, p. 328.
4. See Tim Pat Coogan, *The Man Who Made Ireland: The Life and Death of Michael Collins* (Niwot, CO: Roberts Rinehart, 1992).
5. Benedict J. Kerkvliet, *The Huk Rebellion: A Study of Peasant Revolt in the Philippines* (Berkeley, CA: University of California, 1977), p. 238.
6. Richard Stubbs, *Hearts and Minds in Guerrilla Warfare: The Malayan Emergency of 1948–1960* (Singapore: Oxford University, 1989), Chapter 7. Cynthia McClintock seems to believe that insurgencies can succeed even in countries with a "peaceful path." Concerning Sendero Luminoso and similar groups, she writes that "these movements are likely to reject elections—criticizing their procedural flaws as well as their failures to produce effective governments—and rather base their claims to legitimacy on quasi-religious and ideological grounds." Consequently, "at century's end, 'democracy'—defined as elections—is not enough to doom revolution." But of course the point is not that free elections and a peaceful path will always prevent the *rise* of insurgencies, but rather that they will prevent their *success.* The fate of Sendero as of 2004 seems to reinforce the view of Guevara and many others that insurgencies against democratic or even pseudo-democratic regimes must eventually fail. See Cynthia McClintock, *Revolutionary Movements in Latin America: El Salvador's FMLN and Peru's Shining Path* (Washington, DC: U.S. Institute of Peace, 1998), pp. 306, 312.
7. Jeffrey Herbst, *States and Power in Africa: Comparative Lessons in Authority and Control* (Princeton, NJ: Princeton University, 2000), p. 85.

8. See John Coates, *Suppressing Insurgency: An Analysis of the Malayan Emergency 1948–1954* (Boulder, CO: Westview, 1994), p. 83.

9. See F.F. Liu, *A Military History of Modern China 1924–1949* (Princeton, NJ: Princeton University, 1956); Suzanna Pepper, *Civil War in China: The Political Struggle, 1945–1949* (Berkeley, CA: University of California, 1978); Joes, *War for South Viet Nam.*

10. John McCuen, *The Art of Counter-Revolutionary War: The Strategy of Counterinsurgency* (London: Faber and Faber, 1966).

11. On Moro society and its wars, see Bacevich, "Disagreeable Work"; T.J. George, *Revolt on Mindanao: The Rise of Islam in Philippine Politics* (Kuala Lumpur: Oxford University Press, 1980); Vic Hurley, *Swish of the Kris: The Story of the Moros* (New York: Dutton, 1936); George W. Jornacion, *The Time of the Eagles: United States Army Officers and the Pacification of the Philippine Moros* (Doctoral dissertation, UCLA, 1973); Brian McAllister Linn, *Guardians of Empire: The U.S. Army and the Pacific, 1902–1940* (Chapel Hill, NC: University of North Carolina, 1997); Donald Smythe, *Guerrilla Warrior: The Early Life of John J. Pershing* (New York: Scribner's 1973); Vandiver, *Black Jack.*

12. *The Art of War*, chapter VII. Machiavelli agrees: see his *The Art of War* (New York: Da Capo, 1990 [orig. 1521]), p. 178.

13. General Abdul H. Nasution, *Fundamentals of Guerrilla Warfare* (Praeger, 1965 [orig. 1953]), p. 64.

14. Richard L. Clutterbuck, *The Long, Long War: Counterinsurgency in Malaya and Viet Nam* (New York: Praeger, 1966), p. 176.

15. John Morgan Gates, *Schoolbooks and Krags: The United States Army in the Philippines 1898–1902* (Westport, CT: Greenwood, 1973), p. 271.

16. Harmon, "Illustrations of Learning in Counterinsurgency Warfare," p. 32.

17. See James S. Corum and Wray R. Johnson, *Air Power in Small Wars: Fighting Insurgents and Terrorists* (Lawrence, KS: University Press of Kansas, 2003); and see Philip Anthony Towle, *Pilots and Rebels: The Use of Aircraft in Unconventional Warfare, 1918–1988* (London: Brassey's, 1989). And see footnote 15 in chapter 5, "Foreign Involvement with Insurgency."

18. Quoted in S.Y. Teng, *The Nien Army and Their Guerrilla Warfare, 1851–1868* (Paris: Mouton, 1961), p. 213. For more on the great Nien rebellion and its pacification, see *The Cambridge History of China*, ed. Denis Twichett and J.K. Fairbank (Cambridge: Cambridge University Press, 1978), vol. 10, part 1, pp. 310–16 and 456–77.

19. Mary C. Wright, *The Last Stand of Chinese Conservatism* (Stanford, CA: Stanford University, 1967), p. 144

20. See Keith Bickel, *Mars Learning: The Marine Corps' Development of Small Wars Doctrine, 1915–1949* (Boulder, CO: Westview, 2001), pp. 80ff.

21. Jeffery Race, "How They Won," *Asian Survey*, v. 10 (August, 1970).

22. Charles Stuart Callison, *Land to the Tiller in the Mekong Delta* (Lanham, MD: University Press of America, 1983), p. 111.

23. See Pye, "The Roots of Insurgency."

24. Joes, *Guerrilla Conflict before the Cold War*, p. 73.

25. Vegetius, *Epitoma rei militaris*, iii.

26. Machiavelli, *Art of War*, Book VII.

27. See among others, Anthony Short, *The Communist Insurrection in Malaya, 1948–1960* (London: Frederick Muller, 1975), p. 378; O'Ballance, *Malaya*, p. 108; Nathan

Leites and Charles Wolf, *Rebellion and Authority: An Analytic Essay on Insurgent Conflicts* (Santa Monica, CA: RAND 1970), p. 77.

28. Joes, *America and Guerrilla Warfare*, p. 110.

29. Sun Tzu, *On War*, XI, 32. John P. Cann emphasizes that prompt medical attention to the wounded, including evacuation by helicopter, had very good effects on the morale of Portuguese soldiers, *Counterinsurgency in Africa*, pp. 177–82.

30. Tito to author Fitzroy Maclean, *Disputed Barricade* (London; Jonathan Cape, 1957), p. 236.

31. Bernard Fall, *Street Without Joy* (Harrisburg, PA: Stackpole, 1964), p. 354.

32. Lucien Bodard, *The Quicksand War*, trans. P. O'Brian (Boston: Little, Brown, 1967), p. 239.

33. George K. Tanham, *Communist Revolutionary Warfare: From the Viet Minh to the Viet Cong* (New York: Praeger, 1967, rev. ed.), p. 90.

34. See the fate of the French garrisons at Cao Bang and Lang Son, in Joes, *Modern Guerrilla Insurgency*, pp. 103–4.

35. "Winter, with no food in the countryside and no leaves on the trees to give cover, is not a good season for guerrillas." Maclean, *Disputed Barricade*, p. 170

36. The famous Confederate guerrilla chief John Mosby wrote that most of his men were in their teens or early twenties because "they haven't the sense to know danger when they see it." Jeffrey D. Wert, *Mosby's Rangers* (New York: Simon and Schuster, 1990), p. 75.

37. Deneys Reitz, *Commando* (New York: Praeger, 1970 [originally published 1929, composed 1903]), p. 223. For the opening of the Smuts invasion of the Cape, see Reitz, *Commando*, pp. 203–14. Reitz's memoirs, beautiful in their simplicity, honesty and clarity, were written immediately after the war, while he was still quite young and an exile in Madagascar.

38. Luis Taruc, *Born of the People* (Westport, CT: Greenwood, 1973 [orig. 1953]), p. 139.

39. U.S. Marine Corps, *Small Wars Manual*, chapter 5–8. The Marines also used aggressive combat patrols in Haiti; see Bickel, *Mars Learning*, pp. 91ff.

40. See the letter written by General Bruce Hamilton in Victor Sampson and Ian Hamilton, *Anti-Commando* (London: Faber and Faber, 1931), pp. 148–51.

41. Christiaan Rudolf De Wet, *Three Years' War* (London: Constable, 1902), p. 263. The National Scouts were Boers of the Transvaal who, concluding that the struggle against British power was hopeless, had surrendered and then volunteered to fight against the guerrillas to hasten the coming of peace. One of these National Scouts was Piet De Wet, younger brother of the famed guerrilla leader. The first National Scouts were raised in 1901, drawn mostly from the lower strata of Boer society; eventually over 2,000 served. Most Boer soldiers looked upon these Scouts as traitors, and if captured they were frequently killed on the spot.

42. De Wet, *Three Years' War*, p. 263. On British flying columns, see Callwell, *Small Wars*, pp. 138ff.

43. Neil Macauley, *The Sandino Affair* (Chicago: Quadrangle, 1967), p. 269.

44. Eliot Cross, *Conflict in the Shadows*, p. 82.

45. Basil Liddell Hart, *The Real War, 1914–1918* (Boston, MA: Little, Brown, 1930), p. 266.

46. See Le Thi Que, A. Terry Rambo, and Gary D. Murfin, "Why They Fled: Refugee Movement during the Spring 1975 Communist Offensive in South Viet Nam," *Asian Survey* 16 (September 1976). In 1975 North Vietnamese Premier Pham Van Dong

allowed that from 50 to 70 percent of the Southern population would need to be persuaded of the benefits of "reunification"; Malcolm Salmon, "After Revolution, Evolution," *Far Eastern Economic Review*, Dec. 12, 1975, pp. 32–34. On the weaknesses of the Communists in the South and the strength of Southern popular opposition to conquest by the North, see also Gabriel Kolko, *Anatomy of a War* (New York: Pantheon, 1985), pp. 250, 482; Robert A. Scalapino, "We Cannot Accept a Communist Seizure of Viet Nam," *New York Times Magazine*, Dec. 11, 1966, p. 46; the CBS survey in Wesley Fishel, *Viet Nam: Anatomy of a Conflict* (Itasca, IL: Peacock, 1968), pp. 653, 659; Howard R. Penniman, *Elections in South Viet Nam* (Washington, DC: American Enterprise Institute, 1972), p. 199; Dennis J. Duncanson, *Government and Revolution in Viet Nam* (New York: Oxford University Press, 1968, p. 13) estimates that the Communists had the support of one-fourth of the South Vietnamese.

47. See Joes, *America and Guerrilla Warfare*, chapter 7, "Viet Nam: A Case of Multiple Pathologies"; and *The War for South Viet Nam* (Westport, CT: Praeger, 2001, 2d edition), Chapter 12, "South Viet Nam on Its Own."

48. Clausewitz, *On War*, Book 1, chapter one.

49. Washington, DC: Department of the Army, March 1962.

50. A hamlet is a subdivision of a village.

51. General Westmoreland does not even mention PROVN in his memoirs. But General Victor Krulak, commander of Fleet Marine Force, Pacific, and Robert Komer, in charge of U.S. pacification efforts, liked PROVN a great deal. See Lewis Sorley, "To Change a War: General Harold K. Johnson and the PROVN Study," *Parameters*, vol. xxviii (Spring 1998); see also *The Pentagon Papers*, vol. IV, pp. 369, 371, 374, 376.

52. Al Hemingway, *Our War Was Different: Marine Combined Action Platoons in Viet Nam* (Annapolis, MD: Naval Institute Press, 1994), p. 178.

53. Invasion is the proper term. If all the North Vietnamese who came down the Ho Chi Minh Trail over a period of years had entered South Vietnam in one day, it would have looked like the Korean invasion of 1950.

54. Norman B. Hannah, *The Key to Failure: Laos and the Viet Nam War* (Lanham, MD: Madison Books, 1987); Harry Summers, *On Strategy: A Critical Analysis of the Viet Nam War* (Novato, CA: Presidio, 1982); Sir Robert Thompson, "Regular Armies and Counterinsurgency" in Ronald Haycock, ed., *Regular Armies and Insurgency* (London: Croom Helm, 1979).

55. Chen Jian, "China's Involvement in the Viet Nam War, 1964–1969," *China Quarterly*, no. 142 (June 1995).

56. Sir Robert Thompson, *Defeating Communist Insurgency: The Lessons of Malaya and Viet Nam* (New York: Praeger, 1966); *No Exit from Viet Nam*; *Peace is Not at Hand* (New York: David McKay, 1974).

57. And if the North Vietnamese had committed the colossal error of trying to outflank the blockage on the Ho Chi Minh Trail by invading Thailand? So much the better!

58. For the CAPs, see F.J. West, *The Village* (New York: Harper and Row, 1972), and *Small Unit Action in Viet Nam* (Quantico, VA: U.S. Marine Corps, 1967); and Stuart A. Herrington, *Silence Was a Weapon: The Viet Nam War in the Villages* (Novato, CA: Presidio, 1982).

59. Basil Liddell Hart, *Strategy*, p. 153.

60. Clausewitz, *On War*, Book VI, Chapter One.

61. See the geographical distribution of U.S. casualties in Thayer, *War Without Fronts*.

EPILOGUE: CONFLICT IN IRAQ

1. *Los Angeles Times*, January 4, 2004.

2. Free elections have served as an effective path to peaceful change. But they also precipitated the conflicts in Northern Ireland after 1969, in Spain in 1936, and in the U.S. in 1861. Free elections brought the German National Socialists to power, and may install a militant fundamentalist regime in Iraq.

3. From the end of World War II until the overthrow of the monarchy in 1958, Iraq did have a quasi-parliamentary system. See Phebe Marr, *The Modern History of Iraq* (Boulder, CO: Westview, 1985), chapters 4 and 5; also R. James Woolsey, "King and Country," in *The Wall Street Journal*, October 29, 2003.

4. Samuel P. Huntington, *The Clash of Civilizations and the Remaking of World Order* (New York: Simon and Schuster, 1996).

5. Thomas Mockaitis, *British Counterinsurgency in the Post-Imperial Era* (Manchester, UK: University of Manchester, 1995), p. 129.

BIBLIOGRAPHY

Abel, Christopher. "Colombia and the Drug Barons: Conflict and Containment." *World Today,* vol. 49 (1993).

Aldis, Anne, ed. *The Second Chechen War.* Camberley, England: Conflict Studies Research Center, 2000.

Alexander, Don W. *Rod of Iron: French Counterinsurgency Policy in Aragon during the Peninsular War.* Wilmington, DE: Scholarly Resources, 1985.

Alexander, Robert J. *Communism in Latin America.* New Brunswick, NJ: Rutgers University Press, 1960.

Alexiev, Alexander. *Inside the Soviet Army in Afghanistan.* Santa Monica, CA: RAND, 1988.

Allen, George W. *None So Blind: A Personal Account of the Intelligence Failure in Viet Nam.* Chicago, IL: Ivan R. Dee, 2001.

Allen, W.E.D. and Paul Muratoff. *Caucasian Battlefields.* Cambridge: Cambridge University Press, 1953.

Amstutz, J. Bruce. *Afghanistan: The First Five Years of Soviet Occupation.* Washington, DC: National Defense University, 1986.

Anonymous. "Reflections on Counterinsurgency in Thailand." *World Affairs,* vol. 146 (1984–1985).

Anderson, Bern. *By Sea and River: The Naval History of the Civil War.* New York: Knopf, 1962.

Andreski, Stanislav. *Military Organizations and Society.* Berkeley, CA: University of California Press, 1968.

Arendt, Hannah. *On Revolution.* New York: Viking, 1963.

Aristotle. *The Politics.*

Armstrong, John. *Ukrainian Nationalism.* New York: Columbia University Press, 1955.

Arnold, Anthony. *The Fateful Pebble: Afghanistan's Role in the Fall of the Soviet Empire.* Novato, CA: Presidio, 1993.

Aulard, A. *The French Revolution: A Political History, 1789–1804.* Trans. Bernard Miall. New York: Scribner's, 1910.

Austin, N.J.E., and N.B. Ravkov. *Exploratio: Military and Political Intelligence in the Roman World from the Second Punic War to the Battle of Adrianople* (London: Routledge, 1995).

Avedon, John F. *In Exile from the Land of Snows*. New York: Knopf, 1984.

Averoff-Tossizza, Evangelos. *By Fire and Axe: The Communist Party and the Civil War in Greece, 1944–1949*. New Rochelle, NY: Caratzas, 1978.

Bacevich, A.J., et al. *American Military Policy in Small Wars: The Case of El Salvador*. Washington, DC: Pergamon-Brassey's, 1988.

Bacevich, Andrew J. "Disagreeable Work: Pacifying the Moros 1903–1906." *Military Review*, vol. 62 (1982).

Baddeley, John F. *The Russian Conquest of the Caucasus*. New York: Russell and Russell, 1969 [orig. 1908].

Baev, Pavel. *The Russian Army in a Time of Troubles*. London: Sage, 1996.

Bailey, David. *Viva Cristo Rey! The Cristero Rebellion and the Church-State Conflict in Mexico*. Austin, TX: University of Texas Press, 1974.

Banning, T.C.W. *Origins of the French Revolutionary Wars*. New York: Longman, 1986.

Barr, Alfred R., and Caesar Sereseres. "U.S. Conventional Warfare Operations and Lessons from Central America, 1980–1990: A Successful Economy of Force Engagement Strategy." *Low Intensity Conflict and Law Enforcement*, vol. 8 (1999).

Bartov, Omer. *Hitler's Army*. New York: Oxford University Press, 1991.

Bass, Robert D. *Gamecock: The Life and Times of General Thomas Sumter*. New York: Holt, Rinehart, Winston, 1961.

———. *Swamp Fox*. New York: Henry Holt, 1959.

Beals, Carlton. *Mexican Maze*. Philadelphia, PA: Lippincott, 1931.

Beaumont, Roger. *Sword of the Raj: The British Army in India, 1747–1947*. Indianapolis, IN: Bobbs Merrill, 1977.

Beckett, Ian F.W. *Modern Insurgencies and Counterinsurgencies: Guerrillas and Their Opponents Since 1750*. New York: Routledge, 2001.

———. "The Portuguese Army: The Campaign in Mozambique, 1964–1974." In Ian F.W., Beckett and John Pimlott, eds., *Armed Forces and Modern Counter-Insurgency*. London: Croom Helm, 1985.

———. "The Soviet Experience." In Ian F.W. Beckett, ed., *The Roots of Counter-Insurgency*. London: Blandford, 1988.

Beckett, Ian F.W., et al. *War in Peace: Conventional and Guerrilla Warfare Since 1945*. New York: Harmony, 1982.

Bedeski, Robert. *State-Building in Modern China: The Kuomintang in the Prewar Period*. Berkeley, CA: University of California Center for Chinese Studies, 1981.

Bell, Sir Charles. *The People of Tibet*. Oxford: Clarendon Press, 1928.

Bell, J. Bowyer. "Endemic Insurgency and International order: The Eritrean Experience." *Orbis*, vol. 18 (1974).

Benda, Harry J. *The Crescent and the Rising Sun*. The Hague: Van Hoeve, 1958.

Bender, Gerald J. "The Limits of Counterinsurgency: An African case." *Comparative Politics*, vol. 4 (1972).

Berdal, Mats, and David Malone, eds. *Greed and Grievance: Economic Agendas in Civil Wars* (Boulder, CO: Lynne Rienner, 2000.

Bergerud, Eric M. *The Dynamics of Defeat*. Boulder, CO: Westview, 1991.

Bergquist, Charles. "Waging War and Negotiating Peace: The Contemporary Crisis in

Historical Perspective." In Charles Bergquist, R. Penaranda, and G. Sanchez, eds., *Violence in Colombia, 1990–2000.* Wilmington, DE: Scholarly Resources, 2001.

Bergquist, Charles, et al. *Violence in Colombia: The Contemporary Crisis in Historical Perspective.* Wilmington, DE: Scholarly Resources, 1992.

———. *Violence in Colombia: Waging War and Negotiating Peace.* Wilmington, DE: Scholarly Resources, 2001

Bickel, Keith. *Mars Learning: The Marine Corps' Development of Small Wars Doctrine, 1915–1949.* Boulder, CO: Westview, 2001.

Black, C.E., et al. *Neutralization in Southeast Asia: Problems and Prospects.* Washington, DC: U.S. Government Printing Office, 1966.

Blank, Stephen J. "Soviet Forces in Afghanistan: Unlearning the Lessons of Viet Nam." In Stephen J. Blank et al., eds., *Responding to Low-Intensity Conflict Challenges.* Maxwell Air Force Base, AL: Air University Press, 1990.

Blank, Stephen J., et al., eds. *Responding to Low-Intensity Conflict Challenges.* Maxwell Air Force Base, AL: Air University Press, 1990.

Blank, Stephen J., and Earl H. Tilford. *Russia's Invasion of Chechnya: A Preliminary Assessment.* Carlisle Barracks, PA: Strategic Studies Institute, 1995.

Blasio, José Luis. *Maximilian Emperor of Mexico: Memoirs of His Private Secretary.* New Haven, CT: Yale University Press, 1934.

Blaufarb, Douglas. *The Counterinsurgency Era: United States Doctrine and Performance 1950 to the Present.* New York: Free Press, 1977.

Bodard, Lucien. *The Quicksand War.* Boston, MA: Little, Brown, 1967.

Boualam, Bachaga. *Les Harkis au service de la France.* Paris: Editions France-Empire, 1963.

Bowler, R. Arthur. *Logistics and the Failure of the British Army in America, 1775–1783.* Princeton, NJ: Princeton University Press, 1975.

Boyer de la Tour, Pierre. *Le Martyre de l'Armée française: de l'Indochine à l'Algérie.* Paris: Presses du Mail, 1962.

Boyle, John Hunter. *China and Japan at War: The Politics of Collaboration.* Stanford, CA: Stanford University Press, 1972.

Bracamonte, José Moroni, and David E. Spencer. *Strategy and Tactics of the Salvadoran FMLN Guerrillas.* Westport, CT: Praeger, 1995.

Bradsher, Henry S. *Afghanistan and the Soviet Union.* Durham, NC: Duke University Press, 1985.

Brandenburg, Frank. *The Making of Modern Mexico.* Englewood Cliffs, NJ: Prentice-Hall, 1964.

Braun, Herbert. *Our Guerrillas, Our Sidewalks: A Journey into the Violence of Colombia.* Niwot, CO: University Press of Colorado, 1994.

Breeze, David J. *The Northern Frontier of Roman Britain.* New York: St. Martin's, 1982.

Breeze, David J., and B. Dobson. *Hadrian's Wall.* London: Allen Lane, 1976.

Brenner, Anita. *Idols Behind Altars.* New York: Harcourt, Brace, 1929.

Brinton, Crane. *The Anatomy of Revolution.* New York: Vintage, 1965 [orig. 1936].

Brown, Lyle C. "Mexican Church-State Relations." *Journal of Church and State,* vol. 6 (1964).

Broxup, Marie, ed. *The North Caucasus Barrier: The Russian Advance toward the Muslim World.* New York: St. Martin's, 1992.

Bruce, Neil. *Portugal: The Last Empire.* New York: Wiley, 1975.

Buchsbajew, Alexander. *Toward a Theory of Guerrilla Warfare: A Case Study of the Ukrainian National Underground in the Soviet Union and Communist Poland.* Ph.D. dissertation, City University of New York, 1984.

Bui Diem. *In the Jaws of History.* Boston: Houghton-Mifflin, 1987.

Bui Tin. *Following Ho Chi Minh: Memoirs of a North Vietnamese Colonel.* Honolulu, HI: University of Hawaii Press, 1995.

———. *From Enemies to Friends.* Annapolis, MD: Naval Institute Press, 2002.

Burggraaff, Winfield J. *The Venezuelan Armed Forces in Politics, 1935–1959.* Columbia, MO: University of Missouri Press, 1972.

Burr, J. Millard, and Robert O. Collins. *Requiem for the Sudan.* Boulder, CO: Westview, 1995.

Butson, Thomas G. *The Tsar's Lieutenant: The Soviet Marshall.* New York: Praeger, 1984.

Buttinger, Joseph. *Viet Nam: A Dragon Embattled.* New York: Praeger, 1967.

———. *Viet Nam: A Political History.* New York: Praeger, 1968.

Byman, Daniel, et al. *Trends in Outside Support for Insurgent Movements.* Santa Monica, CA: RAND, 2001.

Cadena, Marisol de la. "From Race to Class: Insurgent Intellectuals *de provincia* in Peru, 1910–1970." In Steve J. Stern, ed., *Shining and Other Paths: War and Society in Peru, 1980–1995.* Durham, NC: Duke University Press, 1998.

Caesar, Julius. *The Civil War*, in *The Gallic War and Other Writings of Julius Caesar*, trans. Moses Hadas. New York: Modern Library, 1957.

Callison, Charles Stuart. *Land to the Tiller in the Mekong Delta.* Lanham, MD: University Press of America, 1983.

Callwell, C.E. *Small Wars: Their Principles and Practice.* London: Greenhill, 1990 [orig. 1896].

Calvert, Michael. "Counter-Insurgency in Mozambique." *Journal of the Royal United Services Institute for Defence Studies*, vol. 118 (1973).

Cann, John P. *Counterinsurgency in Africa: The Portuguese Way of War, 1961–1973.* Westport, CT: Greenwood, 1997.

Cao Van Vien. *The Final Collapse.* Washington, DC: U.S. Army Center of Military History, 1983.

Cao Van Vien, and Dong Van Khuyen. *Reflections on the Viet Nam War.* Washington, DC: U.S. Army Center of Military History, 1980.

Carlson, E.F. *The Chinese Army.* New York: Institute of Pacific Relations, 1940.

Carr, Raymond. *Spain, 1808–1939.* London: Oxford University Press, 1966.

Carver, Michael. *War Since 1945.* New York: Putnam's, 1981.

Castañeda, Jorge. *Utopia Unarmed: The Latin American Left After the Cold War.* New York: Vintage, 1993.

Castel, Albert. *William Clarke Quantrill: His Life and Times.* New York: Frederick Fell, 1962.

Castro-Communist Insurgency in Venezuela. Alexandria, VA: Georgetown Research Project, Atlantic Research Corporation, n.d.

Catton, Bruce. *Glory Road.* Garden City, NY: Doubleday, 1952.

Centeno, Miguel Angel. *Blood and Debt: War and the Nation-State in Latin America.* University Park, PA: Pennsylvania State University Press, 2002.

Chaliand, Gérard. "The Bargain War in Afghanistan." In Gérard Chaliand, ed., *Guerrilla Strategies.* Berkeley, CA: University of California Press, 1982.

Chamberlin, William Henry. *The Russian Revolution, 1917–1921.* New York: Macmillan, 1935.

Chambers, J.W., ed. *The Oxford Companion to American Military History.* New York: Oxford University Press, 1999.

Chang, Iris. *The Rape of Nanking: The Forgotten Holocaust.* New York: Basic Books, 1997.

Chanoff, David and Doan Van Toai. *Portrait of the Enemy.* New York: Random House, 1986.

Chassin, Ch.-L. *Les pacifications de l'Ouest, 1794–1801.* Mayenne: Floch, 1973 [orig. 1896].

Chauvel, Richard. *Nationalists, Soldiers, and Separatists: The Ambonese Islands from Colonialism to Revolt.* Leiden: KITLV, 1990.

Chen Jian. "China and the First Indo-China War, 1950–1954." *China Quarterly,* no. 133 (1993).

———. "China's Involvement in the Viet Nam War, 1964-1969." *China Quarterly,* no, 142 (1995).

Chi Hsi-sheng. *Nationalist China at War: Military Defeats and Political Collapse, 1937–1945.* Ann Arbor, MI: University of Michigan Press, 1982.

Chiang Kai-shek. *China's Destiny.* New York: Roy Publishers, 1947.

Chlapowski, Dezydery. *Memoirs of a Polish Lancer.* Trans. Tim Simmons. Chicago, IL: The Emperor's Press, 1992 [orig. 1837].

Chorley, Katherine. *Armies and the Art of Revolution.* Boston, MA: Beacon, 1973.

Churchill, Winston. *The Hinge of Fate.* Boston, MA: Houghton Mifflin, 1950.

———. "The Martyrdom of Warsaw." In *Triumph and Tragedy.* Boston, MA: Houghton Mifflin, 1953.

Ciechanowski, Jan M. *The Warsaw Rising of 1944.* Cambridge: Cambridge University Press, 1974.

Cincinnatus (pseud.). *Self-Destruction: The Disintegration and Decay of the United States Army During the Viet Nam Era.* New York: Norton, 1981.

Clarke, Jeffrey J. *Advice and Support: The Final Years, 1965–1973.* Washington, DC: U.S. Army Center of Military History, 1988.

Clausewitz, Carl von. *On War.* Edited and translated by Michael Howard and Peter Paret. Princeton, NJ: Princeton University, 1976.

Cloake, John. *Templer: Tiger of Malaya.* London: Harrap, 1985.

Clubb, O. Edmund. *Twentieth Century China.* New York: Oxford University Press, 1972, 2d ed.

Clutterbuck, Richard L. *The Long, Long War: Counterinsurgency in Malaya and Viet Nam.* New York: Praeger, 1966.

Coates, John. *Suppressing Insurgency: An Analysis of the Malayan Emergency, 1948–1954.* Boulder, CO: Westview Press, 1992.

Cobb, Richard. *The People's Armies.* Trans. Marianne Elliot. New Haven, CT: Yale University Press, 1987.

Cohen, Eliot. "The Strategy of Innocence? The United States, 1920–1945" in Williamson Murray, MacGregor Knox, and Alvin Bernstein, eds. *The Making of Strategy: Rulers, States and War.* Cambridge: Cambridge University Press, 1994.

Cohen, Stephen. *The Indian Army.* Berkeley, CA: University of California Press, 1971.

Collins, J. Lawton. *The Development and Training of the South Vietnamese Army, 1950–1972.* Washington, DC: Department of the Army, 1975.

Conboy, Kenneth, and James Morrison. *The CIA's Secret War in Tibet.* Lawrence, KS: University Press of Kansas, 2002.

Connelley, William Elsey. *Quantrill and the Border Wars.* New York: Pageant, 1956 [orig. 1909].

Connelly, Owen. *Blundering to Glory: Napoleon's Military Campaigns.* Wilmington, DE: Scholarly Resources: 1987.

Connor, Walker. *Ethnonationalism: The Quest for Understanding.* Princeton, NJ: Princeton University Press, 1994.

Coogan, Tim Pat. *The Man Who Made Ireland: The Life and Death of Michael Collins.* Niwot, CO: Roberts Rinehart, 1992.

Coox, A.D. *Nomonhan: Russia Against Japan, 1939.* Stanford, CA: Stanford University Press, 1985.

Cordesman, Anthony H., and Abraham Wagner, eds, *The Lessons of Modern War,* vol. 3, *The Afghan and Falklands Conflicts.* Boulder, CO: Westview, 1990.

Corson, William R. *The Betrayal.* New York: Norton, 1968.

Corti, Egon. *Maximilian and Charlotte of Mexico.* 2 vols. New York: Knopf, 1928.

Corum, James S., and Wray R. Johnson. *Air Power in Small Wars: Fighting Insurgents and Terrorists.* Lawrence, KS: University Press of Kansas, 2003.

Coulter, E. Merton. *The Confederate States of America, 1861–1865.* Baton Rouge, LA: Louisiana State University Press, 1950.

Craig, Mary. *Tears of Blood: A Cry for Tibet.* Washington, DC: Counterpoint, 1999.

Cross, James Eliot. *Conflict in the Shadows: The Nature and Politics of Guerrilla War.* Westport, CT: Greenwood, 1975 [orig. 1963].

Cubides, Fernando. "From Private to Public Violence: The Paramilitaries." In Charles Bergquist, R. Penaranda, and G. Sanchez, *Violence in Colombia, 1990–2000.* Wilmington DE: Scholarly Resources, 2001.

Cumberland, Charles C. *Mexico: The Struggle for Modernity.* New York: Oxford University Press, 1968.

Curtis, Edward E. *The Organization of the British Army in America.* New Haven, CT: Yale University Press, 1926.

Dabbs, Jack Autrey. *The French Army in Mexico, 1861–1867.* The Hague: Mouton, 1963.

Dalai Lama, The. *Freedom in Exile.* New York: Harper Perennial, 1990.

———. *My Land and My People.* New York: McGraw-Hill, 1962.

Daly, M.W. "Broken Bridges and Empty Baskets: The Political and Economic Background of the Sudanese Civil War." In M.W. Daly and A.A. Sikainga, eds., *Civil War in the Sudan*. New York: British Academic Press, 1993.

Davidson, Phillip B. *Viet Nam at War: The History, 1946–1975*. Novato, CA: Presidio, 1988.

Dawson, Alan. *55 Days: The Fall of South Viet Nam*. Englewood Cliffs, NJ: Prentice-Hall, 1977.

Dear, I.C.B., ed. *The Oxford Companion to World War II*. New York: Oxford University Press, 1995.

Degregori, Carlos Ivan. "Harvesting Storms." In Steve J. Stern, ed., *Shining and Other Paths: War and Society in Peru, 1980–1995*. Durham, NC: Duke University Press, 1998.

———. "Shining Path and Counterinsurgency Strategy Since the Arrest of Abimael Guzman." In Joseph S. Tulchin and Gary Bland, eds., *Peru in Crisis*. Boulder, CO: Lynne Rienner, 1994.

De la Gorce, Paul-Marie. *The French Army: A Military-Political History*. New York: George Braziller, 1963.

De Lee, Nigel. "The Far Eastern Experience." In Ian F.W. Beckett, ed., *The Roots of Counterinsurgency*. London: Blandford, 1988.

DeMond, Robert O. *The Loyalists in North Carolina During the Revolution*. Hamden, CT: Archon, 1964.

Deng, Francis Mading. "War of Visions in the Middle East." *Middle East Journal*, vol. 44 (1990).

Desch, Michael, ed. *Soldiers in Cities: Military Operations on Urban Terrain*. Carlisle Barracks, PA: Strategic Studies Institute, 2001.

de Soysa, Indra. "The Resource Curse: Are Civil Wars Driven by Rapacity or Paucity?" In Mats Berdal and D. M. Malone, eds., *Greed and Grievance: Economic Agendas in Civil Wars*. Boulder, CO: Lynne Rienner, 2000.

Devillers, Philippe. *Histoire du Viet-Nam de 1940 à 1952*. Paris: Editions du Seuil, 1952.

De Wet, Christiaan Rudolph. *Three Years' War*. New York: Scribner's, 1903.

Divine, David. *The North-west Frontier of Rome: A Military Study of Hadrian's Wall*. London: Macdonald, 1969.

Dix, Robert H. *Colombia: The Political Dimensions of Change*. New Haven, CT: Yale University Press, 1967.

Djilas, Milovan. *Wartime: With Tito and the Partisans*. Trans. M.B. Petrovich. London: Secker and Warburg, 1977.

Dong Van Khuyen. *The RVNAF*. Washington, DC: U.S. Army Center of Military History, 1980.

Donnell, John C. *Viet Cong Recruitment: Why and How Men Join*. Santa Monica, CA: RAND, 1967.

Doyle, William. *The Oxford History of the French Revolution*. Oxford: Oxford University Press, 1989.

Dreyer, June T. *China's Forty Millions: Minority Nationalities and National Integration in the People's Republic of China*. Cambridge, MA: Harvard University Press, 1976.

Duarte, José Napoleon. *Duarte: My Story*. New York: Putnam's, 1986.

Duiker, William J. *The Communist Road to Power in Viet Nam*. Boulder, CO: Westview, 1981.

Dulles, John W.F. *Yesterday in Mexico: A Chronicle of the Revolution, 1919–1936*. Austin, TX: University of Texas Press, 1961.

Duncanson, Dennis J. *Government and Revolution in Viet Nam*. New York: Oxford University Press, 1968.

Dunkerley, James. *Power in the Isthmus: A Political History of Modern Central America*. New York: Verso, 1988.

Dunlop, John B. *Russia Confronts Chechnya: Roots of a Separatist Conflict*. Oxford: Clarendon Press, 1998.

Dunn, James W. "Province Advisers in Viet Nam, 1962–1965." In Richard A. Hunt and Richard H. Shultz, Jr., eds., *Lessons from an Unconventional War*. New York: Pergamon, 1982.

Eastman, Lloyd. "Nationalist China During the Nanking Decade." In John K. Fairbank, ed., *The Cambridge History of China*, vol. 13, *Republican China, 1912–1949*, part two. Cambridge: Cambridge University Press, 1983.

Ebert, James R. *A Life in a Year: The American Infantryman in Viet Nam, 1965–1972*. Novato, CA: Presidio, 1993.

Eckstein, Harry, ed. *Internal War*. New York: Free Press, 1964.

Eisenhower, John D. *Agent of Destiny: The Life and Times of General Winfield Scott*. New York: Free Press, 1997.

Elsbree, W.H. *Japan's Role in Southeast Asian Nationalist Movements*. Cambridge, MA: Harvard University Press, 1953.

Ely, Paul. *Lessons of the War in Indochina*. 2 vols. Santa Monica, CA: RAND, 1967.

———. *L'Indochine dans la tourmente*. Paris: Plon, 1964.

Emerson, Rupert. *From Empire to Nation*. Cambridge, MA: Harvard University Press, 1960.

Englemann, Larry. *Tears Before the Rain: An Oral History of the Fall of South Viet Nam*. New York: Oxford University Press, 1990.

Evangelista, Matthew. *The Chechen Wars*. Washington, DC: Brookings, 2003.

Evans, Alexander. "The Kashmir Insurgency: As bad as it gets." *Small Wars and Insurgencies*, vol. 11 (2000).

Evans, Ernest. "El Salvador's Lessons for Future U.S. Interventions." *World Affairs*, vol. 60 (1997).

Fairbairn, Geoffrey. *Revolutionary Guerrilla Warfare: The Countryside Version*. Harmondsworth, England: Penguin, 1974.

Fairbank, John K. *The Great Chinese Revolution, 1800–1985*. New York: Harper and Row, 1986.

Fairbank, John K. "Introduction: Maritime and Continental in China's History." In John K. Fairbank, ed., *The Cambridge History of China*, vol. 12, *Republican China 1912–1949*, part one. Cambridge: Cambridge University Press, 1983.

Fairbank, John K., ed. *The Cambridge History of China*, vol. 12, *Republican China 1912–1949*, part one. Cambridge: Cambridge University Press, 1983.

Fairbank, John K., ed. *The Cambridge History of Modern China*, vol. 13, *Republican China 1912–1949*, part two. Cambridge: Cambridge University Press, 1983.

Fall, Bernard. *Hell in a Very Small Place*. Philadelphia, PA: Lippincott, 1967.

―――. *Street Without Joy*. Harrisburg, PA: Stackpole, 1964.

―――. *The Two Viet Nams: A Political and Military Analysis*. New York: Praeger, 1967, 2d ed.

Farwell, Byron. *The Great Anglo-Boer War*. New York: Norton, 1976.

Fauriol, George, ed. *Latin American Insurgencies*. Washington, DC: Georgetown University Press, 1985.

Fellman, Michael. *Inside War: The Guerrilla Conflict in Missouri During the American Civil War*. New York: Oxford University Press, 1989.

Finch, Raymond C. "Why the Russian Military Failed in Chechnya," Fort Leavenworth KS: U.S. Army Foreign Military Studies Office, 1998.

Fishel, Wesley, ed. *Viet Nam: Anatomy of a Conflict*. Itasca, IL: Peacock, 1968.

Fogel, Joshua A., ed. *The Nanjing Massacre*. Berkeley, CA: University of California Press, 2000.

Fortescue, Sir John. *A History of the British Army*. 8 vols. London: Macmillan, 1899-1930.

Freeman, Jr., Charles W. *Arts of Power: Statecraft and Diplomacy*. Washington, DC: United States Institute of Peace, 1997.

Friend, Theodore. *The Blue-Eyed Enemy: Japan Against the West in Java and Luzon, 1942–1945*. Princeton, NJ: Princeton University Press, 1988.

Fuller, J.F.C. *Julius Caesar: Man, Soldier and Tyrant*. New Brunswick, NJ: Rutgers University Press, 1965.

Funston, Frederick. *Memories of Two Wars: Cuban and Philippine Experiences*. New York: Scribner's, 1911.

Furnivall, John. *Colonial Policy and Practice: A Comparative Study of Burma and Netherlands India* [sic]. Cambridge: Cambridge University Press, 1948.

Gabory, Émile. *La Révolution et la Vendée*. Vol. 1: *Les deux Patries*. Paris: Perrin, 1925.

Galeotti, Mark. *Afghanistan: The Soviet Union's Last War*. Portland, OR: Frank Cass, 1995.

Gall, Carlotta, and Thomas de Waal. *Chechnya: Calamity in the Caucasus*. New York: New York University Press, 1998.

Gammer, Moshe. *Muslim resistance to the Tsar: Shamil and the Conquest of Chechnya and Daghestan*. London: Frank Cass, 19943.

Ganguly, Sumir. *The Crisis in Kashmir: Portents of War, Hopes of Peace*. New York: Cambridge University Press, 1997.

Gann, Lewis H. *Guerrillas in History*. Stanford, CA: Hoover Institution on War, Revolution and Peace, 1971.

Garcia, José. "El Salvador: Recent Elections in Historical Perspective." In John Booth and Michael Seligson, eds., *Elections and Democracy in Central America*. Chapel Hill, NC: University of North Carolina Press, 1989.

Garton Ash, Timothy. *The Uses of Adversity*. New York: Vintage, 1990.

Gates, John Morgan. *Schoolbooks and Krags: The United States Army in the Philippines, 1899–1902*. Westport, CT: Greenwood, 1973.

Gentleman, Judith. *The Regional Security Crisis in the Andes: Patterns of State Response*. Carlisle Barracks, PA: Strategic Studies Institute, 2001.

George, T.J. *Revolt on Mindanao: The Rise of Islam in Philippine Politics*. Kuala Lumpur: Oxford University Press, 1980.

Gerson, Noel B. *The Swamp Fox: Francis Marion*. Garden City, NY: Doubleday, 1967.

Girling, John S. *Thailand: Society and Politics*. Ithaca, NY: Cornell University Press, 1981.

———. "Northeast Thailand: Tomorrow's Viet Nam?" *Foreign Affairs*, vol. 47 (1968).

Goldstein, Melvin C. *A History of Modern Tibet, 1913–1951*. Berkeley, CA: University of California Press, 1989.

Goodman, Allan E. *An Institutional Profile of the South Vietnamese Officer Corps*. Santa Monica, CA: RAND, 1970.

Goodwin, Jeff and Theda Skocpol. "Explaining Revolutions in the Contemporary Third World." *Politics and Society*, vol. 17 (1989).

Gorriti, Gustavo. *The Shining Path: A History of the Millenarian War in Peru*. Trans. Robin Kirk. Chapel Hill, NC: University of North Carolina Press, 1999.

Grau, Lester, ed. *The Bear Went Over the Mountain: Soviet Combat Tactics in Afghanistan* Portland, OR: Frank Cass, 1998.

Grau, Lester and Michael A. Gress, trans. and ed. *The Soviet-Afghan War: How a Superpower Fought and Lost*. Lawrence, KS: University Press of Kansas, 2002.

Gray, Colin. *The Leverage of Seapower: The Strategic Advantage of Navies in War*. New York: Free Press, 1992.

———. *Modern Strategy*. New York: Oxford University Press, 1999.

———. "Strategy in the Nuclear Age: The United States, 1945–1991." In Williamson Murray et al., eds., *The Making of Strategy: Rulers, States, and War*. Cambridge: Cambridge University Press, 1994.

Grayson, G.W. "Portugal and the Armed Forces Movement." *Orbis*, vol. 19 (1975).

Greene, G.W. *Life of Nathanael Greene*. Cambridge, MA: Hurd and Houghton, 1871.

Grenier, Yves. "From Causes to Causers: The Etiology of Salvadoran Internal War Revisited." *Journal of Conflict Studies*, vol. 16 (1996).

Griffith, Samuel B. *Mao Tse-tung on Guerrilla War*. New York: Praeger, 1961.

Gross, Jan. *Polish Society Under German Occupation*. Princeton, NJ: Princeton University Press, 1979.

Gruening, Ernest. *Mexico and Its Heritage*. New York: Century, 1921.

Grunfeld, A. Tom. *The Making of Modern Tibet*. London: Zed, 1987.

Guevara, Ernesto. *Guerrilla Warfare*. New York: Vintage, 1960.

Guillebaud, J.C. "Les Harkis oubliés par l'histoire." *Le Monde*, July 3, 1979.

Guyot, Dorothy. "The Burman Independence Army: A Political Movement in Military Garb." In Josef Silverstein, ed., *Southeast Asia in World War II*. New Haven, CT: Yale University Press, 1966.

Hagedorn, Herman. *Leonard Wood*. 2 vols. New York: Harper, 1931.

Hallion, Richard. *The Naval Air War in Korea*. Baltimore, MD: Nautical and Aviation Publishing, 1986.

Hammer, Ellen J. *The Struggle for Indochina, 1940–1955*. Stanford, CA: Stanford University Press, 1966.

Hannah, Norma B. *The Key to Failure: Laos and the Viet Nam War*. Lanham, MD: Madison Books, 1987.

Hanrahan, Gene Z. *Japanese Operations Against Guerrilla Forces.* Chevy Chase, MD: Operations Research Office, Johns Hopkins University, 1954.

Harmon, Christopher. "Illustrations of Learning in Counterinsurgency Warfare." *Comparative Strategy*, vol. 11 (1992).

Harries, M., and S. Harries. *Soldiers of the Sun: The Rise and Fall of the Imperial Japanese Army.* New York: Random House, 1991.

Hart, Albert Bushnell. "Why the South was Defeated in the Civil War." In *Practical Essays on American Government.* New York: Longmans, Green, 1893.

Heggoy, Alf Andrew. *Insurgency and Counterinsurgency in Algeria.* Bloomington, IN: Indiana University Press, 1972.

Heinz, Wolfgang. "Guerillas, Political Violence, and the Peace Process in Colombia." *Latin American Research Review*, vol. 24 (1989).

Hemingway, Al. *Our War Was Different: Marine Combined Action Platoons in Viet Nam.* Annapolis, MD: Naval Institute Press, 1994.

Hendriksen, Thomas H. "Lessons from Portugal's Counterinsurgency Operations in Africa." *Journal of the Royal United Services Institute for Defence Studies,* vol. 123 (1978).

———. "Portugal in Africa: Comparative Notes on Counterinsurgency." *Orbis*, vol. 21 (1977).

Herbst, Jeffrey. *States and Power in Africa: Comparative Lessons in Authority and Control.* Princeton, NJ: Princeton University Press, 2000.

Herrington, Stuart A. *Silence Was a Weapon: The Viet Nam War in the Villages.* Novato, CA: Presidio, 1982.

Hickey, Gerald C. *The American Military Advisor and His Foreign Counterpart: The Case of Viet Nam.* Santa Monica, CA: RAND, 1965.

———. *Village in Viet Nam.* New Haven, CT: Yale University Press, 1964.

Higginbotham, Dan, ed. *Reconsiderations on the Revolutionary War.* Westport, CT: Greenwood, 1978.

Hinojosa, Ivan. "On Poor Relations and the Nouveau Riche: Shining Path and the Radical Peruvian Left." In Steve J. Stern, *Shining and Other Paths: War and Society in Peru, 1980–1995.* Durham, NC: Duke University Press, 1998.

Hinsley, F.H. *British Intelligence in the Second World War.* 5 vols. London: Her Majesty's Stationery Office, 1979–1990.

Hoang Ngoc Lung. *The General Offensives of 1968–1969.* Washington, DC: U.S. Army Center of Military History, 1981.

———. *Intelligence.* Washington, DC: U.S. Army Center of Military History, 1982.

Holt, P.M. *The Mahdist State in Sudan.* Oxford: Oxford University Press, 1958.

Horne, Alistair. *A Savage War of Peace: Algeria 1954–1962.* Harmondsworth, England: Penguin, 1987.

Horowitz, Donald L. *Ethnic Groups in Conflict.* Berkeley, CA: University of California Press, 1985.

Hosmer, Stephen T. *The Army's Role in Counterinsurgency and Insurgency.* Santa Monica, CA: RAND, 1990.

———. *Viet Cong Repression and Its Implications for the Future.* Santa Monica, CA: RAND, May 1970.

Hosmer, Stephen T., K. Kellen, and B.M. Jenkins. *The Fall of Saigon.* New York: Norton, 1990.

Howard, Michael. "When Are Wars Decisive?" *Survival*, vol. 41 (1999).

Howe, Sonia. *Lyautey of Morocco.* London: Hodder and Stoughton, 1931.

Hsieh Jan-chih. *The Kuomintang: Selected Historical Documents, 1894–1969.* New York: St. John's University Press, 1970.

Hsu Long-Hsuen and Chang Ming-Kai, eds. *History of the Sino-Japanese War, 1937–1945.* Taipei: Chung Wu Publishers, 1971.

Hu Pu-yu. *A Brief History of the Chinese National Revolutionary Forces.* Taipei: Chung Wu Publishing, 1971.

Hunt, Richard A. *Pacification: America's Struggle for Viet Nam's Hearts and Minds.* Boulder, CO: Westview, 1995.

Hunt, Richard A., and Richard H. Shultz Jr., eds. *Lessons from an Unconventional War.* New York: Pergamon, 1982.

Huntington, Samuel P. *Political Order in Changing Societies.* New Haven, CT: Yale University Press, 1968.

Hough, Richard Lee. "Development and Security in Thailand: Lessons from Other Asian Countries." *Asian Survey*, vol. 9 (1969).

Hurley, Vic. *Swish of the Kris: The Story of the Moros.* New York: Dutton, 1936.

Hutt, Maurice. *Chouannerie and Counter-Revolution.* Cambridge: Cambridge University Press, 1993.

Hyman, Anthony. *Afghanistan Under Soviet Domination.* London: Macmillan, 1984.

International Commission of Jurists. *The Question of Tibet and the Rule of Law.* Geneva: International Commission of Jurists, 1959.

Isby, David C. "Soviet Strategy and Tactics in Low Intensity Conflict." In Richard H. Shultz, Jr., et al., eds., *Guerrilla Warfare and Counterinsurgency: U.S.-Soviet Policy in the Third World.* Lexington, MA: Lexington Books, 1989.

James, C.L.R. *Black Jacobins: Toussaint L'Ouverture and the San Domingo Revolution.* 2d ed. New York: Vintage, 1963.

James, Daniel, ed. *The Complete Bolivian Diaries of Che Guevara and Other Captured Documents.* New York: Cooper Square Press, 2000.

Joes, Anthony James. *America and Guerrilla Warfare.* Lexington, KY: University Press of Kentucky, 2000.

———. *From the Barrel of a Gun: Armies and Revolutions.* Washington, DC: Pergamon-Brassey's, 1986.

———. *Guerrilla Conflict Before the Cold War.* Westport, CT: Praeger, 1996.

———. *Guerrilla Warfare: A Historical, Biographical and Bibliographical Sourcebook.* Westport, CT: Greenwood, 1996.

———. *Modern Guerrilla Insurgency.* Westport, CT: Praeger, 1992.

———, ed., *Saving Democracies: U.S. Intervention in Threatened Democratic States.* Westport, CT: Praeger, 1999.

———. *The War for South Viet Nam, 1954–1975.* Westport, CT: Praeger, rev. ed., 2001.

Johnson, Chalmers. *Autopsy on People's War.* Berkeley, CA: University of California Press, 1973.

———. *Peasant Nationalism and Communist Power*. Stanford, CA: Stanford University Press, 1961.

Johnson, Douglas H., and Gerard Prunier. "The Foundation and Expansion of the Sudan People's Liberation Army." In M.W. Daly and A.A. Sikainga, eds., *Civil War in the Sudan*. New York: British Academic Press, 1993.

Jomini, Antoine-Henri. *The Art of War*, trans. G.H. Mendell and W.P. Craighill. Westport, CT: Greenwood, n.d. [orig. 1838].

Jones, Archer. *The Art of War in the Western World*. New York: Oxford University Press, 1987.

Jordan, Donald A. *The Northern Expedition: China's National Revolution, 1926–1928*. Honolulu, HI: University of Hawaii Press, 1976.

Jornacion, George W. *Time of the Eagles: United States Army Officers and the Pacification of the Philippine Moros*. Ph.D. dissertation, UCLA, 1973.

Joshi, Manoj. *The Lost Rebellion*. New Delhi: Penguin, 1999.

Kahin, G.M. *Nationalism and Revolution in Indonesia*. Ithaca, NY: Cornell University Press, 1959.

Kahn, Herman. "If Negotiations Fail." *Foreign Affairs*, vol. 46 (1968).

Karnes, Thomas L. *The Failure of Union: Central America, 1824-1975*. Chapel Hill, NC: University of North Carolina Press, 1976.

Karp, Craig. *Afghanistan: Eight Years of Soviet Occupation*. Washington, DC: U.S. Department of State. 1987.

———. *Afghanistan: Seven Years of Soviet Occupation*. Washington, DC: U.S. Department of State, 1986.

Kautilya. *The Arthashastra*.

Keegan, John. *Intelligence in War*. New York: Knopf, 2003.

———. *Dien Bien Phu*. New York: Ballantine, 1974.

———. *Six Armies in Normandy*. New York: Viking, 1982.

Kelly, Brian. *The Cristero Rebellion*. Ph.D. dissertation, University of New Mexico, 1973.

Kelly, George. *Lost Soldiers: The French Army and Empire in Crisis*. Cambridge, MA: MIT Press, 1965.

Kerkvliet, Benedict J. *The Huk Rebellion: A Study of Peasant Revolt in the Philippines*. Berkeley, CA: University of California Press, 1977.

Keyes, Charles F. *Isan: Regionalism in Northeast Thailand*. Ithaca, NY: Cornell University Press, 1967.

———. *Thailand: Buddhist Kingdom as Modern Nation-State*. Boulder, CO: Westview, 1987.

Khalid, M. *John Garang Speaks*. London: KPI, 1987.

Kirby, Stanley Woodburn. *Singapore: The Chain of Disaster*. New York: Macmillan, 1971.

———. *The War Against Japan*, vol. V. London: H. M. Stationery Office, 1969.

Kirk, Robin. "The Deadly Women of the Shining Path." *San Francisco Examiner*, March 22, 1992.

Kissinger, Henry, et al. *Report of the Bipartisan Commission on Central America*. Washington, DC: Government Printing Office, 1984.

Kitson, Frank. *Low Intensity Operations*. London: Faber and Faber, 1971.

Knaus, John Kenneth. *Orphans of the Cold War: Americans and the Tibetan Struggle for Survival*. New York: Public Affairs, 1999.

Koch, Jeannette A. *The Chieu Hoi Program in South Viet Nam, 1963–1971*. Santa Monica, CA: RAND, 1973.

Kolko, Gabriel. *Anatomy of a War: Viet Nam, the United States, and the Modern Historical Experience*. New York: Pantheon, 1985.

Komer. Robert W. *Bureaucracy at War: U.S. Performance in the Viet Nam Conflict*. Boulder, CO: Westview, 1986.

———. *The Malayan Emergency in Retrospect: Organization of a Successful Counterinsurgency Effort*. Santa Monica, CA: Rand, 1972.

Komorowski, Tadeusz [nom de guerre: Bor]. *The Secret Army*. New York: Macmillan, 1951.

Korbonski, Stefan. *Fighting Warsaw*. New York: Funk and Wagnalls, 1968.

Kousoulas, D. George. *Revolution and Defeat: The Story of the Greek Communist Party*. New York: Oxford University Press, 1965.

Krepinevich, Andrew. *The Army and Viet Nam*. Baltimore, MD: Johns Hopkins University Press, 1986.

Kunstadter, Peter, ed. *Southeast Asian Tribes, Minorities and Nations*. Princeton, NJ: Princeton University Press, 1967.

Lambert, Robert Stansbury. *South Carolina Loyalists in the American Revolution*. Columbia, SC: University of South Carolina Press, 1987.

Lancaster, Donald. *The Emancipation of French Indochina*. London: Oxford University Press, 1961.

Lansdale, Edward. *In the Midst of Wars: An American's Mission to Southeast Asia*. New York: Harper and Row, 1972.

Laqueur, Walter. *Guerrilla: A Historical and Critical Study*. Boston, MA: Little, Brown, 1977.

Lavergne, M., ed. *Soudan Contemporaine*. Paris: Karthala, 1989.

Le Thi Que, A., Terry Rambo, and Gary D. Murfin. "Why They Fled: Refugee Movement during the Spring 1975 Communist Offensive in South Viet Nam." *Asian Survey*, vol. 16 (1976).

Lebra, Joyce. *Japanese-Trained Armies in Southeast Asia: Independence and Volunteer Forces in World War II*. New York: Columbia University Press, 1977.

Lee, Chong-Sik. *Counterinsurgency in Manchuria: The Japanese Experience, 1931–1940*. Santa Monica: RAND, 1967.

Lee, Rensselaer. *The White Labyrinth: Cocaine and Political Power*. New Brunswick, NJ: Transaction, 1989.

Lefebvre, Georges. *The Coming of the French Revolution*. Princeton, NJ: Princeton University Press, 1947.

———. *The French Revolution*. 2 vols. New York: Columbia University Press, 1962-1964.

———. *Napoleon from Tilsit to Waterloo*. Trans. J.E. Anderson. New York: Columbia University Press, 1969.

LeGro, William E. *Viet Nam from Ceasefire to Capitulation.* Washington, DC: U.S. Army Center of Military History, 1981.

Leites, Nathan. *The Viet Cong Style of Politics.* Santa Monica, CA: RAND, 1969.

Leites, Nathan, and Charles Wolf. *Rebellion and Authority: An Analytic Essay on Insurgent Conflicts.* Santa Monica, CA: RAND, 1970.

LeMoyne, James. "El Salvador's Forgotten War." *Foreign Affairs,* vol. 66 (1989).

Lenin, V.I.. *Collected Works,* vol. 31. Moscow: Progress Publishers, 1966.

Leoni, Raúl, and John D. Martz. *The Venezuelan Elections of December 1, 1963.* Washington, DC: Institute for the Comparative Study of Political Systems. 1964.

Leung, Edwin, ed. *Historical Dictionary of Revolutionary China, 1839–1976.* Westport, CT: Greenwood, 1992.

Lewin, Ronald. *Hitler's Mistakes.* New York: William Morrow, 1984.

Lewis, William F. *Francisco Xavier Mina: Guerrilla Warrior for Romantic Liberalism.* Ph.D. dissertation, University of California Santa Barbara, 1968.

Lewy, Guenter. *America and Viet Nam.* New York: Oxford University Press, 1978.

———. *Religion and Revolution.* New York: Oxford University Press, 1974.

Li, Lincoln. *The Japanese Army in North China, 1937–1941: Problems of Political and Economic Control.* Tokyo: Oxford University Press, 1975.

Liddell Hart, Basil H. *History of the Second World War.* New York: Da Capo, 1999 [orig. 1970].

———. *The Real War 1914–1918.* Boston: Little, Brown, 1930.

———. *Scipio Africanus.* New York: Da Capo, 1994.

———. *Strategy.* London: Faber and Faber, 1967

———. *Thoughts on War.* London: Faber and Faber, 1944.

Lieuwen, Edwin. *Arms and Politics in Latin America.* New York: Praeger, 1960.

———. *Mexican Militarism: The Political Rise and Fall of the Revolutionary Army, 1910–1940.* Westport, CT: Greenwood, 1981 [orig. 1968].

Lieven, Anatol. *Chechnya: Tombstone of Russian Power.* New Haven, CT: Yale University Press, 1998.

Linn, Brian McAlister. *Guardians of Empire: The U.S. Army and the Pacific, 1902–1940.* Chapel Hill, NC: University of North Carolina Press, 1997.

———. *The Philippine War, 1899–1902.* Lawrence, KS: University Press of Kansas, 2000.

———. *The U.S. Army and Counterinsurgency in the Philippine War, 1899–1902.* Chapel Hill, NC: University of North Carolina Press, 1989.

Lippmann, Walter. "The Church and State in Mexico: The American Mediation." *Foreign Affairs,* vol. 8 (1930).

Liu, F.F. *Military History of Modern China, 1924-1949.* Princeton, NJ: Princeton University Press, 1956.

Lomperis, Timothy J. *The War Everyone Lost—and Won.* Baton Rouge, LA: Louisiana State University, 1984.

———. *From People's War to People's Rule: Insurgency, Intervention, and the Lessons of Viet Nam.* Chapel Hill, NC: University of North Carolina Press, 1996.

Longer, V. *Red Coats to Olive Green: A History of the Indian Army, 1600–1974.* Bombay: Allied Publishing, 1974.

Lovelace, Daniel D. *China and 'People's War' in Thailand, 1964–1969.* Berkeley, CA: University of California Press, 1971.

Lovett, Gabriel H. *Napoleon and the Birth of Modern Spain.* 2 vols. New York: New York University Press, 1975.

Lukas, Richard. *The Forgotten Holocaust: The Poles Under German Occupation, 1939–1945.* Lexington, KY: University Press of Kentucky, 1986.

Luttwak, Edward N. *The Grand Strategy of the Roman Empire.* Baltimore: Johns Hopkins University Press, 1976.

MacAleavy, Henry. *The Modern History of China.* London: Weidenfeld and Nicolson, 1968.

Macauley, Neil. *The Sandino Affair.* Chicago, IL: Quadrangle, 1967.

Macdonnell, A.G. *Napoleon and His Marshals.* New York: Macmillan, 1934.

Machiavelli, Niccolo. *The Art of War.* New York: Da Capo, 1990 [orig. 1521].

———. *The Prince.*

Mackesy, Piers. *The War for America, 1775–1783.* Cambridge, MA: Harvard University Press, 1965.

Maclean, Fitzroy. *Disputed Barricade.* London: Jonathan Cape, 1957.

Malia, Martin. *The Soviet Tragedy.* New York: Free Press.

Malleray, Henri de. *Les cinq Vendées.* Paris: Plon-Nourrit, 1924.

Manchester, William. *American Caesar: Douglas MacArthur, 1880–1964.* Boston, MA: Little, Brown, 1978.

Manrique, Nelson. "The War for the Central Sierra." In Steve J. Stern, ed., *Shining and Other Paths: War and Society in Peru, 1980–1995.* Durham, NC: Duke University Press, 1998.

Manwaring, Max. *Implementing Plan Colombia.* Carlisle Barracks, PA: Strategic Studies Institute, 2000.

———. *Internal Wars: Rethinking Problem and Response.* Carlisle Barracks, PA: Strategic Studies Institute, 2001.

———. *Nonstate Actors in Colombia.* Carlisle Barracks, PA: Strategic Studies Institute, 2002.

———. *U.S. Security Policy in the Western Hemisphere.* Carlisle Barracks, PA: Strategic Studies Institute, 2001.

Manwaring, Max G., and Courtney E. Prisk. *A Strategic View of Insurgencies: Insights from El Salvador.* Washington, DC: Institute for National Strategic Studies, 1990.

———, eds. *El Salvador at War: An Oral History.* Washington, DC: National Defense University, 1988.

Mao Tse-tung. *Basic Tactics.* Trans. Stuart Schram. New York: Praeger, 1966.

———. "On the Protracted War." In *Selected Works of Mao Tse-tung.* Peking: People's Publishing House, 1952.

———. *Selected Military Writings.* Peking: Foreign Languages Press, 1966.

Marc, Henri, and Pierre Cony. *Indochine française.* Paris: Editions France-Empire, 1946.

Marcella, Gabriel. *The United States and Colombia: The Journey from Ambiguity to Strategic Clarity.* Carlisle Barracks, PA: Strategic Studies Institute, 2003.

Marcella, Gabriel, and David Schulz. *Colombia's Three Wars: U.S. Strategy at the Crossroads.* Carlisle Barracks, PA: Strategic Studies Institute, 1999.

Marchand, Jean. *L'Indochine en guerre.* Paris: Pouzet, 1955.

Margolis, Eric S. *War at the Top of the World: The Struggle for Afghanistan, Kashmir and Tibet.* New York: Routledge, 2000.

Mark, Eduard. *Aerial Interdiction: Air Power and the Land Battle in Three American Wars.* Washington, DC: Center for Air Force History, 1994.

Markham, Felix. *Napoleon.* New York: New American Library, 1963.

Marks, Thomas A. *Colombian Army Adaptation to FARC Insurgency.* Carlisle Barracks, PA: Strategic Studies Institute, 2002.

———. *Counterrevolution in China.* London: Frank Cass, 1998.

———. *Maoist Insurgency Since Viet Nam.* Portland, OR: Frank Cass, 1996.

Marston, R. "Resettlement as a Counter-Insurgency Technique." *Journal of the Royal United Services Institute for Defence Studies,* vol. 124 (1979).

Martin, Jean-Clement. *La Vendée et la France.* Paris: Editions du Seuil, 1987.

Martin, Percy. *Maximilian in Mexico.* New York: Scribner's, 1914.

Martz, John D., and David Meyers. "Venezuelan Democracy and the Future." In John D. Martz and David Meyers, eds., *The Democratic Experience.* New York: Praeger, 1977.

Mathiez, Albert. *The French Revolution.* Trans. C.A. Phillips. New York: Russell and Russell, 1962 [orig. 1928].

Maullin, Richard. *Soldiers, Guerrillas and Politics in Colombia.* Lexington, MA: Lexington Books, 1973.

Maurois, Andre. *Lyautey.* New York: Appleton, 1931.

Maxwell, Neville. *India's China War.* New York: Anchor, 1972.

May, Glenn Anthony. *Battle for Batangas: A Philippine Province at War.* New Haven, CT: Yale University Press, 1991.

McAlister, John T. *Viet Nam: The Origins of Revolution.* Garden City, NY: Doubleday Anchor, 1971.

McBeth, John. "A Battle for Loyalty in the Jungles." *Far Eastern Economic Review,* June 8, 1979.

———. "Counting on Nearby Friends." *Far Eastern Economic Review,* July 13, 1979.

McChristian, Joseph A. *The Role of Military Intelligence, 1965–1967.* Washington, DC: Department of the Army, 1974.

McClintock, Cynthia. *Revolutionary Movements in Latin America: El Salvador's FMLN and Peru's Shining Path.* Washington, DC: U.S. Institute of Peace, 1998.

McCuen, John J. *The Art of Counter-Revolutionary Warfare.* Harrisburg: Stackpole, 1966.

McManners, John. *The French Church and the Revolution.* Westport, CT: Greenwood, 1982.

McPherson, James M. *Battle Cry of Freedom.* New York: Oxford University Press, 1988.

Mecham, J. Lloyd. *Church and State in Latin America.* Chapel Hill, NC: University of North Carolina Press, rev. ed., 1966.

Menon, Rajan, and Graham E. Fuller. "Russia's Ruinous Chechen War." *Foreign Affairs,* vol. 79 (March/April 2000).

Meyer, Jean A. *The Cristero Rebellion*. New York: Cambridge University Press, 1976.

Michael, Franz. *The Taiping Rebellion: History and Documents*. 3 vols. Seattle, WA: University of Washington Press, 1966-1971.

Military History Institute of Viet Nam. *Victory in Viet Nam: The Official History of the People's Army of Viet Nam, 1954-1975*. Trans. Merle Pribbenow. Lawrence, KS: University Press of Kansas, 2002.

Millett, Richard L. *Colombia's Conflicts: The Spillover Effects of a Wider War*. Carlisle Barracks, PA: Strategic Studies Institute, 2002.

Mitchell, Harvey. "The Vendée and Counterrevolution: A Review Essay." *French Historical Studies*, vol. 5 (1968).

Mockaitis, Thomas R. *British Counterinsurgency, 1919–1960*. New York: St. Martin's, 1990.

———. "From Counterinsurgency to Peacemaking: New Applications for an Old Approach." In Anthony James Joes, ed., *Saving Democracies: U.S. Intervention in Threatened Democratic States*. Westport, CT: Praeger, 1999.

Montagnon, André. *Les guerres de Vendée, 1794–1832*. Paris: Perrin, 1974.

———. *Une guerre subversive: La guerre de Vendée*. Paris: La Colombe, 1959.

Moore, Albert B. *Conscription and Conflict in the Confederacy*. New York: Macmillan, 1924.

Moraes, Frank. *The Revolt in Tibet*. New York: Macmillan, 1960.

Morison, Samuel Eliot. *The Oxford History of the American People*. New York: Oxford University Press, 1965.

Mosby, John S. *The Memoirs of Col. John S. Mosby*. Nashville: J.S. Sanders, 1995.

Mullik, B.N. *My Years with Nehru: The Chinese Betrayal*. Bombay: Allied Publishers, 1971.

Murray, Williamson, MacGregor Knox and Alvin Bernstein, eds. *The Making of Strategy*. Cambridge: Cambridge University Press, 1994.

Napier, W.F.P. *History of the War in the Peninsula and in the South of France*. 6 vols. London: Frederick Warne, 1890–1892.

Nasution, Abdul H. *Fundamentals of Guerrilla Warfare*. New York: Praeger, 1865 [orig. 1953].

Navarre, Henri. *Agonie de l'Indochine*. Paris: Plon, 1956.

Nelson, William H. *The American Tory*. Oxford: Clarendon Press, 1961.

Nevins, Allan. *The War for the Union: The Improvised War 1863–1864*. New York: Scribner's, 1959.

———. *The War for the Union: The Organized War to Victory 1864–1865*. New York: Scribner's, 1971.

Newberg, Paula R. *Double Betrayal: Repression and Insurgency in Kashmir*. Washington, DC: Carnegie Endowment for International Peace, 1995.

Ngo Quang Truong. *Territorial Forces*. Washington, DC: U.S. Army Center of Military History, 1981.

Nguyen Cao Ky. *Buddha's Child*. New York: St. Martin's, 2002.

Nicolson, Harold. *Dwight Morrow*. New York: Harcourt Brace, 1935.

Norbu, Jamyang. *Warriors of Tibet*. London: Wisdom, 1986.

Nuechterlein, Donald E. *Thailand and the Struggle for Southeast Asia*. Ithaca, NY: Cornell University Press, 1965.

Nunez, Joseph R. *Fighting the Hobbesian Trinity in Colombia: A New Strategy for Peace*. Carlisle Barracks, PA: Strategic Studies Institute, 2000.

O'Ballance, Edgar. *The Algerian Insurrection, 1954–1962*. Hamden, CT: Archon, 1967.

———. *The Greek Civil War*. London: Faber and Faber, 1966.

———. *The Indo-China War, 1945-1954*. London: Faber and Faber, 1964.

———. *Malaya: The Communist Insurgent War*. Hamden, CT: Archon, 1966.

———. *The Secret War in the Sudan*. Hamden, CT: Archon, 1977.

———. *The War in Viet Nam*. New York: Hippocrene, 1981.

Obando, Enrique. "Defeating Shining Path: Strategic Lessons for the Future." In Anthony James Joes, ed., *Saving Democracies: U.S. Intervention in Threatened Democratic States*. Westport, CT: Praeger, 1999.

Oliker, Olga. *Russia's Chechen Wars 1994–2000: Lessons for Urban Combat*. Santa Monica, CA: RAND, 2001.

Oman, Charles. *A History of the Peninsular War*. 7 vols. Oxford: Clarendon Press, 1902-1930,

Oquist, Paul. *Violence, Conflict and Politics in Colombia*. New York: Academic Press, 1980.

Orwell, George. *1984*. New York: Harcourt, 2000.

Osterling, Jorge. *Democracy in Colombia: Clientelist Politics and Guerrilla Warfare*. New Brunswick, NJ: Transaction, 1989.

Ott, Thomas R. *The Haitian Revolution*. Knoxville, TN: University of Tennessee Press, 1973.

Overy, Richard. *Why the Allies Won*. New York: Norton, 1995.

Pakenham, Thomas. *The Boer War*. New York: Random House, 1979.

Palmer, Bruce, Jr. U.S. *Intelligence in Viet Nam*. Special Issue of *Studies in Intelligence*, vol. 28 (1984).

Palmer, Dave Richard. *Summons of the Trumpet: U.S.–Viet Nam in Perspective*. Novato, CA: Presidio, 1978.

Palmer, David Scott. "The Revolutionary Terrorism of Peru's Shining Path." In Martha Crenshaw, ed., *Terrorism in Context*. University Park, PA: Pennsylvania State University Press, 1995.

Pancake, John S. *This Destructive War: The British Campaign in the Carolinas, 1780–1782*. University, AL: University of Alabama Press, 1985.

Panikkar, K.M. *Asia and Western Dominance*. London: Allen and Unwin, 1959.

Paret, Peter. *French Revolutionary Warfare from Indochina to Algeria: An Analysis of a Political and Military Doctrine*. New York: Praeger, 1964.

———. *Internal War and Pacification: The Vendée, 1789–1796*. Princeton, NJ: Princeton University Center of International Studies, 1961.

Paret, Peter, ed. *Makers of Modern Strategy: From Machiavelli to the Nuclear Age*. Princeton, NJ: Princeton University Press, 1986.

Pareto, Vilfredo. *Sociological Writings*. New York: Praeger, 1966.

Parrish, R.D. *Combat Recon: My Year with the ARVN*. New York: St. Martin's, 1991.

Passage, David. *The United States and Colombia: Untying the Gordian Knot*. Carlisle Barracks, PA: Strategic Studies Institute, 2000.

Pateman, Roy. *Eritrea: Even the Stones Are Burning*. Trenton, NJ: Red Sea Press, 1990.

Patterson, George N. *Peking Versus Delhi*. New York: Praeger, 1964.

———. *Requiem for Tibet*. London: Aurum, 1990.

———. *Tibet in Revolt*. London: Faber and Faber, 1960.

Peissel, Michel. *The Secret War in Tibet*. Boston: Little, Brown, 1973.

Penniman, Howard R. *Elections in South Viet Nam*. Washington, DC: American Enterprise Institute, 1972.

Pentagon Papers, The. Gravel Edition. Boston, MA: Beacon, 1971.

Pepper, Suzanne. *Civil War in China: The Political Struggle, 1945–1949*. Berkeley, CA: University of California Press, 1978.

Peters, Ralph. "Heavy Peace." *Parameters*, vol. 29 (1999).

———. "Our Old New Enemies." *Parameters*, vol. 27 (1997).

———. "Our Soldiers, Their Cities." *Parameters*, vol. 26 (1996).

———. "The Culture of Future Conflicts." *Parameters*, vol. 25 (1995–1996).

———. "The New Warrior Class." *Parameters*, vol. 24 (1994).

Peterson, Michael E. *Combined Action Platoons: The U.S. Marines' Other War in Viet Nam*. New York: Praeger, 1989.

Phipps, Ramsay Weston. *The Armies of the First French Republic and the Rise of the Marshals of Napoleon I*. Westport, CT: Greenwood, 1980.

Pike, Douglas. *PAVN: People's Army of Viet Nam*. Novato, CA: Presidio, 1986.

———. *Viet Cong: The Organization and Techniques of the National Liberation Front of South Viet Nam*. Cambridge, MA: M.I.T. Press, 1966.

———. *The Viet Cong Strategy of Terror*. Saigon: Private Monograph, 1970.

Pilloni, John R. "Burning Corpses in the Streets: Russia's Doctrinal Flaws in the 1995 Fight for Grozny." *Journal of Slavic Military Studies*, vol. 13 (2000).

Pimlott, John. "The British Experience." In Ian F. W. Beckett, *The Roots of Counter-Insurgency: Armies and Guerrilla Warfare, 1900–1945*. London: Blandford, 1988.

Pino, Ponciano del. "Family, Culture, and 'Revolution': Everyday Life with Sendero Luminoso." In Steve J. Stern, ed., *Shining and Other Paths: War and Society in Peru, 1980–1995*. Durham, NC: Duke University Press, 1998.

Poole, Peter. *The Vietnamese in Thailand: A Historical Perspective*. Ithaca, NY: Cornell University Press, 1970.

Popkin, Samuel. *The Rational Peasant*. Berkeley, CA: University of California Press, 1979.

Porch, Douglas. "Bugeaud, Gallieni, Lyautey: The Development of French Colonial Warfare." In Peter Paret, ed., *Makers of Modern Strategy: From Machiavelli to the Nuclear Age*. Princeton, NJ: Princeton University Press, 1986.

———. *The Conquest of Morocco*. New York: Fromm, 1982.

———. *The Portuguese Armed Forces and the Revolution*. Stanford, CA: Hoover Institution on War, Revolution and Peace, 1977.

Pouget, Jean. *Nous étions à Dien Bien Phu.* Paris: Presses de la Cité, 1964.

Prunier, Gerard. "Le Sud-Soudan depuis l'Indépendence (1956–1989)." In Marc Lavergne, ed., Soudan Contemporain. Paris: Karthala, 1989.

Puri, Balraj. *Kashmir Toward Insurgency.* New Delhi: Orient Longman, 1993.

Pye, Lucian. *China.* New York: HarperCollins, 1991, 4th ed.

———. *Guerrilla Communism in Malaya.* Princeton, NJ: Princeton University Press, 1956.

———. "The Roots of Insurgency." In Harry Eckstein, ed., *Internal War.* New York: Free Press, 1964.

———. *Warlord Politics.* New York: Praeger, 1971.

Qiang Zhai. *China and the Viet Nam Wars 1950–1975.* Chapel Hill, NC: University of North Carolina Press, 2000.

Quirk, Robert E. *The Mexican Revolution and the Catholic Church.* Bloomington, IN: Indiana University Press, 1973.

Race, Jeffrey. "How They Won." *Asian Survey,* vol. 10 (1970).

———. *War Comes to Long An: Revolutionary Conflict in a Vietnamese Province.* Berkeley, CA: University of California Press, 1972.

———. "War in Northern Thailand." *Modern Asian Studies,* vol. 8 (1974).

Rajagopalan, R. "Restoring Normalcy: The Evolution of the Indian Army's Counterinsurgency Doctrine." *Small Wars and Insurgencies,* vol. 11 (Spring 2000).

Ramage, James. *Gray Ghost: The Life of Colonel John Singleton Mosby.* Lexington, KY: University Press of Kentucky, 1999.

Ramsey, Russell W. "Critical Bibliography on the Violence in Colombia." *Latin American Research Review,* vol. 8 (1973).

Ranelaugh, John. *The Agency: The Rise and Decline of the CIA.* New York: Simon and Schuster, 1987.

Rangel Bandiera, Antonio. "The Portuguese Armed Forces Movement: Historical Antecedents, Demands, and Class Conflict." *Politics and Society* vol. 6 (1976);

Rankin, Hugh F. *Francis Marion: The Swamp Fox.* New York: Crowell, 1973.

Rashid, Ahmed. "The China Factor." *Far Eastern Economic Review,* January 13, 1994.

Reitz, Deneys. *Commando.* London: Faber and Faber, 1929.

Rempe, Dennis M. "An American Trojan Horse? Eisenhower, Latin America, and the Development of U.S. Internal Security Policy, 1954–1960." *Small Wars and Insurgencies,* vol. 10 (1999).

———. "Guerillas, Bandits and Independent Republics: U.S. Counterinsurgency Efforts in Colombia, 1955-1965." *Small Wars and Insurgencies,* vol. 6 (1995).

———. "The Origin of Internal Security in Colombia." *Small Wars and Insurgencies,* vol. 10 (1999).

———. *The Past as Prologue? A History of U.S. Counterinsurgency Policy in Colombia, 1958–1966.* Carlisle Barracks, PA: Strategic Studies Institute, 2002.

Richani, Nazih. "The Political Economy of Violence: The War System in Colombia." *Journal of Interamerican Studies and World Affairs,* vol. 39 (Summer 1996).

Richardson, H.E. *A Short History of Tibet.* New York: E. P. Dutton, 1962.

Ridley, Jasper. *Maximilian and Juàrez.* New York: Ticknor and Fields, 1992.

Robbins, James S. *Soviet Counterinsurgency in Afghanistan*. Ph.D. dissertation, Tufts University, 1991.

Rocelle, P. *Pourquoi Dien Bien Phu?* Paris: Flammarion, 1968.

Roeder, Ralph. *Juárez and His Mexico*. 2 vols. New York: Viking, 1947.

Roguet, Christophe. *De la Vendée militaire*. Paris: J. Coreard, 1834.

Romulo, Carlos P. *Crusade in Asia*. New York: John Day, 1955.

Romulo, Carlos P., and Marvin M. Gray. *The Magsaysay Story*. New York: John Day, 1956.

Roy, Jules. *The Battle of Dien Bien Phu*. New York: Harper and Row, 1965.

Roy, Olivier. *Islam and Resistance in Afghanistan*. Cambridge: Cambridge University Press, 1986.

Russell, Bertrand. *Power*. London: Allen and Unwin, 1962.

Russian General Staff, The. *The Soviet-Afghan War*. Trans. and ed. by Lester W. Grau and Michael A. Gress. Lawrence, KS: University Press of Kansas, 2002.

Ryan, Henry Butterfield. *The Fall of Che Guevara: A Story of Soldiers, Spies and Diplomats*. New York: Oxford University Press, 1998.

Saikal, Amin, and William Maley. *The Soviet Withdrawal from Afghanistan*. Cambridge; Cambridge University Press, 1989.

Salmon, Malcolm. "After Revolution, Evolution." *Far Eastern Economic Review*, December 12, 1975.

Sampson, Victor, and Ian Hamilton. *Anti-Commando*. London: Faber and Faber, 1931.

Sanchez, Gonzalo. "La Violencia in Colombia: New Research, New Questions." *Hispanic American Historical Review*, vol. 65 (1985).

Scalapino, Robert. "We Cannot Accept a Communist Seizure of Viet Nam." *New York Times Magazine*, December 11, 1966.

Scham, Alan. *Lyautey in Morocco*. Berkeley, CA: University of California Press, 1970.

Schama, Simon. *Citizens: A Chronicle of the French Revolution*. New York: Knopf, 1989.

Schmitter, Philippe S. "Liberation by Golpe." *Armed Forces and Society*, vol. 2 (1975).

Schofield, Victoria. *Kashmir in Conflict*. London: Tauris, 2000.

Schultz, Duane. *Quantrill's War*. New York: St. Martin's, 1996.

Schwarz, Benjamin. *American Counterinsurgency Doctrine and El Salvador: The Frustrations of Reform and the Illusions of Nation Building*. Santa Monica, CA: RAND, 1991.

Scigliano, Robert. *South Viet Nam: Nation Under Stress*. Boston: Houghton Mifflin, 1964.

Secher, Reynald. *Le Génocide Franco-français: La Vendée-Vengé*. Paris: Presses Universitaires de France, 1988. 2d ed.

Sen, Chanakya. *Tibet Disappears: A Documentary History of Tibet's International Status, the Great Rebellion, and Its Aftermath*. New Delhi: Asia Publishing House, 1960.

Sereseres, Caesar. "The Highlands War in Guatemala." In George Fauriol, ed., *Latin American Insurgencies*. Washington, DC: Georgetown University Press, 1985.

————. "Lessons from Central America's Revolutionary Wars, 1972–1984." In Robert E. Harkavy and Stephanie G. Newman, eds., *The Lessons of Recent Wars in the Third World*. Lexington, MA: Lexington Books, 1985.

Shakabpa, T. *Tibet: A Political History*. New Haven, CT: Yale University Press, 1967.

Shakya, Tsering. *The Dragon in the Land of Snows*. New York: Columbia University, Press, 1999.

Shaplen, Robert S. *The Road from War: Viet Nam, 1965–1970*. New York: Harper and Row, 1970.

Sheahan, John. *Patterns of Development in Latin America: Poverty, Repression and Economic Strategy*. Princeton, NJ: Princeton University Press, 1987.

Sherman, Richard F. *Eritrea in Revolution*. Ph.D. dissertation, Brandeis University Press, 1980.

Sheridan, James E. *China in Disintegration: The Republican Era in China 1912–1949*. New York: Free Press, 1975.

————. "*The Warlord Era: Politics and Militarism Under the Peking Government, 1916–1928.*" In John K. Fairbank, ed., *The Cambridge History of China*, vol. 12, *Republican China 1912–1949*, part one. Cambridge: Cambridge University Press, 1983.

Sherwig, John M. *Guineas and Gunpowder: British Foreign Aid in the Wars with France, 1793–1815*. Cambridge, MA: Harvard University Press, 1969.

Shifter, Michael. "Colombia on the Brink: There Goes the Neighborhood." *Foreign Affairs*, vol. 78 (1999).

Short, Anthony. *The Communist Insurrection in Malaya, 1948–1960*. New York: Crane, Russak, 1975.

Shultz, Richard H., Jr., et al., eds. *Guerrilla Warfare and Counterinsurgency: U.S.-Soviet Policy in the Third World*. Lexington, MA: Lexington Books, 1989.

Shy, John. "American Society and Its War for Independence." In Dan Higginbotham, ed., *Reconsiderations on the Revolutionary War*. Westport, CT: Greenwood, 1978.

Siepel, Kevin H. *Rebel: The Life and Times of John Singleton Mosby*. New York: St. Martin's, 1983.

Simpson, Howard R. *Dien Bien Phu: The Epic Battle America Forgot*. Washington, DC: Brassey's 1996.

Skocpol, Theda. *States and Social Revolutions: A Comparative Analysis of France, Russia and China*. New York: Cambridge University Press, 1979.

Slade, Stuart. "Successful Counterinsurgency: How the Thais Burnt the Books and Beat the Guerrillas." *International Defence Review*, vol. 22 (1989).

Slim, William. *Defeat into Victory*. London: Cassell, 1956.

Smith, Michael. "Taking the High Ground: Shining Path and the Andes." In David Scott Palmer, ed., *Shining Path of Peru*. New York: St. Martin's, 1994.

Smith, Paul. *Loyalists and Redcoats: A Study in British Revolutionary Policy*. Chapel Hill, NC: University of North Carolina Press, 1964.

Smith, Warren. *Tibetan Nation: A History of Tibetan Nationalism and Sino-Tibetan Relations*. Boulder, CO: Westview, 1996.

Smuts, Jan Christian. *Selections from the Smuts Papers*. Ed. W.K. Hancock and Jean van der Poel. Cambridge: Cambridge University Press, vol. 1, 1966.

Smythe, Donald. *Guerrilla Warrior: The Early Life of John J. Pershing.* New York: Scribner's, 1973.

Snow, P. "Nomonhan—The Unknown Victory." *History Today,* July 1990.

Soboul, Albert. *The French Revolution, 1788-1799.* Trans. A. Forrest and C. Jones. New York: Random House, 1975.

Solé, Jacques. *Questions of the French Revolution.* New York: Pantheon, 1989.

Sorley, Lewis. *A Better War. The Unexamined Victories and Final Tragedy of America's Last Years in Viet Nam.* New York: Harcourt, Brace, 1999.

———. "To Change a War: General Harold K. Johnson and the PROVN Study." *Parameters,* vol. 28 (1998).

Spector, Ronald. *Advice and Support: The Early Years, 1941–1960.* Washington, DC: U.S. Army Center of Military History, 1983.

Spencer, David E. *Colombia's Paramilitaries: Criminals or Political Force?* Carlisle Barracks, PA: Strategic Studies Institute, 2001.

———. *From Viet Nam to El Salvador: The Saga of the FMLN Sappers and Other Guerrilla Special Forces in Latin America.* Westport, CT: Praeger. 1996.

Sprout, Harold and Margaret. *The Rise of American Naval Power, 1776–1918.* Princeton, NJ: Princeton University Press, 1967 [orig. 1939].

Starn, Orin. "Villagers at Arms: War and Counterrevolution in the Central-South Andes." In Steve J. Stern, ed., *Shining and Other Paths: War and Society in Peru, 1980–1995.* Durham, NC: Duke University Press, 1998.

Starner, Frances Lucille. *Magsaysay and the Philippine Peasantry.* Berkeley, CA: University of California Press, 1961.

Statesman's Yearbook 1953. New York: St. Martin's, 1953.

Statesman's Yearbook 1994–1995. New York: St. Martin's, 1994.

Stein, Stanley, and B.H. Stein. *The Colonial Heritage of Latin America.* New York: Oxford University Press, 1970.

Stern, Steve J., ed. *Shining and Other Paths: War and Society in Peru, 1980–1995.* Durham, NC: Duke University Press, 1998.

Stoecker, Sally W. *Forging Stalin's Army: Marshal Tukhachevsky and the Politics of Military Innovation.* Boulder, CO: Westview, 1998.

Stubbs, Richard. *Hearts and Minds in Guerrilla Warfare: The Malayan Emergency, 1948–1960.* New York: Oxford University Press, 1989.

Sullivan, John F. *Of Spies and Lies: A CIA Lie Detector Remembers Viet Nam.* Lawrence, KS: University of Kansas Press, 2000.

Summers, Harry. *On Strategy: A Critical Analysis of the Viet Nam War.* Novato, CA: Presidio, 1982.

Sun Tzu. *The Art of War,* trans. Samuel B. Griffith. New York: Oxford University Press, 1963.

Sutherland, C.H.V. *The Romans in Spain.* Westport, CT: Greenwood, 1982 [orig. 1939].

Sutherland, Donald. *The Chouans: The Social Origins of Popular Counterrevolution in Upper Brittany, 1770–1798.* Oxford: Oxford University Press, 1982.

Tamari, Dov. "Military Operations in Urban Environments: The Case of Lebanon, 1982." In Michael C. Desch, ed., *Soldiers in Cities: Military Operations on Urban Terrain.* Carlisle Barracks, PA: Strategic Studies Institute, 2001.

Tang Tsou. *America's Failure in China, 1940–1950*. Chicago, IL: University of Chicago Press, 1963.

Tanham, George K. *Communist Revolutionary Warfare: From the Viet Minh to the Viet Cong*. 2d ed. New York: Praeger, 1967.

———. *Trial in Thailand*. New York: Crane, Russak, 1974.

Taruc, Luis. *Born of the People*. Westport, CT: Greenwood, 1973 [orig. 1953].

———. *He Who Rides the Tiger*. New York: Praeger, 1967.

Taylor, Jan. *China and Southeast Asia: Peking's Relations with Revolutionary Movements*. New York: Praeger, 1976, 2d ed.

Taylor, Maxwell. *Swords and Plowshares*. New York: Norton, 1972.

Tec, Nechama. *When Light Pierced the Darkness: Righteous Christians and the Polish Jews*. New York: Oxford University Press, 1988.

Teitler, Gerke. *The Dutch Colonial Army in Transition*. Rotterdam: Erasmus University Press, 1980.

Teng, S.Y. *The Nien Army and Their Guerrilla Warfare*. Westport, CT: Praeger, 1984 [orig. 1961]

Thayer, Thomas C. "Territorial Forces." In W. Scott Thompson and Donaldson D. Frizzell, *The Lessons of Viet Nam*. New York: Crane, Russak, 1977.

———. *War Without Fronts: The American Experience in Viet Nam*. Boulder, CO: Westview, 1985.

Theobald, A.B. *The Mahdiya*. London: Longmans, 1962.

Thiers, Louis Adolphe. *The History of the French Revolution*. Trans. Frederick Shoberl. Philadelphia: Lippincott, 1894.

Thomas, Hugh. *The Cuban Revolution*. New York: Harper and Row, 1977.

Thomas, Timothy. "The Battle for Grozny: Deadly Classroom for Urban Combat." *Parameters*, vol. xxix (1999).

Thompson, Sir Robert. *Defeating Communist Insurgency: The Lessons of Malaya and Viet Nam*. New York: Praeger, 1966.

———. *Lessons from the Viet Nam War*. London: Royal United Services Institute, 1966.

———. *No Exit From Viet Nam*. New York: David McKay, 1969.

———. *Peace Is Not at Hand*. New York: David McKay, 1974.

———. "Regular Armies and Insurgency." In Ronald Haycock, ed., *Regular Armies and Insurgency*. London: Croom Helm, 1979.

———. *Revolutionary War in World Strategy*. New York: Taplinger, 1970.

Thompson, W. Scott, and Donaldson D. Frizzell. *The Lessons of Viet Nam*. New York: Crane, Russak, 1977.

Thoumi, Francisco. *Political Economy and Illegal Drugs in Colombia*. Boulder, CO: L. Rienner, 1995.

Thucydides. *The Peloponnesian Wars*. In Robert B. Strassler, ed., *The Landmark Thucydides*. New York: Free Press, 1996.

Tien Hung-mao. *Government and Politics in Kuomintang China, 1927–1937*. Stanford, CA: Stanford University Press, 1972.

Tien Hung Nguyen, and Jerrold Schechter. *The Palace File*. New York: Harper and Row, 1986.

Tilly, Charles. "Does Modernization Breed Revolution?" *Comparative Politics*, vol. 5 (April 1973)

Todd, Olivier. *Cruel April. The Fall of Saigon*. New York: Norton, 1990.

Tone, John Lawrence. *The Fatal Knot: The Guerrilla War in Navarre and the Defeat of Napoleon in Spain*. Chapel Hill, NC: University of North Carolina Press, 1994.

Towle, Philip Anthony. *Pilots and Rebels: The Use of Aircraft in Unconventional Warfare, 1918–1988*. London: Brassey's, 1989.

Tranie, J., and J.-C. Carmigniani *Napoleon's War in Spain*. Trans Janet Mallender and J. Clements. London: Arms and Armour, 1982.

Trotsky, Leon. *History of the Russian Revolution*. Trans. Max Eastman. New York: Simon and Schuster, 1933.

Truong Nhu Tang. *A Viet Cong Memoir*. New York: Harcourt, 1987.

Tuck, Jim. *Holy War in Los Altos: A Regional Analysis of Mexico's Cristero Rebellion*. Tucson, AZ: University of Arizona, 1982.

Tulchin, Joseph S., and Gary Bland, eds. *Peru in Crisis*. Boulder, CO: L. Rienner, 1994.

Urban, Mark. *War in Afghanistan*. New York: St. Martin's. 1988.

U.S. Department of State. *Afghanistan: Soviet Occupation and Withdrawal*. Washington, DC: U.S. Department of State. 1988.

——. *Foreign Relations of the United States 1950*, vol. VI: East Asia and the Pacific. Washington, DC: U.S. Government Printing Office, 1976.

——. *Foreign Relations of the United States, vol. XIX : China 1958-1960*. Washington, DC: U.S. Government Printing Office, 1996.

U.S. Marine Corps. *Small Wars Manual*. Washington, DC: U.S. Government Printing Office, 1940.

Valeriano, Napoleon, and Charles T.P. Bohannan. *Counter-Guerrilla Operations: The Philippine Experience*. New York: Praeger, 1962.

Van Creveld, Martin L. *The Sword and the Olive: A Critical History of the Israeli Defense Force*. New York: Public Affairs, 1998.

Van der Kroef, Justus. "Guerrilla Communism and Counterinsurgency in Thailand." *Orbis*, vol. 18 (1974)

Vandiver, Frank E. *Black Jack: The Life and Times of General John J. Pershing*. College Station, TX: Texas A & M University Press, 1977.

Van Dyke, Carl. "Kabul to Grozny: A Critique of Soviet (Russian) Counterinsurgency Doctrine." *Journal of Slavic Military Studies*, vol. 9 (1996).

Van Hollen, Eliza. *Afghanistan: Three Years of Occupation*. Washington, DC: U.S. Department of State, 1982.

Van Slyke, Lyman P. "China Incident." In *The Oxford Companion to World War II*. Ed. I.C.B. Dear. New York: Oxford University Press, 1995.

——. *The Chinese Communist Movement: A Report of the U.S. War Department* July 1845. Stanford, CA: Stanford University Press, 1968.

Van Tien Dung. *Our Great Spring Victory*. New York: Monthly Review, 1977.

Van Tyne, C.H. *The Loyalists in the American Revolution*. New York: Peter Smith, 1929.

Vegetius, Flavius. *Epitoma Rei Militaris*. Ed. and Trans. Leo F. Stelten. New York: P. Lang, 1990.

Viorst, Milton. "Sudan's Islamic Experiment." *Foreign Affairs*, vol. 74 (1995).

Vo Nguyen Giap. *Dien Bien Phu*. Hanoi: Foreign Languages Publishing House, 1964.

———. *How We Won the War*. Philadelphia, PA: Recon, 1976.

Vulliamy, C.E. *Crimea: The Campaign of 1854-1856*. London: Jonathan Cape, 1939.

Waghelstein, John. *El Salvador: Observations and Experiences in Counterinsurgency*. Carlisle Barracks, PA: U.S. Army War College, 1985.

Walt, Stephen. *Revolution and War*. Ithaca, NY: Cornell University Press, 1997.

Walton, C. Dale. *The Myth of Inevitable U.S. Defeat in Viet Nam*. London: Frank Cass, 2002.

War of the Rebellion: A Compilation of the Official Records of the Union and Confederate Armies, Series 1, vol. 51, Part 1. Washington, DC: U.S. Government Printing Office, 1897.

Ward, Christopher. *The War of the Revolution*. New York: Macmillan, 1952.

Warner, Denis. *Certain Victory: How Hanoi Won the War*. Kansas City, KS: Sheed, Andrews and McMeel, 1978.

Warner, Philip. *The Crimean War: A Reappraisal*. New York· Taplinger, 1972.

Webre, Stephen A. *José Napoleon Duarte and the Christian Democratic Party in Salvadoran Politics, 1960–1972*. Baton Rouge, LA: Louisiana State University, 1979.

Webster, Graham. *The Roman Imperial Army*. 3d ed. Totowa, NJ: Barnes and Noble, 1985.

Wei, William. *Counterrevolution in China: The Nationalists in Jiangxi during the Soviet Period*. Ann Arbor, MI: University of Michigan, 1985.

Weigley, Russell F. *The Partisan War: The South Carolina Campaign of 1780–1782*. Columbia, SC: University of South Carolina Press, 1970.

———. "A Strategy of Attrition: George Washington." *The American Way of War*. Bloomington, IN: Indiana University Press, 1977.

Wert, Jeffrey D. *Mosby's Rangers*. New York: Simon and Schuster, 1990.

West, F.J. *Small Unit Action in Viet Nam*. Quantico, VA: U.S. Marine Corps, 1967.

———. *The Village*. New York: Harper and Row, 1972.

Westmoreland, William. *A Soldier Reports*. Garden City, NY: Doubleday, 1976.

Wheal, Elizabeth-Anne, et al., eds. *A Dictionary of the Second World War*. New York: Peter Bedrick, 1990.

Wheeler, Douglas L. "African Elements in Portugal's Armies in Africa, 1961–1974." *Armed Forces and Society*, vol. 2 (1976).

Whitson, William P. *Lessons from China*. N.D., N.P.

Wickam-Crowley, Timothy. *Guerrillas and Revolutions in Latin America: A Comparative Study of Insurgents and Regimes Since 1956*. Princeton, NJ: Princeton University Press, 1991.

Wilbur, C. Martin. "The Nationalist Revolution: From Canton to Nanking, 1923–1928." In *The Cambridge History of China*, vol. 12,. *Republican China,1912–1949*, part one. Cambridge: Cambridge University Press, 1983.

Wilkie, James W. "The Meaning of the Cristero Religious War Against the Mexican Revolution." *Journal of Church and State*, vol. 8 (1966).

———. "Statistical Indicators of the Impact of the National Revolution on the Catholic Church in Mexico, 1910–1967." *Journal of Church and State*, vol. 12 (1970).

Williams, Glanmor. *Owen Glendower*. London: Oxford University Press, 1961.

Wirtz, James J. *The Tet Offensive: Intelligence Failure in War*. Ithaca, NY: Cornell University Press, 1991.

Wit, Daniel. *Thailand: Another Viet Nam?* New York: Scribner's, 1968.

Wolff, Tobias. *In Pharaoh's Army: Memories of a Lost War*. London: Picador, 1994.

Woodhouse, C.M. *The Struggle for Greece, 1941–1949*. London: Hart-Davis, MacGibbon, 1976.

Woodward, Ralph Lee. *Central America: A Nation Divided*. New York: Oxford University Press, 1976.

Wright, Mary C. *The Last Stand of Chinese Conservatism*. Stanford, CA: Stanford University Press, 1967.

Xiaoming Zhang. "The Viet Nam War, 1964–1969: A Chinese Perspective." *Journal of Military History,* vol. 60 (1996).

Young, Arthur N. *China and the Helping Hand, 1937–1945*. Cambridge, MA: Harvard University Press, 1963.

Young, Victor. "The Victors and the Vanquished: The Role of Military Factors in the Outcome of Modern African Insurgencies." *Small Wars and Insurgencies,* vol. 7 (1996).

Yu, George T. *Politics in Republican China: The Kuomintang, 1913–1924*. Berkeley, CA: University of California Press, 1966.

Zawodny, J.K. *Death in the Forest*. South Bend, IN: University of Notre Dame Press, 1962.

———. *Nothing But Honor*. Stanford, CA: Hoover Institution on War, Revolution and Peace, 1978.

INDEX